Learn to Program with Python™

John Smiley

Smiley Publishing
Philadelphia

Smiley Publishing

PO Box 2062

Riverton, NJ 08077-2062

U.S.A.

smileypublishing@johnsmiley.com

Learn to Program with Python

ISBN: 978-1-61274-071-3

Other books by John Smiley:

How I taught Katy Perry (and others) to program in Python

How I taught Katy Perry (and others) to program in C#

How I taught Katy Perry (and others) to program in Java

How I taught Katy Perry (and others) to program in JavaScript

How I taught Katy Perry (and others) to program in Visual Basic 2010 Express

How I taught Katy Perry (and others) to program in Visual C# 2010 Express

Learn to Program with C#

Learn to Program with C++

Learn to Program with Java

Learn to Program with Java SE6

Learn to Program with JavaScript

Learn to Program with VB.Net 2010 Express

Learn to Program with Visual Basic 6

Learn to Program with Visual Basic 6 Examples

Learn to Program with Visual Basic 6 Objects

Learn to Program with Visual Basic 6 Databases

Learn to Program with Visual Basic 2010 Express

Learn to Program with Visual C# 2010 Express

My Climb To The Top (of the Bell Atlantic Tower)

Programming for Seniors

The Complete Book of Stair Climbing (2012 Edition)

10 9 8 7 6 5 4 3 2 1

Credits

Author:
John Smiley

Technical Editor:
Kevin Smiley

Technical Reviewer:
Lynda Dehring

Layout and Proof:
John Smiley

Cover:
John Smiley

Index:
John Smiley

This book is dedicated to my wife Linda

About the Author

John Smiley, a Microsoft Certified Professional (MCP) and Microsoft Certified Solutions Developer (MCSD) in Visual Basic, has been programming and teaching for more than 20 years. He is the President of John Smiley and Associates, a computer consulting firm serving clients both large and small in the Philadelphia Metropolitan area. John is an adjunct professor of Computer Science at Penn State University, Philadelphia University, and Holy Family College, and also teaches in a variety of Internet venues including SmartPlanet and ElementK.

On the writing front, John is the author of the immensely popular **Learn to Program with Visual Basic 6**, along with Learn to Program with Visual Basic Examples, Learn to Program Databases with Visual Basic 6, Learn to Program Objects with Visual Basic 6, Learn to Program with Java, Learn to Program with VB.Net 2002/2003, Learn to Program with VB.Net 2005 Express, Learn to Program with C#, Learn to Program with Python and Learn to Program with JavaScript..

Feel free to visit John's Web Site at

http://www.johnsmiley.com

or contact him via email at johnsmiley@johnsmiley.com. He religiously answers all of his emails, although not necessarily instantaneously!

Contents

Acknowledgments

I want to thank first and foremost my wife Linda for her love and support, and putting up with my harangues about "having to write an hour today."

Many thanks to my son Kevin Smiley, one of the world's great Python experts, who patiently put up with many questions from me as I learned, and later grew to love, this wonderful language.

Many thanks to my friend Lynda Dehring, one of my students and reader of previous books, who patiently read through the many drafts of this book and found errors and offered suggestions on how to make it better. It wouldn't be nearly as good as it is without her!

Many thanks to a number of people who kept asking how I was making out with the book, particularly Fred Forshee and Rich Blitz. Knowing someone was waiting for the book to be finished helped me continue writing it.

Many thanks also go to the thousands of students I've taught over the years for your tireless dedication to learning the art and science of Computer Programming. Your great questions and demanding persistence in getting the most out of your learning experience truly inspired me, and has contributed greatly to my books. Many of you dragged yourself to class after a long hard day of work, or Rose early on your Saturday day off to learn Visual Basic and the other programming languages I have taught. You have my greatest respect and admiration.

I also want to thank the many readers of my many books who have taken the time to write or email me about the books. Most of the time, the correspondence is incredibly glowing---I truly appreciate hearing from each of you, and I want you to know that I read and respond to each email I receive.

I want to thank all the members of my family for their continued belief in and support of me over the years, in particular my mother, who always prayed for the success of my books. She is no longer with us here, but I see her light every morning when I jog in the dark, and I'm sure she is now with my father, surely together flipping through the pages of this book now.

It's been over forty years since I last saw my father---and his role in the writing of this and my others books can never be understated. He and my mother were a great inspiration and role model for me.

I know that the God who made us all will someday permit us to be together again.

Organizations/Conventions Used in the Book

Each chapter of the book follows in a session in a make-believe college classroom. Read along and learn the material with the rest of the students.

Every chapter has example programs and practical exercises for you to complete. I encourage you to follow along with the example programs---and by all means complete the exercises in the book as well. If typing is not your strong suit, you can download both the completed examples and exercises via this link

http://www.johnsmiley.com/main/mybooks.htm

Care to take a quiz to test your knowledge? Follow this link and you can take a series of multiple choice quizzes drawn from the book

http://www.johnsmiley.com/tester/login.asp

Finally, if the book isn't enough for you to get going with Python, consider joining me in an Internet-based Python class. My introductory classes are held several times throughout the year---and I'll be teaching these classes for as long as I'm sojourning in this dimension. For more information, follow this link...

http://www.johnsmiley.com/main/training.htm

Chapter 1---Where Do I Begin?

"Where do I begin?" is a question I am frequently asked by my students, and this seems like a good question to tackle right at the beginning of this book. In this first chapter, we'll look at the development process of an actual working program through the eyes and ears of my University Computer Programming class and you will also be introduced to our 'class project'. By the end of the book, we'll have taken a real-life application through from the concept all the way to the finished product!

> **NOTE: Occasionally, my students become disillusioned when they hear that we won't be diving straight in and coding our application. However, when I remind them that programming is much the same as writing a report (or in other words, it is a two stage process of planning and then producing) they tend to settle down.**

Where Do We Begin?

As part of answering the question, "Where do we begin?" this chapter looks at the Systems Development Life Cycle, which is a popular methodology that has been developed to ensure that Computer Systems are developed in a methodical, logical and step-by-step approach. We'll be looking at the Systems Development Life Cycle in quite a bit of detail, since the majority of this book will be spent in developing a real-world application. In this chapter we'll meet with a prospective client and conduct a preliminary interview with him. From that interview (and a subsequent one!) we'll develop a Requirements Statement, which provides details as to what the Computer Program should do. This Requirements Statement will form the basis of the Computer Program that we will develop throughout the rest of the book

> **NOTE: From this point on, you will follow me as I lead a group of my University students in an actual class on Python. If I do my job right, you will be a part of the class, learning along with them as we complete a thirteen-week course about programming in Python.**

Computer Programming Many books on Computer Programming have the reader, perhaps as early as the first chapter, code a program which 'cutely' displays a message box that says 'Hello World'. Then the author will point to the fact that within the first few minutes of reading his or her book, the reader has already written a working program. I'm not so naive as to believe that writing such a program makes you a Computer Programmer. Therefore, we'll opt for a slower approach. Simple programs, although great for the ego, are not the programs that are found in the real world. Real-world programs are written to meet someone's needs. These needs are frequently complex and difficult to verbalize. In this book, you and I will embark on a journey together that will see us complete the prototyping stage of a real-world project. I believe that this is the best way to learn programming.

In my University classes, I don't usually introduce the class project until several weeks into the semester. When I finally do introduce the class project, I give my students a Requirements Statement. I don't tell my students exactly how the application should look, or how to program it. I tell them only what is required. In other words, I complete the hard part for them - gathering the User Requirements.

Programming the Easy Way

When I first began to teach Computer Programming, some of my students would tell me that they just didn't know where to begin when they first started to work on their programming assignments. They would start to program the application, then stop. Some of them would find themselves re-writing their code and re-designing their application several times. Then they would change it again. Face to face I could usually clear things up for them by giving them a gentle nudge or hint in the right direction. However, their work would show a definite lack of direction. Why the problem? They lacked a plan.

As soon as I realized this, I began to teach my students more than just Computer programming. I began to teach them the Systems Development Life Cycle (SDLC), the methodology I mentioned earlier. You see, programmers need blueprints or maps. Programmers need something tangible, usually in writing, before they can begin a project. Just about all of my students agree that having a blueprint like this makes the development process that much easier.

Sometimes I'll meet former students of mine at the University, and I'll ask them how their other Computer Programming classes are coming along. Occasionally, they'll tell me that they're working on a great real-world assignment of some kind, but they just don't know where to begin. At that point, I'll remind them of what I told them in class - that they should begin with the design of the user interface, observe the default behavior of the design and then add code to fill in the gaps. That's not the problem, they tell me. The problem is that they don't know how to gather the user requirements for the system. They don't really know what the system should do.

Often the real problem is that the client isn't prepared to give the programmers a detailed enough Requirements Statement. In class the professor distributes a well-defined Requirements Statement but in the real world, programmers need to develop this themselves. Unfortunately, they may not know how to sit down with the prospective user of their system to determine what is required to satisfy the user's needs.

That skill, to listen to the user and determine their needs, is something that I now teach to some extent in all of my computer classes - whether they are programming courses, courses on Systems Analysis and Design, or Database Management.

Planning a Program is Like Planning a House

A friend of mine is a general contractor and home-builder. His job is similar to that of a programmer or system designer. He recently built an addition to a customer's house. He wouldn't think of beginning that work without first meeting with the owner of the house to determine their needs. He couldn't possibly presume to know what the owner wants or needs. The builder's role, in meeting with the owner, is largely to listen and then to advise.

My friend the home builder tells me that certain home owners may want a design that is architecturally unsound - either because their ideas and design are unsafe and would violate accepted building code regulations, or because they would violate local zoning regulations for their neighborhood. In some cases, he tells me, owners ask for features that he is certain they will later regret - and for which they probably hold him responsible. His role as an advisor demands that he inform the homeowner of these problems.

As soon as my friend believes that he understands what the owner wants, then he prepares a set of blueprints to be reviewed by the homeowner. Frequently the owner, after seeing his own vision on paper, will decide to change something, such as the location of a window or the size of a closet. The concrete characteristics of the blueprints make an agreement between the builder and owner easier to arrive at. The same can be said of a concrete plan for the writing of a program or the development of a system.

The big advantage of developing a plan on paper is that, while the project is still on paper, it's relatively painless to change it. Once the house has been assembled and bolted together, it becomes much more of a problem to change something.

The same is true of a computer program. Although it's not physically nailed or bolted together, once a programmer has started to write a program, changing it becomes very labor-intensive. It's much easier to change the design of a system prior to writing the first line of code.

In the world of software development, you would be surprised how many programmers begin work on an application without really having listened to the user. I know some programmers who get a call from a user, take some quick notes over the phone, and deliver an application without ever having met them! It could be that the user's requirements sound similar to something the programmer wrote last year, so the developer feels that will be good enough for the new client.

Other developers go a step further, and may actually meet with the client to discuss the user's needs. Nevertheless, sometimes the developer may not be a good listener, or just as likely, the user may communicate their needs poorly. The result may be that the user receives a program that doesn't come close to doing what they wanted it to do.

In this course, we'll develop a prototype for a real-world application called the Grades Calculation Program, and then take it through to the complete product. As we progress through the course together, we will work through one possible solution, but I want you to know that in Python programming, the number of solutions is almost infinite. As I tell my students all the time, there are many ways to paint a picture. One of the things I love about teaching Python is that I have never received the same solution to a project twice. Everyone brings his or her own unique qualities to the project.

I want you to feel free to take the Grades Calculation Program and make your solution different from mine. In fact, I encourage it, but you should stick close to the Requirements Statement that we are going to develop in this chapter.

We Receive a Call from our 'Client'

During my Fall Semester Visual Basic class, I had been lucky enough to be contacted by a client, Joe Bullina, owner of the Bullina China Shop, who needed a fairly high tech computer program written to produce price quotations for the customers in his shop, and I had used the development of his program as the class project for my Visual Basic course.

Python, by its very nature, is a bit more difficult to learn than Visual Basic, and although I knew I could ask the students in my Python class to write the same program in Python, I also knew that incorporating every feature found in the Visual Basic version of the China Shop program would be difficult to 'squeeze' into an eight week Python course. Furthermore, I also knew that many of those same Visual Basic students would be present in the Python class, and most likely they would be in the mood for a fresh 'challenge'--not a rehash of the China Shop program.

And so I was glad when one Monday morning, about a week before meeting with my Python class for the first time, I received a phone call from Frank Olley, a fellow professor at the University, and Dean of the English Department. Frank and I knew each other well--in fact, at one time he had been a teacher of mine. Frank was wondering if I could write a program that he could use to calculate student grades.

I asked Frank if he had considered using a spreadsheet program like Excel to do the calculations---his requirement sounded like a fine application for that.

He told me he had considered Excel, but he ultimately wanted the program to be able to prompt the user for the correct grade "pieces" necessary to calculate the student's final grade—something he didn't know how to do in Excel.

Frank and I agreed to meet on Tuesday afternoon in his office.

We Meet with Our 'Client'

I arrived at Frank Olley's office around 2 p.m. on a sunny Tuesday afternoon. Entering the Liberal Arts building, a large brick building brought back pleasant memories of my college years. I hadn't been in the Liberal Arts building since I graduated some years back--the Computer Science building was now my haunt.

I found Frank's office, and was greeted by his secretary.

"Hi, I'm John Smiley; I'm here to meet Frank Olley."

"Just a minute Mr. Smiley, Mr. Olley is expecting you."

A few moments later, Frank came out of his office.

"Sorry to keep you waiting, John" Frank said, warmly extending his hand. "I was on the phone with Robin Aronstam and David Burton--I believe you know who they are."

Indeed I did---Robin Aronstam was the chairman of the Mathematics Department and David Burton was the chairman of the Science Department.

"I hope you don't mind if Robin and David attend our meeting," Frank continued, "I think they may want to 'piggyback' some requirements of their own on top of mine."

"Piggyback?" I asked.

"That's right, John," Frank replied. "I saw them both in the Faculty dining room today at lunch, and I mentioned to them that you were coming over to discuss writing a program to calculate student grades---they were wondering if you could include their requirements in the program also."

"I don't see why not," I said. Just then Robin and David arrived. During the course of the next twenty minutes or so the three of them laid out for me their unique requirements. There was a commonality in that each one required a program that could calculate the final grade for a student in their own department---English, Math and Science. On the other hand, each had their own requirements.

NOTE: This project, though 'real world' has been toned down a bit for learning purposes.

"The English Department," Frank Olley explained, "calculates the Final grade for a student taking an English course as 25% of their Midterm grade, 25% of their Final Examination grade, 30% for a semester long Research paper, and--because we expect our students to be able to speak in public and make oral presentations---20% for a half hour long Class presentation."

"The Science Department is similar," David chimed in, "except that we don't require a Class presentation. We calculate the grade for a student taking a Science course as 40% of their Midterm grade, 40% of their Final Examination grade, and 20% for a semester long Research paper."

Robin then explained that for a student taking a Math course, only a Midterm and Final Examination grade entered into the equation. "Each counts 50% toward their final grade," Robin said.

"Those requirements don't seem terribly complicated," I assured them. "Do you have any details in your mind as to what you want the program to look like?"

"Not really," Frank said. "I guess we were hoping that you could take care of those details. Don't get us wrong. We know what we want the program to do, that is, calculate a student's grade. Beyond that, our biggest requirement is that the program be simple to use."

"Can you think of anything else?" I asked.

"Eventually, we'd like to have the program be accessible from the Web" David added. He hesitated for a moment and then added hopefully. "What do you think? The program doesn't sound too difficult, does it?"

Famous last words, I thought to myself. "No David, it doesn't," I said, "I could probably write this program in an hour or so...."

Robin noticed that my voice had trailed off.

"What's wrong?" she asked.

"Nothing's wrong," I said, "I was just thinking..."

I explained to Frank, Robin and David that on Saturday I would be meeting with my 'Introduction to Programming with Python ' Spring Semester class for the first time. I then went on to explain to them that in my Fall Semester Visual Basic course, the class and I had developed a real-world application for a client in West Chester.

"Perhaps," I said, "this time around, we could have them work on your requirements as their class project."

Frank looked excited and nervous at the same time.

"How would that work?" he asked.

"Well," I said, "each semester I give my Python programming students a project to work on. Python is a bit more complicated than Visual Basic, so although I was tempted to have them work on the same project as my Fall Semester Visual Basic students, I thought that might be too much for a first Python class. However, your project sounds ideal, and I think it will excite them. It's better than anything I could ever dream up, because it's real, with a real 'client'--you--- expecting real results. And your requirements, though they seem simple enough from a user point of view, have a few 'quirks' that will make it pretty challenging from a Python programming perspective."

I looked at the group for a reaction. I saw a look of unease on David's face.

"I can take these requirements," I continued, "distribute them to my students on Saturday, and over the course of the eight Week Semester, they can write the program for you. By the end of the Semester, you'll have your program, and they'll have some real experience under their belts. Unless of course, you're in a huge hurry..."

"No," Frank said, "as long as they finish the program by the end of the Spring Semester, we can use the program to calculate the grades in each of our departments. Of course, I'm guessing that the program your students write won't be as sophisticated as one that you would write. After all, your students are just beginners."

"To some degree that's true, Frank," I said. "Most notably, the program we produce for you won't have a Windows user interface. It will be something that in the Python world we call a Console Application."

"Like an old DOS program?" Robin chimed in.

"That's right, Robin," I said. "Developing a Windows user interface in an introductory Python program is way beyond the scope of the class. However, since you eventually want this program to be available on the Web, that's something we can easily do in the JavaScript class I'll be teaching this summer."

"So we'll start out with a Python Console Application to calculate the spring semester grades," Frank said, "and then have a Web version available for the Fall Semester?"

"That shouldn't be a problem Frank," I said. "And I'll be working with them every step of the way. You can expect a top-notch program, and I have no doubt that we can finish the first version on time for you to use in May."

I must have said the magic words; at this Frank smiled, extended his hand and said, "That sounds like a deal to me."

"There's just one more thing Frank," I said sheepishly.

"What's that John?" he asked.

"Would it be possible to 'pay' my students something for the development of the program?" I asked. "It doesn't have to be much---but paying them will permit them to legitimately cite this experience as paid professional experience."

"I'm sure there's something in the English Department budget to pay them," Frank said smiling. "How about the Math and Science departments?"

"That shouldn't be a problem," Robin said. "You mentioned that your Fall Semester Visual Basic class wrote a program for a local business. How much did you charge him?"

"He paid us $540," I said. "I was able to give each one of my eighteen students $30 each."

"That sounds like a bargain to me," David said, "I'm sure each of our departments will be able to kick in $180 for your students work---sounds like a great idea to me."

As I prepared to leave, I warned the group that what we had done this afternoon merely represented the first step, the tip of the iceberg, so to speak, in a six step process known as the Systems Development Life Cycle (SDLC). The first phase, the Preliminary Investigation, had begun and ended with our initial interview. Five phases of the SDLC remained.

As I walked to the door, Frank and I mutually agreed that I would deliver to him, in a week or so, a Requirements Statement drawn from the notes taken at today's meeting. I warned the group that when they read the Requirements Statement that I would send to them, the possibility existed that they would find some things that I had misinterpreted, and perhaps some things that they would be sure they had mentioned that wouldn't appear at all. I told him that the Requirements Statement would act as a starting point for their project. Until I received a confirmation from them confirming the Requirements, neither my student team nor I would proceed with the development of the program.

As I walked out the door of Frank's office, we all exchanged warm 'good byes'. Frank, David and Robin were all genuinely likable people, and I hoped this experience would be a rewarding one for them and the students in my class. I left Frank, Robin and David discussing an upcoming Freshman Social, and I headed off to teach a late afternoon class at the University.

The Systems Development Life Cycle (SDLC)

During my walk to my late afternoon class, I gave a great deal of thought to Frank's program. The more I thought about it, the more I believed that having my students write the program was a great idea, and I was sure they would think so too. Working on a real-world application would be a great practical assignment for them. Even more so than something I made up, this project would give each of them a chance to become deeply involved in the various aspects of the SDLC. For instance:

- someone in the class would need to work on the user requirements

- someone else would be involved in a detailed analysis of the Grading program

- everyone would be involved in coding the program

- some students would work on installing the software

- some students would be involved in training and implementation

Four days later, on Saturday morning, I met my 'Introductory Programming with Python' class for the first time.

As is my custom during my first class, I took roll, and asked each of the students to write a brief biography on a sheet of paper. Doing this gives me a chance to get to know them, without the pressure of having to open themselves up to a room full of strangers, although many of them will become good friends during the course of the class.

I only called out their first names as I like to personalize the class as much as possible. Usually, I have some duplicated first names, but this semester, that wasn't a problem.

"Valerie, Peter, Linda, Steve, Katherine Rose."

"If you don't mind, just call me Rose," Rose said.

"Rhonda, Joe, John."

"Jack, if you don't mind."

"Barbara, Kathy, Dave, Ward, Blaine, Kate, Mary, Chuck, Lou, Bob."

A total of eighteen students.

After giving them 15 minutes to write, I collected their biographies and began to read them. A few had some programming experience, using programming languages that were a bit dated. A number were looking to get into the exciting world of Computer Programming, either because they had an opportunity at work, or believed one would open up shortly. A couple of them were people looking to get into the work force after years away from it. One of the students, Chuck, was just fifteen, a local high school student. Another student, Lou, was permanently disabled, and although he didn't look it, he wrote that his disability would probably end up restricting him to a wheelchair.

My classroom is about 40 feet by 20 feet and there are three rows of tables containing PCs. Each student has their own PC, and at the front of the room I have my own, cabled to a projector that enables me to display the contents of my video display.

My first lecture usually involves bringing the class up to a common level so that they feel comfortable with both the terminology and methodology of using a PC-based environment. This time, however, instead of waiting a few weeks before introducing the class project, I could hardly wait to tell them. In the first few minutes of class, I introduced the students to the Grades Calculation Program. Just about everyone in the class seemed genuinely excited at the prospect of developing a real-world application. They were even more excited after I offered to split the profits with them. For most of the class, this was their first programming course---and at its conclusion, they would all be paid as professionals, with a legitimate project to add to their resumes.

"You mean this course isn't going to be the usual 'read the textbook, and code the examples' course," Ward said.

"Exactly," I said, "we'll be developing a real world application, and getting paid for it!"

"How will we know what to do?" Rose asked nervously.

I explained that in today's class, we'd actually develop a Requirements Statement.

"A Requirements Statement," I said, "is an agreement between the contractor (in this case us) and the customer (in this case Frank, Robin and David) that specifies in detail exactly what work will be performed, when it will be completed, and how much it will cost."

I continued by explaining that at this point, all we had were my notes from my initial interview with them. For the most part, this was just a quick sketch of the program. While we might very well have produced a quick sketch of the user interface in the following hour or so, we still did not know how to write a single line of code in Python. There was still much to learn! Furthermore, while we could probably pretty easily come up with a sketch of what the program would look like, we still needed to concern ourselves with the processing rules (e.g., the calculated grades of the various student types) which Frank, Robin and David had given to me during our meeting.

> **TIP: Processing rules are known either as Business Rules or Work Rules.**

"Can you give us an example of a Business Rule?" Peter asked.

"Sure Peter," I answered. "A good example would be a web-based ticket purchasing Web site, where customers are typically restricted from ordering large quantities of tickets. The Web site might have a business rule that prohibits the same customer from purchasing more than 4 tickets to the same event."

"That very thing happened to me just last week," Valerie said. "I tried to purchase an entire row of tickets to the upcoming Elton John concert, but the Web site restricted me to just 4."

I pointed out that I had agreed to drop off the Requirements Statement to Frank Olley sometime before we met for class next Saturday. I told my class that there was the possibility that the Requirements Statement would have some mistakes in it, and even some missing items. Frank might very well see something on the Requirements Statement that would cause him to think of something else he wants the program to do. I cautioned them not to be too hasty at this point in the project. There was still a great deal of planning left to do!

"Such hastiness," I said, "is exactly why the Systems Development Life Cycle was developed."

> **TIP: The SDLC was developed because many systems projects were developed which did not satisfy user requirements and the projects that did satisfy user requirements were being developed over budget or over time.**

I saw some puzzled looks. I explained that the Systems Development Life Cycle (SDLC) is a methodology that was developed to ensure that systems are developed in a methodical, logical and step-by-step approach. There are six steps, known as *phases*, in the Systems Development Life Cycle:

> **NOTE: Different companies may have different 'versions' of the SDLC. The point is that just about everyone who does program development can benefit from one form or other of a structured development process such as this one.**

- The Preliminary Investigation Phase

- The Analysis Phase

- The Design Phase

- The Development Phase

- The Implementation Phase

- The Maintenance Phase

I continued by explaining that out of each phase of the SDLC, a tangible product, or *deliverable*, is produced. This deliverable may consist of a Requirements Statement, or it may be a letter informing the customer that the project cannot be completed within their time and financial constraints. An important component of the SDLC is that at each phase in the SDLC, a conscious decision is made to continue development of the project, or to drop it. In the past, projects developed without the guidance of the SDLC were continued well after 'common sense' dictated that it made no sense to proceed further.

"Many people say that the SDLC is simply common sense," I said. "Let's examine the elements of the SDLC here. You can then judge for yourself."

Phase 1: The Preliminary Investigation

I told my class of my meeting with Frank, Robin and David, which essentially constituted the Preliminary Investigation Phase of the SDLC.

"This first phase of the SDLC," I said, "may begin with a phone call from a customer, a memorandum from a Vice President to the director of Systems Development, or a letter from a customer to discuss a perceived problem or deficiency, or to express a requirement for something new in an existing system. In the case of the Grades Calculation program, it was a desire on the part of Frank Olley to develop a 'program' to calculate grades of English students in his department---of course, you already know how it's quickly grown beyond that to include the Math and Science departments."

I continued by explaining that the purpose of the Preliminary Investigation is not to develop a system, but to verify that a problem or deficiency actually exists, or to pass judgment on the new requirement. The duration of the preliminary investigation is typically very short, usually not more than a day or two for a big project, and in the instance of the Grades Calculation Program, about an hour.

The end result, or deliverable, from the Preliminary Investigation phase is either a willingness to proceed further, or the decision to 'call it quits'. What influences the decision to abandon a potential project at this point? There are three factors, typically called *constraints*, which result in a go or no-go decision.

- <u>Technical</u>. The project can't be completed with the technology currently in existence. This constraint is typified by Leonardo Da Vinci's inability to build a helicopter even though he is credited with designing one in the 16th century. Technological constraints made the construction of the helicopter impossible.

- <u>Time</u>. The project can be completed, but not in time to satisfy the user's requirements. This is a frequent reason for the abandonment of the project after the Preliminary Investigation phase.

- <u>Budgetary</u>. The project can be completed, and completed on time to satisfy the user's requirements, but the cost is prohibitive.

"In the case of the Grades Calculation Program," I told my students, "Frank and I never came close to dropping the project. This is a project that all of us really wanted to pursue. And paying us something to do the programming is just icing on the cake!"

Needless to say, the students and I formally decided to take on the project, and proceed with the second phase of the SDLC.

Phase 2: Analysis Phase

The second phase of the SDLC, the Analysis phase, is sometimes called the Data Gathering phase.

> **NOTE: In this phase we study the problem, deficiency or new requirement in detail. Depending upon the size of the project being undertaken, this phase could be as short as the Preliminary Investigation, or it could take months.**

I explained that what this meant for my class was potentially another trip to the Liberal Arts building to meet with Frank, Robin and David to gather more detailed requirements, or to seek clarification of information gathered during the Preliminary Investigation.

> **WARNING: As a developer, you might be inclined to believe that you know everything you need to know about the project from your preliminary investigation. However, you would be surprised to find out how much additional information you can glean if you spend just a little more time with the user.**

You might be inclined to skip portions of what the SDLC calls for, but it forces you to follow a standardized methodology for developing programs and systems. As we'll see shortly, skipping parts of the SDLC can be a big mistake, whereas adhering to it ensures that you give the project the greatest chance for success.

I told them that while some developers would make the case that we have gathered enough information in Phase 1 of the SDLC to begin programming; the SDLC dictates that Phase 2 should be completed before actual writing of the program begins.

"The biggest mistake we could make at this point would be to begin coding the program. Why is that? As we'll see shortly, we need to gather more information about the business from the 'owner'---in this case Frank, Robin and David. There are still some questions that have to be asked."

In discussing the SDLC with the class, I discovered that one of my students, Linda Schwartzer, had some Systems Analysis experience. Linda offered to contact Frank Olley, to set up an appointment to spend part of the day with the person who currently calculates the grades for the English department. This meeting would fulfill the data-gathering component of the Analysis Phase. In the short time I had spent with Linda, I sensed a great communicative ability about her, and so I felt very comfortable with Linda tackling the Analysis phase of the SDLC.

Typically, our first class meeting is abbreviated, and since we were basically frozen in time until we could complete Phase 2 of the SDLC, I dismissed the class for the day. Prior to Linda's meeting with Frank Olley, I sent him the following email:

Hi Frank,

I want to thank you for taking the time to meet with me last Tuesday afternoon. As I discussed with you at that time, it is my desire to work with you in developing a program that can calculate student grades for the English, Math and Science departments.

The program will be developed as part of my Introduction to Python computer class at the University. As such, your costs will be $540, payable upon final delivery of the program. In return, you agree to allow me to use your contract to provide my students with a valuable learning experience in developing a real-world application.

Sometime during the coming week, one of my students, Linda Schwartzer, will be contacting you to arrange to spend time meeting with the person who currently calculates grades in the English department. Although you may not see the necessity in this additional meeting, it will satisfy the next phase of the Systems Development Life Cycle I discussed with you at our meeting. Adhering strictly to the SDLC will result in the best possible program we can develop for you.

I'd like to take this opportunity to highlight the major points we discussed last week. We will develop a PC-based program, for you, with an eye toward web enabling it also. Here are the major functions that the developed program will perform:

1. This program will provide the user with a user-friendly interface for calculating a student's grade.

2. The user will be requested to designate the type of student--English, Math or Science---for which they wish to calculate a grade.

3. If the user indicates they wish to calculate the grade for an English student, the interface will prompt them for a Midterm examination grade, a Final examination grade, a Research Paper grade, and a Presentation grade. The final grade will be calculated as 25% of the Midterm examination grade, 25% of the Final examination grade, 30% of the Research Paper grade, and 20% of the Presentation grade.

4. If the user indicates they wish to calculate the grade for a Science student, the interface will prompt them for a Midterm examination grade, a Final examination grade, and a Research Paper grade. The final grade will be calculated as 40% of the Midterm examination grade, 40% of the Final examination grade, and 20% of the Research Paper grade.

5. If the user indicates they wish to calculate the grade for a Math student, the interface will prompt them for a Midterm examination grade, and a Final examination grade. The final grade will be calculated as 50% of the Midterm examination grade and 50% of the Final examination grade.

6. Once calculated, the grade will be displayed on the interface.

I think I've covered everything that we discussed last Tuesday. If I have missed anything, please let Linda know when she arrives in your office.

Regards,

John Smiley

This email, in essence, will become the Requirements Statement that we will formally develop shortly. The next day I received the following fax from Frank Olley:

Dear John

I reviewed your email, and everything looks fine.

One thing we forgot to mention last Tuesday is that the numeric grades need to be converted to 'letter' grades for report card purposes. Complicating matters is that the letter grade equivalents of all the departments are different. Here is a table explaining the breakdown.

DEPT	ENGLISH	MATH	SCIENCE
A	93 OR GREATER	90 OR GREATER	90 OR GREATER
B	85 TO 93	83 TO 90	80 TO 90
C	78 TO 85	76 TO 83	70 TO 80
D	70 TO 78	65 TO 76	60 TO 70
F	LESS THAN 70	LESS THAN 65	LESS THAN 60

Regards,

Frank Olley

Complicate the program? Sure, a bit. I was sure Linda would more than likely find other surprises as well. This new 'requirement' was about par for the course. I checked my notes, and Frank was correct---he never mentioned it. Of course, a good developer can anticipate requirements such as these. I just missed it.

Linda called me on Monday morning to tell me that she had arranged to meet with Frank Olley on Thursday morning. That Thursday evening Linda called to tell me that her observations of the English, Math and Science Department's current operations had gone well. Contrary to what I expected, she saw nothing in her observations of their day-to-day operation that contradicted the notes that I took during my preliminary investigation.

However, Linda reported that nothing out of the usual occurred. She did tell me that from her observations, it was obvious that the program would pay for itself in no time. All three departments had work-study students performing the calculations manually---and making lots of mistakes.

That Saturday, I again met with our class. After ensuring that I hadn't lost anyone in the intervening week (yes, everyone came back), we began to discuss the third phase of the SDLC---the Design phase.

Phase 3: Design Phase

"Phase 3 of the SDLC is the Design phase," I said.

I explained that design in the SDLC encompasses many different elements. Here is a list of the different components that are 'designed' in this phase:

- Input
- Output
- Processing
- File

"Typically," I said, "too little time is spent on the design phase. Programmers love to start programming." I continued by saying that you can hardly blame them, writing a program is exciting, and everyone wants to jump in and start writing code right away. Unfortunately, jumping immediately into coding is a huge mistake.

"After all," I said, "you wouldn't start building a house without a blueprint, would you? You simply cannot and should not start programming without a good solid design."

> **NOTE: Even though at this point the class knew very little about Python, they were already familiar with computer applications of one kind or other--either Microsoft Windows program, Macintosh programs, Linux programs or Web based programs (knowledge of one of these is a requirement for the course). Designing and developing the 'look' of an application program is independent of the tool that you'll use to program it.**

I should point out here that my role in the Design Phase was to act as a guide for my students. Frank Olley had told us what he wanted the program to do. Like any 'client', he described his program requirements in functional terms that he understood.

My students were already familiar with computer applications, but at this point in our course, they were not Python experts. However, knowing how to use a program was not sufficient for them to know how Frank Olley's requirements translated into the terms of a Python program. Ultimately, it was my job to help them translate those requirements into Python terms.

I pointed out that critics of the SDLC agree that it can take months to complete a house, and making a mistake in the building of a house can be devastating; writing a Python program, on the other hand, can be accomplished in a matter of hours, if not minutes. If there's a mistake, it can be corrected quickly.

Critics of the SDLC further argue that time constraints and deadlines can make taking the 'extra' time necessary to properly complete the Design Phase a luxury that many programmers can't afford.

"I answer that criticism in this way," I said, citing a familiar phrase that you have probably heard before. "It seems there is never time to do something right the first time, but there's always time to do it over."

The exceptional (and foolish) programmer can begin coding without a good design. Programmers who do so may find themselves going back to modify pieces of code they've already written as they move through the project. They may discover a technique halfway through the project that they wish they had incorporated in the beginning, and then go back and change code. Worse yet, they may find themselves with a program that 'runs' but doesn't really work, with the result that they must go back and start virtually from the beginning.

"With a good design," I said, "the likelihood of this nightmare happening will be reduced dramatically. The end result is a program that will behave in the way it was intended, and generally with a shorter program development time."

Armed with our notes from the Preliminary Investigation, Linda's notes from the Detailed Analysis, and Frank Olley's emails, my students and I began the Design Phase of the SDLC in earnest. By the end of the design phase, we hoped to have a formal Requirements Statement for the program, and perhaps even a rough sketch of what the user interface will look like.

I reminded my students that the Requirements Statement would form the basis of our agreement with Frank, Robin and David. For some developers, the Requirements Statement becomes the formal contract to which both they and the customer agree, and sign.

Linda began the design phase by giving the class a summary of the three or four hours she spent in the English, Math and Science departments. Linda said that she felt comfortable in stating that nothing she had observed that day contradicted the view expressed in my notes, and in my email to Frank Olley.

Not everyone in the class had had the benefit of seeing my notes or the email, so I distributed to the class copies of my notes, my email to Frank Olley, and his reply email to me. I gave my students a few minutes to review and digest the material.

We began to discuss the program requirements. I could see there was some hesitation as to where to begin, so I began the process with a question.

"Let's begin by making a statement as to what we are trying to accomplish here," I said.

"We need to write a program to display the calculated final grade for a student in the English, Math or Science departments," Dave said.

"Excellent," I said. Dave had hit the nail squarely on the head. The primary purpose of the program was to calculate a student's grade. To be sure, there would be more to the program than that, but from Frank Olley's point of view, all he needed the program to do was to display a student's grade.

"To clarify," Kate said, "we should probably state the student's 'letter grade' as opposed to the student's numeric grade."

"Good clarification Kate," I said, "Frank did add that in his email didn't he."

Frequently, new programmers are unable to come to grips as to where they should begin in the Design Phase. I suggested to my class that most programs are designed by first determining the output of the program. The reasoning behind starting with the output is that if you know what the output of the program should be, you can determine the input needed to produce that output pretty easily. Once you know both the output from, and the input to the program, you can then determine what processing or calculations that need to be performed to convert that input to output.

Output Design

I told my students that we were fortunate, in that the class's first project was one where the output requirements could be stated so simply: a grade calculation.

"Where will the grade calculation go?" I asked.

"To a printer?" Jack suggested.

"On the computer screen," Rose countered.

"I agree with Rose," I said, "probably to the computer screen."

Some of the students seemed perplexed by my answer.

"Probably?" Dave asked.

I explained that Frank Olley and I had never formally agreed where the grade calculation would be displayed. The issue had never come up.

"Let's be sure," I said, "to explicitly specify a display of the grade calculation in the Requirements Statement. Speaking of which…would anyone care to volunteer to begin to write up the specifications for it?"

Dave volunteered to begin writing our Requirements Statement, so he started up Microsoft Word and started typing away.

Rhonda made a suggestion for the color and font size for the program's calculated grade display, but Peter said that it was probably a bit premature to be talking about colors and font sizes at this point in our design. I agreed, pointing out that in this class, we would be creating a Python Console Application.

"Do you mean a DOS program?" Peter asked.

"That's one way of looking at it, Peter," I answered. "For this introductory-level Python class, writing a Microsoft Windows program is definitely beyond its scope. We need to concentrate on learning good fundamental, object-oriented programming techniques. There are advanced courses here at the University that can teach you how to develop a program that has a Microsoft Windows user interface; however, in this class, you'll learn to write a Python Console application, which will resemble an old-time DOS program."

"Will there be any other output from the program?" Rhonda asked, after several moments went by.

"I'd like to suggest that we display the date and time on the computer screen," Valerie suggested.

"Good idea," Mary said.

However, Linda disagreed, arguing that the display of the date and time was unnecessary considering the fact that the PC's at the University were all running Windows---and displayed the current time on the Windows Taskbar anyway.

"We could display the current date and time," I said, "but I'm inclined to agree with Linda---all of the PC's at the University that will run our program are Microsoft Windows based---and capable of displaying a date and time on their own. And while it's true that the beauty of the Python programs we will learn how to write in this class are that they can run on virtually any operating system---I can't think of any environment in which the user can't be aware of the current date and time if they so desire."

The majority of the class agreed.

"Getting back to the display of the grade," Peter said, "do you think it would be a good idea to display the calculated numeric grade as well as the letter grade?"

"Yes, I think that's a great idea," Kathy added.

Taking a moment to consider, I said, "I agree also. So we now have two output requirements---a grade calculation, where we display both the calculated numeric grade for the student, and the corresponding letter grade. I can't think of anything else from an output point of view, can you?"

"What about the individual components that makes up the grade?" Rhonda asked. "Should we display those?"

"Great idea, Rhonda," I said.

"But won't the user be inputting those values?" Blaine responded. "Is it necessary to repeat them?"

"I think it's a good idea to display the values that the user has input," I said. "That way, the user can be sure what component pieces make up the final grade that is being displayed."

I waited to see whether there were any questions, but there were none.

"I think we now have enough information to proceed to our next step," I said. "What's that? Anyone?"

Barbara suggested that because we seemed to have the output requirements identified—the component grade pieces that the user has entered, along with a calculated final grade—we should move on to a discussion of processing.

"As I explained earlier, it will be easier for us if we discuss input into the program prior to discussing processing," I said. "It's just about impossible to determine processing requirements if we don't know our input requirements."

Input Design

"So does anyone have any suggestions as to what input requirements we need?" I asked the class.

Dave quickly rattled off several input requirements: a Midterm grade, a Final Examination grade, a Research Paper grade, and a Presentation grade.

"Excellent," I said, "of course, those requirements will vary depending upon the type of student that is being calculated."

"Is that another piece of Input?" Mary suggested, "The type of student whose grade is being calculated."

"Excellent observation Mary," I said. "Only for an English student will all four grades be required. A Science student's final grade is comprised of three component pieces---Midterm Final Examination and Research Paper, and a Math student's final grade is comprised of only two pieces---the Midterm and Final Examination grades."

"Anything else?" I asked.

"How will the input be entered into the program?" Kathy asked. "How will the user of the program let the program know what type of student they are entering?"

Designating the type of Student

Several students suggested that the user of the program could designate the type of student by entering the type using the computer's keyboard.

"My motto is to have the user do as little typing as possible," I said. "If we ask the user of the program to use the keyboard to enter the type of student into the program, we're going to have to insist that each user of the program type it consistently---that's something we can't count on. For instance, one user may type 'Math', another may type 'Mathematics', and still a third may type 'Calculus'."

"I see what you mean," Rhonda said. "But what's our alternative?"

I could see that some of the students were perplexed about the alternatives to entering the type of student via the PCs keyboard.

"Can we prompt the user to enter a number instead?" Kathy asked.

"What do you mean, Kathy?" Rhonda asked.

"Well," Kathy said, "instead of asking the user to type 'English,' 'Math,' or 'Science,' why not have them type the number 1 for English, the number 2 for Math, and the number 3 for Science? There's only one way to type the numbers 1, 2, and 3—that should cut down on user input error."

"Excellent, Kathy," I said. "That's certainly one way—and probably the best way—to handle this dilemma."

Designating the Component grades

OK," Ward said. "Now that we have come up with a way for the user to identify the student type, what happens next?"

"I'd like to suggest," Dave said, "that depending on the value the user enters—1, 2 or 3—that the program then prompt the user for the appropriate component grades—midterm examination, final examination, research paper, and presentation."

"What do you mean by appropriate component grades, Dave?" Rhonda asked.

"Well," Dave replied, "if the user tells the program that they wish to calculate the grade for an English student, then the program needs to prompt for all four component pieces—midterm examination, final examination, research paper, and presentation. If the user tells the program that they wish to calculate the grade for a math student, then the program needs to prompt for just two component pieces—midterm examination and final examination. Finally, if the user tells the program that they wish to calculate the grade for a science student, then the program needs to prompt for three component pieces—midterm examination, final examination, and research."

"Excellent, Dave," I said.

"This sounds like it's all going to be a lot of fun," Rhonda said. "I just wish I could envision what the interface will look like. Do we have to wait until we write the program to see what the interface will actually look like?"

"Good question, Rhonda," I said. "No, we don't have to wait that long. There's no rule that says we can't sketch the user interface using pencil and paper well before that."

"How can we have an interface if we aren't designing our program as a Windows program?" Kate asked.

"I see your point, Kate," I answered, "but even though our program won't have a Windows look and feel, we still need to make some design decisions about how the program will interface with the user of our program. Without a good interface—whether it be Windows or not—a program is doomed to failure."

The First Interface Design

As it turned out, during the course of our discussions, Barbara had been sketching a preliminary interface design. Upon hearing my remarks about sketching the interface, she offered to show the class what she had sketched so far, and I displayed it on the classroom projector.

```
Enter student type (1=English, 2=Math, 3=Science): 1

Enter the Midterm Grade: 100
Enter the Final Examination Grade: 100
Enter the Research Grade: 100
Enter the Presentation Grade: 100

Final Numeric Grade is: 100
Final Letter Grade is: A
```

"That looks great, Barbara," Rhonda said. "Seeing the interface design on paper makes this easier for me to envision."

"I agree, Rhonda," I said. "And you'll find that having a blueprint like this will make programming the interface much easier later on."

I then asked Barbara if she would mind explaining the interface design to the rest of the class.

"It's kind of basic," Barbara said, "but based on our previous discussion, I figured the first thing we would want to do is to ask the user the type of grade they wished to calculate. I did that by displaying a message asking them to enter 1 for an English student, 2 for a math student, and 3 for a science student. In the sketch, I've presumed they've selected 1 for an English student, and after they've typed the number 1, the program then prompts them to enter the component grade pieces for an English student. I hope this is OK."

"It's great, Barbara," I said, "Exactly what I had in mind. Does anyone have any suggestions? Don't be shy now—this sort of collaborative effort is the way things are frequently done in the real world."

"I have a suggestion, but I don't want to appear to be picky," Blaine said.

"Go ahead Blaine," Barbara answered. "I realize this is a bit rough."

"I was going to suggest that there's no title or identifying caption for the program," he answered. "Someone walking by the PC wouldn't know what the user was working on. I guess the interface, while perfectly functional, just seems a bit 'unfriendly' to me."

"Blaine's right," Barbara answered. "I didn't include any such element in the sketch. Should I be that detailed here?"

"It can't hurt," I said. "It's one less thing to forget when it comes time to actually write our code."

"I can fix that," Barbara said, and in a minute, version 2 of the interface design was displayed for my students to see—this one having a welcome message, and a thank-you for using the program.

```
WELCOME TO THE GRADES CALCULATION PROGRAM

Enter student type (1=English, 2=Math, 3=Science): 1

Enter the Midterm Grade: 100
Enter the Final Examination Grade: 100
Enter the Research Grade: 100
Enter the Presentation Grade: 100

Final Numeric Grade is: 100
Final Letter Grade is: A

THANKS FOR USING THE GRADES CALCULATION PROGRAM!
```

"Anything else?" I asked.

"I'd like to suggest," Dave said, "that we repeat the grades that the user has entered, and that we right justify both the grades and the calculated answer."

"I'm not sure what you mean Dave," Barbara said. "Why don't you take over here?" She then handed Dave her sketchpad.

"I'm not much of an artist," Dave said, but in a minute or two he had modified Barbara's sketch to look like this.

```
WELCOME TO THE GRADES CALCULATION PROGRAM

Enter student type (1=English, 2=Math, 3=Science): 1

Enter the Midterm Grade: 100
Enter the Final Examination Grade: 100
Enter the Research Grade: 100
Enter the Presentation Grade: 100

**** ENGLISH STUDENT ****

Midterm Grade:          100
Final Examination Grade: 100
Research Grade:          100
Presentation Grade:      100

Final Numeric Grade is:  100
Final Letter Grade is:   A

THANKS FOR USING THE GRADES CALCULATION PROGRAM!

|
```

"Oh, I see," Rhonda said, "Dave's changes have 'neatened up' the interface quite a bit."

"This is starting to shape up quite nicely," Steve said.

That seemed to be the majority opinion of the class. I waited to see if there were any other suggestions.

"I have a question." Chuck said. "Is the program going to end after the user calculates just one grade? Shouldn't we ask the user if they have any more grades to calculate?"

"Chuck's right," Barbara said, "I never thought of that!"

"That's a great point, Chuck," I said, "I'd like to suggest that the first thing we do is ask the user if they have a grade to calculate. If they answer 'No,' we immediately thank them for using the program, and end it. If they answer 'Yes,' then we ask them the type of student they wish to calculate. After prompting them for the appropriate data, we display the final grade, and then ask them if they have another grade to calculate. If they answer 'Yes,' then once again we prompt them to tell us the type of student they wish to calculate...."

"And we repeat the process all over again," Dave chimed in. "Sounds like a perfect application for a loop?"

"A what?" Rhonda asked.

"A Loop is a programming Structure," I said smiling, "and it's something that you'll learn about a few weeks from now. Until then, please don't worry about it."

I noticed that Barbara had finished making my suggested changes to on her sketch, and I took it from her and displayed it on the classroom projector.

```
WELCOME TO THE GRADES CALCULATION PROGRAM

Do you want to calculate a grade? YES

Enter student type (1=English, 2=Math, 3=Science): 1

Enter the Midterm Grade: 100
Enter the Final Examination Grade: 100
Enter the Research Grade: 100
Enter the Presentation Grade: 100

**** ENGLISH STUDENT ****

Midterm Grade:              100
Final Examination Grade: 100
Research Grade:            100
Presentation Grade:       100

Final Numeric Grade is:   100
Final Letter Grade is:     A

Do you have another grade to calculate? NO

THANKS FOR USING THE GRADES CALCULATION PROGRAM!
```

"This project is beginning to shape up," Ward said. "Did we forget anything?"

"I can't think of anything," I said. "But the great thing about doing the design on paper first is that if you do forget anything, it's a matter of making some changes to a sheet of paper, not to your program code."

I waited to see if there were any questions, but there were none.

The Requirements Statement

We had been working pretty intensely and, in my opinion, making some excellent progress, so I suggested that we take a break. Before adjourning, I asked Dave, the student who was developing the Requirements Statement, to let us see what he had developed so far. I made copies of his work. After the break, I handed these out to the rest of the class for discussion. Here is the copy of the Requirements Statement I gave to my students:

<u>REQUIREMENTS STATEMENT</u>

Grades Calculation Program

GENERAL DESCRIPTION

The program will consist of an Interface in which the user will be asked if he or she has a grade to calculate.

If the answer is No, the program will thank them and immediately end.

If the answer is Yes, the program will prompt the user for the type of student for whom they wish to calculate a grade. Depending upon the answer, the user will then be prompted to enter the appropriate component grades (see Business Rules below)

After displaying both a calculated numeric and letter grade, the program will ask the user if they have another grade to calculate.

If the answer is Yes, once again the program will prompt the user for a student type.

If the answer is No, the program will thank them and immediately end.

OUTPUT FROM THE SYSTEM

The student's final numeric grade and letter grade will be displayed. In addition, the program will indicate the type of student for which it has displayed a grade, and repeat (or echo back) the values it used to calculate the grade.

INPUT TO THE SYSTEM

The user will specify the type of student whose grade is to be calculated by entering 1 for an English student, 2 for a Math student, or 3 for a Science student.

If an English student, the Midterm, Final Examination, Research Paper, and Class Presentation grades will be prompted for and entered by the user.

If a Math student, the Midterm and Final Examination grades will be prompted for and entered by the user.

If a Science student, the Midterm, Final Examination, and Research Paper grades will be prompted for and entered by the user.

BUSINESS RULES

An English student's grade is calculated as 25% of the Midterm grade, 25% of the Final examination grade, 30% of the Research Paper grade and 20% of the Class Presentation grade.

A Math student's grade is calculated as 50% of the Midterm grade and 50% of the Final examination grade.

A Science student's grade is calculated as 40% of the Midterm grade, 40% of the Final examination grade, and 20% of the Research paper grade.

Each department has unique letter grade equivalents for the student's calculated final numeric average. Here is a table of the letter grade equivalents:

DEPARTMENT	ENGLISH	MATH	SCIENCE
A	93 OR GREATER	90 OR GREATER	90 OR GREATER
B	85 TO 93	83 TO 90	80 TO 90
C	78 TO 85	76 TO 83	70 TO 80
D	70 TO 78	65 TO 76	60 TO 70
F	LESS THAN 70	LESS THAN 65	LESS THAN 60

I explained to the class that the Requirements Statement can easily form the basis of a contract between the customer and the developer of the program. The Requirements Statement should list all the major details of the program. You should take care not to paint yourself into any unnecessary programming corners by including any window dressing. These can just get you into trouble later. For instance, notice here that we didn't specify the exact text of how we would thank the user for using our program, and we didn't mention the welcome message the program would display (although we did include these details on our sketch). Suppose, for instance, we later decided against displaying a welcome message—theoretically, deviating from the Requirements Statement could be construed as a violation of contractual terms.

I asked for comments on the Requirements Statement, and everyone seemed to think that it was just fine. My students agreed that the project was coming along quite nicely, but as they say, the proof is in the pudding. It's only the customer's opinion that counts, and we'd have to see how Frank, Robin, and David felt about it. With no more comments or suggestions on the user interface or the Requirements Statement, we set about completing the Design phase of the SDLC by looking at processing.

Processing Design

"Processing is the conversion of inputs to outputs, the conversion of Data to Information," I said. "At this point in the Design phase of the SDLC, we should have now identified all of the output from the program---a calculation of the student's grade---and all of the input necessary to produce that output--the component pieces of the grade."

I explained that just as a good novel will typically have several subplots; a Python program is no exception. It contains several processing 'subplots' as well.

We have the main 'plot', that is the calculation of the student's grade, but we also have 'subplots' such as:

- Determining the type of student whose grade is being entered

- Selectively displaying the appropriate prompts for component grades based on the student type selected

- Ensuring that valid data is entered as a response to the prompts

- Making the appropriate calculation

- Displaying the calculated grade

It's important to note that in Processing Design, we don't actually write the program. That's done later. In Processing Design, we specify the processes that need to be performed to convert input into output.

Looking at Processing in Detail

"Let's look at a simple example which isn't part of the Grades Calculation Program," I said, "that most of you are probably familiar with, the calculation of your paycheck."

I continued by saying that if you want to calculate your net pay, you need to perform several steps. Here are the steps or functions necessary to calculate your net pay:

1. Calculate gross pay

2. Calculate tax deductions

3. Calculate net pay

> NOTE: Programming is done in the next phase of the SDLC, the Development Phase. Specifying how processing is to occur is not as important in this phase as specifying what is to occur. For instance, this sequence identifies the 'what' of processing, not the how. The 'how' is a part of the Development phase.

These functions can be broken down even further. For instance, the calculation of your gross pay will vary depending upon whether you are a salaried employee or an hourly employee. If you are an hourly employee, your gross pay is equal to your hourly pay rate multiplied by the number of hours worked in the pay period. The specification of these functions is exactly what the designer must detail in the Processing Design phase of the SDLC.

When it comes to processing design, documenting the processing rules is crucial because translating processing rules into a narrative form can sometimes result in confusion or misinterpretation. Over the years, systems designers have used various 'tools' to aid them in documenting the design of their systems.

Some designers have used tools called *flowcharts*. Flowcharts use symbols to graphically document the system's processing rules. Here are the net pay processing rules we discussed earlier depicted using a flowchart. (My apologies to any accountants reading this; these calculations have been simplified for illustration purposes.)

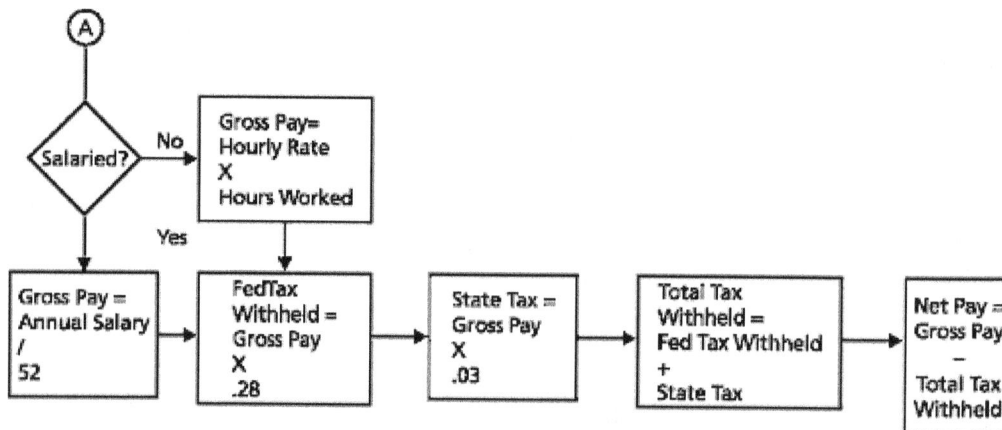

Other designers favor Pseudocode. Pseudocode is an English-like language that describes in non-graphical form how a program should execute. Here are the same net pay processing rules depicted using Pseudocode:

Assumption: Pay is calculated on a weekly basis (52 pay periods per year).

Assumption: Salaried employee pay is Annual Salary divided by 52.

Assumption: Hourly employee pay is Hourly Rate multiplied by hours worked.

1. If employee is salaried, then go to Step 4

2. Employee is hourly, then calculate gross pay equal to hourly wage rate multiplied by hours worked in pay period

3. Go to Step 5

4. Employee is salaried, so calculate Gross Pay equal to Annual Salary divided by 52

5. Calculate Federal Tax withheld equal to Gross Pay multiplied by 0.28

6. Calculate State Tax withheld equal to Gross pay multiplied by 0.03

7. Calculate Total Tax withheld equal to Federal Tax withheld + State Tax withheld

8. Calculate Net Pay equal to Gross Pay less Total Tax withheld

> NOTE: Both of these techniques found favor in the era of the Procedural Program.

> A Procedural Program is one that executes from top to bottom virtually without interruption. A procedural program ordains to the user exactly how they will interact with your program. For instance, in the Grades Calculation Program, the user will select a type of student, and then enter values for component grade pieces such as the Midterm or Final Examination grade.

> I frequently find students who have a strong programming background writing procedural programs. Procedural Programming (using languages like Basic, Fortran and COBOL) is like taking a ride on a tour bus, where all of the destination stops are pre-determined, and pre-ordered.

> Windows programs are Event-Driven programs. Event-Driven programs (using languages such as Visual Basic, C# and Python) don't force the user to behave in a certain way, but rather react to the user.

> An event-driven program does not attempt to 'dictate' to the user what they should do in the program, and when they should do it. Instead an event-driven program presents the user with a visual interface that permits them to interact with the program. This is more like choosing the rides at a carnival.

> Once entry has been gained, the rides they go on and the order in which they ride them is entirely up to the user. An event-driven program must be able to work and respond to any eventuality.

"In my classes," I said, "I don't require the use of either flowcharting or Pseudocode. All that I ask from you is that you give careful thought to the processing that is necessary to solve the problem before beginning to code in Python."

I could see some happy faces and I continued by saying that invariably, this means working out a solution on a piece of paper prior to coding it. Some students are more 'visual' than others, preferring to design their solution in graphical terms. Other students are less 'visual' and their solutions look very much like the Pseudocode we saw earlier. The point is, without some written plan, the programming process can go awry.

I cited this example. Several years ago, I was teaching a class on another language called COBOL, and I gave my students the following programming problem:

> Write a program to calculate the net wage of a laborer who works 40 hours at a pay rate of $5 per hour. Income tax at the rate of 20% of the gross pay will be deducted. What is the net pay?

The correct answer is $160. Forty hours multiplied by $5 per hour results in a gross pay of $200. The income tax deduction is 20% of $200, which is $40. $200 less the $40 income tax deduction results in a net pay of $160.

A number of students calculated the net pay as $240. Instead of deducting the income tax deduction of $40 from the gross pay, they added it instead. When I questioned the methodology behind their incorrect answer, most of them told me they thought the problem had been so simple, that they hadn't bothered to work out the solution on a piece of paper ahead of time. They just started coding. Had they taken the time to work out the solution on paper first, they would have known what the answer should be and they wouldn't have submitted a program to me that calculated the results incorrectly.

"This is what I'm suggesting to you," I said. "Take the time to work out the solution on paper. You'll be happy that you did."

Back to the Grades Calculation Program

We continued by discussing processing design. I reminded my students that, in general, design is an iterative process. It's rare that the designer or programmer hits the nail perfectly on the head the first time. It's very possible that after going through processing design, you will discover that you are missing some crucial piece of input necessary to produce a piece of output. In this case, you would need to look at your input processing again. For instance, with the Grades Calculation Program, we could have forgotten to ask the user to specify the type of student whose grade they wished to calculate--such an omission would have catastrophic consequences.

As a starting point in our processing discussion, we agreed to begin with our primary goal: *To calculate a student's grade.* We had already determined that in order to calculate a grade, we needed to know the type of student, and once we knew that, the individual grade components that made up the final grade.

We started with a hypothetical user entering a hypothetical student's information.

"Can anyone tell me," I asked "what the final grade for an English student would be if he or she scored an 88 on their midterm examination, a 90 on their final examination, an 85 on their Research paper, and a 75 on their Class presentation? Plus, can you tell me how you arrive at the result?"

"If I were solving this problem using pencil and paper," Ward said, "I would take the score for the student's midterm grade-88--and multiply it by .25, giving me a result of 22 which I would then set aside. I would then take the score for the final examination--90---and multiply it by .25, giving me a result of 22.5, which I would then set aside. I would then take the score for the student's Research paper---85---and multiply it by .3, giving me a result of 25.5, which I would then set aside. I would then take the score for the Class Presentation---75---and multiply it by .2, giving me a result of 15, which I would then set aside. Finally, I would take the four 'set aside' results---22, 22.5 25.5 and 15, and add them together to arrive at a sum of 85--which, if we refer to the Requirements Statement, equates to the letter 'B' for an English student."

"That's excellent Ward," I said.

"I think we've got a problem here," Chuck said. "I went through the same process Ward just did--but I come up with a letter grade of 'C'."

Sure enough, we did have a problem. In looking over the Requirements Statement, it indicated that for an English Student, the numeric grade of 85 equated to both the letter 'B' and the letter 'C'.

"How did that happen?" Kate asked.

"Those are the numbers that Frank Olley supplied in his email," I said, "unfortunately, I missed catching this. Right now we have a little problem---but I happen to know that Frank is in his office today---hopefully he can give us a quick solution to the problem."

I pulled out my cell phone (ah, the conveniences of modern living!) and gave Frank a quick call. Fortunately, he was still in his office. I explained that in his email to me outlining the numeric grade-letter equivalents, he had used the phrase '78 to 85' to describe the letter grade of 'C' for an English student---and then the phrase '85 to 93' to describe the letter grade of 'B'--what happens if the student scores a final numeric grade of '85' right on the nose.

I had to explain the problem once more for Frank--and then he apologized and explained that a numeric grade of '85' was the starting point for a 'B'---anything less than '85' was a C. I asked him if the same applied to the other categories--since we also had overlapping there. Frank said that it did, and based on our discussion, the class and I re-worked that table from the Requirements Statement to look like this...

DEPARTMENT	ENGLISH	MATH	SCIENCE
A	>= 93	>= 90	>= 90
B	< 93 and >= 85	< 90 and >= 83	< 90 and >= 80
C	< 85 and >= 78	< 83 and >= 76	< 80 and >= 70
D	< 78 and >= 70	< 76 and >= 65	< 70 and >= 60
F	< 70	< 65	< 60

"That's better," I said, admiring my work.

"Maybe for you," Rhonda responded, "this reminds me of Algebra, and I think the table is a lot more difficult to read this way. Do we have to express the rules for the letter grade computations this way? Those less than and greater than symbols always confused me."

"In the long run, we'll be better off," I said, "the way we've phrased the rules for forming the letter grades isn't much different from the Python code we'll write. Plus, these are expressed in certain terms--unlike the previous version of the table which had the overlapping values."

"Have we missed anything with the grade calculation?" I asked.

"Suppose," I added, "the user selects a student type of 'English' and enters value for a Midterm, a Final examination, and a Research paper--but fails to enter a value for the Class presentation--what should the program do?"

"How can that happen?" Kate asked. "I mean, doesn't the user have to respond to the prompts that are displayed?"

"That's true Kate," I said, "but it's possible for the user to simply press the ENTER key, thereby not providing a value for that particular grade component."

My students agreed that we needed to display some sort of error message if we didn't have all the ingredients necessary to arrive at a valid grade calculation—either because the user simply pressed the ENTER key or they entered an invalid value (a value less than 0 or greater than 100). An error message is another form of output.

Now it seemed as though we were gaining momentum. As I mentioned earlier, during the course of processing design, we may uncover holes in the input or output design, such as the overlapping grade. That had been the case here. Although it's certain that we would have eventually noticed these holes when we were coding the program, fixing these flaws while we were still in the design phase of the SDLC is much easier and cheaper than fixing them in the midst of programming the application.

In large projects particularly, portions of a project may be given to different programmers or even different teams of programmers for coding. It could be some time before flaws in the design are uncovered—in some cases weeks or even months. The longer it takes to discover these flaws, the more likely it is that some coding will have to be scrapped and redone. A well thought-out Design phase can eliminate many problems down the line.

We'd plugged the hole in the grade calculation processing—now it remained to be seen if there were any other processing design issues.

"What about ending the program?" Steve asked. "Do we need to write code for that?"

I explained that we would need to write a few lines of Python code to end the program--but that there was no need to formally state that in the Requirements statement. After a few moments of silence, it seemed that we were finished with the Design phase of the SDLC. Here is the **Final Requirements Statement** that the class approved:

REQUIREMENTS STATEMENT
Grades Calculation Program

GENERAL DESCRIPTION

The program will consist of an Interface in which the user will be asked if he or she has a grade to calculate.

If the answer is No, the program will thank them and immediately end.

If the answer is Yes, the program will prompt the user for the type of student for whom they wish to calculate a grade. Depending upon the answer, the user will then be prompted to enter the appropriate component grades (see Business Rules below)

After displaying both a calculated numeric and letter grade, the program will ask the user if they have another grade to calculate.

If the answer is Yes, once again the program will prompt the user for a student type.

If the answer is No, the program will thank them and immediately end.

OUTPUT FROM THE SYSTEM

The student's final numeric grade and letter grade will be displayed. In addition, the program will indicate the type of student for which it has displayed a grade, and repeat (or echo back) the values it used to calculate the grade.

INPUT TO THE SYSTEM

The user will specify the type of student whose grade is to be calculated by entering 1 for an English student, 2 for a Math student, or 3 for a Science student.

- If an English student, the Midterm, Final Examination, Research Paper, and Class Presentation grades will be prompted for and entered by the user.

- If a Math student, the Midterm and Final Examination grades will be prompted for and entered by the user.

- If a Science student, the Midterm, Final Examination, and Research Paper grades will be prompted for and entered by the user.

BUSINESS RULES

An English student's grade is calculated as 25% of the Midterm grade, 25% of the Final examination grade, 30% of the Research Paper grade and 20% of the Class Presentation grade.

A Math student's grade is calculated as 50% of the Midterm grade and 50% of the Final examination grade.

A Science student's grade is calculated as 40% of the Midterm grade, 40% of the Final examination grade, and 20% of the Research paper grade.

Each department has unique letter grade equivalents for the student's calculated final numeric average. Here is a table of the letter grade equivalents:

DEPARTMENT	ENGLISH	MATH	SCIENCE
A	>= 93	>= 90	>= 90
B	< 93 and >= 85	< 90 and >= 83	< 90 and >= 80
C	< 85 and >= 78	< 83 and >= 76	< 80 and >= 70
D	< 78 and >= 70	< 76 and >= 65	< 70 and >= 60
F	< 70	< 65	< 60

I polled the class to see if everyone agreed with the Requirements Statement, and then revealed that we were now done with the Design Phase of the SDLC. I once again reminded my students that the Design Phase of the SDLC tends to be an iterative process, and that we might find ourselves back here at some point. We then moved on to a discussion of the fourth phase of the SDLC--the Development Phase.

Phase 4: Development Phase

I told my class that we would not spend a great deal of time discussing the Development Phase here since the rest of the course would be spent in developing the Grades Calculation Program, in which they would play an active role!

"The Development phase is," I said, "in many ways the most exciting time of the SDLC. During this phase, computer hardware is purchased, if necessary, and the software is developed. Yes, that means we actually start coding the program during the Development phase, and in this class, we'll be using Python as our development tool."

I explained that during the Development Phase, we'd constantly examine and re-examine the Requirements Statement to ensure that we were following it to the letter, and I encourage all of them to do the same. I explained that any deviations (and there may be a surprise or two down the road) would have to be approved either by the project leader (me) or by our clients (Frank, Robin and David.)

Everyone in the class seemed anxious to begin, but they promised me they would remain patient while I discussed the final two phases of the SDLC.

Phase 5: Implementation Phase

The Implementation Phase is the phase in the SDLC when the project reaches fruition. I explained to my students that after the Development phase of the SDLC is complete, we begin to actually implement the system. In a typical project, what this means is that any hardware that has been purchased will be delivered and installed in the client's location.

In the instance of our clients," I said, "they already have the equipment. So instead, during the Implementation phase, the Python program that we write will be loaded onto their PC's."

Not surprisingly, everyone in the class agreed that they wanted to be there for that exciting day.

Barbara raised the issue of program testing. During the Implementation phase, both hardware and software is tested. We agreed that students in the class would perform most of the testing of the program, as we agreed that it would be unreasonable and unfair to expect our clients to test the software that we had developed in a 'live' situation. Naturally, our goal was that when the software was installed in the English, Math and Science departments, that the program should be bug (problem) free.

On the other hand, I cautioned them, almost invariably, the user will uncover problems that the developer has been unable to generate. I told them we would discuss handling these types of problems in more detail in our class on Error Handling.

> NOTE: As you'll see later on in the book, the official Python term for Error Handling is Exception Handling

"I've heard the term 'debugging used among the programmers at work," Valerie said. 'Is that something we'll be doing?"

"Most definitely Valerie," I said. "Debugging is a process in which we run the program, thoroughly test it, and systematically eliminate all of the errors that we can uncover. We'll be doing this prior to delivering the program to Frank, Robin and David."

I then explained that during the Implementation phase, we would also be training the users of the program-most likely work study students in the English, Math and Science departments---but perhaps Frank, Robin and David as well. Again, everyone in the class wanted to participate in user training. One of my students noted that she thought that there needed to be two levels of training performed:

Several students thought that it would be a good idea to have a student observing the users of the program during its first week of operation, in order to assist users in the operation of the system, and to ease any 'computer' anxiety that the users might be suffering. I thought this was a great idea, and also pointed out these observations would provide valuable feedback on the operation of the program from the most important people in the loop, the end users.

In fact, the mention of the word 'feedback' led quite naturally into a discussion of the final phase of the SDLC--- Audit (sometimes called Feedback) and Maintenance.

Phase 6: Audit and Maintenance Phase

Phase 6 of the SDLC is the Audit and Maintenance Phase. In this phase, someone, usually the client, but sometimes a third party such as an auditor, studies the implemented system to ensure that it actually fulfills the details of the Requirements Statement. The bottom line is that the developed system should have solved the problem or deficiency, or satisfied the desire that was identified in Phase 1 of the SDLC - the preliminary investigation.

More than a few programs and systems have been fully developed that, for one reason or another simply never met the original requirements. The Maintenance portion of this phase deals with any changes that need to be made to the system.

Changes are sometimes the result of the system not completely fulfilling its original requirements, but it could also be the result of customer satisfaction. Sometimes the customer is so happy with what they have got that they want more. Changes can also be forced upon the system because of governmental regulations, such as changing tax laws, while at other times changes come about due to alterations in the business rules of the customer.

As I mentioned in the previous section, we intended to have one or more members of the class in the English, Math and Science departments during the first week of system operation. That opportunity for the user to provide direct feedback to a member of the development team would more than satisfy the Audit portion of Phase 6.

In the future, we hoped that Frank, Robin and David would be so happy with the program that we had written for them, that he would think of even more challenging requirements to request of the class.

Where To From Here?

It had been a long and productive session for my students. I told them that in our next meeting we would start to discuss how a computer works, and we would actually begin to work with Python.

Ward asked me how the progression of the project would work, that is, would we finish the project during our last class meeting, or would we be working on it a little bit each week? I said that I thought it was important that we develop the program incrementally. Each week we meet, we would attempt to finish some portion of the project.

Developing the project in steps like this would hold everyone's interest, and give us a chance to catch any problems well before the last week of class.

Summary

The aim of this chapter was to tackle the question "Where do I begin?" We saw that the design of an application is best done systematically, with a definite plan of action. That way, you know that everything has been taken into account.

A good place to begin is with a Requirements Statement, which is a list of what the program has to be able to do. Usually, you get the information for this from whoever is asking you to write the program. It's a good idea to keep in continuous contact with this person, so that any changes they want can be tackled before it becomes too much of a problem.

A good systematic approach is embodied in the systems development life cycle (SDLC), which consists of six phases:

· The Preliminary Investigation: Considering the technical, time, and budgetary constraints and deciding on the viability of continuing development of the application.
· The Analysis Phase: Gathering the information needed to continue.
· The Design Phase: Creating a blueprint of the program's appearance and program structure without actually starting any programming.
· The Development Phase: Creating the application, including all interface and code.
· The Implementation Phase: Using and testing the program.
· The Maintenance Phase: Making refinements to the product to eliminate any problems or to cover new needs that have developed.

Using the SDLC methodology can make any problems you encounter in your design more obvious, making it easier for you to tackle them at a more favorable point in your design, rather than changing existing code.

Chapter 2--- Getting Comfortable With Python

In this chapter, we'll follow my computer class as they take their first look at the Python environment. The purpose of this chapter is to give you an overview of how to create a Python program using Windows Notepad (or any editor of your choice if you are using a Mac or a Unix PC) and how to run it. Throughout this chapter, as the class and I entered various commands into our PCs, I displayed the results of what we entered on the classroom projector that shows the contents of my video display. These results are shown throughout this chapter where appropriate.

Installing Python

I began our second class by getting straight to the point.--at least I thought I was, until I discovered that my Computer Lab Assistant had failed to install Python on the classroom computers.

"No problem," I said, "Python is easy to install, and we'll be up and running in no time."

The first step is to use a Web Browser (we were using Firefox) to navigate to the official Python Website

http://www.python.org/downloads

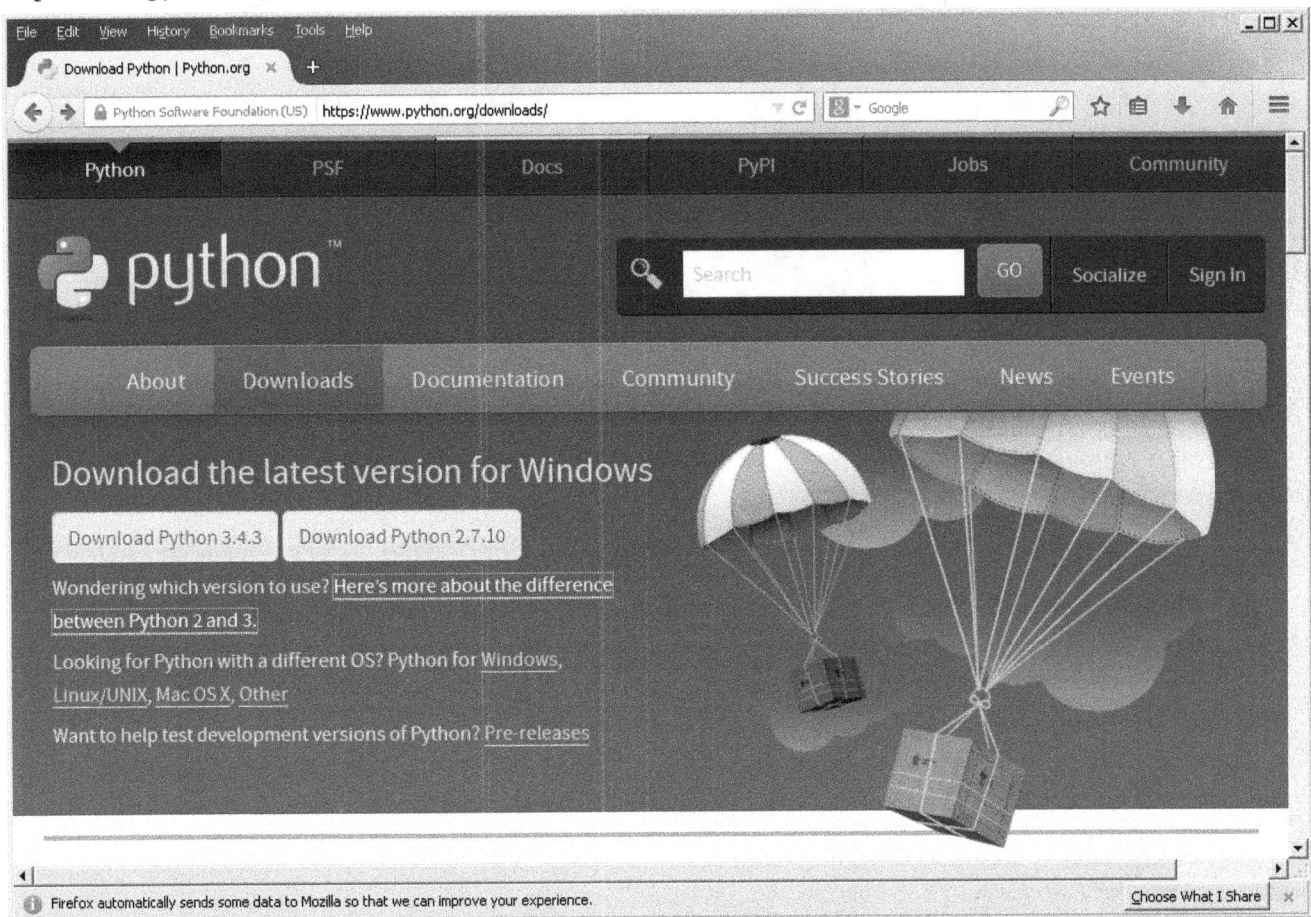

"Notice how this website presumes we want the Windows version," I said. "But it also offers Python for Linux/Unix and the Mac OX, along with the ever popular 'Other'. We'll be selecting the Windows version/"

"Why are there 2 versions?" Dave asked.

"Python has been around for a while," I answered, "and there are a bunch of programs that have been written using what I'll call 'classic Python.'. Python purists will tell you that if all you want to do is run old Python programs, download Version 2.7.10, which is the last of the Version 2 builds of the program. If you are interested in writing new Python programs that have even more functionality, you'll want to download the latest and greatest Python version, which today happens to be 3.4.3."

> NOTE: That was the case when I started writing this book. When I checked today, the latest was 3.6. That's the beauty of Python, it's always be improved upon, but the basics for an introductory book like this, remain the same. Feel free to download the latest version you see.

I then clicked on the "Download Python 3.4.3" tab.

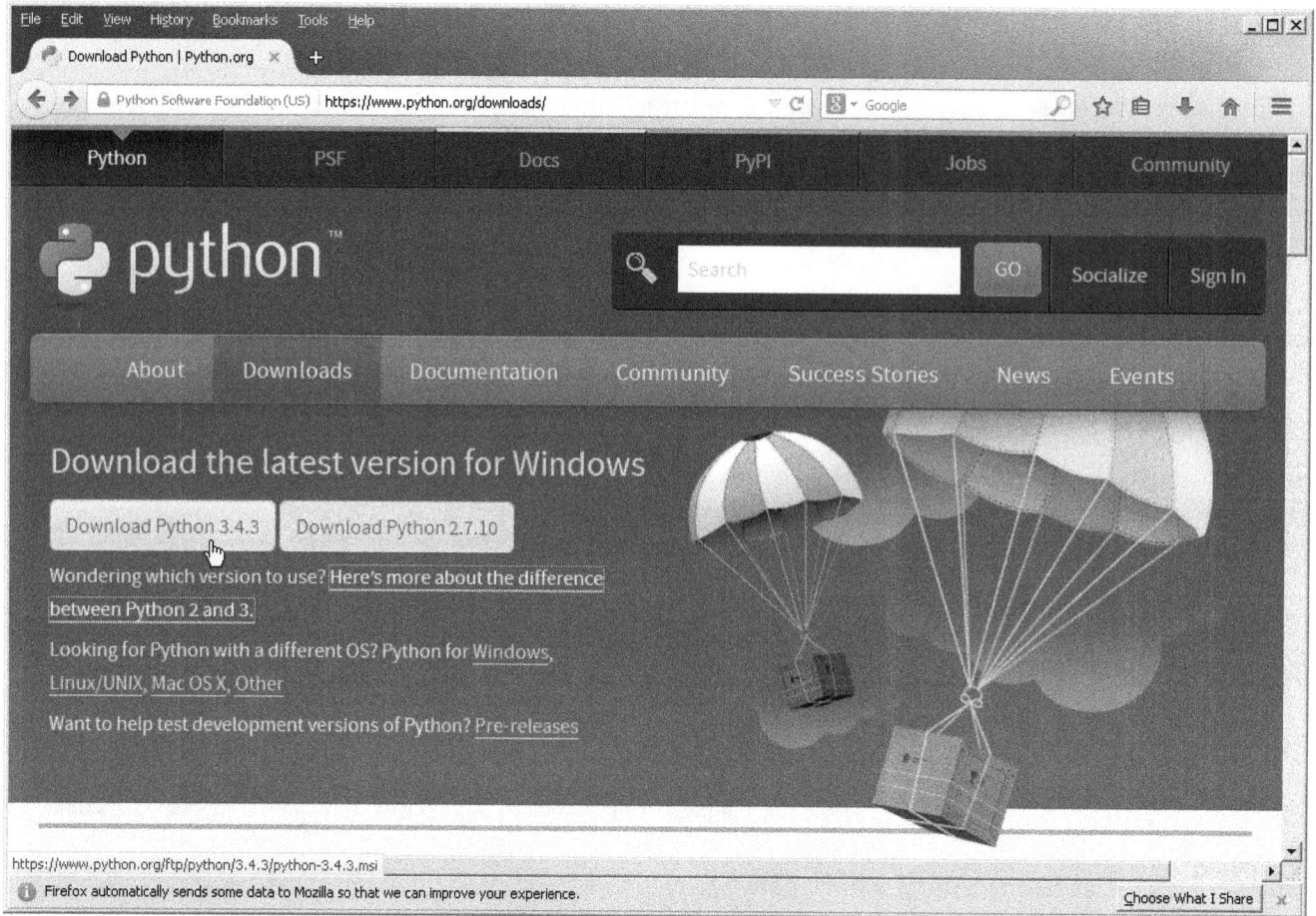

A message box appeared, indicating that I would be opening a Windows Installer Package called python-3.4.3.msi

That's fine, and so I clicked on the "Safe File" button...

At this point, it was just a matter of finding the file (depending upon where your browser saves it) and double clicking on the installer file...

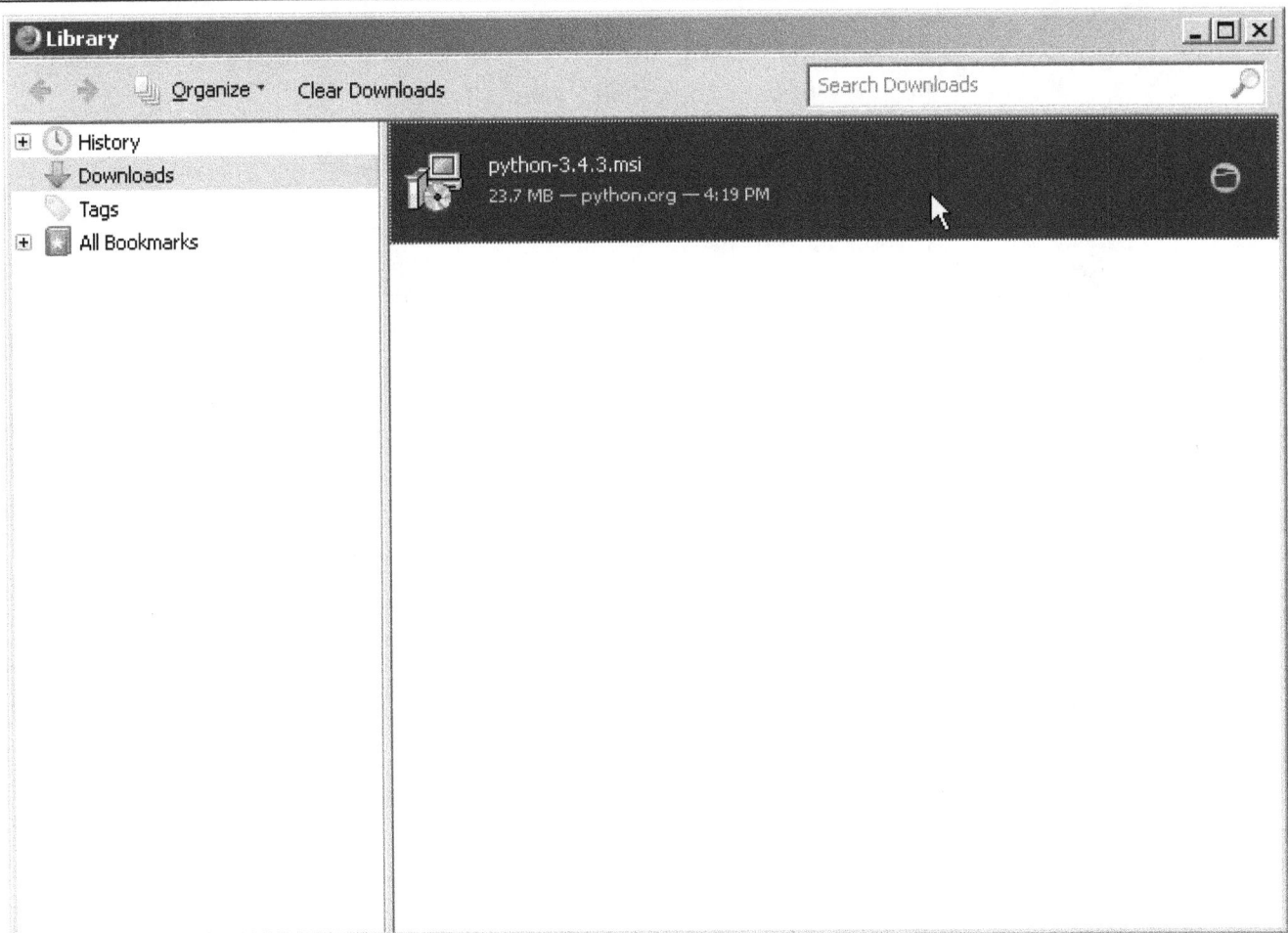

Firefox recognized that the installer file is an executable file. A warning appears. I clicked on the OK button to continue with the installation...

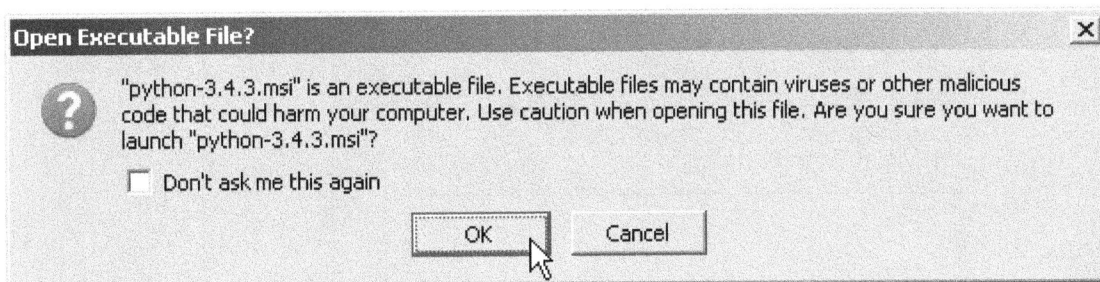

The Python setup program appears. You can choose to install Python for just the currently logged in user or for every user who may use the PC. I selected "Install for all users."

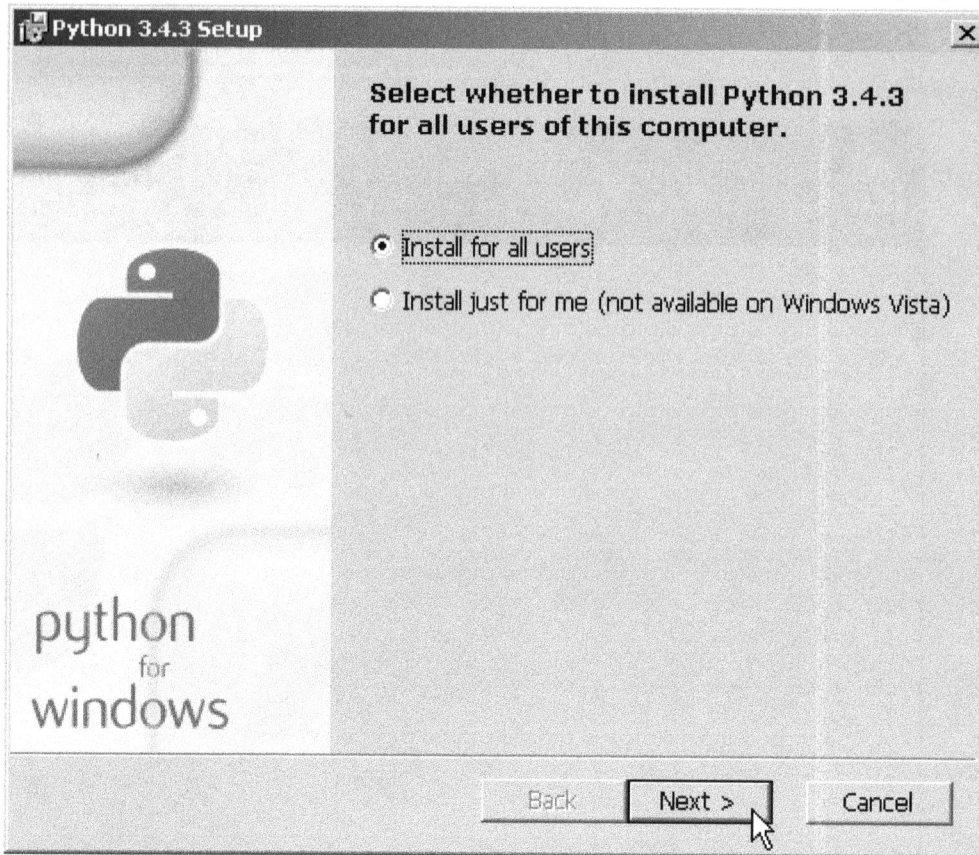

The Python installer then asks where we want to install Python---I accepted the default folder of C:\Python34 by clicking the Next button

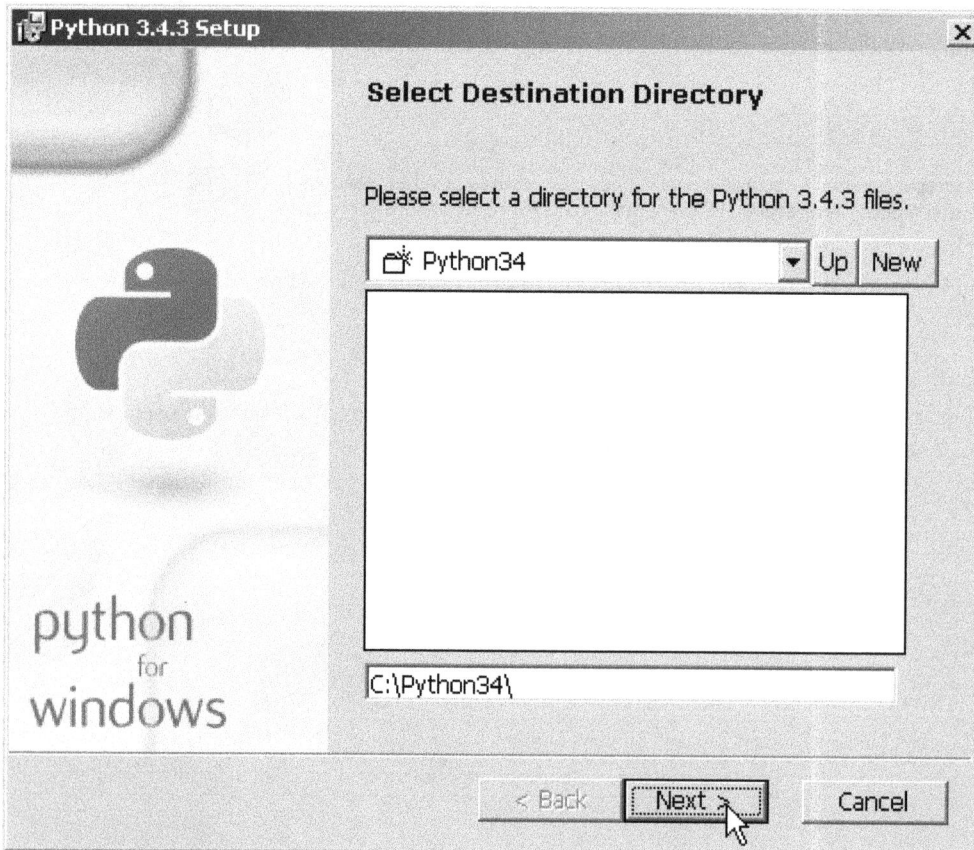

We have the ability to customize the Python installation---again, I just accepted the default installation by clicking on the Next button...

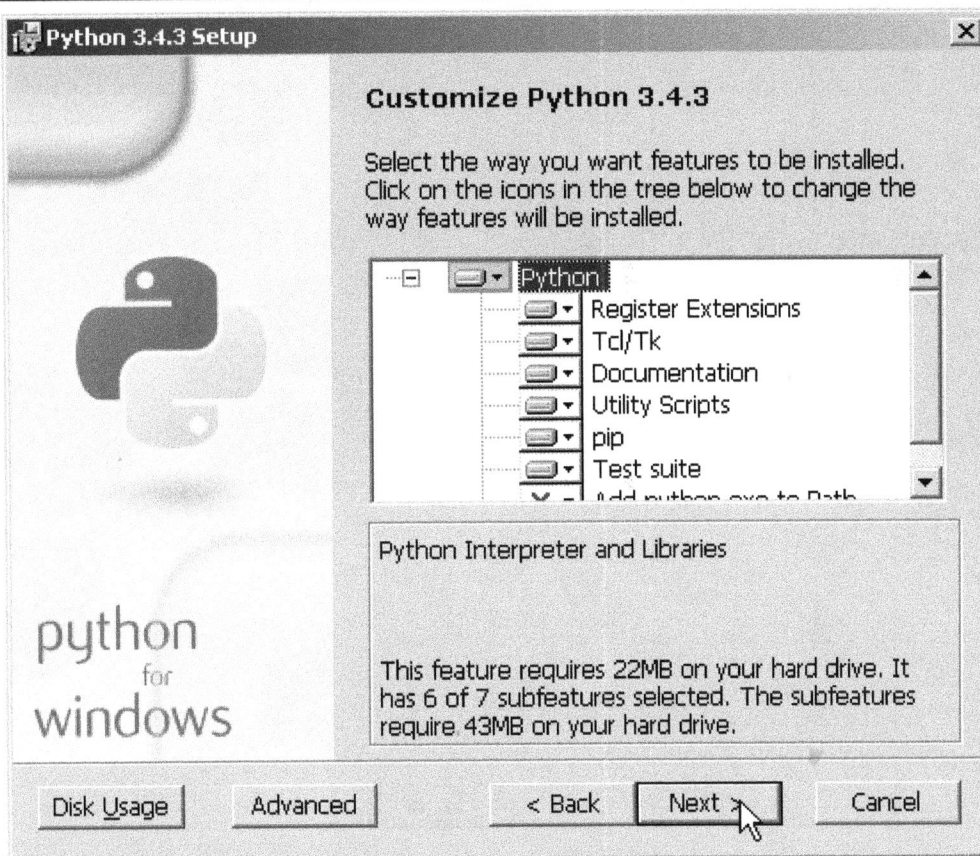

The Python installation now begins in earnest. This only takes a few minutes...

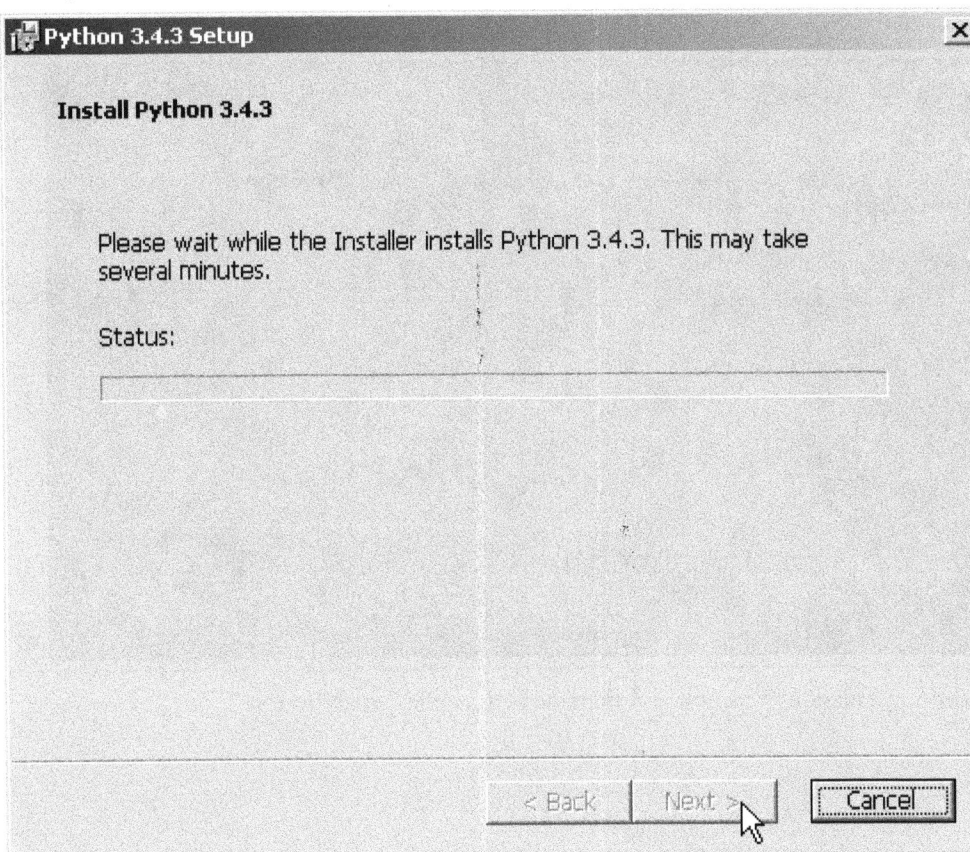

Files are copied...

```
Python 3.4.3 Setup                                          ×

    Install Python 3.4.3


       Please wait while the Installer installs Python 3.4.3. This may take
       several minutes.

       Status:  Copying new files

       ■■■■■■■■■■■■■■■

                                < Back    Next >       Cancel
```

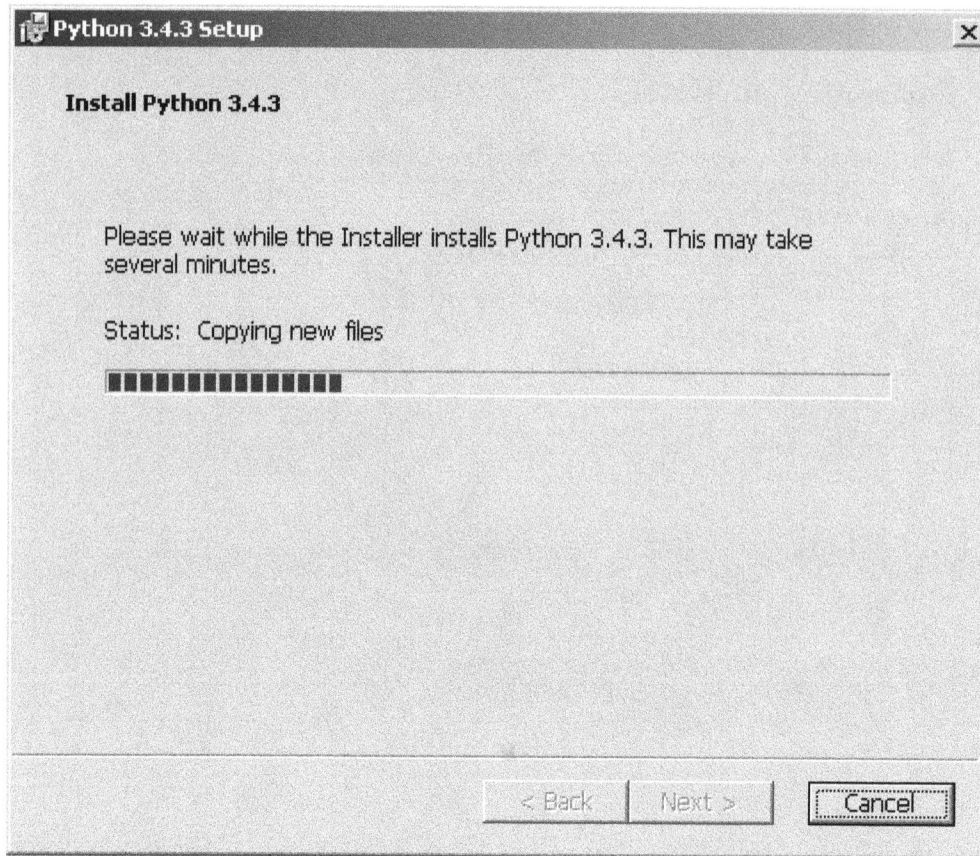

A command (DOS) window appears in the background---nothing to worry about...

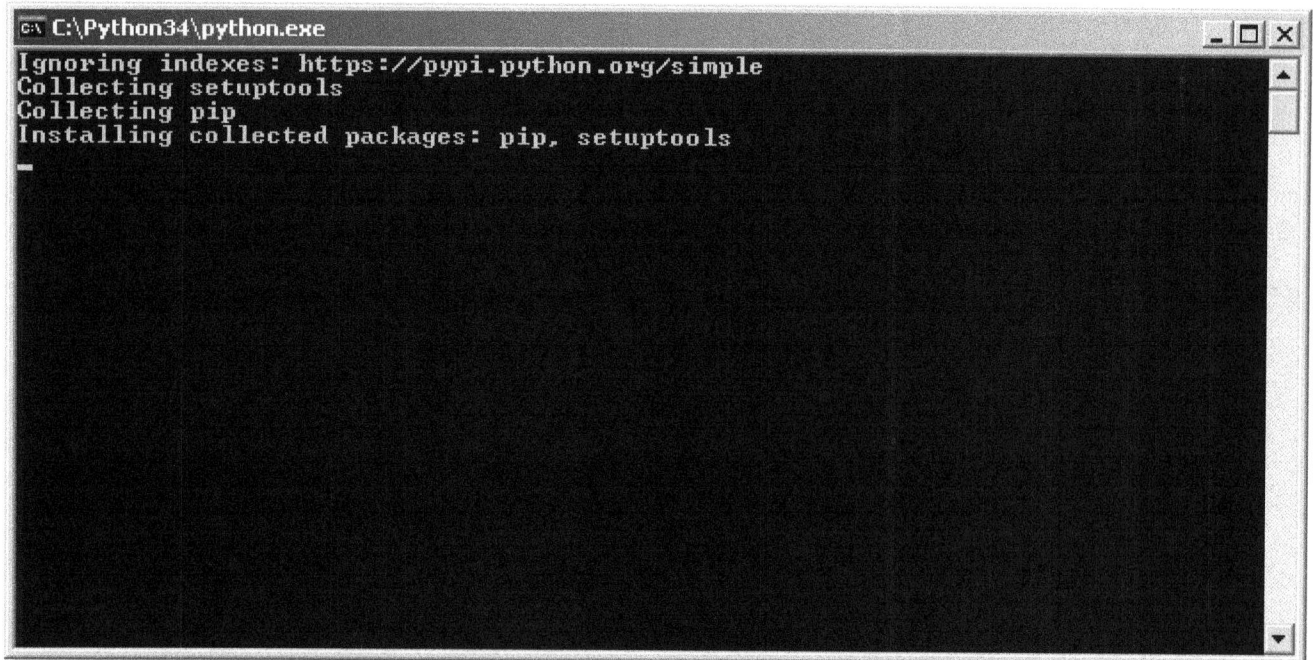

```
C:\Python34\python.exe                                    _□×
Ignoring indexes: https://pypi.python.org/simple
Collecting setuptools
Collecting pip
Installing collected packages: pip, setuptools
▄
```

Just a few minutes later, the Python installation is complete. I then clicked on the Finish button.

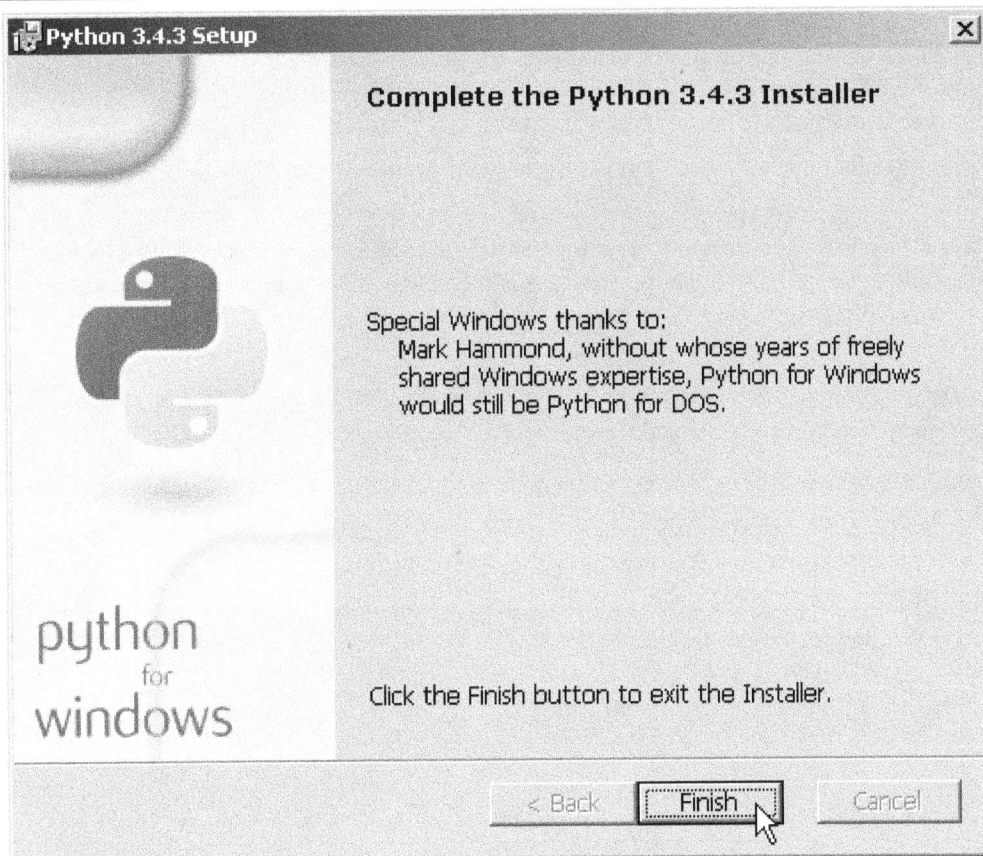

If you navigate to the Windows Program Manager, you'll see a Python 3.4 group containing 5 items. Interestingly, we'll never use any of these, although I encouraged my students to read through the Python 3.4. Manuals.

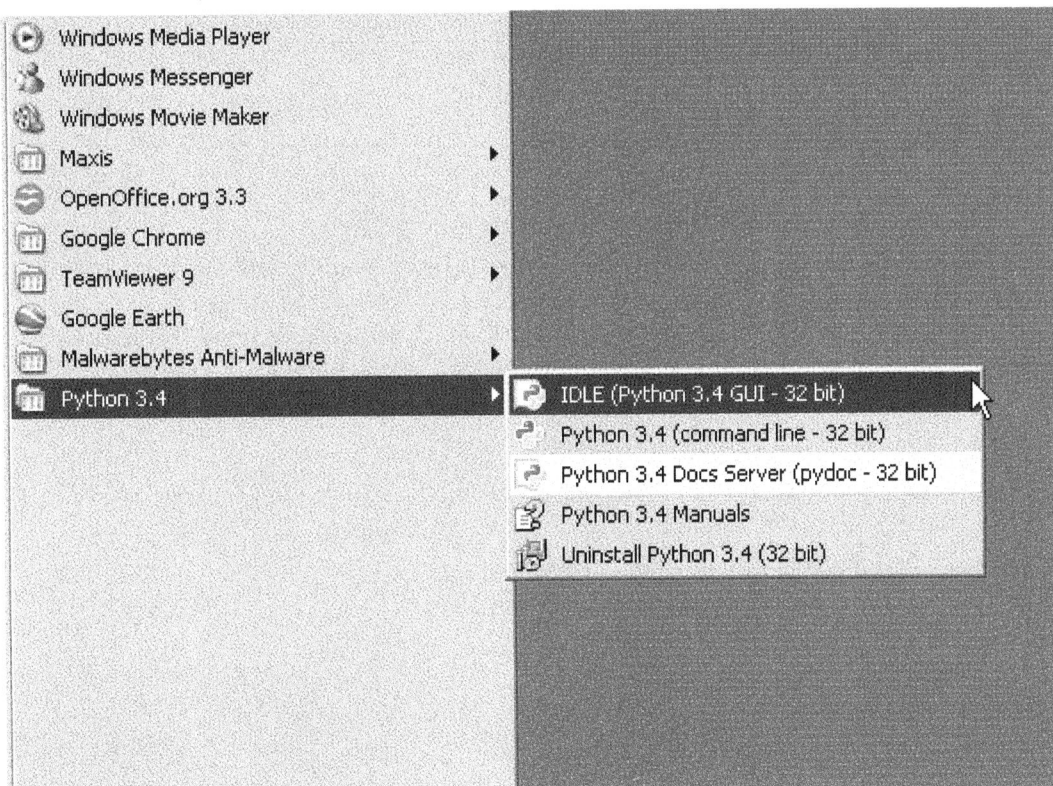

Let's talk about IDLE

"What is IDLE", Linda asked, obviously looking at the first item in the Python Program group.

"IDLE is a Python IDE, or Integrated Development Environment" I said. "Within IDLE, you can write a Python program, although in this class we'll be writing our programs using either Windows Notepad or Notepad++, and running or executing our programs in a Windows Command Window. The main thing most programmers like about IDLE is that it does permit you to test your code to observe how it runs."

Dave chimed in. "Does that mean if you are having a problem executing your program in a Windows Command Window you can test it in IDLE?"

"Exactly Dave," I answered. "IDLE reminds me very much of the very early BASIC Interpreter window, which some of you may have used. The only time we'll use IDLE in our class is today, when we compose and test our first Python program. After that, we'll write our programs in Notepad or Notepad++ and execute them in a Windows Command Window."

> NOTE: For those of you following along with a MAC or Unix/Linux PC, you will use the editor of your choice to compose your Python programs.

"Dave's been reading ahead again," Rhonda said. "For the rest of us, what's a Windows Command Window?"

"Sorry Rhonda," Dave said. "Correct me if I'm wrong Professor, but a Windows Command Window is a window in which we can directly interact with the Operating System to execute our Python programs. Is that right?"

"I couldn't have said it better myself Dave," I said. "In a few moments, after we are done discussing IDLE, we'll be opening up a Windows Command Window to do exactly that."

Getting Comfortable with Python

"With the Python Interpreter installed, it's now time to turn our attention to writing our first Python program," I said.

"Interpreter?", Kate asked. "How is that different from a compiled program that we created in our C++ class last semester?

"Good question Kate," I responded, as I looked out the classroom window and noticed a wasp trying to enter through a crack in the pane. "Python programs are not compiled prior to executing them. In the Python world, whether running programs in IDLE or via a Windows Command Window, the source code is interpreted by the Python Interpreter before it is executed, essentially executing the program line by line."

> NOTE: Python purists will no doubt point out that a first pass of the program results in a Byte Code file that is then executed in a second pass of the Python Interpreter, similar to the way Java works.

"I would think that means Python programs run slower than C++ programs," Steve said.

"That's right Steve," I answered, "but with today's fast PC's, it's not a very big deal. You wouldn't **notice** a difference between the speed of the first program we write today in Python versus the same program written in C++, although the actual speed difference is significant---perhaps 100 times slower. However, it does mean that no commercial grade game programs, heavily dependent upon graphics, will be created using Python. But it's still a great language to learn."

Content that the wasp had not entered the classroom, I continued on.

"In today's class," I said, "we're going to concentrate on writing our first Python program. And for the one and only time in this class, we'll be using IDLE to do it. Let's do that now."

I then started IDLE by clicking on it in the Python Program Group, and the following screen shot was displayed.

```
Python 3.4.3 Shell                                    _ | □ | X
File  Edit  Shell  Debug  Options  Window  Help

Python 3.4.3 (v3.4.3:9b73f1c3e601, Feb 24 2015, 22:43:06) [MSC v.1600 3
2 bit (Intel)] on win32
Type "copyright", "credits" or "license()" for more information.
>>>




                                                      Ln: 3 Col: 4
```

"This is IDLE,'" I said. "As you can see, IDLE is pretty full featured. The menu bar reads Python 3.4.3 Shell, and it has a full featured menu. In the IDLE window itself, there's some information displayed, along with an IDLE prompt that consists of 3 greater than signs."

"Is that where we write our program?" Kate asked.

"Exactly Kate," I said. "Our first program today is going to be a single line of code, expressing our love for this wonderful programming language."

I then typed the single line of code into IDLE, following the three greater than signs, and hit the ENTER key.

```
Python 3.4.3 Shell                                    _ | □ | X
File  Edit  Shell  Debug  Options  Window  Help

Python 3.4.3 (v3.4.3:9b73f1c3e601, Feb 24 2015, 22:43:06) [MSC v.1600 3
2 bit (Intel)] on win32
Type "copyright", "credits" or "license()" for more information.
>>> Print ("I love Python!")
Traceback (most recent call last):
  File "<pyshell#0>", line 1, in <module>
    Print ("I love Python!")
NameError: name 'Print' is not defined
>>> |

                                                      Ln: 8 Col: 4
```

"What happened," Rhonda asked. "Looks like there's an error."

"Oops," I exclaimed.

Maybe the wasp trying to get into the classroom had distracted me. They can be nasty in enclosed spaces, and they love the heat that our computers generate.

"I made a mistake," I said. "Python is case sensitive, and Python knows that the word print---in Python terms the **print()** function---should be spelled in lower case letters, not with a leading capital letter. Let's correct this and try again."

This time I wrote the correct line of code into the IDLE window and hit the ENTER key. The results were better.

```
Python 3.4.3 Shell                                              _ □ ×

File  Edit  Shell  Debug  Options  Window  Help

Python 3.4.3 (v3.4.3:9b73f1c3e601, Feb 24 2015, 22:43:06) [MSC v.1600 3
2 bit (Intel)] on win32
Type "copyright", "credits" or "license()" for more information.
>>> Print ("I love Python!")
Traceback (most recent call last):
  File "<pyshell#0>", line 1, in <module>
    Print ("I love Python!")
NameError: name 'Print' is not defined
>>> print ("I love Python!")
I love Python!
>>>

                                                        Ln: 10 Col: 4
```

"As you can see," I said, "after entering the code correctly this time, and hitting the ENTER key, 'I love Python!' was displayed in the IDLE window. This single line of code doesn't do much. It's intended to display the phrase 'I love Python', using the Python **print()** function. Because we are coding this line of code in IDLE, the result will also be displayed in the IDLE window. Notice that the word 'print' is displayed in purple, the 'argument' to the **print()** function is displayed in green and the output of the **print()** function is displayed in blue."

"Cool," I heard Joe say.

"It doesn't look like you can execute a multiple line program in IDLE" Dave said.

"In the interactive mode I just demonstrated that's true," I said, "but before this class is over today I'll show you it is possible to execute a multi-line program in IDLE. It just requires some additional work. For now, though, I'd like to write the same basic program we just executed here in Notepad, and then execute it in a Windows Command Window."

"Are you talking about the MS-DOS prompt," Rhonda said with a worried look on her face. "I know next to nothing about DOS."

"Don't worry, Rhonda," I said. "You don't need to be an expert at DOS (or Windows) to write and execute your Python programs. Once you have the Python Interpreter installed, executing your programs isn't difficult. I'll be showing you how to do that today—and you'll have some exercises to complete later on in the class for reinforcement."

I waited to see if I was about to lose any of my students. No one got up in a panic to leave the classroom (you think I'm kidding, but I've seen it happen!), and so I began again.

Writing Our First Python program Using Notepad (or Notepad++)

"Creating a Python program is a <u>two</u> step process," I said.

1. Create the source file in Notepad or Notepad++, saving it with a filename extension of .py
2. Execute the program in a Windows Command Window

Create the Source File with a file name extension of .py

"First, we use a text editor—Notepad is easiest one to use in the Microsoft Windows environment— to create what is known as a *source* file. A source file is an ordinary text file containing Python instructions. We then save the Python source file to the hard drive of our computer, giving it a name of our choice. However, the name of a Python source file must end with a period, followed by the letters py; this is called its filename extension. Shortly, we'll create a Python source file whose name is ILovePython.py..."

> **NOTE: Be sure to name your Python source file with the filename extension .py**

"...where the period followed by the letters .py is the filename extension."

I paused to see if I had lost anyone.

"Once we have created the source file," I continued, "we can then execute our program by typing its name in a Windows Command Window---provided, of course, we have installed Python on our computer."

Again I paused to see if there were any questions before continuing.

"Using Notepad (or Notepad++) to write our first Python program is a snap," I said. "As we did a moment ago in IDLE, let's write a Python program that will display the message, 'I love Python!'. This version of the program will include some program comments."

I then started Notepad and entered the following code.

```
# This program displays "I love Python!"

print ("I love Python!")
```

"Let's save this file," I said, "by selecting File | Save As from Notepad's menu bar, which will then display this window."

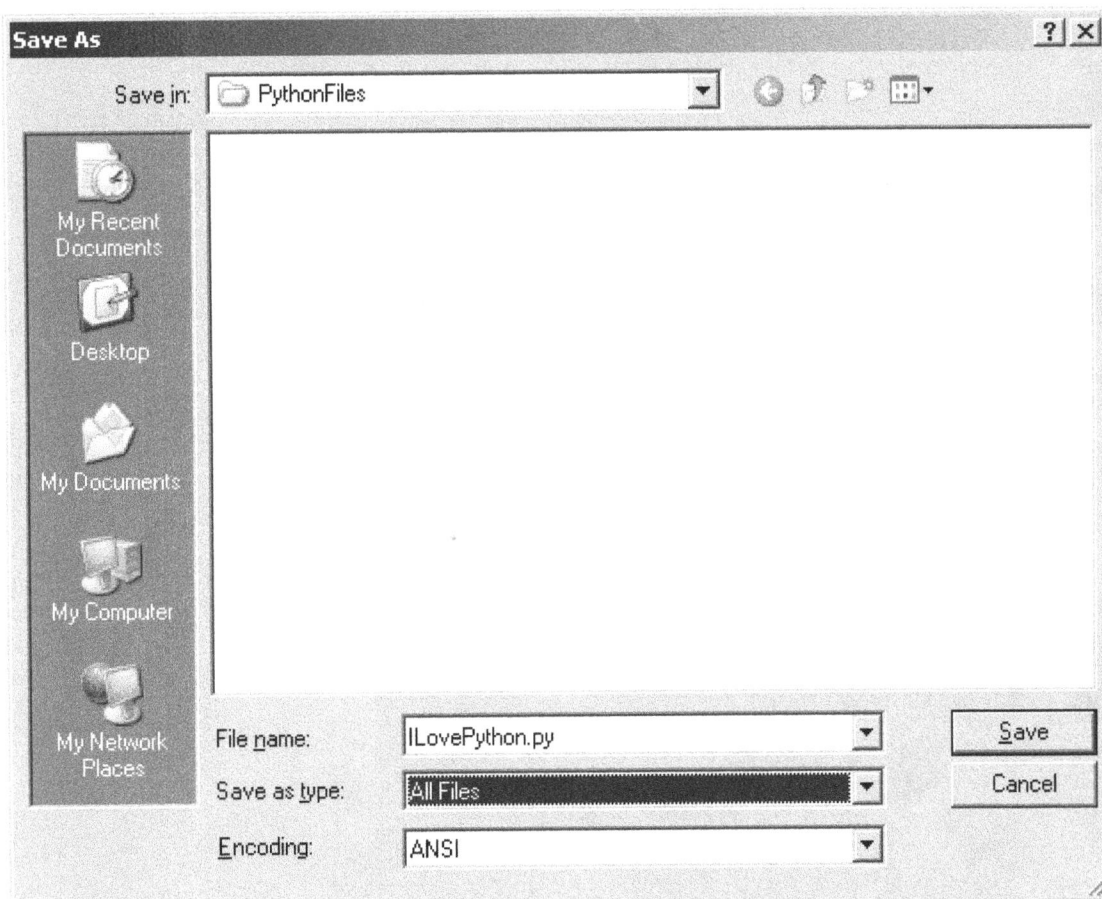

File name: ILovePython.py

Save as type: All Files

Encoding: ANSI

"I like to save all of my Python source files in a folder called PythonFiles," I said, "which is why I'm specifying 'PythonFiles' in the 'Save in:' drop-down List box. (I previously created that folder.) Notice how I have named my Python source file with the filename extension py. I also need to specify 'All Files' in the 'Save as type' drop-down List box. After clicking the Save button, you should notice that the Notepad Title Bar now reflects the new filename."

```
ILovePython.py - Notepad

File  Edit  Format  View  Help

# This program displays "I love Python!"

print ("I love Python!")
```

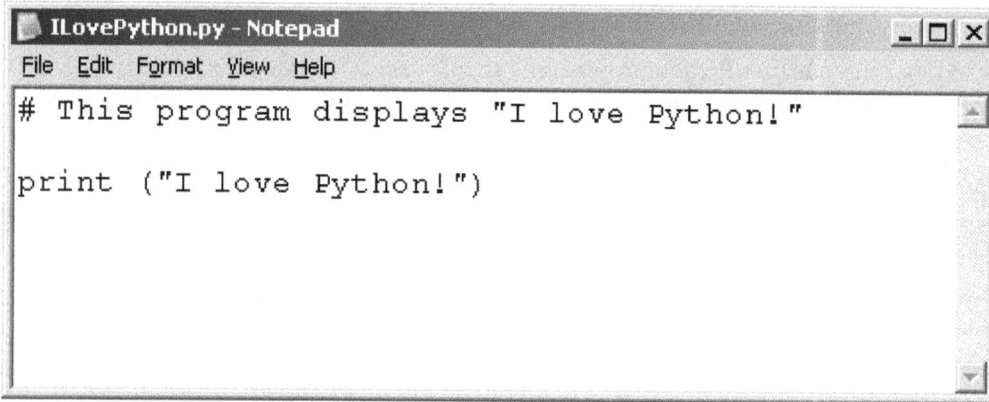

"Now that we have a good Python source file saved," I said, "our next and final step is to execute this source file from a Windows Command Window. Provided a Python Interpreter is installed, Python will then interpret the source code, and attempt to execute it."

"So there's no need to generate an executable file like there is in some other languages?" Kate asked.

"That's right Kate," I answered. "Python interprets the source code line by line and executes our code that way."

> **NOTE: Python purists will no doubt point out that a first pass of the program results in a Byte Code file that is then executed in a second pass of the Python Interpreter, similar to the way Java works.**

I paused to make sure I hadn't lost anyone, before continuing.

"Let's open a Windows Command Window now," I said. "The easiest way to that is to click the Windows Start | Run button, and enter **cmd**"

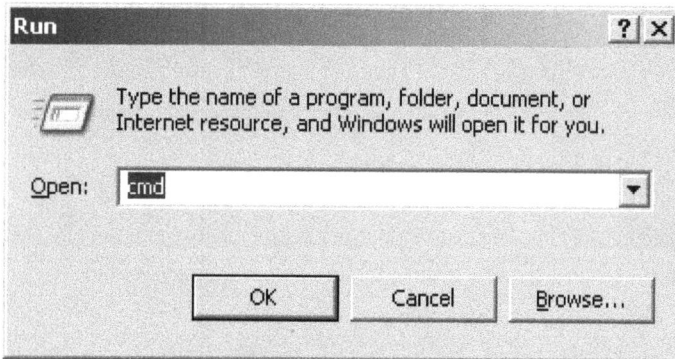

```
Run                                          ? X

      Type the name of a program, folder, document, or
      Internet resource, and Windows will open it for you.

Open:  cmd

           OK          Cancel        Browse...
```

"...then click the OK button. This will launch a Windows Command Window which should look like this."

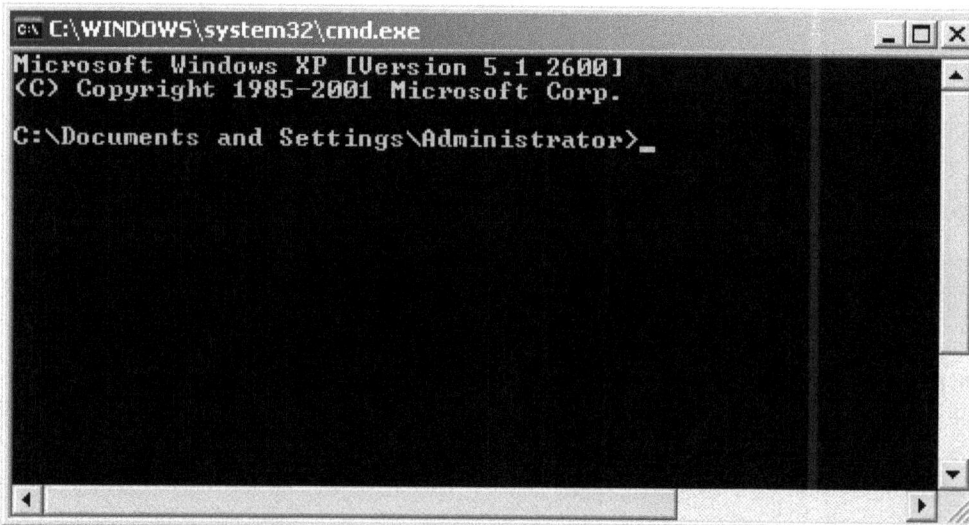

```
C:\WINDOWS\system32\cmd.exe                    _ □ X

Microsoft Windows XP [Version 5.1.2600]
(C) Copyright 1985-2001 Microsoft Corp.

C:\Documents and Settings\Administrator>_
```

"Within the Windows Command Window," I said, "is a brief message about the version of the Windows Operating System you are running, and also a prompt that shows you the 'Current Directory'. Exactly what that is will be dependent upon the computer you are using. Here in our classroom, we're still running Windows XP, and the current directory is typically the Home Directory of the account that is logged in. In my case, I'm the Administrator of the PC. Regardless of what we see here, we need to change the current directory to the folder where our Python source code file is located. To do that, we enter this command

CD C:\PythonFiles

"...at the Windows Command Window and press ENTER. The prompt will now change, reflecting the new 'Current Directory'. Another name for Directory is Folder.

```
C:\WINDOWS\system32\cmd.exe                                    _ □ X
Microsoft Windows XP [Version 5.1.2600]
(C) Copyright 1985-2001 Microsoft Corp.

C:\Documents and Settings\Administrator>cd C:\PythonFiles

C:\PythonFiles>
```

NOTE: I've named the directory in mixed case, and Windows isn't terribly picky about the spelling of PythonFiles. However, Unix/Linux is case sensitive, so you will need to be very precise about the naming and spelling of folders and source code.

"At this point, we can confirm the location of our Python source file by entering

DIR

At the Windows Command Window and pressing ENTER. DIR is a command that displays the contents of the Current Directory or Folder. As you can see, it currently contains just one file called ILovePython.py."

```
C:\WINDOWS\system32\cmd.exe                                    _ □ X
Microsoft Windows XP [Version 5.1.2600]
(C) Copyright 1985-2001 Microsoft Corp.

C:\Documents and Settings\Administrator>cd C:\PythonFiles

C:\PythonFiles>dir
 Volume in drive C has no label.
 Volume Serial Number is C40F-9ECD

 Directory of C:\PythonFiles

06/28/2015  01:24 PM    <DIR>          .
06/28/2015  01:24 PM    <DIR>          ..
06/28/2015  01:24 PM                72 ILovePython.py
               1 File(s)             72 bytes
               2 Dir(s)   7,980,060,672 bytes free

C:\PythonFiles>
```

Execute the Python Program

"Now that we are 'in' the correct directory or folder on our computer" I said, "we can now find and run or execute our program simply by typing its name at the prompt."

```
C:\WINDOWS\system32\cmd.exe                                          _ □ ×

Microsoft Windows XP [Version 5.1.2600]
(C) Copyright 1985-2001 Microsoft Corp.

C:\Documents and Settings\Administrator>cd C:\PythonFiles

C:\PythonFiles>dir
 Volume in drive C has no label.
 Volume Serial Number is C40F-9ECD

 Directory of C:\PythonFiles

06/28/2015  01:24 PM    <DIR>          .
06/28/2015  01:24 PM    <DIR>          ..
06/28/2015  01:24 PM                72 ILovePython.py
               1 File(s)             72 bytes
               2 Dir(s)   7,980,060,672 bytes free

C:\PythonFiles>ILovePython
I love Python!

C:\PythonFiles>
```

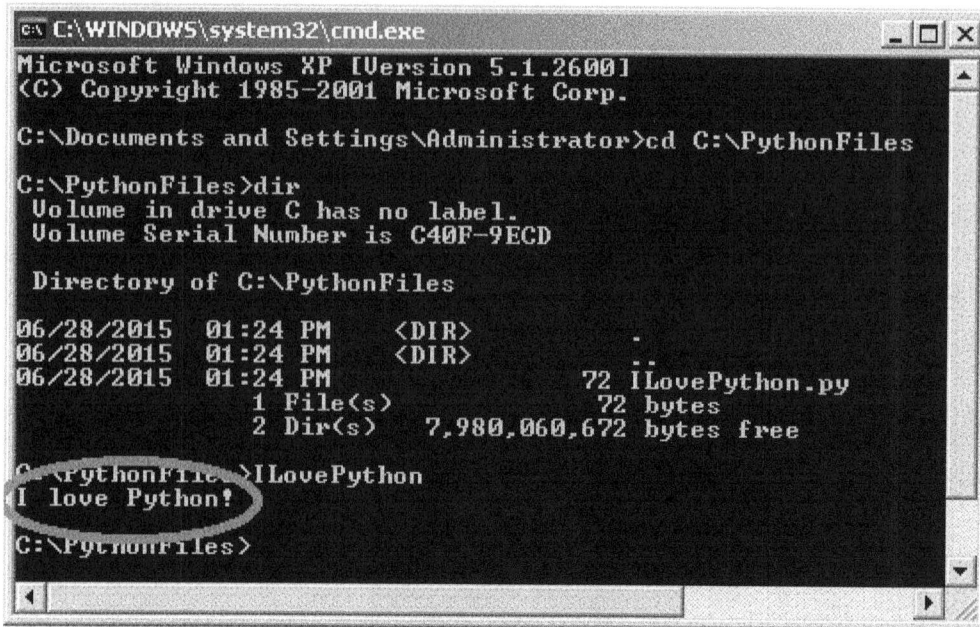

"That worked!" I heard Rhonda say excitedly.

"Why didn't we type '.py' at the end of the filename?" Kate asked.

"It's not necessary," I answered, "although we could have typed it that way. Also, although we went to some trouble to name our program using mixed case—that is, a mixture of upper- and lowercase letters to make the name more readable—we could type the name of the source file in all lower case letters, and it would still run. That's true in Windows, but other Operating Systems, such as UNIX and Linux are much more case sensitive, and you would have to exactly match the name of the source code there."

I then executed our program by typing its name in all lower case letters, this time including the py file extension. It executed successfully.

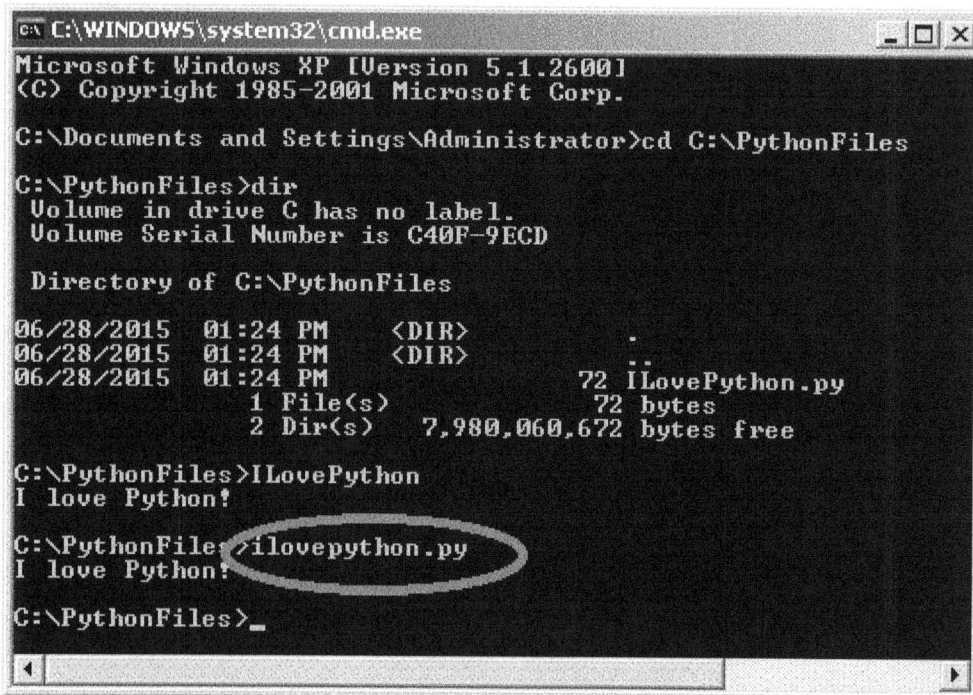

```
C:\WINDOWS\system32\cmd.exe                                          _ □ ×

Microsoft Windows XP [Version 5.1.2600]
(C) Copyright 1985-2001 Microsoft Corp.

C:\Documents and Settings\Administrator>cd C:\PythonFiles

C:\PythonFiles>dir
 Volume in drive C has no label.
 Volume Serial Number is C40F-9ECD

 Directory of C:\PythonFiles

06/28/2015  01:24 PM    <DIR>          .
06/28/2015  01:24 PM    <DIR>          ..
06/28/2015  01:24 PM                72 ILovePython.py
               1 File(s)             72 bytes
               2 Dir(s)   7,980,060,672 bytes free

C:\PythonFiles>ILovePython
I love Python!

C:\PythonFiles>ilovepython.py
I love Python!

C:\PythonFiles>_
```

"As you can see," I said, "we still got the same result."

Joe had a question:

"I expected that I could run this program by using Windows Explorer," Joe said, "but when I double clicked on the python source file name using Windows explorer, a window opened up and then quickly closed. It seemed as if nothing happened."

"Joe is correct," I said. "If we attempt to run our Python program by double clicking it in Windows Explorer, the program runs so fast that a window opens and closes before we can see the results. There is a way around this problem, and it's to add a single line of code requesting that the user press the ENTER key in order to continue, like this…"

I displayed this altered code on the classroom projector and saved it.

```
# This program displays "I love Python!"

print ("I love Python!")
input ("\n\nPress the ENTER key to exit.")
```

"If we now double click on the modified source file in Windows Explorer," I explained, "I love Python!' will be displayed in a window, and this time the window will stay open until we press the ENTER key. Actually, pressing any key will do, but we'll learn more about that when we discuss the **input()** function later on."

I then double clicked the source file in Windows Explorer, and the following screen shot appeared on the classroom projector.

```
I love Python!

Press the ENTER key to exit.
```

I pressed the ENTER key and the window disappeared.

"Ordinarily," I said, "we use the **input()** function to 'accept' a character or characters from the user before he or she hits the ENTER key. Because every function in Python returns a value back to the program that calls it, ordinarily we would do something with these characters. However, in this case, this was just a 'trick' to keep the window open long enough for us to observe the result of our **print()** function. No other entry besides the ENTER key was required."

"I've noticed," Linda said, "that you called the **print()** and **input()** statements 'functions'. Is that intentional?"

"Yes it is Linda," I answered. "These are Python functions---slightly different from Python statements. The differences is the concept of a return value---that is, a value that is passed back to the program that calls the function. In the case of the **input()** function, the return value is a character or characters that are accepted from the user. In the case of the **print()** function, the return value is directed to the Python Console window. We'll learn more about return values throughout the course."

I could sense some restlessness in the class and there was just one more thing I wished to cover before taking a short break.

"I promised that I would show you how to execute a multi-line program within IDLE," I said. "Our program now contains 3 lines of code---4 if you count the blank line. Let's start up IDLE again and see how easy it is to execute this program."

I then started IDLE, and the following screen shot was displayed as it had been earlier.

```
Python 3.4.3 Shell                                              _ □ X

File  Edit  Shell  Debug  Options  Window  Help

Python 3.4.3 (v3.4.3:9b73f1c3e601, Feb 24 2015, 22:43:06) [MSC v.1600 3
2 bit (Intel)] on win32
Type "copyright", "credits" or "license()" for more information.
>>>




                                                          Ln: 3 Col: 4
```

"As Dave noted earlier," I reminded the class, "you can't compose a multi line program using the Python Shell because as soon as you hit the ENTER key, IDLE will execute that line of code. However, if you click on File-Open..."

```
Python 3.4.3 Shell                                              _ □ X

File  Edit  Shell  Debug  Options  Window  Help

  New File        Ctrl+N       73f1c3e601, Feb 24 2015, 22:43:06) [MSC v.1600 3
  Open...         Ctrl+O       its" or "license()" for more information.
  Recent Files          ▶
  Open Module...  Alt+M
  Class Browser   Alt+C
  Path Browser

  Save            Ctrl+S
  Save As...      Ctrl+Shift+S
  Save Copy As... Alt+Shift+S

  Print Window    Ctrl+P                                   Ln: 3 Col: 4
```

"...and specify the location and name of the Python file you wish to execute and the click the Open button..."

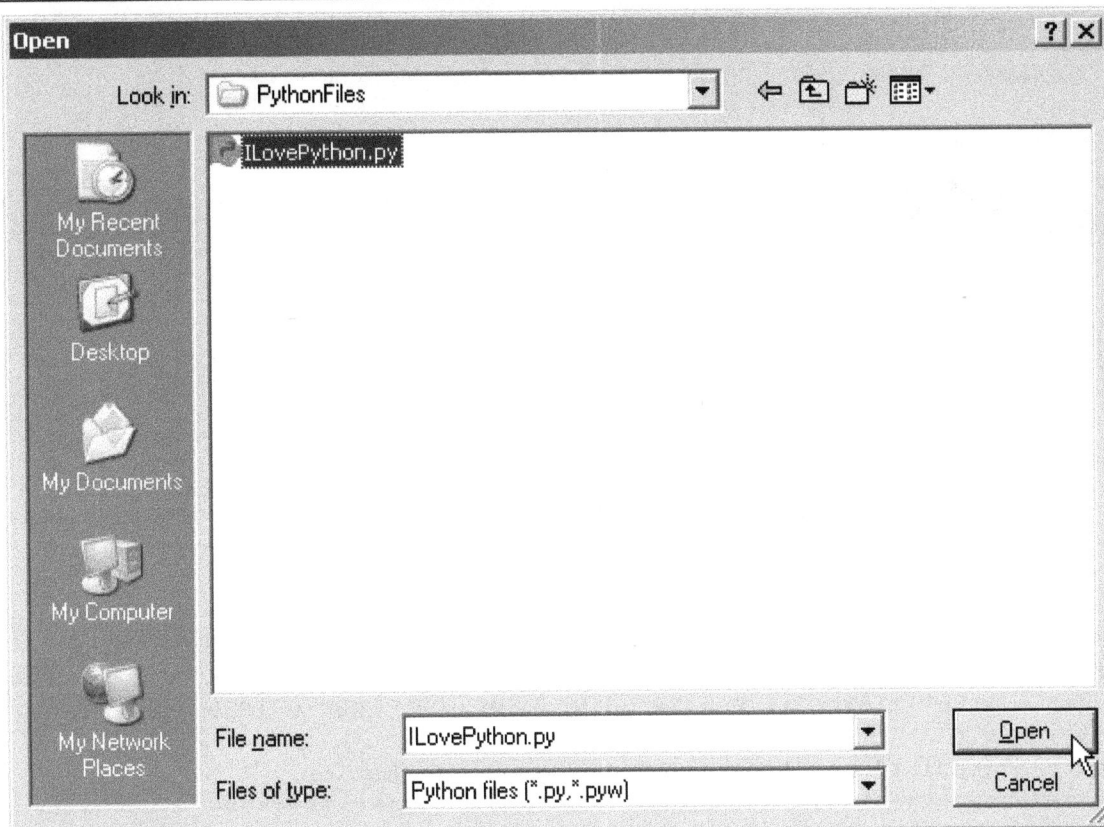

"...IDLE will 'load' your program into a window like this..."

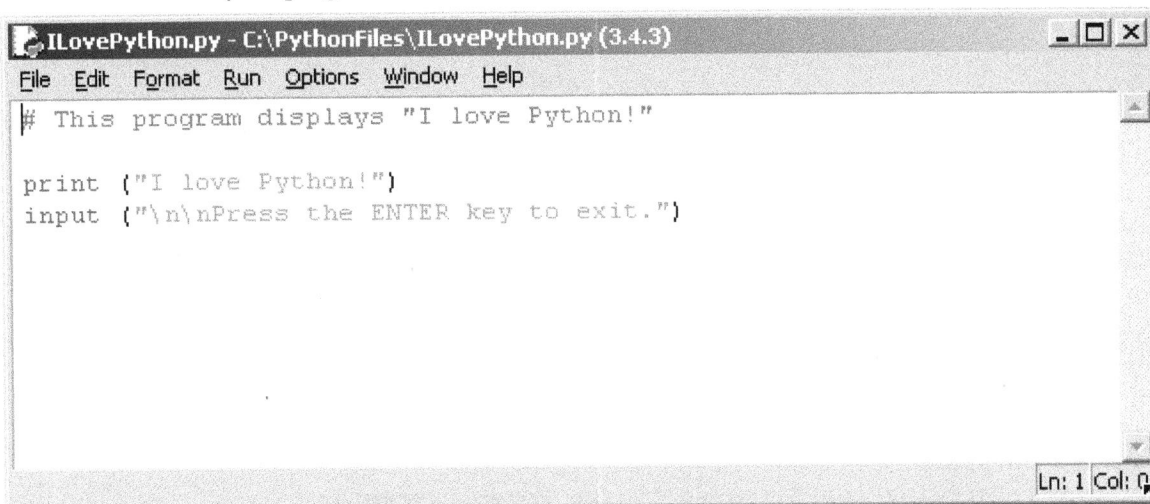

"This looks like the IDLE window." I said, "But it's not. It's called a Script window, and you can see that the menu items here are different from those in the IDLE Shell window. At this point, you can click the Run-Run Module menu item, or just press the F5 function key and your program will run."

```
ILovePython.py - C:\PythonFiles\ILovePython.py (3.4.3)          _ □ X
File  Edit  Format  Run  Options  Window  Help
# This progr┌─────────────── Python!"
             │  Python Shell
print ("I lo │
input ("\n\n │  Check Module  Alt+X    y to exit.")
             │  Run Module    F5
             └───────────────
                          ⤴
                                                        Ln: 1 Col: 0
```

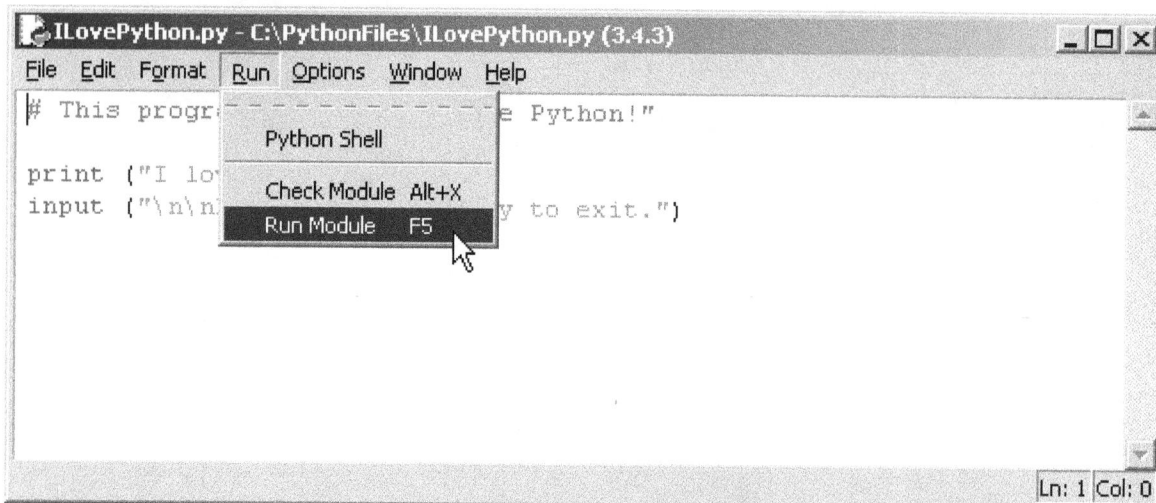

Programmers generally like to do things the easy way, so I pressed the F5 function key and our program was executed. A Python Shell window appeared, with the output of our program.

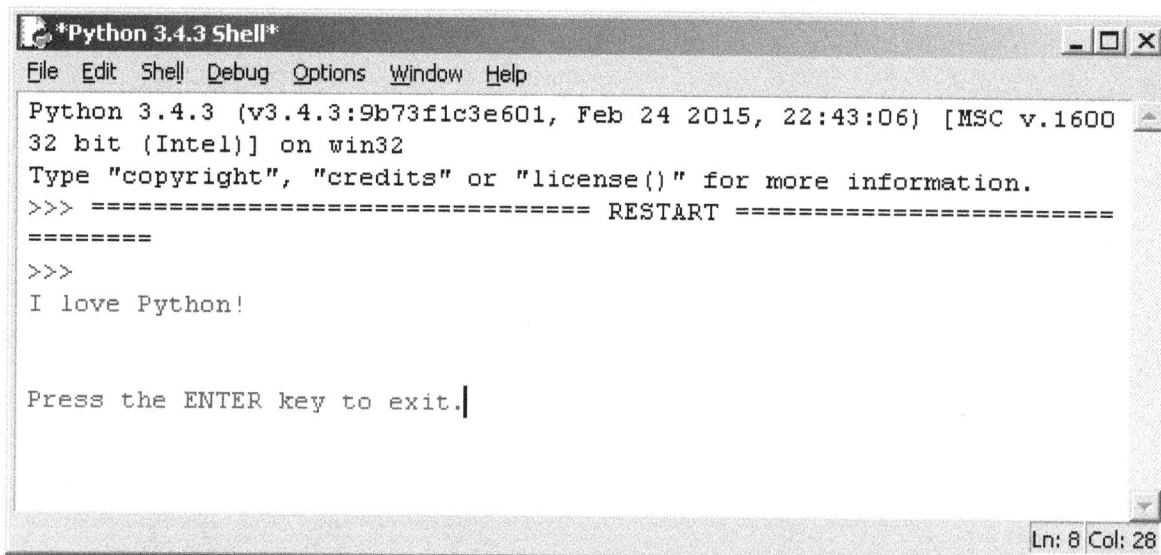

```
*Python 3.4.3 Shell*                                          _ □ X
File  Edit  Shell  Debug  Options  Window  Help
Python 3.4.3 (v3.4.3:9b73f1c3e601, Feb 24 2015, 22:43:06) [MSC v.1600
32 bit (Intel)] on win32
Type "copyright", "credits" or "license()" for more information.
>>> ============================ RESTART ========================
========
>>>
I love Python!


Press the ENTER key to exit.|

                                                        Ln: 8 Col: 28
```

I pressed the ENTER key and the program finished, leaving us with the IDLE >>> prompt.

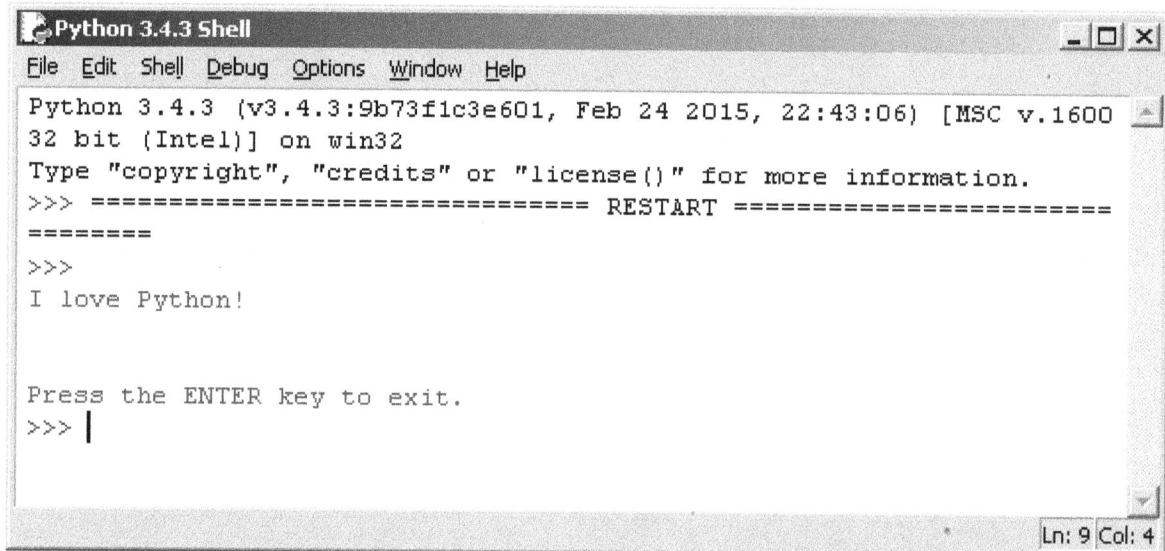

```
Python 3.4.3 Shell                                            _ □ X
File  Edit  Shell  Debug  Options  Window  Help
Python 3.4.3 (v3.4.3:9b73f1c3e601, Feb 24 2015, 22:43:06) [MSC v.1600
32 bit (Intel)] on win32
Type "copyright", "credits" or "license()" for more information.
>>> ============================ RESTART ========================
========
>>>
I love Python!


Press the ENTER key to exit.
>>> |

                                                        Ln: 9 Col: 4
```

"I should point out," I said, "that if we select File-New from the IDLE menu, we could have written our program from scratch that way..."

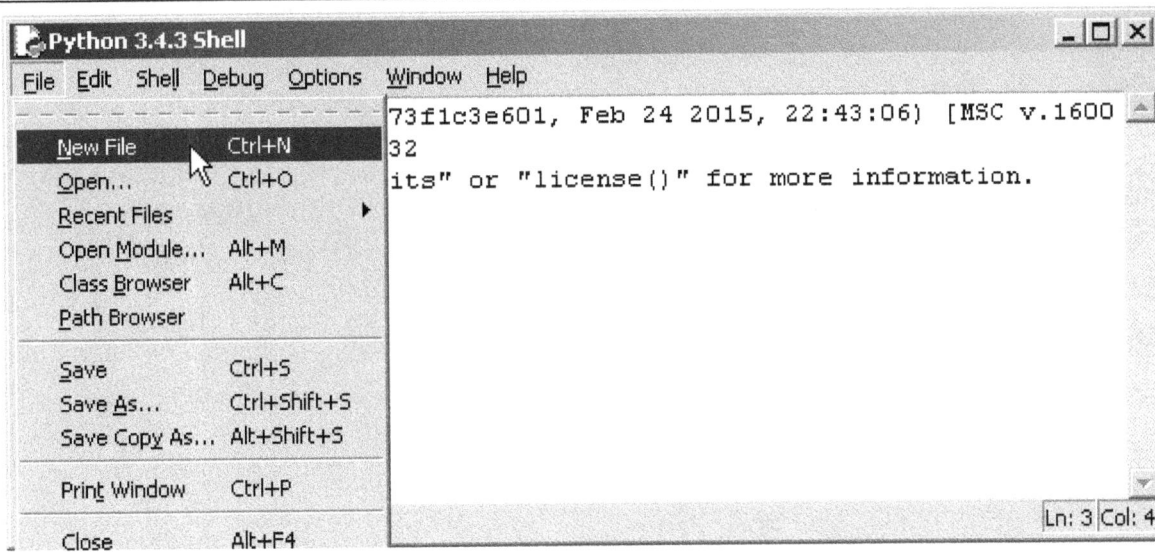

"Selecting New File opens up an untitled Script window where we can then code our program from scratch…"

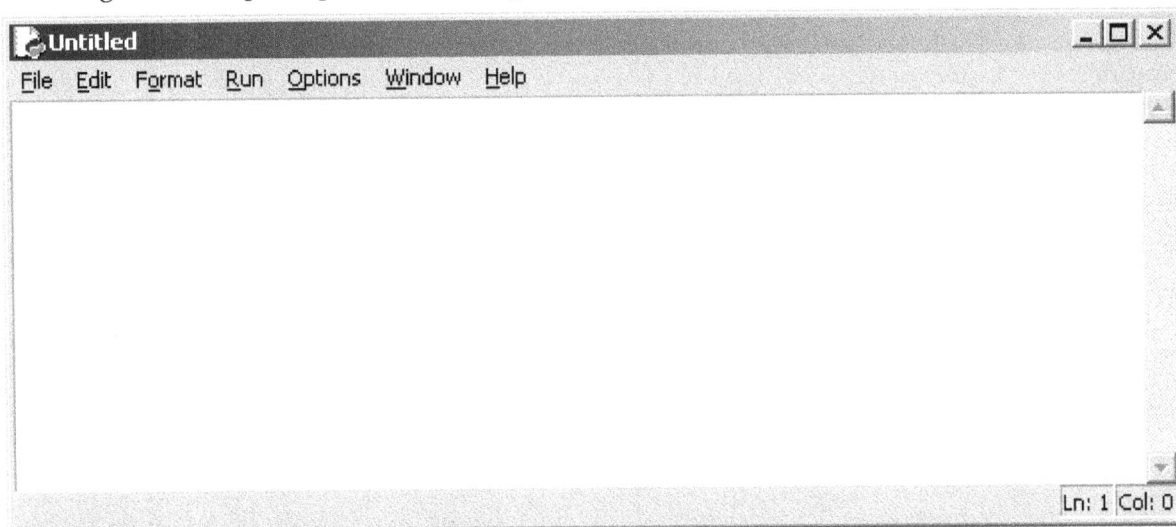

"…Once we code it, we can then save it with a name in our PythonFiles folder or directory. Again, my preference--- and what we'll be doing for the remainder of our class---is to code our programs in Notepad and execute them via a Windows Command Window, but if IDLE is your preference, I have no objection to you using it."

> **NOTE: My preference is to code my Python source files using either Notepad or Notepad++ and to execute them in a Windows Command Window.**

"Are you going to explain this code?" Rose asked.

"You bet," I answered.

I suggested that because we had been working for a while, it would be a great time to take a break.

Elements of a Python program

Fifteen minutes later, I began a discussion of the code we had written earlier. I displayed it on the classroom projector.

```
# This program displays "I love Python!"

print("I love Python!")
input("\n\nPress the ENTER key to exit.")
```

Jack had a comment: "I was just comparing this Python program to the first one we wrote in our C++ class," Jack said. "This is so much simpler to do the same thing."

I agreed.

"Python is definitely a programming language more suitable for the beginner programmer than C++," I said, "but it's also very full featured as well. One thing you may notice is that although Python <u>does have</u> Object Oriented features, using them are not required as it is in some other languages. In fact, in this class, we won't be using any objects features of Python. We'll save that for our next class called 'Doing Objects in Python."

"I think I like that," Rhonda said. "Classes, Objects, Methods and Properties confused me at first in our C++ and Java classes. I like the idea of learning the language itself before we delve into Object Oriented programming."

"Let's examine our 3 line program," I said, "beginning with the first line of code which is simply a Program comment...."

Program Comments

"...Program comments are explanatory statements that you can include in the Python programs that you write. All programming languages allow for some form of comments. The trick is how to tell Python that the statement you are entering is a comment and not a Python command. In Python, there are two ways to specify a comment. The first one we've already seen."

```
# This program displays "I love Python!"
```

"Is that what the pound sign (#) indicates?" Mary asked.

"That's right, Mary," I said. "The pound sign (#) character tells Python that everything that follows after it is a program comment."

"Can a comment only appear on a line by itself," Dave asked, "or can it follow after a Python statement?"

"You can place a comment after a Python statement," I answered. "Just follow the Python statement with the pound sign (#) characters, like this."

```
print("I love Python!")     #Displays an output message
```

"...Quite frequently, you may want to include more than one line of comments. I typically include comments in my program to indicate what the program does, who wrote the program, and when it was written. That's easy to do in Python, like this..."

```
# This program displays "I love Python!"
# This program written by John Smiley
# This program was written on June 30, 2016
```

"...There's another way to do this, called a block comment. It's a bit more obscure, and looks like this, using triple quotation marks to delimit the beginning and the end of the comment..."

```
""" This program displays "I love Python!"
    This program written by John Smiley
    This program was written on June 30, 2016 """
```

"...Do you see how the triple quotation marks at the beginning of the first line of the comment, and another set of triple quotation marks at the end of the comment on the third line?"

"I do, but you're right, that does look confusing," Mary said.

"I agree with you Mary," I replied, "which is why I don't use this format myself. But it is available."

"Should comments always appear at the top of the code, or can they appear anywhere?, Rose asked"

"There no requirement that they appear at the top," I answered. "but that is my preference. As we saw here, some programmers include a comment at the top of their code, indicating the author of the program, the date the program was written, and anything else they—or someone reading the program code later—might find useful. Some programmers never comment their code. At a minimum, I routinely include comments with my name, the date the program was written, and what it's intended to do. I also freely use comments within my program whenever I write code that I either needed to look up online or in a reference manual. I figure that if I needed to go to that extreme to write it, explaining the code via a comment will be helpful the next time I or someone else views the code. By the way, some programmers make their comments elaborate by using pound signs to draw something that is sometimes called a 'flower box', like this."

```
###############################################################
# Programmer: John Smiley
```

```
# Date Written: December 19, 2016
# This program displays "I love Python!"
###################################################/
```

"I know you said earlier that we would be doing exercises of our own for practice," Kathy said. "Will we be required to code comments in the exercises that we do?"

"I encourage comments , but they're not required," I said. "I've already noticed that some of you are not the fastest typists in the world. I'll leave it up to you to insert the comments of your choice as you complete the exercises."

"Did you say that Python ignores comments?" Rhonda asked. "Are you saying that the first few lines of code in our Python program don't mean anything? Python just ignores them?"

"Exactly right, Rhonda" I answered. "As far as Python is concerned, any line of code that begins with a pound sign (#) is meaningless. When the Python Interpreter sees the pound sign (#) it doesn't attempt to translate and execute it. Python just ignores it."

No one had any other questions about comments.

The print() Function

"Let's move onto that second line of code now," I said. "This line of code, when executed by the Python Interpreter, results in the phrase "I love Python!" being displayed in a Python Console Window...."

```
print("I love Python!")
```

"...**print()** is a Python function. A function is essentially a command that does something. Python functions can also be 'qualified' through the use of an argument, which is additional information that optionally may be passed to the function within the parentheses. In this case, the argument to the **print()** function is what we want displayed, "I love Python!".

> NOTE: With the print() function, and in Python in general, text such as 'I love Python!' needs to be enclosed within either double or single quotation marks. This text is called a String Literal. Later on, you'll see that we can also use the print() function with numbers, variables and Lists. More on that later.

"...Python comes with a bunch of built in functions that have been designed by the authors of the Python language to perform common, useful operations, such as displaying text in a Python Console Window, accepting input from the user, calculating the number of days between two dates---the list goes on and on. And, one more thing---later on, you'll see that you can write your own functions."."

> NOTE: For a list of all the built-in Python functions, follow this link.
> http://docs.python.org/3/library/functions.html

I looked around for signs of confusion before adding,

"If this doesn't make perfect sense to you, don't worry a great deal about it—we'll be examining functions in more detail later on in the course."

The input() Function

"This last line of code completes our work for our first simple program," I said.

```
input("\n\nPress the ENTER key to exit.")
```

"As we saw with the **print()** function," I said, "we follow the name of the Python function---in this case **input()**---with a pair of parentheses, within which is a phrase that is enclosed within quotation marks. You may have notices that when this line of code was executed in our program, the phrase 'Press the ENTER key to exit' was displayed in our Python Console Window."

I paused before continuing.

"What is the meaning of the pair of backslash n's"? Joe asked.

"Good question Joe," I replied. "The Backslash+n character pattern is called an escape sequence. When our program is executed, this combination of characters tells Python to first display a blank line in our Python Console

Window before displaying anything else. Since we have 2 Backslash+n sequences, Python first displays 2 blank lines before displaying the phrase 'Press the ENTER key to exit.'."

"Didn't we see something similar in our C++ class?," Dave asked.

"Right you are Dave," I said, "This escape sequence is a programming technique fairly common in all programming languages. The backslash character in combination with the character that follows it is called an escape sequence, and it designates something 'special', in this case a new line. There are other escape sequences, such as backslash+t which generates a tab character in a Python Console window."

"The word 'input' seems to imply," Kate said "that something is received from the user when they are typing. Is that true?"

"You're correct Kate," I said. "That's exactly what the **input()** function does, although here we are using it as a way to prevent our program, when run from Windows Explorer, from starting, quickly displaying 'I love Python!', and then quickly ending. Until the **input()** function detects that the user has pressed the ENTER key, the program is just sitting around waiting for something to happen. In fact, we could have typed our name and pressed the ENTER key. It doesn't matter. It's the press of the ENTER key that 'completes' the **input()** function, and allows our program to end."

"That doesn't seem very useful," Rhonda said. "Shouldn't the **input()** function do more than that?"

"The **input()** function will be very useful to us later on in the course," I said. "Using it, we'll be able to accept the component grades for our Grades Calculation Program. But that's a few weeks away."

"How important is indentation?" Ward asked. "I've heard from the programmers in work that indentation is very important in a Python program."

"You're right about that Ward," I said. "In other programming languages, indentation is used to make the program easier to read. However, in Python indentation is an integral part of the language. At times, indentation is required, most often when we are creating something called blocks. We use blocks to create logical units in our code. In a few weeks, when we discuss Selection Structures, which is code that allows our program to behave differently depending upon whether a specific condition has been met or not, you'll see how important Blocks---and indentation---are.

"What is white space?" Kate asked. "Some of the Python programmers at work refer to this from time to time."

"White space refers to space between Python statements, and also blank lines in the code," I answered. "Programmers use white space to make their code more readable. For instance, in this simple program we just wrote, we had white space between our comments and the first 'real' line of code in our program, the **print()** function. If had wanted to, we could have placed a blank line between the lines containing the **print()** and **input()** functions, like this…"

```
# This program displays "I love Python!"

print("I love Python!")

input("\n\nPress the ENTER key to exit.")
```

"Is there a line continuation character in Python like there is in Visual Basic?" Rose asked. "In Visual Basic, if we want to split up a long line of code into two pieces, we can use an underscore character. Does Python have something similar?"

"Yes there is Rose," I said. "In Python, you can use the backslash (\) character to 'split' a long line of code into multiple lines. However, most times it's not necessary (although it will be for us as we develop the Grades Calculation program.) Because of the 'white space' nature of Python code, most times if you want to split up a single line of code into two or more lines, you can just hit the ENTER key—Python doesn't care. But be careful NOT to indent it. As I've mentioned, indentation in Python has special meaning for Python For instance, the line of code…"

```
print("I love Python!")
```

"…can be broken up into two lines of code, like this."

```
print
("I love Python!")
```

"…But be careful. If you indent your code to make it prettier like this…"

```
print
    ("I love Python!")
```

"...this code will generate a Python Interpreter error when you try to execute it..."

```
C:\WINDOWS\system32\cmd.exe                          _ □ ×

C:\PythonFiles>ILovePython
  File "C:\PythonFiles\ILovePython.py", line 4
    ("I love Python!")
     ^
IndentationError: unexpected indent

C:\PythonFiles>_
```

"...Remember, indentation has special meaning in Python. One other thing, you can't 'split' the line of code within the middle of a quoted String—the code between the quotation marks that is displayed on the console, and you can't 'split' a line of code using this technique in the middle of a mathematical Operation. For instance, this code split in the middle of a quoted String..."

```
print("I
Love Python!")
```

"... would also result in an error when you tried to execute it..."

```
C:\WINDOWS\system32\cmd.exe                          _ □ ×

C:\PythonFiles>ILovePython
  File "C:\PythonFiles\ILovePython.py", line 3
    print "I
           ^
SyntaxError: Missing parentheses in call to 'print'

C:\PythonFiles>
```

"How would that code look with the line continuation backslash character?" Dave asked.

"Thanks for reminding me Dave," I said. "It would look like this..."

```
print \
("I love Python!")
```

"...This would also work..."

```
print \
   ("I love Python!")
```

"Take my advice," I continued. "It's a rare instance where you will need to split your code into multiple lines, although because of the nature of our Grades Calculation Program, we will need to do so. In that case, we'll use the line continuation character."

"You mentioned earlier that Python is case sensitive— I guess my question is, How case sensitive is it?" Mary asked.

"Python is very case sensitive," I replied. "You need to be very careful about the spelling of function names in Python. For instance, this line of code ..."

```
print ("I love Python")
```

"...is not the same as this line of code."

```
Print("I love Python")
```

"Spelling 'print' as 'Print' with a Capital letter 'P' will confuse Python," I said, "Python expects function names to be in all lower case letters. Spelling them with an initial capital letter will result in a Python Interpreter error when you try to execute your program, like this..."

```
C:\WINDOWS\system32\cmd.exe                                    _ □ X

C:\PythonFiles>ILovePython
Traceback (most recent call last):
  File "C:\PythonFiles\ILovePython.py", line 3, in <module>
    Print ("I love Python!")
NameError: name 'Print' is not defined

C:\PythonFiles>
```

"The same thing would happen," I continued, "if we spelled **input()** with a capital letter 'I'.

> NOTE: Later on in the course, next week in fact, we'll be creating Python variables and Pseudo Constants. We can name variables and Pseudo constants almost anything we want, but once named, we must then refer to them spelled identically to the way we created them.

"Can we use a single quote here--an apostrophe---instead of a double quote when we specify the argument to the **print()** function?" Dave asked.

"Dave," I said, "that's a great question. In Python, you can use single quotes, double quotes, and even triples quotes whenever you are dealing with String Literals like this. For instance, all three of these Python statements will generate the same output. This one with double quotes.."

```python
print("I love Python!")
```

"...this one with single quotes.."

```python
print('I love Python!')
```

"... and finally, this one with triple quotes, which is three consecutive double quotes."

```python
print("""I love Python!""")
```

"Do you have a preference?" Valerie asked.

"My preference is to use double quotes," I said "The problem with single quotes is that if you have a String Literal that itself contains an apostrophe (a single quote), using a single quote to 'sandwich' the String Literal like this..."

```python
print('Sally's string is broken')
```

"will confuse Python and cause it to generate an error message. On the other hand, using single quotes does allow you to use a String Literal that itself contains quotation marks, like this..."

```python
print('He was overheard to say "not now!!!" quite Loudly!')
```

"Of the three options," I said, "using triple quotes gives us the most flexibility, in that we can easily specify a String Literal that contains either double quotes or single quotes without confusing Python, like this String Literal..."

```python
print("""He was overheard to whisper "She isn't well" """)
```

"Ultimately," I said, "whether you use single quotes or double quotes is up to you--but my preference---and one that we'll follow throughout the rest of the course, is to use double quotes with out String Literals. If for some reason, we need to display double quotes in our Python Console window, we'll either use single quotes or triple quotes at that time."

I waited to see if there were any other questions, but no one had any.

"What I'd like to do now," I said, "is to give you a chance to write and execute a Python program of your own. As we'll do during the remainder of the course, I have a series of exercises for you to complete that will lead you through the process."

I then distributed this exercise for the class to complete.

Practice 2-1 Writing your first Python program---Grades.py

In this exercise you'll write your first Python program--which will form the basis of our class project.

If typing these long examples and exercises isn't something you want to do, feel free to follow this link to find and download the completed solutions for all of the examples and exercises in the book. Just click on the Python book, then follow the link entitled exercises ☺

http://www.johnsmiley.com/main/books.htm

1. Create a folder on your hard drive called \PythonFiles\Grades. This will be the "home" of our class project, the Grades Calculation Program.

2. Using the editor of your choice (if you are using Windows, use Notepad or Notepad++), enter the following code (be extremely careful of the capitalization):

```
# Grades.py
# After Chapter 2

print("It's not much, but it's a start!")
```

3. Save your source file as <u>Grades.py</u> in the \PythonFiles\Grades folder (select File-Save As from Notepad's Menu Bar). Be sure to save your source file with the file name extension 'py'.

Discussion

There were some minor problems completing the exercise---some people in the class weren't very familiar with Notepad---but all in all, this exercise went pretty smoothly. In just a few minutes, everyone in the class had completed coding their first Python program—the Grades program. This source file, although very simplistic, would eventually form the basis of the Grades Calculation program we would give to Frank, Robin, and Dave on the last week of class.

"Is this the program we'll be using to calculate grades for the English, Math, and Science departments?" Mary asked. "It looks like all this does is display a message in the Python Console."

"That's right, Mary," I said. "It's just a single line of code, but we'll build on from there…"

```
print("It's not much, but it's a start!")
```

"Have you heard the expression," I said, "that the journey of a thousand miles begins with the first step? This is the first step—the creation of the Grades Calculation program. From here, everything else will be built. And even though displaying this message isn't part of the user requirements, I wanted the program to do 'something' when you executed it—just to prove to you that there is some activity going on in there."

There were no questions about the actual coding of the program. It was almost identical to the example we had been working on. So, I then distributed this exercise for the class to complete.

Practice 2-2 Executing (Running) Grades.py

In this exercise, you'll execute the program you coded in Practice 2-1, Grades.py.

1. Bring up the Windows Command Window.

2. In the Windows Command Window, change to the directory (folder) containing your Grades.py source file by entering

```
CD C:\PythonFiles\Grades
```

and pressing the ENTER key (pressing the ENTER key is necessary for all of the Windows Command Window steps).

> **NOTE: If you saved your source file to another drive, substitute that drive letter for 'C'**

3. Confirm the existence and location of your Python source file by entering

```
DIR
```

at the Windows Command Window and pressing ENTER. You should see an entry for Grades.py similar to this screenshot:

```
C:\WINDOWS\system32\cmd.exe                              _ □ ×

C:\PythonFiles\Grades>dir
 Volume in drive C has no label.
 Volume Serial Number is C40F-9ECD

 Directory of C:\PythonFiles\Grades

07/03/2015  04:02 PM    <DIR>          .
07/03/2015  04:02 PM    <DIR>          ..
07/03/2015  04:40 PM               59 Grades.py
               1 File(s)             59 bytes
               2 Dir(s)   7,510,474,752 bytes free

C:\PythonFiles\Grades>
```

If you don't see your source file listed, something went wrong in Practice 2-1 and you will need to verify your work there before proceeding.

4. Now execute your program by entering

Grades

at the Windows Command Window, and pressing ENTER. You should see the following screenshot displayed on your computer.

```
C:\WINDOWS\system32\cmd.exe                              _ □ ×

C:\PythonFiles\Grades>Grades
It's not much, but it's a start!

C:\PythonFiles\Grades>
```

Discussion

This exercise went pretty smoothly, but there were a few problems. The typical errors were the ones I had warned my students about, but warning students about problems is different from having them experience them on their own. Experience is the great teacher! And so I gave them some extra time to try to complete this exercise on their own.

Some students had problems "finding" the Python code they created in the previous exercise. One student failed to properly create a folder (or directory) for his project. One student forgot to name their source code with a .py extension. As I feared (and predicted,) a couple of students (I won't mention any names) spelled the **print()** function with a capital letter P. One student forgot to follow the function name with a pair of parentheses, and another student forgot the quotation marks. Despite the problems, just about everyone had a great time resolving their errors----this is, after all, how we learn.

"I know we haven't done all that much," Rhonda said, "but I feel pretty good about what we've done so far. My programming friends all told me how difficult computer programming can be—but so far, so good."

"I'm not sure I agree with your friends Rhonda," I said. "Computer Programming requires attention to detail. If you can do that, you're well on your way. And Python is as easy a language to learn as there is. And, as you may know, here at the University we have a reputation for doing a pretty good job with beginner programmers. One step at a time, I always say, and the next logical step is next week's class where I will give you a Python code overview to show you what this marvelous programming language can do."

It had been a very productive class—my students now had the beginnings of the Grades Calculation Program in place. It had also been a pretty long class, and as I glanced up at the clock on the wall of our Computer Lab, I realized our class was over. I then dismissed class for the day.

Summary

In this chapter, you were exposed to the "nitty gritty" of the Python environment. You saw that writing a program in Python is pretty basic. You use an editor (in our case, Notepad or Notepad++) to create a Python source file, then run or execute the program from a Windows Command Window just by entering its name and pressing the ENTER key.

In the next chapter, you'll learn about computer data--and how your Python program works with it.

Chapter 3---Data

In a computer program, data is extremely important. As we learned in Chapter 1, data is input into a computer program to be processed into some form of meaningful output. In this chapter, we'll discuss the concept of data in a computer program. You'll learn about program variables, Pseudo Constants, the different types of Python data, and the many operations that can be performed on that data.

Computer Data

"Data can be a very complex topic," I said to the class at the beginning of our third class meeting, "but it's an extremely important one. Failure to understand data can lead to problems with your programs down the line. What you learn today may seem very theoretical to you, but it will be vital for your future programming career. Even if you don't see an immediate application for it, look at the information you receive today as something that you can tuck into your programming back pocket for future use."

Variables

"In the Python programs that we write," I said, "the data with which we work will potentially come from three places: the user, in the form of selections that they make, either via a console program or selections from objects such as buttons or List boxes in a window; external sources, such as disk files or databases; and sometimes internal sources in the form of variables."

"Variables?" Rhonda asked.

I explained that variables are placeholders in the computer's memory where we can temporarily store information. Values—such as numbers and characters, for example—are stored in variables while our program is running. As the name implies, the values of these variables can change at any time.

"I'm a little confused as to why we would create a variable in the first place," Barbara said. "Isn't all the data that we need—especially in the program we're writing in this class—entered by the user? Why do we need to store anything temporarily?"

"That's a good question, Barbara," I said. "And to a great degree, you're right. Most of the data that computer programs need is entered by the user, or it comes from a disk file or database. However, there may be times when your program will need to create and use a variable to store the answer to a question that you have asked of the user or the result of a calculation, or, as you'll learn in a few weeks, to keep track of a counter, which is a variable that counts something."

"You said that variables enable us to store information temporarily," Kate said. "I assume that means until our program ends. A variable can't last beyond the running of a program, can it?"

"That's right Kate," I said. "Variables, and the data they contain, go away when our program stops running."

I paused before continuing.

"There are two types of variables," I said. "Local variables and Global variables. Today we'll be learning how to create Global variables. A Global variable is a variable created within the main body of our Python program. Global variables can be seen or accessed in any part of our program. Local variables are variables created within user-defined functions we write on our own (or also within a Class, something we'll learn about in our Objects course). Local variables can only be accessed within the function where they are created. User-defined Functions, and how to create them, we will learn about in Week 6. At that point we'll examine Local variables defined within functions of our own.

> **NOTE: Python programmers don't spend a great deal of time categorizing their variables as Global or Local. They just create them. Python doesn't require that you specify a variable as Global or Local---Python decides that for you based on where the variable is created. If it's created in a function, the variable is Local, and can't be seen or accessed outside of the function. If it's created within the main body of your program, outside of any function, the variable is Global and can be seen or accessed anywhere within your program, including functions.**

"You used the term 'created' in regards to variables," Dave said. "Don't you mean to say declare?"

"Good point Dave," I said. "Many, if not most programming languages, insist that you formally 'declare' a variable with a name and its Data Type before you can begin working with it. Python is different. Variables are created simply by assigning a value to them. There's no need to formally 'declare' a variable in Python with a name and a Data Type prior to that."

"In other words, just assign a value to a variable and it's created?" Jack asked.

"That's right Jack," I answered. "That's all it takes. But be careful. Just because you don't need to formally 'declare' a variable doesn't mean you can refer to one which hasn't been assigned a value. Doing so will generate a Python error."

I paused before continuing.

"Regardless of Local or Global variables," I said, "creating and working with either type of variable is essentially the same. The difference between Global and Local variables, as we'll see later on in the course, is their Scope. Scope means where a variable can be seen or accessed within our program."

Our first variable: The Global Variable

I asked my students to consider a hypothetical program that I hoped would illustrate the need for variables in a program.

"Let's write a Python program," I said, "designed to take two numbers and display their sum in the Python Console Window (hereafter referred to as just the Python Console.) Later on in the course (next week, in fact), you'll learn that there are ways for the user to communicate with our running program (for instance, using the **input()** function,) but for now, let's create two numeric variables by assigning values to them, and then display their sum in the Python Console. I should warn you that most of what you will see in this program you haven't learned yet, but you will today."

I then displayed this program on the classroom projector:

```
# Example3_1.py

number1 = 12
number2 = 23

print(number1 + number2)
```

I saved the program as Example3_1.py, and ran it for the class. The following screen shot was displayed on the classroom projector:

```
C:\Windows\system32\CMD.exe

C:\PythonFiles\Examples>Example3_1
35

C:\PythonFiles\Examples>_
```

Creating/Initializing a Variable

"Let me explain what's going on here," I said. "The first thing we did, after including a comment in our program, was to create a variable called **number1** and assign a value to it using this line of code..."

```
number1 = 12
```

"...To create a variable, we simply type its name, in this case *number1*, and assign a value to it using the equals to sign."

I paused before continuing.

"As I said just a few minutes ago," I repeated, "you don't need to formally declare a variable before assigning a value to it. Just about every other programming language I've used requires you to first declare a variable with a name and a Data Type prior to using it, but Python is different. Python allows you to create a variable just by assigning a value to it."

"What about the Data Type?" Dave asked.

"The Data Type of the variable that Python creates is based on the data you assign to the variable," I said. "This is called Dynamic-Data Typing. In this example, we've assigned the number 12 to the variable called *number1*. As a result, *number1* is created as an Integer variable."

"Integer?" Rose asked.

"An <u>Integer</u> is a whole number," I said, "without a fractional part or a decimal. A number with a fraction—such as 12.2---is called a Floating Point number and a variable assigned that value would be created as a Floating point variable (also called a float.)"

I gave the class a moment to think this over.

"We'll be discussing Integers more in just a few moments," I said. "Now let's take a look at the creation and assignment of our second variable which is very similar to our first."

```
number2 = 23
```

"Finally," I said, "here's something you haven't seen before. This line of code takes the values of the variables *number1* and *number2*, adds them together, and then, using the **print()** function we learned about last week, displays the result in the Python Console. It's just an Addition Operation used with the **print()** function."

```
print(number1 + number2)
```

"You can do that?" Lou asked.

"Yes we can Lou," I said. "Python performs (or in technical terms, executes) the addition within the pair of parentheses first. Python 'looks up' the values contained in the variables referenced, does the addition, then displays the result using the **print()** function."

"There are no quotation marks around the variable names?" Rhonda said. "Last week when we used the **print()** function, 'I love Python!' appeared inside quotation marks. This is different. And why didn't the words *number1* and *number2* appear in the Python Console?"

"Last week, Rhonda" I answered, "we used the **print()** function to display a String Literal, which was sandwiched within Quotation marks. A String Literal is just that---something that we want printed literally, the way it appears within Quotation Marks. Here, *number1* and *number2* are the names of variables, so quotation marks are not required. Also, because *number1* and *number2* are variables whose value is a number, we can sum their values using the Addition Operator---the plus sign---then display that result in the Python Console."

"What would have happened if we had sandwiched *number1* and *number2* within quotation marks?" Barbara asked.

"We would have a much different result than the number 35," I answered. "Let me show you."

I then displayed this modified code on the classroom projector:

```
# Example3_2.py
# Quotation marks in the print() function

number1 = 12
number2 = 23

print("number1 + number2")
```

I then saved the program as <u>Example3_2.py</u>, and ran it for the class. The following screen shot was displayed on the classroom projector:

```
C:\Windows\system32\CMD.exe

C:\PythonFiles\Examples>Example3_2
number1 + number2

C:\PythonFiles\Examples>
```

"What happened to the display of the number 35?" Steve asked.

"By placing quotation marks around 'number1+ number2'," I said, "we created a String Literal, and told Python to literally print that String of characters in the Python Console. Of course, what we actually wanted to do here was to add the values of two variables and display the result. I think we can all agree that our original version of the program was the way to do that."

"That makes sense," Blaine said. "Although I must confess, I'm still not totally clear on this concept of a variable."

"Sometimes Blaine," I said, "it helps to think of a variable like a Post Office Box. For my business, I rent a Post Office Box. When I paid for my Post Office Box, the Post Office assigned me a Box Number. When mail for my Post Office Box arrives, the Postal Clerk places my mail in my box according to the number I've been assigned. If I need to retrieve my mail, knowing the number of my box, I can use my key to retrieve it. Variables in Python are very similar in concept. For instance, this code..."

```
number1 = 12
```

"...tells Python that we wish to create an Integer type variable with the name *number1*, and assign it the value 12. Assigning a value to a variable for the first time is called initializing its value. This is similar to going to the Post Office, renting a box, and receiving a key. The name of the variable is essentially the key for the Python Program. And the great thing about Python (and most other programming languages) is that you can create a variable with an easy-to-remember name that you can easily use later. Thereafter, whenever you need to interact with the variable (either retrieving its value or updating it,) you use its easy-to-remember variable name."

> **NOTE: Assigning an initial value to a variable is called initialization.**

"You said earlier that would be a problem if we didn't initialize a variable, but then tried to work with it," Mary said. "What would happen if we didn't initialize the variables *number1* and *number2* in this example?"

"A picture is worth a thousand words," I said. I then modified our program to look like this:

```
# Example3_3.py
# Printing variables that haven't been initialized

print(number1 + number2)
```

"Notice how I've removed the two lines of code that initialize the values of the variables *number1* and *number2*," I said. "Notice also how I am referring to these two variables in the **print()** function."

I then saved the program as Example3_3.py, and ran it for the class. The following screenshot was displayed on the classroom projector:

```
C:\WINDOWS\system32\cmd.exe

C:\PythonFiles\Examples>Example3_3
Traceback (most recent call last):
  File "C:\PythonFiles\Examples\Example3_3.py", line 4, in <module>
    print (number1 + number2)
NameError: name 'number1' is not defined

C:\PythonFiles\Examples>
```

"What happened?" Ward asked. "I wasn't expecting that. I know in some other programming languages uninitialized variables are considered to have a value of zero?"

"You're right, Ward" I said. "In some programming languages, the value of an uninitialized variable is zero, but Python isn't like that. Python displays what is known as a NameError Exception, complaining that *number1* is not defined. This is because we're trying to refer to a variable that doesn't exist---it was never created because we never assigned a value to it. Notice also that Python displays the NameError Exception only for the variable *number1*. The Python interpreter gave up after encountering its first 'fatal error'. A fatal error is an error which prevents the Python Interpreter from running the rest of the program."

"What's an Exception?" Bob asked.

"An Exception is Python's fancy term for an error," I said. "We'll learn a lot more about Exceptions as we go through the class, and even more in Week 8 when almost the entire class is devoted to them."

> **NOTE: An Exception is Python's fancy term for an error.**

"Why does Python say the name '*number1*' is not defined," Kathy asked. "Why doesn't Python say the variable 'number1' is not defined."

"It's a little complicated," I said, "but the Python Interpreter first scans our code prior to running it to make sure it's OK to run. The Interpreter ignores Comments, then looks in our code for Python statements (which do something), Python functions (which do something but also return a message back to the program that calls them), Python Operators (such as Addition and Subtraction). Anything Python cannot identify as one of these it presumes to be the name of a Variable, or the name of some other Python Objects we haven't learned about yet, such as Lists, Tuples, Dictionaries and Classes. It looks for the name in the program's Namespace, which is where, among other things, Variables, Lists, Tuples, Dictionaries and Classes are defined. If a name isn't found in the Namespace, Python displays the NameError Exception to say that it couldn't find the name there."

I paused before continuing.

"By the way," I said, "if we were to initialize a value for the variable *number1*, but still forgot to initialize *number2*, and then ran the program, the Python Interpreter would then complain that *number2* is not defined."

I modified the program to do exactly that...

```
# Example3_4.py
# Printing variables that haven't been initialized

number1 = 12

print(number1 + number2)
```

I then saved the program as Example3_4.py, and ran it for the class. The following screenshot was displayed on the classroom projector:

```
C:\WINDOWS\system32\cmd.exe                                    _ □ X

C:\PythonFiles\Examples>Example3_4
Traceback (most recent call last):
  File "C:\PythonFiles\Examples\Example3_4.py", line 6, in <module>
    print (number1 + number2)
NameError: name 'number2' is not defined

C:\PythonFiles\Examples>
```

"As predicted," I said, "the Python Interpreter is now complaining that the name '*number2*' isn't defined. Of course, we know it means the variable *number2*."

"So the lesson to be learned here," Blaine said, "is not to forget to initialize your variables before trying to use them."

"That's right, Blaine," I said. "Variables don't have to be formally declared with a Data type in Python, but their values must be initialized before referring to them."

I paused before continuing.

"Something else I'd like to show you," I said, "is how to make our output in the Python Console a little fancier. Let's compare this code to Example3_1.py"

I displayed the code on the classroom projector:

```
# Example3_5.py

number1 = 12
number2 = 23

print("The answer is")
print(number1 + number2)
```

I then saved the program as Example3_5.py, and ran it for the class. The following screenshot was displayed on the classroom projector:

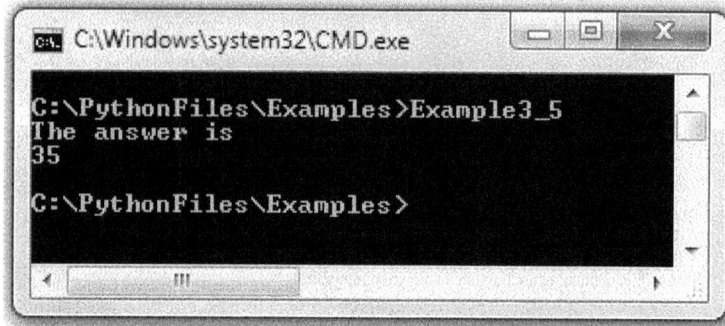

"We're still displaying the number 35 in the Python Console," I said, "but in this case, we're also using the **print()** function to display a message—'The answer is'—before we display the value of the addition of the variables *number1* and *number2*."

"Oh I see," Kate said. "The text contained within the quotation marks of the **print()** function is a String Literal, and is displayed in the Python Console. Is that right?"

"Exactly, Kate," I said. "Text that appears within quotation marks is called a String Literal, and as the name implies, it's displayed literally in the Python Console."

"The next line doesn't have quotation marks" Barbara said. "It's identical to Example3_1, and the number 35 is printed on the next line."

"That's right Barbara," I said, "When Python sees the second **print()** function, it knows to start a new line. As a result, there was no need to use the Backslash+n escape sequence we learned about last week."

I gave my students a chance to think that over.

"Is there any way to have the answer 35 appear on the same line as the phrase 'The answer is?" Mary asked.

"Mary, you read my mind," I said. "Let me show you."

I then displayed this code on the classroom projector:

```
# Example3_6.py

number1 = 12
number2 = 23

print("The answer is", number1 + number2)
```

I then saved the program as Example3_6.py, and ran it for the class. The following screenshot was displayed on the classroom projector:

"The number 35," I said, "the result of the addition of the values of the variables *number1* and *number2*—is now displayed on the same line as the phrase 'The answer is.' We did that with just a single **print()** function. But we did something we haven't done before. We placed a comma after the String Literal to tell Python to display a space, followed by the result of the addition of the values of *number1* and *number2*."

```python
print("The answer is", number1 + number2)
```

"The comma tells Python to display a space, followed by the result of the addition," I continued. "That's a nice feature of the **print()** function."

I could see Steve studying his monitor intently.

"What's wrong Steve?" I asked, preemptively.

"I'm wondering," Steve said, "why you didn't enclose 'number1 + number2' within a pair of parentheses. I think I would have done that just by habit."

"We could have done that, Steve" I agreed, "Some programmers---you included---might have written the **print()** function like this."

```python
print("The answer is", (number1 + number2))
```

"The result would be the same." I said. "The parentheses around 'number1 + number2' are not required here, although some programmers, as you point out, might have done so to improve the program's readability. We'll be discussing why and when parentheses are needed a little later on when we discuss the Order of Operations."

Now Rhonda had a problem.

"I've been following along with you as you've been coding these examples and doing pretty well so far," Rhonda said, "but when I ran my version of the Example3_6 program, there were two spaces between the word 'is' and the number 35 in my Python Console. Can you tell me what I did wrong?"

"Did you include a space after the word 'is' in your String Literal?" I guess. "Notice how my version looks. There's no space after the letter 's' in the word 'is'."

```python
print("The answer is", number1 + number2)
```

"I bet yours looks like this, with a space after the letter s in the word is."

```python
print("The answer is ", number1 + number2)
```

"You're absolutely right," Rhonda said a moment later. "I don't know why I thought I needed to insert a space after the word 'is'."

"There will be times when we need to insert a space the way you did here Rhonda," I said. "In this case, it wasn't necessary, because the comma told Python to display a space."

"Is it possible." Steve asked, "to assign a value to more than one variable on the same line of code?"

"Yes you can, Steve," I said. "Although I don't recommend it. You can use a semicolon to do so, like this…"

```python
number1 = 12; number2 = 23
```

"In fact, you can take this to the extreme by writing an entire Python program with a single line of code. I've seen some students do that. Here's Example3_6.py written with a single line…"

```python
number1 = 12; number2 = 23; print("The answer is", number1 + number2)
```

"This version of the program runs fine," I said, "and produces the same result, but I think you'll agree with me that we've sacrificed a great deal of readability."

"Readability?" Blaine asked. "By that do you mean that this version of the program is harder to follow and understand?"

"Exactly Blaine," I replied, "The original version of this program is very readable, and therefore easier to follow and understand. The single line version is another story. A program written with multiple statements appearing on a single line of code, separated by semicolons, is much harder for the human brain to decipher. This makes modifying programs more difficult. It's frequently a programmer other than the original programmer who may be asked to make modifications to the brilliant code you've written ☺ You want that programmer to be able to, as much as possible, determine at a glance, what you were doing with the code you originally wrote."

Rules For Naming Variables

"You said earlier that we can name our variables virtually anything we want," Jack said. "What are the rules for naming a variable?"

"By convention," I said, "variable names are all lower case letters. Variable names may not begin with a number, but may begin with any letter of the alphabet, even with an underscore, although variable names may not begin with a number, they may contain a number, such as we've seen with our variable named *number1*. Stylistically, although not required, variable names should begin with a lowercase letter. Variable names can be of any length, but variables with long names make coding more difficult, because most times, you'll need to refer to that variable name again somewhere else in your code. Typing a long variable name increases the chance of typing it wrong, and generating a Python error when you execute your program. For that reason, make your variable names as short as possible. Name your variables so that they describe the data they are holding. The more descriptive the better. Many times, it makes sense to use more than one word in your variable name---such as *salestax*. If you do so, separate each word with an underscore character, to make it more readable, such as *sales_tax*. You should also consider avoiding the use of single character variable names, although you will see these used quite a bit in program examples that you see in books and on Internet. In fact, we'll use single character variable names a bit in this course---but I'm doing so to make your typing of our exercises easier. To summarize:"

- Variable names should be all lower case letters

- Variable names <u>may not</u> begin with a number

- Variable names may begin with any letter of the alphabet, even with an underscore

- Although variable names <u>may not</u> begin with a number, they may contain a number

- Stylistically, variable names should begin with a lowercase letter.

- Variable names can be of any length, but variables with long names make coding more difficult. The shorter the better.

- Name your variables so that they describe the data they are holding. The more descriptive the better.

- Many times, it makes sense to use more than one word in your variable name. If you do so, separate each word with an underscore character, to make it more readable.

- Avoid the use of single character variable names, although you will see these used quite a bit in program examples that you see in books and on Internet. Such variable names are known as throwaway variables.

NOTE: Python programmers use variable names beginning with an underscore or single character to denote that their use, within the program, is short-lived, most likely just one time. For this reason, they are known as throwaway variables.

Pseudo Constants

"Are there Constants in Python the way there are in some other programming languages?" Dave asked.

"The answer is no," I said. "Python doesn't have true Constants the way other programming languages do, although it is possible to simulate a Constant by creating a variable, and giving it a name in ALL CAPS. I call these simulated constants Pseudo Constants."

"ALL CAPS?", Steve asked.

"That's right Steve," I said, "in the programming languages that are true Constants, by convention Constants are given names in ALL CAPS. If we simulate a constant in Python, we do the same thing---name the constant with all capital letters."

"But what is a Constant?" Rhonda asked. "You haven't really explained it."

"Like a variable," I answered, "a Constant is a placeholder in memory that holds something, like a number or a name. Unlike a variable, whose value can change, a Constant's value is not permitted to change. That's where the name Constant comes from---Constant value. However, as I said, Python doesn't support the notion of a Constant. If we want to create a variable whose value we don't want to change, the best we can do is 'simulate' a Constant by naming the variable in ALL CAPS."

"So we're relying on the fact that the variable is named in all Capital Letters as a way to alert and prevent us (and other programmers) from writing code to change it?" Joe asked.

"Exactly Joe," I said. "The Python community has found it to be quite useful. Whenever a Python programmer sees a variable named in all CAPS, he or she knows that the author of the program has intended that the variable's value should not change."

"Can we see an example of a Pseudo Constant?" Valerie asked.

"Great idea Valerie," I said. "Let's write a program that simulates a Constant."

I then displayed the following code on the classroom projector:

```
# Example3_7.py
# Simulating a Constant in Python

number1 = 12
BOOSTER = 100

print("The answer is", number1 + BOOSTER)
```

I saved the program as Example3_7.py, and ran it for the class. The following screenshot was displayed on the classroom projector:

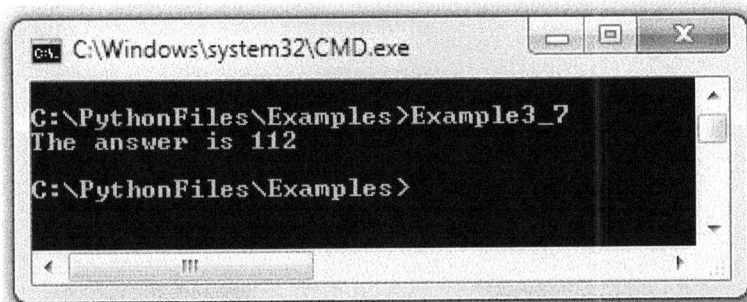

"This is a pretty simple example," I said. "All we're doing here is creating a variable called *number1*, and assigning it the value of 12..."

```
number1 = 12
```

"...Creating another variable called *BOOSTER* and assigning it the value of 100. Because we're naming the variable in all CAPS, we are serving notice to ourselves and any other programmer who reads our code that it's our intention to simulate a Constant here..."

```
BOOSTER = 100
```

"...As I mentioned earlier," I said, "in many languages Constants are named using all capital letters, and that's what I'm doing here. To the Python Interpreter, *BOOSTER* is an ordinary variable, like *number1*, but to a Python programmer, the fact that it's named in all CAPS is an alert that its value should never be changed, but remember Python won't stop you from doing so."

I paused before continuing.

"Once we've created and initialized our Pseudo Constant," I said, "we can then use it in our code the same way we would a variable. In this case, we take the value of *BOOSTER*, add it to the value of the variable *number1*, and display the result in the Python Console."

```
print("The answer is", number1 + BOOSTER)
```

"I see what you're doing here," Steve said, "but my question is: When should we create a Constant?"

"A good rule of thumb is this," I said. "Whenever you find yourself creating a variable and assigning it a value that never changes, and you refer to that variable more than once in your program, it's probably a Constant, and therefore you should probably name it in All CAPS."

"What do you mean by refer to it more than once in your program?" Blaine asked.

"Use it in your code more than once," I said, "For instance, in multiple calculations."

"Getting back to the example program," Kate said, "I was going to ask why you didn't simply take the number 100 and add it to the value of the variable *number1* instead of first assigning it to *BOOSTER*?"

"That's a great question Kate," I said. "We could have used the number 100 itself (called a <u>Numeric Literal</u>) in our calculation, but using a Constant with a meaningful name makes your program much more readable and because of that, more easy to modify if the need arises. To a programmer reading your code, Numeric Literals are just ordinary numbers. Variables---or Pseudo Constants---with meaningful names, on the other hand, make it a lot easier for other programmers to decipher what your program is doing. The bottom line: avoid using Numeric Literals in your program code whenever possible. Create a Pseudo Constant instead."

> **NOTE: Avoid using Numeric Literals in your program code. Create a Pseudo Constant instead."**

"Can you give us an example to illustrate why a Pseudo Constant makes your program easier to modify than one with a Numeric Literal?" Linda asked.

"Sure thing, Linda," I replied. "Let's say you are writing a program to calculate payroll for a company. Let's assume that there's a State Income Tax Rate equal to 1 percent of an employee's Gross Pay. Somewhere in your program, perhaps multiple places, you are going to need to multiply the Gross Pay amount by 0.01. In Python, that would look something like..."

```
gross_pay_amount * .01
```

"...where *gross_pay_amount* is a variable in which we've stored the employee's Gross Pay. Now, further suppose we perform this same calculation in several different places in our program, each time multiplying the value of the *gross_pay_amount* variable by the number 0.01."

I paused before continuing.

"Now let me ask you this question?", I said. "What happens if the State Income Tax rate changes from 1 percent to 2 percent?"

"Obviously," Dave said, "we would have to modify our program and change the number we've been using from 0.01 to 0.02."

"That's right, Dave," I agreed, "and because we have that number hard-coded as a Numeric Literal in several places in our program, we would need to go through our program, possibly line by line, looking for the value 0.01 and then change it to 0.02. Using a Constant, or a variable that appears to be one, can make that process a lot easier."

> **NOTE: Sharp readers will undoubtedly point out that we could do a Search and Replace of .01 for .02. That's true, but even that process is not without hazards**

"How so?" Steve asked.

"Instead of using the Numeric Literal 0.01 in one or more places in our program," I answered, "instead we could create a Pseudo Constant called *STATE_TAX_RATE*, assign it the value of 0.01, and then use that Constant in all of our calculations instead, like this."

```
gross_pay_amount * STATE_TAX_RATE
```

"I think I understand now," Rhonda said. "If the State Tax Rate changes, because we used the Pseudo Constant in our calculations and not the number 0.01, we only need to change the assignment statement for the Pseudo Constant once to reflect the new value."

"That's perfect, Rhonda," I said.

"Can we see assignment for the **STATE_TAX_RATE** constant?" Barbara asked.

I displayed the assignment on the classroom projector:

```
STATE_TAX_RATE = .01
```

"I believe this is the first time that we've assigned a number with a fractional part to a variable, isn't it?" Kate asked

"I think you're right Kate," I said. "Unlike some other programming languages, we don't need to do anything differently here when we assign a number with a fraction to a variable. Behind the scenes, Python creates the variable with a Data Type based on the value you assign to it. This is called **Dynamic Data typing**."

"So *STATE_TAX_RATE* is created as a Floating Point Data Type?" Steve asked.

"That's right Steve," I said, "*STATE_TAX_RATE* is dynamically created as a Floating Point Data Type. Having said that, I need to warn you that although Python supports Dynamic Data Typing, it also enforces something called Strong Data Typing. That means Python is extremely 'picky' about the types of operations that can be performed on data. That means that mathematical Operations can only be performed on numeric data (Integer or Floating Point) and other operations (such as String and List Operations we'll learn about in a few weeks) can be performed only on Strings or Lists. For that reason, although Python takes care of creating the appropriate data type for your variable based on the data that is assigned to it, you will need to be conscious of the Data Type that Python creates for you."

"Wow, I had no idea working with data could be so complicated," Peter said.

"For the most part," I said, "it's not usually a problem. But you will need to be aware of the Data Type that Python has assigned to a variable you create."

I realized that we had been working pretty intensely for some time and, because there were no more questions, I suggested that we take a short break.

Python Data Types

"Let's take a closer look at the Data Types in Python," I said, resuming after a 15 minutes break. "An understanding of the Python Data Types and their characteristics is important. In our simple examples this morning, we referred to the Integer and Floating Point Data Types. Now it's time to review the others"

I paused before continuing.

"Normally," I said, "at this point I would discuss in detail the various Data Types in Python. However, in Python, the topic is not nearly as critical is in other languages."

"Why is that?" Dave asked. "Is it because of the Dynamic Typing you mentioned earlier?"

"That's exactly right Dave," I replied. "In other languages, you must first declare a Data Type for a variable prior to assigning a value to it. That means the programmer is responsible for choosing the correct Data Type to 'hold' the value of the variable. Unfortunately, in those other languages, that also means that the programmer can declare the variable with the wrong Data Type. However, as we've seen, Python, because of its Dynamic Typing, determines the correct Data Type for you based on the value you assign the variable. You can't go wrong. While it's important to understand what's going on behind the scenes, and to be aware of the Data Type of your variable, it's not nearly as critical as it is in other languages. Ultimately, Python will figure it out for you. After the variable is created by Python with an appropriate Data Type, the programmer needs to be careful to use only the appropriate operations for the Data Type of the variable. This will be a continual discussion as we go through the class."

"Is there a way to determine what type of Data Type Python has created for our variable?" Barbara asked.

"That's a great question Barbara," I said. "The answer is yes. You can use the **type()** function to determine the Data Type of a variable. Here's an example program using the **type()** function. We'll create five variables, then see what the Data Type is that Python has determined for them."

I then displayed the following code on the classroom projector:

```
# Example3_8.py
# What's my Data Type?

value1 = 12
value2 = 3.4
value3 = "John Smiley"
value4 = True
value5 = False

print("The data type of value1 is", type(value1))
print("The data type of value2 is", type(value2))
```

```
print("The data type of value3 is",  type(value3))
print("The data type of value4 is",  type(value4))
print("The data type of value5 is",  type(value5))
```

I then saved the program as Example3_8.py, and ran it for the class. The following screenshot was displayed on the classroom projector:

```
C:\PythonFiles\Examples>Example3_8
The data type of value1 is <class 'int'>
The data type of value2 is <class 'float'>
The data type of value3 is <class 'str'>
The data type of value4 is <class 'bool'>
The data type of value5 is <class 'bool'>

C:\PythonFiles\Examples>
```

"We used the **type()** function," I said, "along with the **print()** function, to display the Data Type of each of our five variables. We designated the name of our variable as an 'argument' to the type function by placing it within parentheses. The 'return value' of the **type() function** is the Data Type of the variable. We then use the **print()** function to display the Data Type in the Python Console. We'll be discussing arguments and return values of functions later on in the course."

"So the names within the brackets," Jack said, "are the Data Types that Python has assigned for the variables we've created?"

"That's right Jack," I said. "The four that we see here, int, float, str and bool are the four Data Types we'll be working primarily with in this class: int or Integer; float, or Floating Point Numbers; str, or Strings, and bool, or Boolean, which is either True or False. By the way, don't worry about the word 'class' that precedes the name of the Data Type. Python is Object-Oriented, and behind the scenes, all Data Types are actually Python Objects. You'll learn more about Objects, including how to make your own, in our Python Classes and Objects course offered here at the University."

int and float

"int and float." Kate said. "Those are numeric Data Types, correct?"

"That's right Kate," I said. "In Python, there are two numeric Data Types---int(which are Integers) and float (Floating Point.) Integers are 'whole numbers' and Floating Points are numbers that have a fractional part. Python determine the type of variable to create based on the assignment of the variable. A whole number assigned to a variable creates an Integer Data Type. A number with a fractional part creates a Floating-point Data Type variable."

bool

"Can we take a closer look at this bool type?" Steve said. "I'm not sure I'm getting it."

"Sure thing Steve," I said. "A bool Data Types can have only two possible values: True or False. In Python, True and False are special values that can be directly assigned to a variable. Let's take a look at another example."

I displayed this code on the classroom projector:

```
# Example3_9.py
# Working with Boolean Variables

married = True
retired = False

print("The value of married is",  married)
print("The value of retired is ",  retired)
```

I then saved the program as Example3_9.py, and ran it for the class. The following screenshot was displayed on the classroom projector:

"What we've done here," I said, "is to create two bool variables: one called *married* to represent someone's marital status and the other called *retired* to represent their retirement status. The bool variable is ideal to use when the value of the variable can only be a True/False or Yes/No outcome. Notice how the assignment of True or False to a bool variable is made without enclosing it within quotation marks or apostrophes. Furthermore, notice how the value of the variables married and retired are displayed as True and False respectively in the Python Console."

I was just about to point out that True and False were both spelled <u>starting with a Capital</u> letter when Rhonda raised her hand.

"I've been following along with you," Rhonda said, "but obviously I've done something wrong. I received an error message saying that 'true' is not defined when I tried to run my version of the program."

I suspected I knew what the problem was. I took a walk to Rhonda's work station (it wasn't far, she sat right in the front row) and saw immediately what the problem was.

"I see the problem Rhonda," I said. "In your code, you spelled the word True in all lower case letters, like this…"

For the benefit of everyone in the class, I displayed Rhonda's code on the classroom projector.

```
# Example3_10.py
# Working with Boolean Variables
# True and False intentionally spelled wrong

married = true    # Intentionally spelled wrong
retired = false   # Intentionally spelled wrong

print("The value of married is",  married)
print("The value of retired is ",  retired)
```

"This is a very understandable mistake to make," I said. "Other programming languages, such as Java and C++ spell True and False in all lower case letters, but Python wants True spelled with a capital T and False spelled with a capital F, otherwise you will get this NameError message."

I then saved the program as <u>Example3_10.py</u>, and ran it for the class. The following screenshot was displayed on the classroom projector:

"As you can see," I said, "the spelling of the word 'true' in all lower case letters has confused Python. By the way, notice that the Python Interpreter hasn't gotten a chance to be confused by the spelling of the word 'false' yet—but believe me, if we correct the spelling to 'True' and leave the word 'false' in all lower case, we'll receive a similar NameError message."

In the meantime, Rhonda had corrected her program, and she reported success when she changed the spelling of the word 'true' to 'True'.

"Every programming language has its quirks," I said, "and I warned you that Python can be picky. Obviously, the author of Python didn't care that those of you coming from the Java and C++ worlds would be confused by the spelling."

"I must be doing something similar," Steve said. "I'm getting a NameError message also. But I spelled both true and false in lower case letters."

I took a quick walk to Steve's workstation (he was in the last row of the classroom.) As Steve had indicated, he had a NameError message, but his message said that the name 'married' was not defined., and it targeted the line with the **print()** function as the one in error.

"I see the problem Steve," I said. "You assigned a value to a variable called *married* spelled with 2 r's. However, you're trying to print the value of a variable called 'maried' spelled with just one 'r'. They're not the same, and with this NameError message, Python is telling you that the variable whose value you are trying to display doesn't exist."

I coded up a quick example of Steve's program for the rest of the class and displayed it on the classroom projector:

```
# Example3_11.py
# Trying to display the value of a variable that doesn't exist

married = True
retired = False

print("The value of married is",  maried)
print("The value of retired is ",  retired)     #Intentionally spelled wrong
```

I then saved the program as Example3_11.py, and ran it for the class. The following screenshot was displayed on the classroom projector.

All Steve needed to do was correct the spelling of 'maried' to 'married' and his program worked fine.

I waited to see if there were any more questions before moving onto a discussion of the String Data Type.

Strings

"We've covered numbers and True/False values," Blaine said. "What's next?"

"That would be the String Data Type," I said. "Any text that isn't a number, or isn't a True/False or Yes/No value should be enclosed within quotation marks. This tells Python to create a String variable to store it. Let me show you."

I displayed the following code on the classroom projector.

```
# Example3_12.py
# A String variable

string1 = "John Smiley"
print("The value of string1 is",  string1)
```

I then saved the program as Example3_12.py, and ran it for the class. The following screenshot was displayed on the classroom projector:

"Notice," I said, "that assignments to a String Variable are done by enclosing the character or characters within quotation marks. You can also use apostrophes if you like, but I prefer quotation marks for reasons that I'll explain shortly."

> NOTE: String variables should be enclosed within quotation marks. You can also enclose them within apostrophes (single quote) if you like, but I prefer quotation marks (double quote.)

"Suppose you forget the quotation marks?" Mary asked.

"In that case," I responded, "you'll totally confuse Python, and generate a SyntaxError Exception. Let's take a look."

I quickly coded up an example of an attempt to assign my name to a variable without the use of quotation marks or apostrophes.

```
# Example3_13.py
# A String variable

string1 = John Smiley
print("The value of string1 is", string1)
```

I then saved the program as Example3_13.py, and ran it for the class. The following screenshot was displayed on the classroom projector:

"As predicted," I said, "Python is confused. A String Literal, in this case my name, needs to be sandwiched between quotation marks, like this...."

```
string1 = "John Smiley"
```

"I just realized," Rhonda said, "that when we assign a number to a variable, we don't use apostrophes or quotation marks."

"That's right, Rhonda," I said. "Numbers (also called Numeric Literals) do not have to be enclosed within quotation marks.

I then displayed this code on the classroom projector:

```
number1 = 12
```

"But String Variables must be."

"What about a telephone number or a Social Security Number?" Ward asked. "Both of those contain numbers but are usually written with dashes in them. What about those?"

"That's a great question Ward," I said. "Although both of the examples you cite contain numbers, neither a phone number nor a Social Security Number is actually a number, in the sense that it would be used in a mathematical calculation of some time. As you pointed out, both are typically written with dashes, that aren't numbers at all. Because of that, both of your examples should be assigned to a String Variable sandwiched between Quotation Marks the way we did with the name 'John Smiley' when we assigned it to *string1* in the previous example. The assignment of a Phone Number to a variable would look like this…"

```
phone_number = "215-231-3131"
```

"…Python would then create a String Data Type Variable called *phone_number.*"

> **NOTE: Python style guides recommend, for variable names that contain more than one word, separating the words with an underscore, as we did here between the word phone and the word number.**

"Suppose," Dave said, "we forget the quotation marks in this Phone Number example? That Phone Number looks suspiciously like a Mathematical Calculation. What will happen then? Will Python be confused like it was when we tried to assign your name to a variable without quotation marks?"

"Another great question," I said. "Let's see. We can use the **type()** function to determine what Python believes is going on behind the scenes."

I then coded up this example, using the **type()** function to display the Data Type of a variable…

```
# Example3_14.py
# Assigning a phone number to a variable

phone_number1 = "215-331-3131"
phone_number2 = 215-331-3131

print("The data type of phone_number1 is ",  type(phone_number1))
print("The value of phone_number1 is", phone_number1)

print("The data type of phone_number2 is ",  type(phone_number2))
print("The value of phone_number2 is", phone_number2)
```

"Notice," I said, "that I've assigned a String value to a variable called *phone_number1,* and tried to do the same assignment to a variable called *phone_number2.* However, with the second value I 'forgot' to sandwich the Phone Number within quotation marks. I wonder what will happen?"

I then saved the program as <u>Example3_14.py</u>, and ran it for the class. The following screenshot was displayed on the classroom projector:

```
C:\Windows\system32\CMD.exe

C:\PythonFiles\Examples>Example3_14
The data type of phone_number1 is  <class 'str'>
The value of phone_number1 is 215-331-3131
The data type of phone_number2 is  <class 'int'>
The value of phone_number2 is -3247

C:\PythonFiles\Examples>
```

"I don't see any error messages, or I should say Exceptions" Ward said.

"You're right Ward," I replied, "there aren't any error messages displayed. The program ran fine, and the **type()** function tells us that *phone_number1* is a str (String) Data Type, but *phone_number2* is an int (Integer) Data Type."

"What happened?" Rhonda asked. "Shouldn't they both be Strings?"

"That's what you might think," I said. "Because of the quotation marks, <u>215-331-3131</u> was assigned to a String variable called *phone_number1.* However, as Dave suspected, *phone_number2* is a different story. Because there were no quotation marks around 215-331-3131, Python believed that we were telling it to assign the <u>result</u> of a numeric calculation to the variable called *phone_number2.*"

"You can do that?" Steve asked. "Like a calculator?."

"Exactly Steve," I said. "Because we forgot to place quotation marks around the phone number, Python performed a calculation on it, and the result of the calculation of 215 minus the number 331 minus the number 3131 is then stored in the variable called *phone_number2*."

215 minus 331 = -116 minus 3131 = -3247

"I just used my calculator to verify that result," Rhonda said. "Python is correct—the answer is negative 3247."

"Python did exactly what we told it to do," I said, "that unfortunately, may not be what we actually wanted it to do ☺"

No one had any other questions about Python Data Types, and so, after a 15-minute break, we moved onto a discussion of what we can do with the various types of Python Data---Data Operations.

Operations on Data

"Because you now all know something about Python Data Types," I said, after our break, "it's now time to learn what we can do with that data. This is called Data Operations. Let's start with Mathematical Operations, which are operations that are performed on data stored in numeric variables---either int (Integers) or flt (Floating Points)."

Mathematical Operations

"You can't perform Mathematical Operations on any other kind of data besides numbers," I said. "Now let's look at the various Mathematical Operations available in Python, which are Addition, Subtraction, Multiplication, Division and the Remainder Operation."

I paused a moment before continuing.

"Mathematical Operations," I said, "are performed on a pair of Operands. Operands appear on either side of an Operator, such as a + sign, like this simple Addition Operation."

4 + 2

"The number 4 is one Operand," I said, "the plus sign is an Operator designating Addition, and the number 2 is the second Operand. When the Mathematical Operation is executed, a result is generated. You have <u>three</u> choices as to what to do with this result. First, you can choose to discard it or just ignore it. Secondly, you can assign it to a variable, or thirdly, you can use the result in an expression of some kind, as we did earlier today when we displayed the result of an Addition Operation in the Python Console by using it as an argument to the **print()** function."

"What's an expression?" Linda asked.

"An expression is any combination of numbers, variables or Operations that produces a result," I said. "The example we just saw 4 + 2 is an expression that produces a result of 6. That's a simple expression. Some expressions can be very complex, consisting of many numbers, variables, Operands and Operations."

Here's a list of the Python Mathematical Operators:

Operator	**Meaning**	**Example**
+	Addition	11 + 22
–	Subtraction	22 – 11
*	Multiplication	5 * 6
/	Division	21 / 3
%	Remainder	12 % 2

The Addition Operation (+)

"The Addition Operation (+) adds two Operands and produces a result," I said, as I displayed this example of the Addition Operation on the classroom projector:

number3 = number1 + number2

"In this example," I said, "we're taking the result of the addition of the variables *number1* and *number2* and assigning that resulting value to the variable *number3*. Notice that I didn't say that the Addition Operation adds two numbers—that's not necessarily the case, as it isn't here. In Python, an Operand can be a number, a variable, a Pseudo Constant, or any expression that results in a number. Ultimately, as long as Python can evaluate the expression as a number, the Addition Operation will work."

"What do you mean when you say evaluate?" Kate asked.

"When Python evaluates an expression," I replied, "it examines the expression, substituting actual values for any variables or constants that it finds in order to produce a result."

I took a moment to emphasize that Python performs Operations on only one pair of Operands at a time, which means that even a complex expression like this one will be done one step at a time:

```
number4 = number1 + number2 + number3
```

"We'll learn more about complex expressions like this later," I promised.

"What's an Operand, again?" Ward asked.

"An Operand is something to the left or right of the Operation symbol," I said. "In the assignment statement I just showed you, *number1, number2* and *number3* are all Operands. No matter how many operators appear in an expression, Python performs an operation on just two Operands at a time."

"That's a little surprising to me," Rhonda said. "Are you saying that no matter how fast my PC is, it still performs Arithmetic the way I was taught in school, one step at a time?"

"That's right, Rhonda," I said. "One step at a time. One Operation at a time. But a computer executes those single steps at the speed of light!"

I then displayed Example3_6.py to my students once more:

```
# Example3_6.py

number1 = 12
number2 = 23

print("The answer is", number1 + number2)
```

"Remember this example from earlier?" I asked. "Here we're taking the result of the Addition Operation of the values of the variables *number1* and *number2* and using it as an argument to the **print()** function."

"In this example," Linda said, "you first assigned values to variables and then performed the Addition Operation on the value of the variables. Is it possible to perform the addition using the Numeric Literals?"

"Yes, you can," I said, as I displayed this code:

```
# Example3_15.py

print("The answer is", 12 + 23)
```

I then saved the program as Example3_15.py, and ran it for the class—once again, the number 35 was displayed in the Python Console.

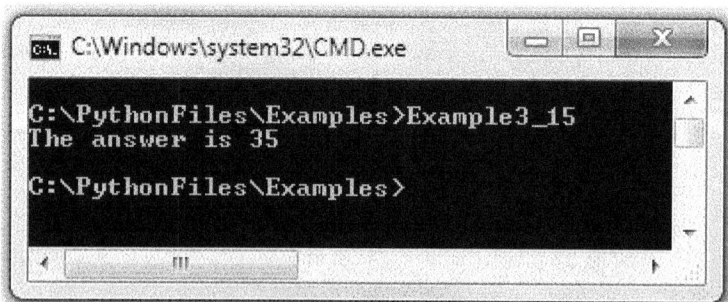

"The result of the addition of 12 and 23 is displayed in the Python Console," I said.

"What are the Numeric Literals that Linda was talking about?" Rhonda asked. "Are those the numbers 12 and 23?"

"Exactly, Rhonda," I replied. "Numeric Literals are literally just numbers."

I waited to see if there were any other questions before moving onto the Subtraction Operation.

The Subtraction Operation (-))

"As you may have guessed," I said, "the Subtraction Operator (–) works by subtracting the Operand on the right side from the Operand on the left and producing a result. Look at this example."

I showed the following code on the class projector:

```
# Example3_16.py

number1 = 44
number2 = 33

result = number1 - number2

print("The answer is",  result)
```

I then saved the program as Example3_16.py, and ran it for the class. The following screenshot was displayed on the classroom projector:

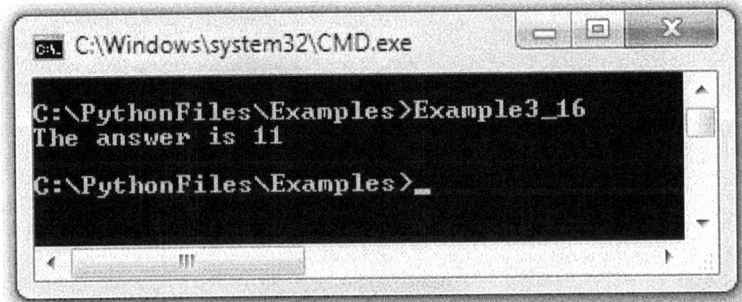

"As you can see," I said, "the value of the variable *number2* was subtracted from the value of the variable *number1* and the result was then…."

"You switched things up a bit here," Ward interrupted.

"What do you mean Ward?" I asked.

"You created an extra variable called *result*, and assigned the result of the Subtraction Operation to it." he answered. "In the previous example, you used the result of the Addition Operation as an argument to the **print()** function."

"That's right," I said. "I wanted to show you that you can assign the result of the Subtraction Operation to another variable. I called the variable *result*, but we could have called it anything we want."

"I noticed that you didn't initialize the *result* variable prior to the assignment?" Ward continued.

"That's right Ward," I said, "The variable *result* is created by the assignment of the result of the Subtraction Operation of the two variables. No prior creation or initialization of the variable is required as is so often required in other programming languages. We then used the value of the result variable as an argument to the **print()** function."

The Multiplication Operation (*)

"The Multiplication Operation (*) multiplies two Operands and produces a result" I said.

"This is a little different from what I used in school," Mary said. "In school, we used the letter X to denote multiplication."

"I did as well," I said, "but with computers---as well as calculators---we use the asterisk instead to designate Multiplication. Except for the use of the asterisk instead of the letter 'X', multiplication in Python works as you would expect."

I displayed the following code on the classroom projector:

```
# Example3_17.py

number1 = 4
number2 = 3

result = number1 * number2

print("The answer is",  result)
```

I then saved the program as Example3_17.py, and ran it for the class. The following screenshot was displayed on the classroom projector:

```
C:\Windows\system32\CMD.exe
C:\PythonFiles\Examples>Example3_17
The answer is 12

C:\PythonFiles\Examples>_
```

"As you can see," I said, "the value of the variable *number1* was multiplied by the value of the variable *number1*. The result was then assigned to the result variable that was then used as an argument to the print() function."

It seemed that Operations, Operands and Operators were becoming "old hat", and so we moved onto Division.

The Division Operation (*)

"The Division Operator (/) works by dividing the Operand on the left by the Operand on the right and returning a result," I said.

```
# Example3_18.py

number1 = 5
number2 = 2

result = number1 / number2

print("The answer is",  result)
```

I then saved the program as Example3_18.py, and ran it for the class. The following screenshot was displayed on the classroom projector:

```
C:\Windows\system32\CMD.exe
C:\PythonFiles\Examples>Example3_18
The answer is 2.5

C:\PythonFiles\Examples>_
```

"5 divided by 2 is 2.5," I said.

"Wow," Linda said. "In C++, our answer likely would have been the whole number 2. Here Python cleverly displays the correct answer, 2.5, even though 5 and 2 are Integer Data Types."

"That's right Linda," I said, "Also, we didn't have to worry about telling Python that the variable *result* should have a fractional part (i.e. Floating Point Data Type.) Python figured it out on its own."

"I might have thought that you would assign a Floating point number for both number1 and number2 to make this work," Ward said. "Like 5.0 and 2.0."

"Totally not necessary Ward," I said. "Python handles everything for us."

The Remainder Operator (%)

"The Remainder Operation," I said, "sometimes called the *Modulus Operation* in other programming languages, deals with remainders. The result of the Remainder Operation is the remainder of a Division Operation. For example, the number 5 divided by the number 2 is 2, with a remainder of 1. The number 23 divided by the number 3 is 7 with a remainder of 2. The number 49 divided by the number 5 is 9 with a remainder of 4. You get the idea. It's that simple. The result of the 'mod' Operation, as it is sometimes called, is the remainder."

"What's the symbol for the Remainder Operation?" Ward asked.

"It's the percent (%) sign," I said. "Let me give you an example of the Remainder Operation."

```
# Example3_19.py

number1 = 49
number2 = 5

result = number1 % number2

print("The remainder is",  result)
```

I then saved the program as Example3_19.py, and ran it for the class. The following screenshot was displayed on the classroom projector:

```
C:\Windows\system32\cmd.exe

C:\PythonFiles\Examples>Example3_19
The remainder is 4

C:\PythonFiles\Examples>
```

"As you can see," I said, "the Remainder Operation has resulted in a value of 4 being displayed in the Python Console."

"I think I'm okay with the mechanics of the Remainder Operation," Rhonda said. "I don't understand why you would want to use it. Can you give us an example?"

"The usefulness of the Remainder Operation," I said, "is not as obvious as the other Mathematical Operations. One of the more common uses of the Remainder Operation is to determine if a number is odd or even. When you perform the Remainder Operation on **Operand1** with the number 2 as **Operand2**, if the result is 0 that means that **Operand1** is an even number. If the result is 1, that means **Operand1** is an odd number."

I gave my students a chance to think about this for a moment.

"So if you 'mod' **Operand1** by the number 2, there are only two possible results, 0 and 1?" Ward asked.

"That's right, Ward," I said. "Let me show you."

I displayed the following code on the classroom projector.

```
# Example3_20.py

odd_number1 = 3
odd_number2 = 5
even_number1 = 4
even_number2 = 6

result = odd_number1 % 2
print("The remainder is",  result)

result = even_number1 % 2
print("The remainder is",  result)

result = odd_number2 % 2
print("The remainder is",  result)

result = even_number2 % 2
print("The remainder is",  result)
```

"What we've done here," I pointed out, "is to declare four variables and assign two of them even numbers and two of them odd numbers. Using the Remainder (or Mod) operator, we can then determine whether the variable is even or odd by examining the result of the Remainder Operation with the number 2. A result of 0 indicates that **Operand1** is an <u>even</u> number, and a result of 1 indicates that **Operand1** is an <u>odd</u> number."

I then saved the program as Example3_20.py, and ran it for the class. The following screenshot was displayed on the classroom projector:

"As you can see," I said, "the result of the Remainder Operation is either a 0 or a 1; 0 indicates an even number, and 1 indicates an odd number."

"It can't be that easy," Ward said. "I think I had a programming assignment like this to do in a class I took several years ago, and as I recall, it was quite difficult to solve. The Remainder Operator. I'll need to remember that one."

The Exponentiation Operator (**)

"Math phobics beware," I said. "It's time to talk about Exponentiation. The Exponentiation Operation (**) raises a number to the power of the exponent. Let's take 2**8 for example. This notation means raise 2 to the power of 8, where 8 is the exponent. When you raise a number to the power of an exponent, you multiply that number by itself the number of times specified by the exponent. In this instance, that means you multiply 2 by itself 8 times, like this:"

$2 * 2 * 2 * 2 * 2 * 2 * 2 * 2 = 256$

"…4 raised to the power of 12 would be 4**12, or 4 multiplied by itself 12 times. The result would be …"

$4 * 4 * 4 * 4 * 4 * 4 * 4 * 4 * 4 * 4 * 4 * 4 = 16777216$

"The Exponentiation Operation," I said, "is typically used in complex scientific and mathematic formulas. Let's see how we would write code to raise 4 to the power of 12 in Python."

I displayed this code on the classroom projector.

```
# Example3_21.py

number1 = 4
number2 = 12

print("The answer is", number1 ** number2)
```

I then saved the program as Example3_21.py and ran it for the class. The following screenshot was displayed on the classroom projector.

"As predicted," I said, "4 raised to the power of 12 is 16,777,216."

Augmented Assignment Operators

"Does Python have the Increment and Decrement Operators that C++ and C# have?" Dave asked.

"Good question Dave," I said. "For those of you who aren't sure what Dave is talking about, both the C++ and C# programming languages allow you to easily add 1 to the current value of a variable with a special Operator called the

Increment Operator. Python, as well as those other programming languages, permit you to add 1 to a variable using this somewhat more cumbersome syntax…"

```
number1 = number1 + 1
```

"I'm not sure I understand how to read that code," Barbara said.

"Read it like this," I answered, "starting with the expression to the right of the equal to sign. Take the current value of the variable **number1**, add 1 to it, then assign that result to the variable *number1*. The result is that the value of the variable **number1** is incremented by 1."

I paused before continuing.

"In C++ and C#," I said, "there's a shortcut notation that automatically adds 1 to the value of that variable *number1* using the ++ Operator. It looks like this…"

```
number1++
```

"Likewise," I continued, "in both languages, we can also easily subtract 1 from the value of the variable *number1* using the -- Operator…"

```
number1--
```

"Unfortunately," I said, "Python doesn't have either the ++ operator or the – operator. However, it does have something similar called Augmented Assignment Operators. Like the ++ and -- operators in C++ or C#, the Python Augmented Assignment Operators can save us a little bit of typing. As a bonus, the Augmented Assignment Operators in Python allow us to increment (add to) or decrement (subtract from) a variable not only by 1, but by any value we choose."

The Augmented Addition Operator (+=)

"The Augmented Addition Operator in Python is the **+=** Operator," I said. "Quite frequently in programming, we find ourselves adding to the value of a variable. Here's the cumbersome version of code to add 1 to the value of a variable."

I displayed the following code on the classroom projector.

```
# Example3_22.py
number1 = 5
number1 = number1 + 1

print("The value of number1 is now",  number1)
```

I then saved the program as Example3_22.py, and ran it for the class. The following screenshot was displayed on the classroom projector:

"The result of 5 plus 1 is 6," I said. "Having created the variable *number1* with a value of 5, we then added 1 to it using this line of code."

```
number1 = number1 + 1
```

"I think you would agree that this code can be confusing," I said. "The expression to the right of the equal to sign is performed first. Read it this way: Take the current value of the variable *number1*, which is 5, add 1 to it, giving a result of 6, and then assign that value to the variable *number1*."

"So that's how that's done," Blaine said. "But what about this Augmented Addition Operator you mentioned?"

"The Augmented Addition Operator is a shortcut version of the code in Example3_22.py," I said. "Take a look at this code."

I then modified the code to look like this:

```
# Example3_23.py

number1 = 10
number1 += 1

print("The value of number1 is now",  number1)
```

I then saved the program as Example3_23.py, and ran it for the class. The following screenshot was displayed on the classroom projector:

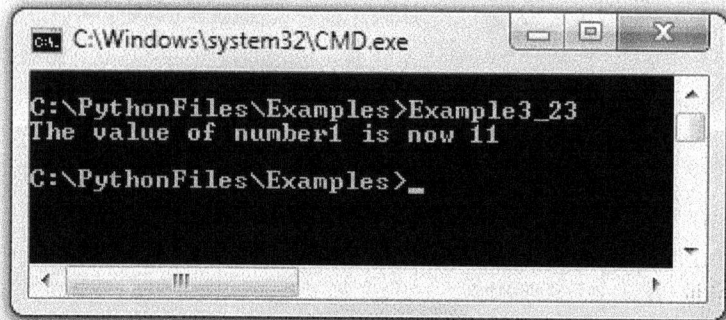

```
C:\Windows\system32\CMD.exe

C:\PythonFiles\Examples>Example3_23
The value of number1 is now 11

C:\PythonFiles\Examples>_
```

"The result of 10 plus 1 is 11" I said. "Having created the variable *number1* with a value of 10, we then added 1 to it with this line of code using the Augmented Addition Operator (+=)..."

```
number1 += 1
```

"It's a shorter version of this code..."

```
number1 = number1 + 1
```

"...but ultimately produces the same result. Which version you use is up to you. Most experienced programmers prefer code that requires less typing :)"

"I must have done something wrong," Rhonda said, "I just typed your example code, but my answer is 1."

I took a quick walk to Rhonda's workstation, and noticed that instead of typing **+=** she had reversed the order and typed **=+** which resulted in her assigning the value 1 to the variable instead of adding 1 to it..

"It's a strange notation," I said, "but you have to be careful to use the correct operator. Remember, it's +=."

Mary had a question: "Did you say that you can add a value other than 1 to the variable?"

"Yes you can Mary," I said, "You can add any value you want using the Augmented Addition Operator. For example, if you want to add 22 to the current value of the variable *number1*, we you do that using this code."

I then modified the code to look like this:

```
# Example3_24.py

number1 = 10
number1 += 22

print("The value of number1 is now",  number1)
```

I saved the program as Example3_24.py, and ran it for the class. The following screenshot was displayed on the classroom projector:

"The result of 10 plus 22 is 32" I said. "Having created the variable *number1* with a value of 10, we then added 22 to it using the Augmented Addition Operator (+=)..."

```
number1 += 22
```

"I think you can see how using the Augmented Addition Operator can save us a few keystrokes," I said. "As I said earlier, Operations to increment variables like this are pretty common in the world of programming."

The Augmented Subtraction Operator (-=)

"And you say we can subtract from a variable the same way?" Linda asked.

"That's right Linda" I said. "That's what the Augmented Subtraction Operator does. In Python, the Augmented Subtraction Operator is -=. Another very common operation is to decrement (subtract from) the value of a variable. This code would be used to subtract 1 from the value of a variable."

I displayed the following code on the classroom projector.

```
# Example3_25.py

number1 = 5
number1 -= 1

print("The value of number1 is now",  number1)
```

I then saved the program as Example3_25.py, and ran it for the class. The following screenshot was displayed on the classroom projector:

"The result of 5 minus 1 is 4" I said. "Having created the variable *number1* with a value of 5, we then subtracted 1 from it using the Augmented Subtraction Operator, giving us a result of 4. This is just a shortcut version of this code."

```
number1 = number1 - 1
```

"As is the case with the Augmented Addition Operator," I said, "we're not restricted to subtracting only 1 from the value of a variable. We can subtract any value we want, like this where we subtract 22 from the value of the variable *number1*..."

I modified the code to look like this:

```
# Example3_26.py

number1 = 5
number1 -= 22
```

```
print("The value of number1 is now", number1)
```

I then saved the program as Example3_26.py, and ran it for the class. The following screenshot was displayed on the classroom projector:

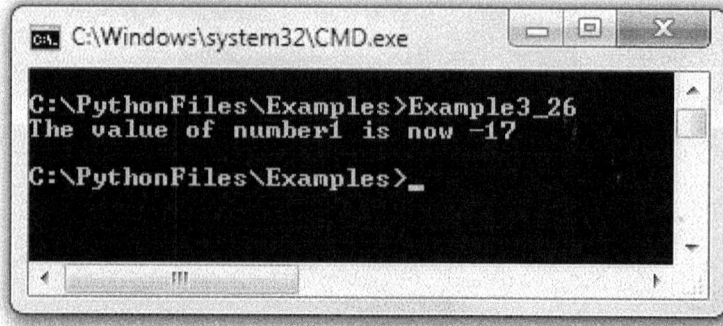

"As you can see," I said, "*number1* was initialized to a value of 5. We then subtracted 22 from it using the Augmented Subtraction Operator, giving us a result of -17. This is a shortcut version of this code."

```
number1 = number1 - 22
```

"In addition to Addition and Subtraction," I said, "Python also has Augmented Multiplication (=*) and Augmented Division (=/) Operators which work in a similar fashion. I will leave you to explore those on your own."

> **NOTE: In addition to the Augmented Addition and Subtraction Operators, Python also supports Augmented Multiplication (=*) and Augmented Division (=/) Operators as well. You may want to explore those out on your own.**

No one seemed to have any problems with either the Augmented Addition or Augmented Subtraction Operators, so I called for a 15-minute break.

Order of Operations

"I mentioned earlier," I said, as we resumed after our break, "that when Python evaluates an expression containing more than one Operation, it can perform only one Operation at a time. The question, then, is in what order does Python perform the Operations?"

"That's right," Jack said. "with multiple operations, how does Python decide which operation to execute first?"

"I would think," Rose said, "that Python would execute the operations from left to right in the expression. That's how I would do it."

"Most people would evaluate an expression that way, Rose," I said, "but that's not the way Python (and other programming languages) do it. Python follows a set of rules, known as the Order of Operations that governs the order in which it performs these operations. Knowing the Order of Operations is critical if you want Python to evaluate your expression the way you intend."

I then displayed this code, containing a complex expression with three Operations, on the classroom projector. Before running the code, I asked everyone in the class to perform the calculation themselves and to tell me the number that they thought would be displayed in the Python Console:

```
# Example3_27.py

print(3 + 6 + 9 / 3)
```

I received a number of different responses.

A number of students suggested that the Division Operation would be executed first, followed by the two Addition Operations, and that the number 12 would be displayed.

The majority of the class said that the Addition Operations would be executed first, left to right, followed by the Division Operation, and that that number 6 would be displayed.

A few students simply couldn't make a guess.

Not wishing to keep the class in suspense any longer, I then saved the program as Example3_27.py, and ran it for the class. The following screenshot was displayed on the classroom projector:

The result 12.0 was displayed.

"It looks as though Python executed the Division first," Dave said, "followed by the two Addition Operations."

"You're right, Dave," I said. "Python evaluated the complex expression and broke it into three distinct Operations:"

1. 3 + 6
2. + 9
3. / 3

"Following the rules for the Order of Operations, Python actually performed the *third* operation, Division, first," I said. "followed by the two Addition Operations. The Order of Operations is determined by the following rules:"

1. Operations in parentheses () are performed first
2. Exponentiation Operations are performed next.
3. Multiplication, Division or Remainder Operations are performed, from left to right in the expression
4. Finally, Addition or Subtraction Operations are performed next, from left to right in the expression

"What does all that mean?" Rhonda asked.

"When Python examines a complex expression," I said, "that is, an expression containing more than one Operation, it checks if there are any Operations within parentheses. If it finds parentheses, it executes the Operations within parentheses first. When all of the Operations within parentheses are executed, Python then looks for any Exponentiation Operations. If it finds any, those are executed next. Python then looks for Operations involving Multiplication, Division or Remainder and executes them. If it finds more than one Multiplication, Division or Remainder Operation, it executes them from left to right. Finally, Python looks for Operations involving Addition or Subtraction and executes them. Once again, it executes each one in turn, starting at the left side of the expression and working its way to the right."

"Can you relate the Order of Operations to the code example you just showed us?" Kathy asked.

"I'd be happy to Kathy," I answered. "Python first looked for parentheses in the expression. Because the entire expression appeared within parentheses as an argument to the **print()** function, this had no impact on the overall evaluation of the expression. Python then looked for any Multiplication or Division Operations. It found just the single Division Operation, and it executed that Operation first."

"So it performed the operation of 9 divided by 3 first?" Valerie asked. "No wonder Python's answer didn't agree with mine."

"That's right Valerie," I said. "And after the Division Operation, Python then looked for any Addition or Subtraction Operations in the expression. It found two of them and executed those Operations from left to right: Therefore, it first added 3 plus 6, giving a result of 9, then added that result to the number 3, which it had previously saved as the result of 9 divided by 3. I think I can show you how this all took place, step by step. Here are the results of the intermediate operations."

I displayed this step by step chart on the classroom projector:

1. Step 1 : 3 + 6 + 9 / 3
2. Step 2 : 3 + 6 + 3
3. Step 3 : 9 + 3
4. Step 4 : 12

"I hope this example shows you," I said, "not only how Python evaluates a complex expression containing multiple Operations, but also how important it is to carefully compose the expressions that you write."

"What do you mean?" Bob asked.

"For instance," I said, "suppose with this code we had intended to calculate the average of three numbers—3, 6, and 9? We know that to calculate an average, we would add 3 plus 6 plus 9 and then divide that result by 3. However, if we were to wager our jobs on getting the average of these three numbers using the Python code we just wrote, we wouldn't have a job very long!"

"You're right about that," Rose said.

"But how could we code the expression to correctly compute the average of 3, 6, and 9?" Jack asked.

"Parentheses," Dave suggested.

"That's right," I said, agreeing with Dave, "we need to place parentheses around the two Addition Operations to force Python to execute the Addition Operations first."

I then modified the code to add parentheses to the complex expression, and displayed it on the classroom projector:

```
# Example3_28.py

print((3 + 6 + 9) / 3)
```

I saved the program as Example3_28.py, and ran it for the class. The following screen shot was displayed on the classroom projector:

"That's better," I said. "The average of 3 plus 6 plus 9 is 6. This time, because we included the two Addition Operations within parentheses, Python executed both Addition Operations prior to the Division Operation--exactly what we intended to happen. Step by step, it looks like this:"

1. Step 1 : (3 + 6 + 9) / 3
2. Step 2 : (9 + 9) /3
3. Step 3 : 18 / 3
4. Step 4 : 6

"Please excuse my dear Aunt Sally," I heard Linda mutter silently.

"What was that Linda?" Rhonda asked. "Please excuse what?"

"**P**lease **E**xcuse **M**y **D**ear **A**unt **S**ally," Linda repeated. "I learned that in my ninth grade Algebra class as a way to remember the Mathematical Order of Operations. **P**arentheses-**E**xponentiation-**M**ultiplication-**D**ivision-**A**ddition-**S**ubtraction. I guess the same rules apply hear."

"I had forgotten all about that mnemonic Linda," I said, "That does summarize the Order of Operations perfectly, and it's an easy way to remember the rules."

> NOTE: A mnemonic is a pattern of letters or words that help you remember something.

"You didn't mention the Remainder Operation in your Aunt Sally's mnemonic," Rhonda said.

"Perhaps," Linda said, "we should modify our mnemonic phrase to read: **P**lease **E**xcuse **M**y **M**other's **D**ear **A**unt **S**ally---**P**arentheses-**E**xponentiation-**M**odulus-**M**ultiplication-**D**ivision-**A**ddition-**S**ubtraction."

"Sounds great to me Linda," Rhonda said, "I don't think I'll be able to forget it now!"

Comparison Operators

"I was talking to a programmer friend of mine at work," Ward said, "and she mentioned something called Comparison Operators. Will we be covering those also?"

"You must be psychic Ward," I replied. "I was just about to introduce Comparison Operators. Arithmetic or Mathematical operators perform an operation on operands to the left and right of an operator and return a result in the form of a number. Comparison Operators <u>compare</u> two expressions to the left and right of a Comparison Operator and return a result. In the case of a Comparison Operator, however, the result isn't a number---it's the value True or False. Here are the six Comparison Operators:"

Symbol	Explanation	Sample Condition	Evaluates To
==	Equal to	22 == 22	True
!=	Not equal to	8 != 22	False
<	Less than	7 < 21	True
<=	Less than or equal to	12 <= 12	True
>	Greater than	4 > 7	False
>=	Greater than or equal to	12 > 7	True

"We'll only be discussing the most common Comparison Operator today: the equal to (==) operator," I said, "although we'll look at some of the others next week when we learn about the If statement, and we'll also be incorporating them into the Grades Calculation Program."

"Is that first Operator correct?" Barbara asked. "Is the Equal to Operator really two equal to signs?"

"That's correct Barbara," I said. "Because the single equal to sign is used to assign a value to a variable in Python, two equal to signs are used to differentiate the Comparison Operator. We haven't learned about If statements yet---we'll do that next week--but in Python, we could use this code to determine if the value of the variable *number1* is equal to 22."

Example3_29.py

```python
number1 = 22

if number1 == 22 :
    print("number1 is equal to 22")
```

"Notice that the assignment statement uses one equal to sign…"

```python
number1 = 22
```

…but within the If statement, we use the double equal to sign (==) to compare the value of *number1* to the literal 22…"

```python
if number1 == 22
```

"So the result of the If statement expression will either be True or False depending upon the comparison of the current value of *number1* to the number 22??" Dave asked.

"That's exactly right Dave," I replied. "If the value of *number1* is equal to 22, the result of the Comparison Operation will be True. As you'll learn next week, when an If statement expression evaluates to True, the Imperative Statement following it---in this case a statement to display a message in the Python Console---is executed."

I then saved the program as Example3_29.py, and ran it for the class. The following screenshot was displayed on the classroom projector:

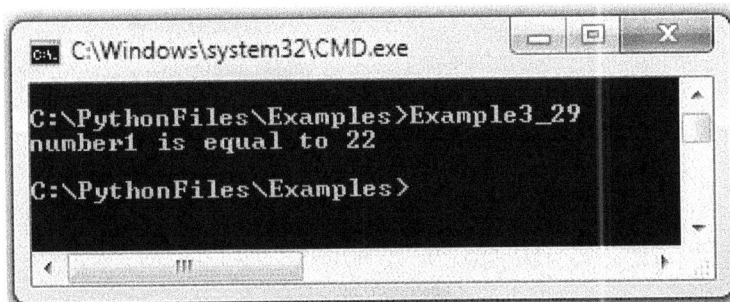

"The variable *number1* is equal to 22 and we display a message saying exactly that," I said. "Now let's modify the program so that we can see the result of the Comparison Operation in the Python Console."

I modified the code and displayed it on the classroom projector.

Example3_30.py

```
number1 = 22

print(number1 == 22)
```

I then saved the program as Example3_30.py, and ran it for the class. The following screenshot was displayed on the classroom projector:

```
C:\Windows\system32\CMD.exe

C:\PythonFiles\Examples>Example3_30
True

C:\PythonFiles\Examples>_
```

"As you can see," I said, "because *number1* is equal to 22, the Comparison Operation returned a result of True, which is what we displayed in the Python Console."

"That's cool," Kate said.

"Likewise," I said, "if the value of *number1* is something other than 22, the result of the Comparison Operation would be False, like this."

I modified the code slightly:

```
# Example3_31.py

number1 = 99

print(number1 == 22)
```

I then saved the program as Example3_31.py, and ran it for the class. The following screenshot was displayed on the classroom projector:

```
C:\Windows\system32\CMD.exe

C:\PythonFiles\Examples>Example3_31
False

C:\PythonFiles\Examples>_
```

"As you can see," I said, "because *number1* is equal to 99, the Comparison Operation returned a result of False, which is what we displayed in the Python Console. The important thing to remember about Comparison Operators, regardless of the Operator you use, is that the result of the Comparison will be either True or False."

> NOTE: I'm not going to explicitly cover the other Comparison Operators. We'll touch upon them in various spots throughout the rest of the course, particularly when we cover the If Statement in Chapter 4.

Boolean Operators

"So far," I said, "we've examined Mathematical Operators and Comparison Operators. Now it's time to look at Boolean Operators."

"Are those the And, Or, and Not Operators?" Blaine asked. "I've been exposed to those in other programming languages."

"That's right, Blaine," I said. "Boolean Operators, sometimes called Logical Operators, , like Comparison Operators, also return a True or False value as the result of performing a Boolean Operation on two Operands. I must warn you that Boolean Operations can be confusing for the beginner. Let's take a look at each one of the three Boolean Operators individually."

NOTE: In addition to the 'And' and 'Or' Boolean Operators we're about to discuss, Python also has 'And' and 'Or' Bitwise Operators. These are entirely different and beyond the scope of this Introductory class.

The Boolean And Operator (and)

"A Boolean And Operation," I said, "returns a True value if the expressions on both sides of the And operator evaluate to True. Here's a preview of the code we'll be running in a few minutes."

```
name == "Smith" and number1 == 22
```

"The And operator in Python," I said, "is the lower case word 'and'. To the left and right of the And Operator is a test expression. Python evaluates each test expression for the 'trueness' or 'falseness' of each. If both the left and right test expressions are True, the entire And Operation is considered True. If the left, the right or both expressions are False, the entire And Operation is considered False."

"Can you give us a real-world example to make this easier to understand?" Ward asked.

"I think so, Ward," I said. I thought for a moment.

"On Wednesday morning," I said, "your best friend Melissa telephones you and invites you to lunch on Friday. You'd love to go, but you have two problems that prevent you from saying yes immediately. First, you and your boss have not been on the best of terms lately, and you don't want to chance taking an extra long lunch on Friday, something that almost always happens when you go to lunch with Melissa (she can really talk.) The only way you can envision going to lunch with her is if your boss will be out of the office on Friday. Recently, she has been taking Friday off to make a long weekend."

"And the second problem?" Barbara asked. "You said there were two problems."

"The second problem," I said, "is that you're short of cash and it's your turn to pick up the tab for lunch. Luckily though, Friday happens to be payday, so cash may not be a problem, provided the direct deposit of your paycheck goes through early Friday morning, something that is 50-50 at best. You decide to call Melissa on Friday at 11 A.M. to let her know for sure if you can make it."

I could see that some of the students were wondering what my heart-felt example had to do with the Python And Operation. I explained that we can express our dilemma in the form of two test expressions joined with the And Operator in this way:

"You can go to lunch with Melissa if your boss is out of the office on Friday AND if the direct deposit of your pay gets into your bank account by 11 A.M. on Friday morning." I said. "In other words, both the left-hand test expression, 'Boss out of office,' and the right-hand test expression, 'Money in bank,' must be True for the And Operation to return a value of True."

```
Boss out of office and Money in bank
```

"So what happens?" Rhonda asked, obviously anxious to hear the end of the story.

"On Friday morning," I said, "you arrive bright and early at the office. Sad for the boss, but happy for you, she has called in to say she has the flu and won't be in the office."

"So the left-hand test expression, 'Boss out of office,' is True," Dave said.

"That's right, Dave," I said. "We're halfway there to the And Operation evaluating to True, and allowing us to go to lunch with Melissa. Now we have to wait on the Direct Deposit. The morning drags by and lunch time gets closer and closer. For the moment though, the And Operation is returning a False value, because the right-hand test expression, 'Money in bank,' is still returning a False value. Remember, the And Operation is True only if both the left-hand test expression and the right-hand test expressions evaluate to True. Only the left-hand test expression, 'Boss out of office,' is True. Unfortunately, the last time you checked your bank balance at 10am, you found that your Direct Deposit still hadn't been made to your bank account, and $1.38 won't buy you and Melissa much of a lunch."

"I wish we could see this graphically," Peter said.

"Good point Peter," I said, "We can express our dilemma in the form of something called a Truth Table. As you suggested Peter, it's a way to graphically express our problem. Here it is."

I displayed the following chart on the classroom projector:

Expression 1	and	Expression 2	Statement
True	and	True	True
True	and	False	False
False	and	True	False
False	and	False	False

"A Truth Table," I said, "shows us that there are four possible outcomes for the And Operation. With the And Operation, there is only *one* way for the And Operation to evaluate to True, and that's if *both* Test Expression 1 (the left-hand side) and Test Expression 2 (the right-hand side) are True. On the other hand, there are *three* ways for the And Operation to evaluate to False, if either Test Expression 1 or Test Expression 2 is False."

"I don't like those odds," Kate said laughing. "I don't think lunch with Melissa looks too promising!"

"Can we re-write the Truth Table in terms of the Boss being out of the office and the money being in the bank?" Rhonda said. "I think that might help me visualize this better."

I took a moment to work up this revised Truth Table and then displayed it on the classroom projector. The current situation as of 10am is highlighted in bold:

Boss Out?	and	Money in Bank?	Go to Lunch?
True	and	True	True
True	**and**	**False**	**False**
False	and	True	False
False	and	False	False

"That's better," Steve said. "This is beginning to make more sense to me now."

"Let's continue on with the story," Rhonda said.

"As of 10:55," I continued, "with no cash in the bank, lunch is now a remote possibility. Just as you're about to call Melissa and tell her 'no' to lunch, you receive a text message from your bank that indicates that the Direct Deposit has finally made it to your bank account. That means that the right-hand test expression is now True. Since both the left-hand and right-hand test expressions evaluate to True, the entire And Operation is True, and you and Melissa can now go off and enjoy a nice, leisurely lunch."

Boss Out?	and	Money in Bank?	Go to Lunch?
True	**and**	**True**	**True**
True	and	False	False
False	and	True	False
False	and	False	False

"Just to confirm," Kate said. "The And Operator in Python is the word 'and'?"

"That's right Kate," I said. "Be sure to spell it in lower case letters."

"Can we see what this looks like in Python?" Mary asked.

I displayed this code on the classroom projector.

```
# Example3_32.py

name = "Smith"
number1 = 99

if name == "Smith" and number1 == 22:
  print("Both sides of the AND expression are True")
```

"I realize we have yet to cover the If statement in detail," I said, "but as we did in Example3_29.py, let's use an If statement to evaluate the truth or falseness of the Boolean Operation we've coded. Here we check if the value of the *name* variable is 'Smith' and the value of the *number* variable is 22. If both the left-hand test expression and the right-hand test expression evaluates to True, the Imperative Statement following the If statement is executed, and we display an appropriate message in the Python Console."

> NOTE: The AND operator is the word 'and' spelled in lower case letters. Spelling it any other way will confuse Python.

I then saved the program as Example3_32.py, and ran it for the class. The following screenshot was displayed on the classroom projector:

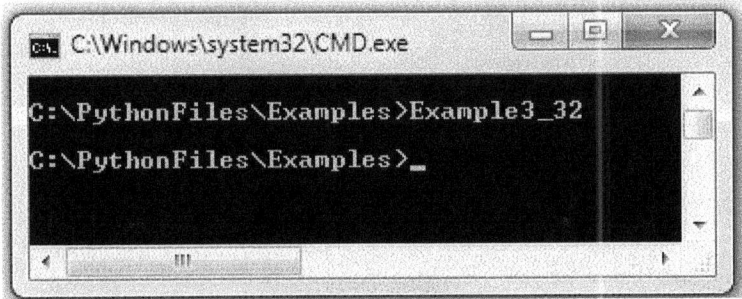

"Nothing seems to have happened," Rhonda said. "No message was displayed."

"You're right Rhonda," I said, "no message was displayed, but Python has done some work in evaluating the And Operation. Let's take a closer look at the And Operation..."

```
if name == "Smith" and number1 == 22:
```

"We created the *name* variable and assigned it the value 'Smith'," I said, "so the left-hand test expression evaluated to True. However, when we created the *number1* variable, we assigned it a value of 99. 99 is most definitely not equal to 22. Therefore, the right-hand test expression evaluated to False. The And Operation is True only if both the left and right-hand test expressions are True. It is considered False if either the left or right-hand test expressions evaluate to False. Because the And Operation evaluated to False, the Imperative Statement following the If statement was never executed, which is why it appears as though nothing happened. Consult our Truth Table to prove this to yourself."

"I see now," Blaine said. "Can we modify the code so that the And Operation evaluates to True?"

"Great idea Blaine," I said. I then changed the code to assign the value 22 to the variable *number1*...

```
# Example3_33.py

name = "Smith"
number1 = 22

if name == "Smith" and number1 == 22:
  print("Both sides of the AND expression are True")
```

I then saved the program as Example3_33.py, and ran it for the class. The following screenshot was displayed on the classroom projector:

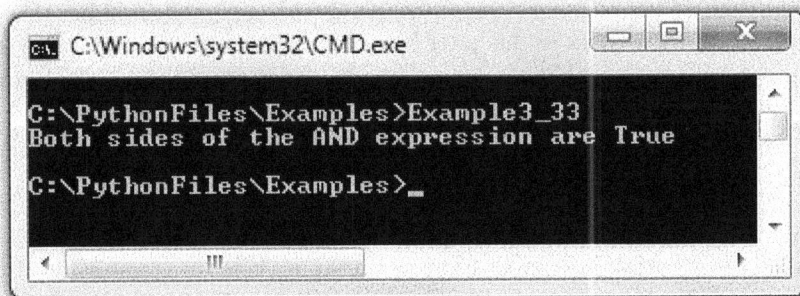

"This time," I said, "a message is displayed in the Python Console. Because both the left and right-hand test expressions are True, the And Operation evaluates to True, and the Imperative Statement following the If statement is executed."

No one seemed to have any problems with the And Operation---time to move onto the Or Operation.

The Boolean Or Operator (or)

"If you're comfortable with the Boolean And Operation," I said, "you won't have much trouble understanding the Boolean Or Operation. The Boolean Or Operation, like the Boolean And Operation, also evaluates expressions to the left and right of an Operator (in this case, the Or Operator,) returning either a value of True or False. Unlike the And Operation, in which only 1 of 4 possible outcomes are True, with the Or Operation, 3 of 4 possible outcomes are True. In fact, there is only one outcome in which the Or Operation is False, and that is if both the left and right-hand test expressions are False. Take a look at the Truth Table for the Or Operation."

I displayed this Truth Table representing the Or Operation on the projector:

Expression 1	or	Expression 2	Statement
True	Or	True	True
True	Or	False	True
False	Or	True	True
False	Or	False	False

"As is the case with the And Operation," I said, "the Truth Table for the Or Operation also has four possibilities. Three out of four combinations evaluate to True. With the Or Operation, there is only one combination that returns a False value, and that's if both the left-hand and right-hand test expressions are False."

"That's pretty much the opposite of the And Operation," Joe observed.

"Can you give us another real-world example to illustrate the Or Operation?" Linda asked. "Although I think it will be pretty hard for you to top that last one where we had a lunch date with Melissa."

I thought for a moment.

"Okay, Linda" I said, "let's try this one. It's Friday morning. While dressing for work, you receive a phone call from the host of an early morning radio show that is running a contest. He tells you that if the month of your birthday ends in r <u>or</u> the last digit of your Social Security Number is 4, you'll be the lucky winner of $10,000!"

"Sounds great to me!" Ward said.

"Let me get this straight," Rhonda said. "To win the $10,000, we need to have just one of those conditions be True—not both---is that right?"

I then displayed this Truth Table to reflect the radio contest. The three outcomes where the Or Operation returns a True value are highlighted in bold.

Birthday Month ends in 'r'	Or	Last Digit of Social Security is '4'?	Win $10,000?
True	**Or**	**True**	**True**
True	**Or**	**False**	**True**
False	**Or**	**True**	**True**
False	Or	False	False

"That's right, Rhonda," I said. "According to the rules of the radio contest, you'll win the $10,000 prize if either the left-hand test expression is True (the month of your birthday ends in the letter R) or the right-hand test expression is True (the last digit of your Social Security Number ends in 4). Unlike the lunch date example, where we needed both the left and right-hand test expressions to be True in order to go to lunch with our friend Melissa, with an Or Operation, only one side of the Or Operation needs to be True. How do you like your odds now, Kate?"

"I love my odds," Kate answered. "If that call were placed to me, I'd win the prize."

Kate wasn't alone—a quick poll of the class revealed that 4 out of the 18 students would win the contest using the Or Operation. However, if the contest had called for the And Operation, none of the students in the class would have won the $10,000 prize!

I took Example3_32.py and modified it by changing the And Operator to an Or operator. In Python, the Or operator is the word 'or' in lower case letters. Spelling it any other way will confuse Python.

> **NOTE:** The Boolean Or operator is the word 'or' spelled in lower case letters. Spelling it any other way will confuse Python.

```
# Example3_34.py

name = "Smith"
number1 = 99

if name == "Smith" or number1 == 22:
  print("One or both sides of the OR expression are True")
```

I then saved the program as Example3_34.py, and ran it for the class. The following screenshot was displayed on the classroom projector.

"Python displays a message indicating that one or both sides of the OR expression are True," I said. "In this case, the left-hand test expression evaluates to True. The *name* variable is equal to 'Smith'. The right-hand test expression evaluates to False because *number1* is equal to 99, not 22. We only need one side of the test expression to evaluate to True in order for the entire Or Operation to be considered True."

I gave my students a chance to think about that.

"Suppose," I suggested, "we change the value of the *name* variable from Smith to Smiley. Now both the left-hand and right-hand test expressions will be False, and the Or Operation will evaluate to False."

I did exactly that, changing the code to look like this:

Example3_35.py

```
name = "Smiley"
number1 = 99

if name == "Smith" or number1 == 22:
  print("One or both sides of the OR expression are True")
```

I then saved the program as Example3_35.py, and ran it for the class. The following screenshot was displayed on the classroom projector:

"Nothing is displayed in the Python console," I said, "because the Or expression evaluates to False. The only way that an Or Operation can return a False value is if <u>both</u> the left-hand and right-hand test expressions evaluate to False. That's the case here—*number*, with a value of 99, is not 22, and *name*, with a value of 'Smiley', is definitely not Smith."

A Problem With The Or Operator

"I just entered some code of my own and I didn't get the correct result," Kathy said.

I took a quick walk to Kathy's PC and saw that she had written the following code. I displayed it for the class on the classroom projector.

Example3_36.py

```
number1 = 99

if number1 == 22 or 88:
  print("One or both sides of the OR expression are True")
```

I gave my students a chance to look at it a moment, then saved the program as Example3_36.py, and ran it for the class. I saw Dave give Kathy a knowing glance, as if he knew what the problem was.

The following screen shot was displayed on the classroom projector:

"What did I do wrong?" Kathy asked. "The message is telling me that one or both sides of the Or Operation are True, but that's not the case. The value of the variable *number1* is 99—that's neither 22 nor 88."

"You're definitely correct there Kathy," I said, "99 is neither equal to 22 nor 88, and you didn't expect to see a message saying that it was. This is a very common error that beginner programmers make---in Python, as well as in other programming languages."

"So what's the problem?" Kathy asked.

"You communicated with Python as if you were talking to a human being," I said. "Your code was very English-like, which is very tempting to write in any programming language. The problem is you don't have two valid expressions on either side of the Or operator."

```
if number1 == 22 or 88:
```

"Your left-hand test expression," I said, "is 'number == 22', which is fine, but your right-hand test expression is just the number 88. That's not a valid expression, it's actually a statement, like saying your name is Kathy. Worse yet, it's a statement that will always evaluate to True. It's as if you asked Python, is 88 equal to 88? Python says yes, 88 is 88!"

I saw some confused looks on the faces of my students.

"Because the right-hand test expression evaluated to True," I continued, "the entire Or Operation was determined to be True."

> **NOTE: Still not clear on this? We'll re-examine this error in Chapter 8 when we deal with common errors that Python Programmers make.**

"So how could I rewrite my code to fix this?" she asked.

"It's very a simple fix," I said. "You need to explicitly code the comparison in the right-hand test expression. That is, compare the variable *number1* to the number 88."

I then displayed the corrected code on the classroom projector.

```
# Example3_37.py

number1 = 99

if number1 == 22 or number1 == 88:
    print("One or both sides of the OR expression are True")
```

I saved the program as Example3_37.py, and ran it for the class. The following screen shot was displayed on the classroom projector:

"That's better," I said, "No message is displayed, which is what we anticipated. 99 is definitely not equal to 22 nor is it equal to 88."

"I see," Kathy said. "The name of the variable *number1* appears in both the left-hand and right-hand test expressions. That was simple, why didn't I think of that?"

"You wrote the code the way you would speak to someone in a conversation," I said, "Unfortunately, as English-like as Python may appear to be, there are still some rules that we need to follow."

I paused before continuing.

Another Problem With The Or Operator

"Kathy's problem highlighted a common error beginners make with the Or Operator," I said. "I should also show you another potential problem with the Or operator. This one occurs when we use the not equal to operator (!=) in an Or Operation."

"Have we worked with the not equal to Operator yet?" Barbara asked.

"Not until now," I said, smiling. "Let's start with a simple example to see how the not equal to operator works. Let's use the **input()** function to prompt the user to enter a number, and then test their entry to determine if it's equal to the number 22. If it is equal to 22, we'll display a message saying that it is equal to 22. If it's not equal to 22, we'll display a message saying that. This example will also introduce you to the Else clause of the If statement, something we'll look at in more detail next week."

I then displayed this code on the classroom projector. (By the way, I'm using the throwaway variable x here to more easily display of the Truth table that I'll show you in a few minutes.)

```
# Example3_38.py

x = int(input("Enter a number from 1 to 100: "))

if x != 22:
  print("Your number is not equal to 22. It is",x)
else:
  print("Your number is equal to 22. It is",x)
```

"There's nothing wrong with this code," I said. "It will produce the result we are seeking."

I then saved the program as Example3_38.py, and ran it for the class.

When prompted for a number, I entered the number 22 and the following screen shot was displayed on the classroom projector:

"No problem here," I said. "We entered the number 22, and Python displayed a message saying that our entry was equal to the number 22. If we run the program again and enter the number 99 (which is not 22,) we should get a message indicating that the value entered is not 22."

I ran the program for the class again, this time entering the number 99. The following screen shot was displayed on the classroom projector:

```
C:\Windows\system32\cmd.exe

C:\PythonFiles\Examples>Example3_38
Enter a number from 1 to 100: 99
Your number is not equal to 22. It is 99

C:\PythonFiles\Examples>
```

"Once again," I said, "the program behaves as expected. 99 is not equal to 22. Python executed the line of code following the Else clause, displaying a message to that effect. Using the not equal to (!=) operator in this simple example worked perfectly."

I paused for a moment.

"No one seems to have noticed." I said, "but we used the **int()** function here for the first time in this program."

```
x = int(input("Enter a number from 1 to 100: "))
```

"That's right," Steve said, "We haven't seen that before. What does it do?"

"The value entered by the user via the **input()** function is a String data type," I said. "If we want to perform numeric comparisons on the number the user enters, we must first convert that String data to a number. We use the **int()** function to convert it to an Integer or whole number. If we were prompting the user to enter a number with a fractional part, we could also use the **float()** function to convert it to floating point data type. Performing numeric comparisons on a String Data type will produce <u>erroneous</u> results."

No one seemed to have any problem with that concept.---numeric comparisons need to be performed against numbers, so if you are prompting the user for a number, convert the value entered via the **input()** function from a String to a number using either the **int()** or **float()** functions.

> NOTE: Numeric comparisons need to be performed against numbers, so if you are prompting the user for a number, convert the value entered via the input() function from a String to a number using either the int() or float() functions.

"So what's the problem with the not equal to Operator?" Blaine asked. "It worked fine here."

"The problem isn't with the not equal to Operator," I said, "the problem is when we use the Or Operator and the left-hand and right-hand test expressions both use the not equal to Operator. To illustrate that, let's modify the program we just wrote. Instead of testing if the user's entry is not 22, let's check if their entry is not 22 or not 44."

"That seems reasonable," Barbara said. "But somehow, I sense this will be a problem."

I then modified the program to look like this and displayed it on the classroom projector.

```
# Example3_39.py

x = int(input("Enter a number from 1 to 100: "))

if x != 22 or x != 44:
  print("Your number is not equal to 22 or 44. It is",x)
else:
  print("Your number is equal to 22 or 44. It is",x)
```

"As you can see," I said, "this program is not much different from Example3_38.py Instead of checking for one value in our If statement, we are now checking for two values---22 or 44. We check for not equal to 22 in the left-hand test expression, and check for not equal to 44 in the right-hand test expression."

> NOTE: Sharp students will undoubtedly realize that we could have written this code using the equality operator (==) and totally avoided the problem we're about to see. More on that in a few minutes ☺

I then saved the program as Example3_39.py, and ran it for the class.

At the prompt, I entered the number 99 and the following screen shot was displayed on the classroom projector:

```
C:\Windows\system32\cmd.exe

C:\PythonFiles\Examples>Example3_39
Enter a number from 1 to 100: 99
Your number is not equal to 22 or 44. It is 99

C:\PythonFiles\Examples>_
```

"No problem here," I said, "99 is neither the number 22 nor the number 44, and we display a message saying exactly that. Now let's run the program again, this time entering the number 22. We should receive a different message.

I ran the program for the class again, this time entering the number 22 at the user prompt. The following screen shot was displayed on the classroom projector:

```
C:\Windows\system32\cmd.exe

C:\PythonFiles\Examples>Example3_39
Enter a number from 1 to 100: 22
Your number is not equal to 22 or 44. It is 22

C:\PythonFiles\Examples>
```

"Uh oh," I heard Rhonda say. "The program is telling us that the number 22 is neither 22 nor 44---but it is one of those numbers."

"That's right Rhonda," I said. "Furthermore, if we run the program again and enter 44 as our entry, the same erroneous message will occur. Python will tell us that our entry of 44 is not equal to 44---but it is!"

I ran the program for the class again, this time entering the number **44**. The following screen shot was displayed on the classroom projector:

```
C:\Windows\system32\cmd.exe

C:\PythonFiles\Examples>Example3_39
Enter a number from 1 to 100: 44
Your number is not equal to 22 or 44. It is 44

C:\PythonFiles\Examples>_
```

"The program isn't working properly," I said, "We don't have time to go through all of the numbers between 1 and 100, but I can assure you that every number we enter will result in a message being displayed that the entry is not equal to 22 or 44, even the two numbers 22 and 44!"

"What's the problem?" Steve asked, "What did we do wrong?"

"We can determine the problem using our old friend, the Truth Table," I said. "With an Or Operation, we evaluate each expression to the left and right hand side of the Or operator. The Or Operation evaluates to True if the expressions on **either** side of the Or operator evaluate to True. The problem with the If statement, as we've constructed it, is that one side or other of the Or expression will <u>always</u> evaluate to True. Therefore, the entire Or statement evaluates to True."

I paused before continuing.

"Let's look at that Truth Table now," I said, "to see how the left and right-hand sides of the Or Operation are evaluated with the 3 values we just entered into our program---99, 22 and 44. The value of the variable *x* appears as the **first** column in our Truth table, the evaluation of x!=22 is the **second** column, the evaluation of x!=44 is the

third column, and the **fourth** column is the evaluation of the entire Or Operation. As you can see, when the value of *x* is equal to 99, the expression x!=22 is True. 99 quite clearly isn't equal to the number 22. Furthermore, the expression x!=44 also evaluates to True, since 99 isn't equal to the number 44 either. Both expressions are True, and so the entire Or statement is True. In this case, the results of the Or Operation are correct"

x	x!= 22	or	x!=44	x!= 22 or x!=44
99	True	Or	True	True

"Now what happens when the user enters 22," I asked. "The value of *x* is 22. The test expression x!=22 evaluates to False, since the value of the variable *x* is quite clearly equal to the number 22. But what about the right-hand test expression x!=44? 22 is not equal to the number 44, so the right-hand test expression evaluates to True. With one side of the Or Operation evaluating to False and one side evaluating to True, the entire Or Operation evaluates to True. Therefore, the Imperative Statement following the If statement is executed, and we display the message that the entered number is not equal to 22 or 44. Of course, this is incorrect, since the entered number was 22."

x	x!= 22	or	x!=44	x!= 22 or x!=44
22	False	Or	True	True

"We will get a similar result," I said, "if the user enters the number 44. Because the value of the variable *x* is equal to 44, the left-hand test expression x!=22 will evaluate to True, since 44 is clearly not equal to the number 22. The right-hand test expression x!=44 will evaluate to False since x is equal to the number 44. With the left-hand test expression of the Or Operation equal to True and the right-hand test expression equal to False, the entire Or Operation evaluates to True. Therefore, the Imperative Statement following the If statement is executed, and we improperly display the message that the entered number is not equal to the number 22 or the number 44. This is incorrect, since the entered number was 44."

x	x!= 22	or	x!=44	x!= 22 or x!=44
44	True	Or	False	True

I paused to make sure I wasn't losing anyone.

"In fact," I said, "there is no way in which the Or Operation that we have constructed will ever evaluate to False. One of the text expressions will always evaluate to True. Look at this Truth Table ion which we test a variety of values for the variable *x*. All of the Or Operations will evaluate to True."

x	x!= 22	or	x!=44	x!= 22 or x!=44
1...21	True	Or	True	True
22	False	Or	True	True
23...43	True	Or	True	True
44	True	Or	False	True
45..100	True	Or	True	True

"Wow, that's amazing," Rhonda said. "What can we do about this?"

"It's a simple change," I said, "And I can summarize it with this rule: Whenever you have 'two not equal to' expressions on either side of an Or Operation, change the Or Operator to an And operator."

> **NOTE: Whenever you have two 'not equal to' expressions on either side of an Or Operation, change the Or operator to an And operator and you'll be fine.**

I gave my students a chance to think about that.

"As we just did with the Or Operation," I said, "let's look at a Truth Table for the And Operation with a variety of values for the variable *x*. With the And Operation, test expressions on **both** sides of the And Operator must evaluate to True in order for the And Operation to be considered True. For values of the variable *x* in the range of 1 to 100, that will only be the case for numbers that are other than 22 or 44. For instance, when the user enters the number 22, the left-hand test expression evaluates to False. When the user enters the number 44, the right-hand test expression evaluates to False. In both cases, for entered values of 22 or 44, the entire And Operation evaluates to False, which is exactly what we want. For the numbers 1 through 21, 23 through 43, and 45 through 100, test expressions on both sides of the And Operation evaluate to True, and the entire And Operation evaluates to True. Therefore, the Imperative Statement following the If statement is be executed and we display the correct message..."

x	x!= 22	and	x!=44	x!= 22 and x!=44
1...21	True	And	True	True
22	False	And	True	False
23...43	True	And	True	True
44	True	And	False	False
45..100	True	And	True	True

I could see some confusion on the faces of my students.

"Let's modify the program to use the And Operator to determine if I'm correct," I said.

I then modified Example3_39.py to look like this, simply changing the word 'or' to 'and'.

```
# Example3_40.py

x = int(input("Enter a number from 1 to 100: "))

if x != 22 and x != 44:
  print("Your number is not equal to 22 or 44. It is",x)
else:
  print("Your number is equal to 22 or 44. It is",x)
```

I then saved the program as Example3_40.py, and ran it for the class.

I entered the number **99** and the following screen shot was displayed on the classroom projector:

"This is correct," I said, "Since the number 99 is neither 22 nor 44, we display a message saying exactly that. Now let's run the program again, this time entering the number 22. Let's see if we receive the correct message this time."

I ran the program for the class again, this time entering the number **22**. The following screen shot was displayed on the classroom projector:

"The program is correct," I said. "22 is most definitely either the number 22 or the number 44. Let's see how the program deals with the number 44."

I ran the program for the class again, this time entering the number **44**. The following screen shot was displayed on the classroom projector:

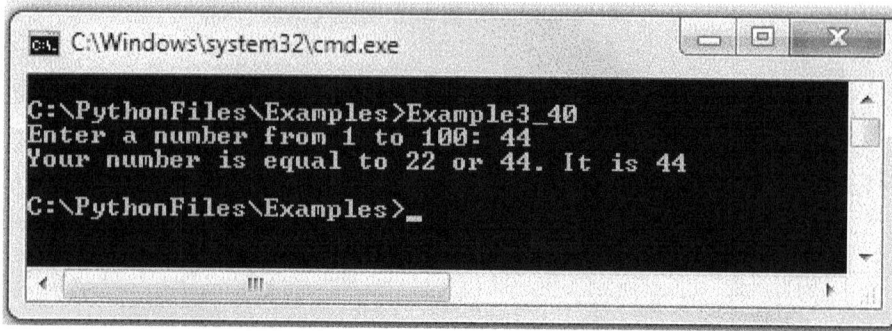

"Again," I said, "the program is correct. 44 is most definitely either the number 22 or the number 44."

After a few moments of silence, Dave had a question.

"Couldn't we have avoided this problem by using the Or Operation with the equal to Operator instead of the not equal to Operator?" Dave asked.

"Dave's correct," I said, "we could have written the code using the equality operator (==) with an Or Operator. By changing the construction of our If statement to first check for the 2 numbers we're looking for (instead of the numbers we're not looking for) and allowing the Else clause to handle all of the other numbers allows us to avoid the troublesome not equal to (!=) Operator. As I often say, there are many ways to paint a picture, and in programming, there is usually more than one way to solve a problem. Dave is suggesting that we could have written Example3_39 like this..."

I then modified Example3_39.py to look like this, changing the not equal to Operator (!=) to the equality Operator (==), and also 'flip flopping' the messages following the If statement and the Else clause."

```
# Example3_41.py

x = int(input("Enter a number from 1 to 100: "))

if x == 22 or x == 44:
  print("Your number is equal to 22 or 44. It is",x)
else:
  print("Your number is not equal to 22 or 44. It is",x)
```

"Let's check the Truth Table for Dave's version," I said, "We are now using the Equality operator (==) in the test expressions with the Or Operation..."

x	x== 22	or	x==44	x== 22 or x==44
1...21	False	Or	False	False
22	True	Or	False	True
23...43	False	Or	False	False
44	False	Or	True	True
45..100	False	Or	False	False

"As you can see," I said, "now the only 2 cases where the Or Operation evaluates to True are those where the value of x is either the number 22 or the number 44. Notice that in addition to that change, we also changed the logic of the program. We now display a message if the value of x is equal to the two values we are looking for---otherwise, we display a message saying that the entered value is not. In the previous version of the program, this logic was reversed."

I then saved the program as Example3_41.py, and ran it for the class.

I entered the number **99** and the following screen shot was displayed on the classroom projector:

"This is correct," I said, "99 is neither the number 22 nor the number 44, and we display a message saying exactly that. Now let's run the program again, this time entering the number **22**."

I ran the program for the class again, this time entering the number 22. The following screen shot was displayed on the classroom projector:

"Again," I said, "the program is correct. 22 is most definitely the number 22 or the number 44."

I ran the program for the class again, this time entering the number **44**. The following screen shot was displayed on the classroom projector:

"Again," I said, "the program is correct. 44 is most definitely either the number 22 or the number 44. I won't run the program through all of the possible values from 1 through 100, but I can assure you that this version of the program will give correct results."

"Dave's version seems a bit easier to follow for me," Bob said. "It's interesting that we can arrive at the same results using different Operators---provided we properly format the test expressions."

"Many people do prefer Dave's version," I said, "Using the not equal to (!=) Operator frequently confuses beginners."

"I'm still not sure I fully understand," Rhonda said, "but I'll be sure to remember your rule of thumb. If we have an Or Operation with a not equal to Operator in the test expressions on both sides of the Or Operation, change the Or Operation to an And Operation."

"That's right Rhonda," I said. "And should you forget, you or one of the users of your program will undoubtedly notice some strange (and incorrect) behavior."

The Boolean Not Operator (not)

"We have one remaining Boolean Operator to discuss today," I continued, "and it's the Boolean Not operator. Unlike the other Boolean Operators which operate on two operands or two test expressions, the Not operator is called a Unary operator because it operates on just a single test expression."

> **NOTE: The Augmented Operators (Addition, Subtraction, Multiplication, and Division) are also called Unary Operators.**

"What does the Not operator do?" Steve asked.

"The Not operator," I replied. "evaluates a test expression, takes the True or False result, and then returns the opposite value. For a test expression that evaluates to True, the Not operator then returns False. If the test expression evaluates to False, the Not operator then returns True."

"Why would you want to do something like that?" Rhonda asked.

"Sometimes test expressions can best be expressed in a negative way," I said. "The Not operator allows you to do that, and can make your code easier to read and understand. Let me give you an example of the Not operator, but before I do that, let's write this simple little program."

I then displayed this code on the classroom projector:

```
# Example3_42.py

number1 = 13

print(number1 == 13)
```

"Can anyone guess what will happen when we execute this code?" I asked.

Dave suggested that the word True would be displayed in the Python Console.

"That's right, Dave" I said. "Because the value of the variable *number1* is 13, Python will evaluate this expression…"

```
number1 = 13
```

"…as True."

I then saved the program as Example3_42.py, ran it for the class, and as Dave had predicted, the word True was displayed in the Python Console.

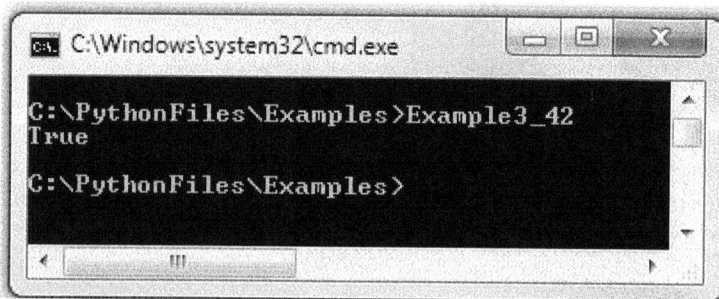

"Now," I said, "let's use the Unary not Operator on that previous expression, and see what happens."

I then modified the code to look like this and displayed it on the classroom projector.

```
# Example3_43.py

number1 = 13

print(not(number1 == 13))
```

"Notice," I said, "that I've inserted the word <u>not</u> in front of the test expression determining if the value of the variable *number1* is equal to 13. What do you think will happen now?"

Dave answered that he thought the word False would be displayed in the Python Console.

"Can you tell us why Dave?" I replied.

"The test expression (number == 13) will evaluate to True," Dave said. "Executing the Not Operation on a test expression that evaluates to True will return a False value, which is what will be displayed in the Python Console."

"Excellent, Dave," I said. "Bill Gates couldn't have stated it any better."

I then saved the program as 'Example3_43.py', ran the program and the following screenshot was displayed on the classroom projector.

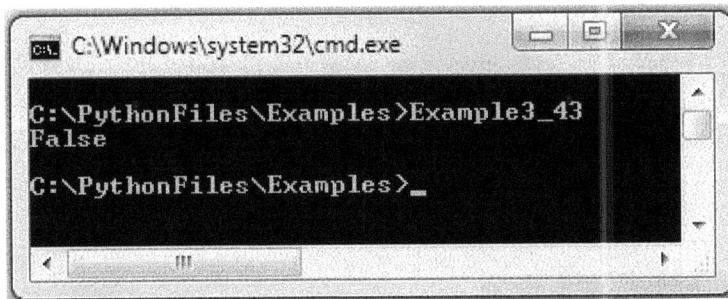

As predicted, Dave was correct; the word False was output in the Python Console.

"Is that all there is to the Not operator?" Barbara asked.

"That's right, Kate" I said.

"Without the Not operator," I said, "determining whether the value of a variable <u>isn't</u> a particular value would require some very hard to read and understand code, like this…"

```python
print(number < 13 or number > 13)
```

"That is pretty cumbersome," Rhonda said. "I can see the benefit of the Not Operator now."

I then suggested that we complete the one and only practice Exercise for the day, the modification of the Grades Calculation Program.

"In this exercise," I said, "you'll have a chance to continue working with the class project—the Grades Calculation Program—which you created last week. We don't have many changes to make to it, but we will enhance it with the creation of some variables and Pseudo Constants."

I then distributed this exercise for the class to complete.

Practice 3-1 Add Variables and Constants to the Grades Calculation Program

In this exercise you'll find and modify the Grades.py program you wrote last week--modifying it to include variable and "constant" creations. For the sake of demonstration, you'll calculate the grade for an English student who has received a midterm grade of 70, a final examination grade of 80, a research grade of 90, and a presentation grade of 100 for the four individual component pieces.

1. Use the editor of your choice (if you are using Windows, use Notepad or Notepad++) and locate and load the Grades.py source file you created last week. It should be located in the \PythonFiles\Grades folder.
2. Modify the code so that it looks like this. Pay careful attention to the line continuation character (the backslash character \) which we are using the calculation of the final numeric grade.

```python
# Grades.py
# After Chapter 3

MIDTERM_PERCENTAGE = .25
FINAL_EXAM_PERCENTAGE = .25
RESEARCH_PERCENTAGE = .30
PRESENTATION_PERCENTAGE = .20
midterm = 70
final_exam_grade = 80
research = 90
presentation = 100
final_numeric_grade = 0

final_numeric_grade = \
    (midterm * MIDTERM_PERCENTAGE) + \
    (final_exam_grade * FINAL_EXAM_PERCENTAGE) + \
    (research * RESEARCH_PERCENTAGE) + \
    (presentation * PRESENTATION_PERCENTAGE)
```

```
print("Midterm grade is : ",  midterm)
print("Final Exam grade is : ",  final_exam_grade)
print("Research grade is : ",  research)
print("Presentation grade is: ",  presentation)
print("\nThe final grade is: ",  final_numeric_grade)
```

3. Save your source file as <u>Grades.py</u> in the \PythonFiles\Grades folder (select File-Save As from Notepad's Menu Bar). Be sure to save your source file with the file name extension 'py'.

4. Execute your program by entering Grades at the command prompt.. (If you have forgotten how to execute your Python program, consult Practice 2-2 from last week.) You should see output similar to this screenshot:

```
C:\Windows\system32\CMD.exe

C:\PythonFiles\Grades>Grades
Midterm grade is :   70
Final Exam grade is :   80
Research grade is :   90
Presentation grade is:   100

The final grade is:   84.5

C:\PythonFiles\Grades>_
```

Discussion

Python is a sensitive language, and as such I didn't expect everything to go smoothly with this exercise. All in all, the exercise went well, although some students, particularly those who didn't follow the exercise precisely, had a number of problems. For instance, it took Rhonda four or five modifications of her source file before she was successfully able to run the Grades program. Most of her problems stemmed from consistently spelling her variable names the same way she created them. And, despite my warning, she typed a forward slash instead of a backslash (\) for the Python line continuation character.

"I admit," Rhonda said, smiling, "I should have paid more attention to the syntax of the variable names. I guess I'm just not used to the case sensitivity of Python."

A number of students had variations of these same problems. After about ten minutes, all the students had finally successfully modified their Grades program, and executed it.

It was now time to discuss what they had done.

"We began our program with a comment," I said, "which was just the name of our program. Some of you, I noticed, also included your name and the date and time you wrote the program. Of course, feel free to include any comment that you find useful."

```
# Grades
```

"This next section of code," I said, "appears to be Constants, but as we learned last week, Python doesn't have true constants, but we can simulate them by typing a variable name in all capital letters, and assigning a value to it."

```
MIDTERM_PERCENTAGE = .25
FINAL_EXAM_PERCENTAGE = .25
RESEARCH_PERCENTAGE = .30
PRESENTATION_PERCENTAGE = .20
```

Moving along to the section of code dealing with variables, Blaine had a question.

"I was a little confused," Blaine said, "about your variable naming conventions. I think I would have begun the variable names with a capital letter."

"By convention," I said, "Python variable names begin with a lowercase letter. If a variable name consists of more than one word, as some of ours do here, then the words are separated with an underscore. That's why we named the variables like this."

```
midterm = 70
final_exam_grade = 80
```

```
research = 90
presentation = 100
final_numeric_grade = 0
```

I had thought that this next section of code where we calculate a numeric grade would give the class problems, but it hadn't, although Mary did have a question:

```
final_numeric_grade =            \
  (midterm * MIDTERM_PERCENTAGE) + \
  (final_exam_grade * FINAL_EXAM_PERCENTAGE) + \
  (research * RESEARCH_PERCENTAGE) + \
  (presentation * PRESENTATION_PERCENTAGE)
```

"I understand what you're doing in this code," Mary said. "You're multiplying the component grade pieces by the applicable constant values, but what's going on with that **backslash** character?"

"The five lines of code you see here are actually just one Python statement," I answered. "It would have been very awkward to write the entire statement on a single line. Using the backslash (\) character, we can break one long line into a more readable five lines. That's what the backslash character does for us."

"Did we really need those parentheses?" Dave asked. "Based on the Order of Operations, wouldn't the Multiplication Operations have been performed before the additions?"

"You're right, Dave," I said. "We could have written the code like this, and the result would still be correct."

```
final_numeric_grade =            \
  midterm * MIDTERM_PERCENTAGE +  \
  final_exam_grade * FINAL_EXAM_PERCENTAGE + \
  research * RESEARCH_PERCENTAGE +  \
  presentation * PRESENTATION_PERCENTAGE
```

"But I'm a big believer in readability. I think the parentheses make the code easier to read and leave no doubt as to our intentions."

I waited to see if anyone had any questions before proceeding.

"Finally," I said, "we use multiple **print()** functions to display the component grade pieces…"

```
print("Midterm grade is : ", midterm)
print("Final Exam grade is : ", final_exam_grade)
print("Research grade is : ", research)
print("Presentation grade is: ", presentation)
```

"…and display the result of our calculated *final_numeric_grade* variable also using the **print()** function…"

```
print("\nThe final grade is: ", final_numeric_grade)
```

"Cool," Barbara said, "very cool. I like what we've done here."

I waited to see if anyone had any questions or additional comments. Most everyone, I could tell, felt the same way Barbara did. Their working Python program was a great source of satisfaction to them.

"Right now," I said, "this program does one thing and one thing only. It will always calculate the same component grade pieces. Next week, we'll learn how to make our program a lot more intelligent through the use of something called Selection Structures."

I then dismissed class for the day.

Summary

This was quite an exhaustive look at the use of data in Python. In this chapter, we learned about the importance of variables in Python. We learned when, where, and how to use variables and about the different Python variable types that you can create. In addition, you discovered how we can use a variety of Operations to manipulate the data contained in those variables.

Variables are defined in memory to hold data or information. Each variable has a Scope that determines what other parts of your program can see the variable and a lifetime that determines when the variable dies.

Global variables are created in the main part of your program and can be seen in all parts of your program, and live for as long as your program runs.

Local variables are created within functions and can be seen only in the function where they are created, and live only for as long as a function executes.

We discussed that there is no need to formally declare and initialize our variables. In Python, variables are created when we assign a value to them. Their Scope is determined by where they are created.

Python Data Types can be categorized in three broad ways:
- **Bool**. True or False values only.
- **Numeric**. Numbers only, which can be Integer (int) and Floating-point (float) Data Types.
- **String**. A set of characters, treated as text. Strings can hold characters representing numbers, but these are not numbers that you can perform arithmetic on.

Python doesn't have true Constants, but you can simulate one by declaring a variable using all capital letters and agreeing (with yourself or your programming team) not to change its value once it's assigned.

Finally, we took a look at Mathematical, Comparison, and Boolean Operators.

Operators act on test expressions and return a result. An example of a Mathematical Operator is the plus sign. We learned that a line of code containing more than one Operation is executed in a defined order called the Order of Operations: Operations in parentheses are performed first, followed by exponentiation, multiplication and division, and finally, addition and subtraction.

An example of a Comparison Operator is the equality Operator, the double equal to sign (==). An example of a Boolean Operator is the <u>and</u> operator.

You should now be familiar with the ways you can manipulate data in Python programs.

In the next chapter, you'll see how Selection Structures permit your program to make decisions and exhibit intelligent behavior.

Chapter 4---Selection Structures

In programming, one of the most important capabilities your program must possess is the ability to adapt to conditions that it encountered while it is running. This is what makes your computer program intelligent. In this chapter, we'll continue to follow my Introductory Python class as we examine Selection Structures—programming constructs that enable your program to adapt to those runtime conditions. Specifically, you'll learn about the If statement. Along the way, you'll also get your first taste of writing a program that accepts input from the user.

Selection Structures

I arrived in the classroom a little later than usual and found a bit of a commotion.

"What's wrong?" I asked, noting that there was a group of students surrounding Rose and Jack.

"As you know," Jack said, "Rose and I are both engineers by trade, and we work for the same company. For the last few months, we've been working on our company's biggest account—overseeing the construction of a new cruise ship in the United Kingdom. Construction is way ahead of schedule, and yesterday our boss told us that we're being called away to participate in the sea trials. So you see, this will probably be our last class!"

"We're both disappointed," Rose said, "because we had hoped to finish the coding for the Grades Calculation Program before we left for the sea trials, but there's no way we'll be near to that point today."

I told both Rose and Jack that we would all be sorry not to have them present all the way through the project, but we hoped they would be able to return in time to see the final version of the Grades Calculation Program implemented in the English, Math, and Science departments.

"But as far as the Grades Calculation Program is concerned," I said, "I have a surprise for you. By the end of today's class, we'll have coded a working prototype of the Grades Calculation Program. It's not quite what we'll be delivering to Frank Olley in a few weeks, but I think you'll be pleased with it—and pretty amazed at just how full featured it is."

As the obvious shock at my last statement subsided, I began our fourth class by telling my students that during the next two weeks, they would be learning about the three types of programming Structures that form the building blocks of all computer programs.

"Structure?" Ward said. "That sounds like a house or a building."

"The building analogy is a good one, Ward," I said. "You've already learned that the first step in developing a program is to develop a 'blueprint' in the form of a Requirements Statement. Many years ago Computer Scientists discovered that any program can be written using a combination of three coding Structures, much like a house can be constructed using a series of standard components. These three Structures—the Sequence structure, the Selection Structure, and the Loop Structure— will form the basis of our discussions over the next few weeks."

"Will we be writing any code ourselves today?" Rhonda asked. "I know we wrote a bit of code last week, but I'm anxious to get going."

"You'll have a chance to write a great deal of code today," I answered. "Whenever possible, I try to have the exercises that we complete here in class ultimately lead to the completion of the Grades Calculation Program. However, from time to time we'll complete some exercises just for practice. So that we don't confuse that work with the Grades Calculation Program, if you want to save your practice exercises, you should save them in the Practice folder you created earlier in the class. Before we get into our examination of the Selection Structure today, I'd like to give you all a chance to work with code that allows you to accept 'input' data into your program.

Getting Input Into Your Program

"Up to this point," I said, "we have written a few programs that accept data from outside of the program while the program is running. In the programming world, this is a very common need. For instance, a program can open and read data from a file on the user's PC or on a network; it can also open and read data from a database, which is a more sophisticated form of a data file. And, as we've already seen, a program can also accept data directly from the user via the **input()** function. Here's an example of a program that prompts the user for a response, then uses the **print()** function to display their answer."

I then wrote and displayed this program on the classroom projector:

```
# Example4_1.py

response = input("What is your favorite programming language? ")
print("You have great taste. " + response + " is a great language.")
```

I then saved the program as Example4_1.py, and ran it for the class.

The following screenshot was displayed on the classroom projector:

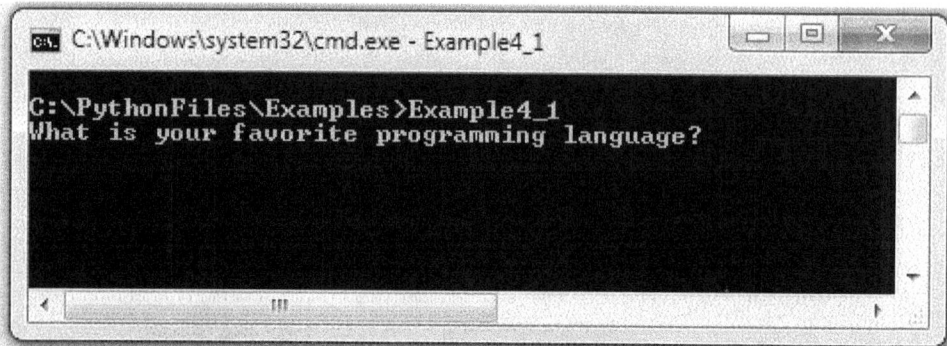

```
C:\Windows\system32\cmd.exe - Example4_1

C:\PythonFiles\Examples>Example4_1
What is your favorite programming language?
```

"The program is prompting us to enter the name of our favorite programming language," I said. "At this point, all we need to do is type our answer and press ENTER."

I did so (entering Python, of course!) and the following screenshot was displayed on the classroom projector:

```
C:\Windows\system32\cmd.exe

C:\PythonFiles\Examples>Example4_1
What is your favorite programming language? Python
You have great taste. Python is a great language.

C:\PythonFiles\Examples>
```

"Nicely done," Dave said. "If I recall, this same program in C++ would probably be 12 lines of code or so. Python is compact."

"You raise a good point Dave," I agreed. "With Python, all we need to do is code the **input()** and **print()** functions, and we're done. A similar program in C++ would be a lot more complicated."

"Can you explain the purpose of *response* with the **input()** function?" Kate asked. "What is *response*?"

"*response*," I said. " is a variable that is used to store the user's response to our question, What is your favorite programming language? Once the user provides us with an answer, we store it in the *response* variable. This is something that we will do quite often in this class."

I paused before continuing.

"There's no need to tell Python in advance that we are creating the *response* variable," I said, "We just place a valid variable name on the left side of the equal to sign, and the user's answer to the **input()** function prompt is assigned to that variable."

> NOTE: As we've seen already, there may be times when you wish to prompt the user for a number. By default, all values returned from the input() function are Strings, so if we want to perform mathematical calculations on the user's response, we need to convert their answer to a number.

"The great thing about the Python **input()** function," I said, "is that, with a single statement, we can ask the user a question, and assign their answer to a variable, in this case the variable we have named *response*. The question, or prompt, is enclosed within quotation marks within the **input()** function."

```
response = input("What is your favorite programming language? ")
```

"Everything that the user types up to the point they hit the ENTER key," I said, "is stored in the variable *response*. Python creates the *response* variable as a String variable, which can cause us problems if we take the user's answer and attempt to perform a mathematical calculation on it. But that's not a big deal to handle, as we saw last week when we learned how to use the **int()** or **float()** functions to convert a String value to a number."

I paused to see if everyone was still with me. They were.

"Finally," I said, turning my attention to the last line of code, "because we now have the user's answer stored in the *response* variable, we can use its value to confirm the user's great taste in a programming language, using the + operator to concatenate the value of the *response* variable to the String 'You have great taste.'"

```
print("You have great taste. " + response + " is a great language.")
```

"Concatenate?" Barbara asked.

"Oh, that's right," I said, "we haven't discussed Concatenation yet. Concatenate means to join together. Strings can be joined, or concatenated, by using the + operator. This isn't a Mathematical Operation we're performing with Strings, it's more like gluing two Strings together. In addition to "gluing" two Strings together, we can also "glue" a String variable to a String by using the + sign. In the case of our **print()** function in this example, we glued a String variable to a String, then glued a String to the end of that combination. Make sense?"

"That's neat," Steve said.

I paused to make sure everyone agreed with him ☺

"Did everyone notice," I said, "the way I included, for formatting purposes, a space after the question mark in the prompt for the **input()** function? Also, in the **print()** function, I included a space after the period following the word 'taste', and included a space before the word 'is' in the concatenated String."

"And why did you do that?" Rhonda asked.

"To ensure that our prompt to the user, and the statement we displayed, looked nice and neat," I said. "Experiment for yourself without the spaces and you'll see that the prompt and the displayed statement look sloppy and poorly formatted without them."

I wanted to give my students a chance to experiment with obtaining input from the user via the Python Console, and so I distributed this exercise for them to complete.

Practice 4-1 Experimenting with Python Input

In this exercise, you'll write a program to ask the user their first name and then generate a custom response to them. You'll discover that if the user makes no response and then presses ENTER, some unsatisfactory results will occur.

1. Create a folder on your hard drive called \PythonFiles\Practice. This will be the home of the Python programs we create here in class that are not part of the Grades Calculation Program.
2. Using Notepad (or Notepad++), enter the following code. Be extremely careful of the capitalization: Python is extremely picky.

```
# Practice4_1.py

response = input("What is your name? ")
print("It's nice to meet you, " + response)
```

3. Save your source file as <u>Practice4_1.py</u> in the \PythonFiles\Practice folder (select File | Save As from Notepad's menu bar). Be sure to save your source file with the filename extension py.
4. Execute your program. When prompted, type your <u>first name only</u> and then press ENTER. A message, including your name, should be displayed in the Python Console.
5. Execute your program again, but this time type your <u>first and last name</u>. What happens? What does Python display in the Python Console?
6. Execute the program once again. When prompted, immediately press the ENTER key. What happens?

Discussion

No one had any major problems completing the exercise. By now all of my students were comfortable with coding a simple Python program and seemed to be having a great time doing it. I ran the program myself, typed my first name, and a message reading "It's nice to meet you, John" was displayed in the Python Console.

```
C:\Windows\system32\cmd.exe

C:\PythonFiles\Practice>Practice4_1
What is your name? John
It's nice to meet you, John

C:\PythonFiles\Practice>
```

Not surprisingly, a few students had minor problems in formatting their display in the Python Console. Rhonda indicated that she had a problem.

"In your version of the program, "Rhonda said, "there was a space between the question and your response, but not in my version."

I took a quick walk to Rhonda's PC.

She had forgotten to include a space after the question mark of her input prompt. Blaine had done the same thing.

```
response = input("What is your name?")
```

I corrected Rhonda's code to look like this---notice the difference.

```
response = input("What is your name? ")
```

"Somehow I thought Python would insert that space for me automatically," Rhonda said.

"In computer programming, very little happens automatically," I emphasized. "Especially when you are dealing with String Literals like this. Whatever you tell Python to display, that's exactly what will be displayed—and that includes spaces."

I paused before continuing.

"Did you notice what happens when you enter both your first and last name?" I asked.

I ran the program again, and this time typed <u>both</u> my first and last name (with a space in between) and then pressed the ENTER key. The following screenshot was displayed on the classroom projector:

```
C:\Windows\system32\cmd.exe

C:\PythonFiles\Practice>Practice4_1
What is your name? John Smiley
It's nice to meet you, John Smiley

C:\PythonFiles\Practice>
```

Both my first and last name were displayed.

"This is a bit different than some other programming languages like C++," Steve said, "which I believe would only have displayed the first word."

"That's right, Steve," I said. "Python has no problem dealing with a response of more than one word. We could have typed a response of any length as our answer to the prompt and Python will gladly accept it. Up until the point the user presses the ENTER key, Python will continue to accept their typed entry as the value for the *response* variable."

"You asked us to run our program and immediately hit the ENTER key," Mary said. "I forgot to do that, what happens?"

"Thanks for reminding me Mary," I said. "Let's see what happens when I do that."

I ran the program again, and this time I immediately hit the ENTER key before typing anything. The following screenshot was displayed on the classroom projector:

"As you can see," I said, "the program runs, but it displays a 'blank' name in its greeting."

"I'm not sure that's such a great thing," Kate said.

"You're absolutely right, Kate," I said. "Being able to detect whether the user immediately presses the ENTER key without typing anything will be very important to us later on, and you'll learn how to handle that in just a few moments."

There were no questions on getting input into our program. It was now time to examine the Python Sequence Structure.

The Sequence Structure---Falling Rock

"I'd like to introduce you to the Python Sequence Structure," I said. "Most teachers (and authors) don't even address the Sequence Structure, but I like to mention it. As you'll learn later on, both the Selection Structure and Loop Structure require a special syntax to implement, but that's not the case with the Sequence Structure. This may seem obvious to you in a minute, but any code that we write is automatically part of a Sequence Structure. By that I mean, each line of code executes one after the other. I like to analogize a Sequence Structure to the behavior of a falling rock."

"Falling rock? What do you mean by that?" Steve said, obviously amused.

"Have you seen signs warning you of falling rock on the highway?" I said. "If you've ever seen rock fall, you know that once it gets rolling, there's no stopping it. The same is true of code in a Python program. Unless we implement either a Selection Structure or a Loop Structure, something we'll examine later on in today's class, code in a Python program executes from top to bottom without stopping."

I paused for a moment before continuing.

"Let's look at the code we wrote last week that calculates the final numeric grade of an English student," I said, "and then displays it in the Python Console:"

I displayed the code for the Grades program on the classroom projector.

```
# Grades.py
# After Chapter 3

MIDTERM_PERCENTAGE = .25
FINAL_EXAM_PERCENTAGE = .25
RESEARCH_PERCENTAGE = .30
PRESENTATION_PERCENTAGE = .20
midterm = 70
final_exam_grade = 80
research = 90
presentation = 100
final_numeric_grade = 0

final_numeric_grade = \
    (midterm * MIDTERM_PERCENTAGE) + \
    (final_exam_grade * FINAL_EXAM_PERCENTAGE) + \
    (research * RESEARCH_PERCENTAGE) + \
    (presentation * PRESENTATION_PERCENTAGE)

print("Midterm grade is : ", midterm)
print("Final Exam grade is : ", final_exam_grade)
```

```
print("Research grade is : ",  research)
print("Presentation grade is: ",  presentation)
print("\nThe final grade is: ",  final_numeric_grade)
```

"This code in Grades.py is a perfect example of the Sequence Structure," I said, "Last week, we saw that the first line of code in Grades.py executes, followed by the second line of code, then the third, and so forth, in *sequence*."

"Oh, I see where the term Sequence Structure comes from now," Valerie said. "You mean each line of code is executed, one after the other. But I have to ask, what else could happen? Isn't every line of code evaluated and then executed by Python?"

"Every line of code is evaluated by Python," I said, "but not every line of code is necessarily executed—or executed only one time for that matter. Some lines of code may be skipped based on conditions found when the program is running (as we saw last week with the Python If statement.). In other cases, lines of code may be executed more than once, as you'll see when you learn about Python Loops next week. The Selection Structure gives intelligence to our program, providing it with decision-making capabilities, which is something the falling rock behavior of a Sequence Structure simply can't do. The Selection Structure allows us to *selectively* execute lines of code based on conditions our program evaluates at runtime. Next week, we'll examine the Loop Structure, which allows us to execute a line or lines of code *repetitively*."

I paused a moment before adding, "In order to illustrate the alternatives to the falling rock behavior of a Sequence Structure, I'd like you to complete a series of exercises based on seven fictitious restaurants in New York City. Pretend that you have been hired by the owners of these seven restaurants to write a program to display their advertisement on a giant display screen in Times Square, but in our case we're going to use the Python Console as our giant display screen. Here's the second exercise of the day, which will illustrate the falling rock behavior of Python code."

I then distributed this exercise for the class to complete.

Practice 4-2 Eat at Joe's – The Sequence Structure---Falling Rock behavior

In this exercise, you'll write a Python program that displays information about the days of operation of seven restaurants in New York City in the Python Console. Pretend that the Python Console is actually a giant display screen in New York City's Times Square.
1. Using Notepad (or Notepad++), enter the following code. Be extremely careful of the capitalization: Python is very picky.

```
# Practice4_2.py


print("Eat at Joe's")
print("Eat at Tom's")
print("Eat at Kevin's")
print("Eat at Rich's")
print("Eat at Rose's")
print("Eat at Ken's")
print("Eat at Melissa's")
```

2. Save your source file as Practice4_2.py in the \PythonFiles\Practice folder (select File | Save As from Notepad's menu bar). Be sure to save your source file with the filename extension py.
3. Execute your program. You should see output similar to this screenshot.

Discussion

Aside from some students' continued anxiety with writing code and some typos, this exercise went pretty smoothly. Having warned them in the instructions for the exercise, my students were very careful with their capitalization.

Only one person had a problem—and that person capitalized the letter 'p' in the word **print**, causing the Python Interpreter to generate an error message.

I gave my students a chance to complete the exercise and then began to explain what we had done with this relatively small program.

"This program seemed pretty straightforward," Rhonda said. "What were you trying to illustrate with it?"

"I wanted to illustrate the Sequence Structure," I answered. "All of the code that makes up the main body of our program represents something known as a Sequence Structure. All that means is that the second line of code executes after the first line of code, the third line after the second line, and so on.

"Falling rock behavior!" Ward chimed in.

"Exactly right, Ward," I said.

NOTE: Unlike the Selection and Loop Structures we'll learn about this week and next week, there's nothing special for you to do to implement a Sequence Structure. Python executes one line after another. Any code not found in a Selection or Loop structure is part of a Sequence Structure.

There were no other questions about the exercise, so I continued, turning my attention to the Python Selection Structure.

"Having written this program for the owners of the seven restaurants," I said, "let us further suppose that the owner of Joe's restaurant goes into semi-retirement and decides to open his restaurant only on Sundays. Tom, the proprietor of Tom's restaurant, hearing the news about Joe, thinks semi-retirement is also a great idea and decides to open his restaurant only on Mondays. Kevin follows suit and opens only on Tuesdays. Soon the rest of the restaurant owners hear about this, figure that one day of work a week is a great idea, and the next thing we know, Rich is open only on Wednesdays, Rose only on Thursdays, Ken only on Fridays, and Melissa only on Saturdays. Hoping to save advertising costs in Times Square, the owner of each restaurant contacts us and informs us that they want to advertise on our giant display screen only on the days of the week that their restaurant is actually open. How can we handle this with our program?"

"I suppose," Peter said, "we could write separate Python programs for the different days of the week—although I'm sure there must be a better way than that."

"You're correct Peter," I said. "We could write a separate Python program for each day of the week. You're also correct that that there must be a better way to handle the problem. We can write a Python program that knows what the current date is—and also the day of the week. Armed with that knowledge, we can then use the Python Selection Structure to decide what restaurant advertisement to display on our giant display screen on any given day."

I could see that my students were obviously impressed---an intelligent computer program!.

The Python Selection Structure---the If Statement

"A Selection Structure," I continued, "using an If statement, can alter the falling rock behavior of a Python program. Implementing a Selection Structure is a little more complicated to write (we saw a preview of it last week.). Selection Structures require that we specify one or more test expressions to be evaluated by our program, along with a statement or statements (called Imperative statements) to be executed if the test expression is determined to be True, and optionally, other statement(s) to be executed if the test expression is determined to be False.."

I gave my students a chance to think about that.

"In our next exercise," I said, "you'll implement a Python Selection Structures using a simple If statement. The test expression that you'll ask Python to evaluate will be the current day of the week. Based on Python's determination of the day of the week, the program will then make a decision as to what restaurant's advertising to display in the Python Console."

I then distributed this exercise for the class to complete.

Don't Forget: If typing these long examples and practice exercises isn't something you want to do, feel free to follow this link to find and download the completed solutions for all of the examples and exercises in the book. Just click on the Python book, then follow the link entitled exercises ☺

Practice 4-3 The If Statement (or what restaurant is open today?)

In this exercise, you'll modify the code from Practice 4-2 to use an If Statement to determine the date, then the day of the week, and therefore the appropriate restaurant to advertise in the Python Console. There are some new keywords and functions introduced in this program (import, datetime, etc.) Don't worry about those for now—we'll be discussing them shortly.

1. Using Notepad enter the following code.

```python
# Practice4_3.py

import datetime

print("Today is: ", datetime.date.today())
print("The day of the week is: ", datetime.date.today().strftime("%A"))
print("The number of the day of the week is: ", datetime.date.today().strftime("%w"))

day_of_the_week = datetime.date.today().strftime("%A")

if day_of_the_week == "Sunday":
  print("Eat at Joe's")

if day_of_the_week == "Monday":
  print("Eat at Tom's")
if day_of_the_week == "Tuesday":
  print("Eat at Kevin's")
if day_of_the_week == "Wednesday":
  print("Eat at Rich's")
if day_of_the_week == "Thursday":
  print("Eat at Rose's")
if day_of_the_week == "Friday":
  print("Eat at Ken's")
if day_of_the_week == "Saturday":
  print("Eat at Melissa's")
```

2. Save your source file as Practice4_3.py in the \PythonFiles\Practice folder (select File | Save As from Notepad's menu bar). Be sure to save your source file with the filename extension py.

3. Execute your program. You should see the current date, the day of the week, the numeric value of the day of the week, along with a restaurant advertisement displayed in the Python Console, similar to this screenshot (what you see will depend on the date and the day of the week it is when you run your program):

```
C:\Windows\system32\cmd.exe

C:\PythonFiles\Practice>Practice4_3
Today is:  2016-01-09
The day of the week is:   Saturday
The number of the day of the week is:  6
Eat at Melissa's

C:\PythonFiles\Practice>
```

Discussion

I gave my students about ten minutes to complete the exercise.

They truly seemed mesmerized with the ability of their program to behave intelligently. Although no one had any trouble completing the exercise, there were still a number of puzzled looks in the classroom.

"This is really cool," Steve said. "I had no idea you could do something like this with a programming language, although I must confess I don't think I understand half the code we just wrote"

"I don't blame you Steve," I said, "there are a number of new keywords and methods introduced in this program and they all center on a special Python object called <u>datetime</u>. <u>datetime</u> is a Python object that we can use to determine our computer's date and time. It allows us to perform all sorts of interesting operations in our Python programs that are dependent on dates and times. Because <u>datetime</u> and its methods (essentially functions) are not something that are used all of the time, (unlike some of the other built-in Python functions, such as **print()** and **input()**,) in order to use the methods of the <u>datetime</u> object, we need to explicitly include the <u>datetime</u> object in our program using the <u>import</u> statement like this..."

```
import datetime
```

"The import statement," I said, "makes available to our program the methods that are part of the <u>datetime</u> object. Methods are nothing more than functions that belong to a Python object. Without the import statement we would not be able to execute these methods (unlike the built-in Python functions that are automatically made available to our program.)"

I paused before continuing.

"I included the next three lines of code in the program," I said, "just so that you could get comfortable with the <u>datetime</u> object and display the results of some of its methods. The first displays the current date in the Python Console using the **today()** method of the <u>date</u> object of the <u>datetime</u> object..."

```
print("Today is: ", datetime.date.today())
```

"That's a mouthful," Rhonda said. "Date object of the datetime object? An object within an object?"

"That's right Rhonda," I said, "this gives us a glimpse into what is known as Object orientation. Objects can themselves be <u>sub objects</u> of other objects. Much like letters are a sub object of a word object, and words are sub objects of a paragraph object. Fortunately, in Python, you don't have to worry a great deal about this concept. Although Python is very much Object Oriented, we can do a lot with the language without having to delve into Objects. Although if you want to, we do that here at the University in our Python Classes and Objects course where you'll learn how to create your own Python objects."

"What's a method?" Joe asked. "Did you say it's like a function?"

"A method is like a function," I answered, "but it's used explicitly in combination with an object name, always following a period or a dot. This syntax is sometimes called <u>dot notation</u>. This is an example of Object Dot Notation where the **today()** method of the date object is executed...

```
datetime.date.today()
```

I paused before continuing to make sure I hadn't lost anyone.

"This next line of code tells Python to display the alphabetic day of the week—that is, Monday, Tuesday, Wednesday, etc. To do that, once again we used the **today()** method of the <u>date</u> object, but this time instead of displaying the date, we passed the date to the **strftime()** method with the special notation "%A" that tells Python to display the alphabetic day of the week."

```
print("The day of the week is: ", datetime.date.today().strftime("%A"))
```

"This next line of code is similar to the previous one, except I wanted to illustrate that the day of the week can also be expressed in terms of numbers, where 0 is Sunday, 1 is Monday, 2 is Tuesday, etc. Again, we use the **today()** method of the date object, but we pass a value to the **strftime()** method with the special notation "%w" that tells Python to display the day of the week in Numeric terms."

```
print("The number of the day of the week is: ", datetime.date.today().strftime("%w"))
```

"All of this makes sense," Jack said. "I think it's just a matter of getting used to all this talk of objects, such as **datetime** and **date**."

"It does take some getting used to," I said. "But remember, although Python is very much Object Oriented, using these objects is fairly easy. Most of the work we will do in this introductory Python course will use the built-in Python functions. As you get more and more skilled with Python, you'll learn that there are literally hundreds of Python Objects that you can import into your programs to do all sorts of magical things."

I waited for questions before continuing.

"The previous 3 lines of code have no bearing on our program," I continued. "I just used them to illustrate the nature of the datetime object. This line of code gets us moving in the correct direction. It takes the alphabetic day of the week, and assigns it to a variable called **day_of_the_week**. Doing this, you will see in a minute, saves us quite a great deal of typing in our If statements, and because of that, reduces the chance of us making a coding error..."

```
day_of_the_week = datetime.date.today().strftime("%A")
```

"At this point," I said, "the *day_of_the_week* variable now contains the current alphabetic day of the week. With the next line of code, we use the Python If statement to determine if the day of the week is Sunday. If it is, we display a message in the Python Console to eat at Joe's restaurant. Notice that the word Sunday is sandwiched within quotation marks and that the following line of code, called an <u>Imperative Statement</u> to be executed if the If statement evaluates to True, is indented."

```
if day_of_the_week == "Sunday":
  print("Eat at Joe's")
```

"Two equal to signs?" Rhonda interrupted. "Is that right? Shouldn't there be just one?"

"Good question, Rhonda," I said. "In Python, we test for equality by using two equal to signs, not a single equal to sign. One equal to sign, as we've seen, is used to assign a value to a variable. Here, we're using the Python If statement to evaluate an expression to determine whether it is True or False and so we use two equal to signs."

"I notice that there is a colon following the closing quotation mark in the word Sunday," Chuck said. "Is that mandatory?"

"Another good question, Chuck," I said. "The answer is yes. The colon is required. If you forget to code the colon, you will generate a Python syntax error when you try to run the program."

> **NOTE: The colon in an If statement is required. The successive Imperative Statement or statements must appear on a subsequent line and must indented**

"What happens if the test expression evaluates to True?" Kate asked.

"If the test expression evaluates to True," I said, "then the indented Imperative Statement following the colon is executed. (There can be more than one Imperative statement, in which case each one is indented.) I need to emphasize how important indentation is here. You must indent the Imperative Statement or statements following the colon, otherwise Python will get confused and generate a syntax error, telling you that it expected an **indented block**."

"Does it matter how many spaces we indent?" Linda asked. "5 spaces, 3 spaces? 1 space?"

"Any number of spaces will work," I answered. "I prefer 2 spaces, but 1 space will also work. If you are using Windows Notepad, using the tab key can sometimes confuse the Python Interpreter, so I avoid using tabs in Notepad. If you use an editor such as Notepad++, it has a nice feature where you can automatically indent selected lines of code in your program. It does so through the use of tabs, which in a program created using Notepad++, causes no problem for the Python Interpreter."

> **NOTE: If you use Notepad++, it has a feature that can automatically indent selected lines of code in your program. It does so through the use of tabs, which Python readily accepts.**

"What's an Imperative Statement?" Rhonda asked.

"An Imperative Statement is a statement (or statements) to be executed if the If statement evaluates to True," I said, "In this example, we coded just a single Imperative Statement to be executed if the day of week is equal to Sunday. You can specify more than one Imperative Statement to be executed if the If statement is True. Just be sure to indent every Imperative Statement."

```
print("Eat at Joe's")
```

"What happens if the test expression evaluates to False?" Joe asked.

"If the test expression evaluates to False," I answered, "the indented Imperative Statement or statements are skipped."

"So the indented Imperative Statements are only executed if the test expression evaluates to True?" Linda asked.

"That's right Linda," I replied.

"And you said you can specify more than one Imperative Statement?" Bob asked.

"That's right," I said. "If you want to execute more than one Imperative Statement, simply code the second statement following the first, the third following the second, etc, like this. Be sure you indent all of them. Like this..."

```
if day_of_the_week == "Sunday":
  print("Imperative Statement #1")
```

```
print("Imperative Statement #2")
print("Imperative Statement #3")
```

"Provided you understand how our first If statement worked," I said, "the remainder of the If statements in the program are pretty straightforward. We're evaluating the value of the variable *day_of_the_week* for each of the other six days of the week. One of these seven If statements have to evaluate to True."

```
if day_of_the_week == "Monday":
  print("Eat at Tom's")
if day_of_the_week == "Tuesday":
  print("Eat at Kevin's")
if day_of_the_week == "Wednesday":
  print("Eat at Rich's")
if day_of_the_week == "Thursday":
  print("Eat at Rose's")
if day_of_the_week == "Friday":
  print("Eat at Ken's")
if day_of_the_week == "Saturday":
  print("Eat at Melissa's")
```

"Is it possible to code an If statement on a single line the way we can do in some other languages?" Dave asked.

"Yes it is Dave," I said. "We could write our code to look like this."

```
if day_of_the_week == "Sunday": print("Eat at Joe's")
```

"That would cut down on the number of lines in our program," Dave observed.

"Yes it would Dave," I said, "Stylistically, I prefer to place the Imperative Statements on separate, indented lines as I showed earlier, but you can use this style if you wish."

"You mentioned earlier," Valerie said, "that if the test expression evaluates to False, the Imperative Statement or statements will be skipped. Is it possible to specify a statement or statements to execute if the test expression is False?"

"Yes," I replied, "we can do that by using the optional Else clause of the If statement. In this program, we didn't specify any statements to execute if the test expression was False."

"So if the If statement evaluates to False," Linda asked, "the Imperative Statement or statements are skipped, and execution of the program picks up with the next line of code following them?

"That's right Linda," I said, "All of the Imperative Statements in the indented block of code are skipped if the test expression evaluates to False. In this program, that meant that the next If statement was executed.""

Valerie had read my mind---it was now time to move onto the Else clause of the If statement.

The If...Else Statement

"With the If statements we've seen so far," I said, "we specified an Imperative Statement to execute if the test expression evaluated to True. Using the optional Else clause, we can specify one or more indented Imperative Statements to execute if the test expression evaluates to False. Let me show you a simple example."

I displayed this program on the classroom projector:

```
# Example4_2.py

response = input("What is your favorite programming language? ")

if response == "Python" :
  print("You have great taste. Python is a great language.")
else:
  print("It's not as good as Python, but " + response + " is also a great language.")
```

I then saved the program as Example4_2.py, and ran it for the class.

The program asked me what my favorite programming language was. I answered Python and was congratulated on my great taste.

"As you can see, " I said, "we used an If Statement to determine if the user's favorite programming language was Python. When I entered Python, the test expression of the If statement evaluated to True, and the single indented Imperative statement following it was executed."

```
if response == "Python" :
  print("You have great taste. Python is a great language".)
```

"Now what happens if the user enters something other than Python in answer to the prompt?" I asked. "Rather than code a series of If statements for every possible programming language (there are hundreds) we handle all other cases with the Else clause by displaying a slightly customized, generic message."

"So the statement or statements following the word Else will be executed if the user enters anything other than Python as their answer to our question?" Kate asked.

"That's right, Kate," I responded. "Anything other than Python will lead to the test expression evaluating to False, in which case the indented Imperative Statement or statements following the word Else are executed. Notice that there is a colon following the word else---the same as there is at the end of the If statement."

```
else:
  print("It's not as good as Python, but " + response + " is also a great language")
```

"By the way," I said, "if the user enters 'Python' any other way than with a capital 'P', followed by the lower case letters 'ython', the program will also interpret that as a False condition. Python is very much case sensitive. In other words, 'python' is not the same as 'Python'. Later on, we'll learn that there are ways to handle this in our program. For now, let's run the program again and answer the program's prompt with a computer language other than Python."

I did exactly that, this time providing an answer of C++ as my favorite language of choice. When I did so, the following screenshot was displayed.

"Because we didn't enter 'Python' as our favorite programming language," I said, "another message was displayed in the Python Console. This message was displayed by the Imperative statement in the Else clause of the If statement. Notice how we cleverly include the user's favorite programming language in the display message. No matter what their response, it will be displayed in the message through the magic of String Concatenation."

```
else:
  print("It's not as good as Python, but " + response + " is also a great language")
```

"I did notice that," Blaine said. "That's pretty cool isn't it?"

"I've heard some of the programmers at work discussing Nested If Statements," Ward asked. "What are those?"

"That is when," I said, "the Imperative statement either in the If statement or the Else clause of the If statement is another If statement. These are called <u>Nested If Statements</u>."

"Wow, that sounds confusing," Barbara said. "Why would we want to do that?"

"Nested If statements allow us to handle complex situations where we have multiple test expressions to evaluate," I answered. "For instance, if we want to display unique messages for a combination of answers that the user provides to us, Nested If statements are ideal. But don't worry---as your experience in Python grows, you'll be coding these in no time. In fact, you'll be coding Nested If statements in the Grades Calculation Program later on today."

No one had any further questions about the If statement or the Else clause.

"Do you remember what happened in Practice 4-1 when we immediately pressed the ENTER key without entering our name?" I said. "Our program displayed a 'blank' name in the Python Console. We can use an If Statement to handle this condition, and that's a skill that will be quite useful to learn."

I then distributed this exercise for the class to do.

Practice 4-4 Using an If statement to check for No Entry

In this exercise, we'll modify the code from Practice 4-1 so that if the user makes no entry for their name and then presses the ENTER key, an appropriate warning message will be displayed in the Python Console.
1. Using Notepad, enter the following code.

```
# Practice4_4.py

response = input("What is your name? ")

if response == "":
  print("You must tell me your name...")
else:
  print("It's nice to meet you, " + response)
```

2. Save your source file as Practice4_4.py in the \PythonFiles\Practice folder (select File | Save As from Notepad's menu bar). Be sure to save your source file with the filename extension py.
3. Execute your program. When prompted, type your full name and then press ENTER. A message, including your full name, should be displayed in the Python Console.
4. Execute your program again, but this time immediately press the ENTER key. What does Python display in the Python Console?

Discussion

I anticipated that a number of students would have issues completing this exercise, and I wasn't wrong :)

A couple of students forgot colons---either after the test expression of the If Statement, or following the word else in the Else Clause of the If statement.

One student placed a space between the pair of quotation marks in the test expression---something that caused his program to not behave as he expected. More on that in a minute.

Indentation proved tricky for a few other students who neglected it altogether and learned quickly how picky Python can be about it.

Finally, one student realized that spelling the words 'if' or 'else' with an initial capital letter would generate a Python syntax error.

"I know you warned us," Rhonda said, "but I guess I didn't realize how serious Python is about spelling and syntax. It pays to be very careful---particularly with colons and indentation. I think I made every mistake it's possible to make in that exercise."

"You're absolutely right, Rhonda," I said, smiling. "However, it's better to learn that now than during your first programming job."

When everyone in the class indicated that they were finished with the exercise, I began my discussion.

"I think you can see that this program exhibits quite a bit of intelligence," I said. "It's essentially the same code from Example4_1, but now we're using an If statement to determine if the user has immediately pressed the ENTER key without typing their name. How do we do that? By checking for what Python calls a null String. A null string is a String variable that contains no characters---nothing---not even spaces. Many beginners believe that a null string contains a single space. That's incorrect. Since we want to determine if the user has entered no characters at our prompt, we check for a null string by using a pair of quotation marks with nothing in between, like this. ..."

```
if response == "":
```

"That was my mistake," Lou said, "I inserted a space in between the quotation marks. Needless to say, my program didn't behave the way I wanted it to work."

"That's an easy error for a beginner to make, Lou" I said. "A test expression with a single space between two quotation marks would evaluate to True only if the if the user pressed the space bar once then hit the ENTER key. What we wanted to check for was if the user immediately pressed the ENTER key without typing a single character. That's the null String we can check for with a pair of quotation marks with nothing in between."

I paused before continuing.

"If the test expression evaluates to True," I said, "we know that the user has pressed the ENTER key without typing any characters, and we display a warning message in the Python Console."

I ran the program myself, immediately pressed the ENTER key, and the following screenshot was displayed:

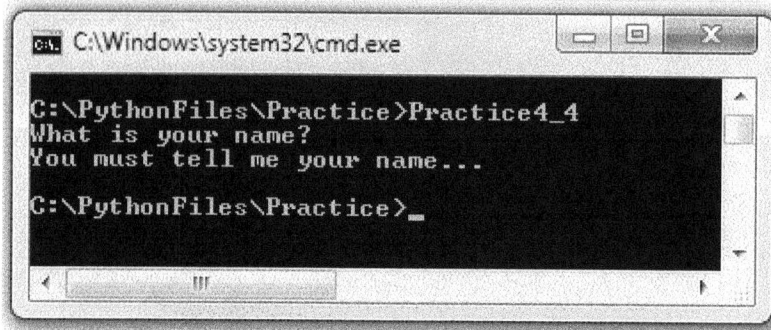

As predicted, hitting the ENTER key without typing any characters produced a warning message.

I scanned the classroom for signs of confusion. There were none. I could see several of my students admiring their work as they ran their programs over and over again.

The elif Clause

"There's another clause of the If Statement I'd like to discuss now," I said. "It's called the **elif** clause, and it's useful when you have a variable that you want to check against a series of possible values."

"I'm not sure I understand what you mean," Joe said. "Series of possible values? Can you show us an example?"

"To make this all a little more understandable," I said, "let me show you what I mean by using Pseudocode to illustrate how we can display, based on his or her age, the number of years until an employee is eligible for retirement."

I saw some puzzled looks.

"We used Pseudocode earlier in the course," I said. "when we were working on the design of the Grades Calculation Program. Pseudocode enables us to express complex problems, in an English-like way, without having to worry about coding the problem in a particular computer language. Then, when we have the problem worked out to our satisfaction, we can then translate the Pseudocode into whatever language in which we are working. Remember, what I'm about to show you isn't Python, so don't try to execute it!"

I then displayed this Pseudocode on the classroom projector:

> **NOTE: Pseudocode is a way of expressing a complex problem in an English-like way, prior to coding it up in an actual programming language.**

There is an employee working for a company. According to the rules of the company:

If the employee's age is 62 or greater
  he/she must be retired
Else If the employee's age is 61
  he/she has 1 year until retirement
Else If the employee's age is 60
  he/she has 2 years until retirement
Else If the employee's age is 59
  he/she has 3 years until retirement

Else
  he/she has a really long time to go

"Are we going to implement this Pseudocode in a Python program?" Linda asked.

"Yes we are," I said. "By using the Elif Clause of the If Statement."

I then distributed this exercise for the class to complete.

Practice 4-5 The Elif Clause

In this exercise, you'll create a program to determine how long an employee has until he or she can retire. See how your finished product mirrors the Pseudocode we just developed.

1. Using Notepad, enter the following code.

```
# Practice4_5.py

response = input("What is your age? ")

if response == "":
  print("You must tell me your age...")
elif int(response) > 61:
   print(response, " - You must be retired")
elif int(response) == 61:
   print(response, " - You have 1 year until retirement")
elif int(response) == 60:
   print(response, " - You have 2 years until retirement")
elif int(response) == 59:
   print(response == " - You have 3 years until retirement")
else:
   print(response , " - You have a long time until retirement")
```

2. Save your source file as Practice4_5.py in the \PythonFiles\Practice folder (select File | Save As from Notepad's menu bar). Be sure to save your source file with the filename extension py.
3. Execute your program multiple times, entering **62**, **61**, **60**, **59**, and **40** as answers to your age. Observe the various messages that are displayed in the Python Console.
4. Execute the program one more time, this time pressing the ENTER key without making an entry for your age. You should receive a warning message.

Discussion

There was probably more code in this exercise than in any of the other exercises we had written so far in the class. Several of my students became confused, lost their places and had to start over.

Fifteen minutes later, though, I was happy to see that everyone in the class had successfully completed the exercise.

I was also happy to see that my students had not made the same mistakes they had made earlier in the class: forgetting colons; spelling 'if', 'else' or 'elif' with initial Capital letters; neglecting to indent the Imperative Statements following the If statement, the Else or the Elif Clauses; inserting a space between the quotation marks of the null String test expression. All of my students even handled the spelling of the new Elif clause perfectly.

"I don't think we've ever written this much code in a single exercise," Rhonda said.

"I think you're right, Rhonda," I replied. "This is probably the longest program we've written so far. As you discovered, when we write programs which test for a number of different values like we did here, it can substantially increase the size of our program. The code we've written for this exercise, though lengthy, is still fairly manageable. Suppose we had a requirement to display a unique message for every age between 1 and 100! That would really increase the size of our code."

Everyone agreed.

It was now time to discuss what we had written.

Displaying the first line of code from our program on the classroom projector, I said "There's nothing new here. This line of code uses the *input()* function to prompt the user to enter his or her age, and then assigns their entry to a variable called *response*."

```
response = input("What is your age? ")
```

"These next two lines of code," I said, "check if the user has pressed the ENTER key without entering their age. That's the so-called null String. If that's the case, the value of the *response* variable will be empty, or null, and we display a warning message in the Python Console."

```
if response == "":
  print("You must tell me your age...")
```

"I noticed," Rhonda said, "that as soon as the warning message is displayed in the Python Console, the program immediately ends. Shouldn't the user be given an opportunity to correct their mistake without having to run the program all over again? Is there a way to do that?"

"There is a way to do that, Rhonda," I said, "but we need to create a Python Loop to do that, and that's something we'll learn how to do next week."

"That next line of code where we check if the value entered is greater than 61?" Ward asked. "That's the **int()** function we learned about last week, isn't it?

```
elif int(response) > 61:
  print(response, " - You must be retired")
```

"Good observation, Ward," I said. "**int()** is the Python function we learned about last week that takes the value of a String variable and returns the <u>Integer</u> equivalent of it. We also could have used its close cousin, the float() function that takes the value of a String variable and returns the Float equivalent of it."

Some of my students seemed confused.

"The **input()** function returns a String value," I said. "and the value residing in the *response* variable is a String. Strings are not numbers. In order to perform any numeric comparison on the value of the *response* variable---as we want to do here---we must work with its numeric equivalent, otherwise Python will display an error message when we try to execute the program. Working with the numeric equivalent of a String is easy. All we need to do is execute the **int()** function on the *response* variable, and then work with its return value, which is an Integer Data Type. We then use the greater than Comparison Operator (>) to determine if its value is greater than 61."

> **NOTE: There's a close cousin of the int() function called the float() function which returns the floating point equivalent of a String value.**

"We learned last week," I said, "that Comparison Operations return either a True or False value. In this program, if the age the user enters is greater than 61, the Comparison Operation returns a True value. If the If Statement evaluates to True, and we then display the user's age, together with the String 'You must be retired' in the Python Console."

```
print(response, " - You must be retired")
```

"What would have happened if we didn't convert the String value in the *response* variable to an Integer?" Kate asked. "Did you say Python would display an error?"

"That's right Kate," I said. "The Python Interpreter would complain that we were trying to perform a Numeric comparison against a String value."

"Can we go back to that line of code where we display the message 'You must be retired'?" Chuck asked. "What's the purpose of the comma following the response variable? Have we covered that before?"

I explained that the comma is a formatting nuance of the **print()** function. We are concatenating the String 'You must be retired' with the value of the *response* variable. The comma automatically inserts a space between the value of the user's response and the String "- You must be retired".

```
print(response, " - You must be retired")
```

"If the number 73 is typed by the user," I said, "the message displayed will read '73 - You must be retired.' Notice the space between the number 73 and the dash in our String Literal."

"That's clever," Steve said. "So we're using the value of the **response** variable in the message, not a Numeric Literal."

"That's right, Steve," I said. "Using the *response* variable in the message makes the message very dynamic. Whatever entry the user makes (provided it's greater than 61) will appear in the message."

"Why is it that we didn't use the **int()** function within the **print()** function to convert the value of the *response* variable to a number?" Rhonda asked.

"The **print()** function requires a String data type as an argument," I said. "And that's already the data type of the *response* variable. Only if we use the value of the response variable in a numeric comparison or a Mathematical calculation do we need to convert (or cast) its Data Type to a number. In fact, if we use a non-String variable in the print() function, we'll trigger a syntax error."

NOTE: The process of converting from one Data Type to another is called casting.

I paused before continuing.

"With the initial If statement," I said, "we're checking if the user's age is greater than 61. If the Comparison Operation evaluates to True, we execute the Imperative Statement following the If Statement, and display a message saying that the user must be retired. If the Comparison Operation evaluates to False, the Imperative statement following the If Statement is bypassed, and the first of our four Elif clauses is executed. The first Elif Clause checks if the user's age is exactly 61..."

```
elif int(response) == 61:
    print(response, " - You have 1 year until retirement")
```

"If it is equal to 61," I said, "we then execute the Imperative Statement to display a message that the user has 1 year until retirement. If the user's entry is not equal to 61, the Imperative Statement following the word elif is bypassed, and the next line of code following it is then executed. This is the second of our four Elif Clauses, this one to check if the value the user has entered is exactly equal to 60. These two lines of code are nearly identical to the previous two lines of code. The test expression is different, as well as the message that we display if the test expression evaluates to True."

```
elif int(response) == 60:
    print(response, " - You have 2 years until retirement")
```

"Likewise," I said, "these next two lines of code work in the same way, checking if the user's age was entered as exactly 59. If it was, we display a message that the user has 3 years until retirement."

```
elif int(response) == 59:
    print(response, " - You have 3 years until retirement")
```

I waited to see if there were any questions.

"Can you imagine how much code we would need to write," I asked, "if we wanted to display a unique message for every possible age from 58 down to 1. Fortunately, the Else clause is a perfect way to handle all of those other possibilities. If the age the user enters is not greater than 61, and it's not equal to 61, 60, or 59, it must be 1 through 58, and is handled by the Imperative statement of the Else clause. Also, to the user, it appears to be customized message since we also display the user's age."

```
else:
    print(response , " - You have a long time until retirement")
```

I waited to see whether there were any other questions. To my surprise, everyone in the class seemed pretty comfortable with the If statement, and its various clauses.

I told my students to take a well-earned 15-minute break.

"When we return from break," I said, "we'll use the Selection Structures we learned about today to enhance the Grades Calculation Program. I think you'll be very pleased with what we're about to do with the project."

Continuing with the Grades Calculation Program

"We now know enough about Python," I said, resuming after our break "to add some intelligence to the Grades Calculation Program. You may remember that last week we added code to the project to calculate the grade for a fictitious English student whose <u>midterm</u> grade was 70, <u>final examination</u> grade was 80, <u>research</u> grade was 90, and <u>presentation</u> grade was 100. We then displayed the student's final grade of 84.5 in the Python Console."

"We hard-coded the component grade pieces in the program code itself," Blaine said.

"That's right, Blaine," I said. "Last week you didn't have the Python skills to allow our program to accept input from a user, so we had no choice but to hard-code the component grade scores directly into the program. After what we've learned today about getting input into our program, and the Python Selection Structures, we'll be able to ask the user what type of student they wish to calculate a grade for and to then accept the appropriate component grade scores from the user based on that student type."

"Wow, are you saying we'll be able to calculate the grade for an actual student today?" Ward asked.

"That's right, Ward" I replied.

"That's very exciting," Rhonda said. "But if I'm not mistaken, after the updates you say we'll be making to the Grades Calculation Program today, won't we be essentially be finished with it?"

"Strictly speaking Rhonda," I said, "you're correct. By the end of today's class, we'll have a working Python program that fulfills the Requirements Statement we developed several weeks ago with Frank Olley."

"What will be doing during the remainder of the class?" Bob asked.

"We still have plenty to learn" I said, "and we'll be able to use those new skills to enhance the basic functionality of our Grades Calculation Program."

I then distributed this exercise for the class to complete.

Don't Forget: If typing these long examples and practice exercises isn't something you want to do, feel free to follow this link to find and download the completed solutions for all of the examples and exercises in the book. Just click on the Python book, then follow the link entitled exercises ☺

http://www.johnsmiley.com/main/books.htm

Practice 4-6 Enhance the Grades Calculation Program

In this exercise, you'll modify the Grades Calculation Program you worked on last week in Practice 3-1, giving it the ability to accept input from the user and calculate grades (both numeric and letter grades) for an English, Math or Science Student.

1. Using Notepad (or Notepad++), locate and open the Grades.py source file you worked on last week. (It should be in the \PythonFiles\Grades folder.)
2. Modify the code so that it looks like this. Be very careful of the indentation in your If statements.

```python
# Grades.py
# After Chapter 4

ENGLISH_MIDTERM_PERCENTAGE = .25
ENGLISH_FINAL_EXAM_PERCENTAGE = .25
ENGLISH_RESEARCH_PERCENTAGE = .30
ENGLISH_PRESENTATION_PERCENTAGE = .20
MATH_MIDTERM_PERCENTAGE = .50
MATH_FINAL_EXAM_PERCENTAGE = .50
SCIENCE_MIDTERM_PERCENTAGE = .40
SCIENCE_FINAL_EXAM_PERCENTAGE = .40
SCIENCE_RESEARCH_PERCENTAGE = .20

print("WELCOME TO THE GRADES CALCULATION PROGRAM")

# What type of student are we calculating?

response = input("\nEnter student type (1=English, 2=Math, 3=Science) :")

if response =="":
  print("You must select a Student Type")
  exit()

if int(response) < 1 or int(response) > 3 :
  print(response, "is not a valid Student Type")
  exit()

#Student type is valid, now let's calculate the grade

#1 is an English Student

if response =="1":
  midterm=int(input("\nEnter the Midterm Grade: "))
  final_exam_grade =  int(input("Enter the Final Examination Grade: "))
```

```python
research = int(input("Enter the Research Grade: "))
presentation = int(input("Enter the Presentation Grade: "))
final_numeric_grade = \
 (midterm * ENGLISH_MIDTERM_PERCENTAGE) + \
 (final_exam_grade * ENGLISH_FINAL_EXAM_PERCENTAGE) + \
 (research * ENGLISH_RESEARCH_PERCENTAGE) + \
 (presentation * ENGLISH_PRESENTATION_PERCENTAGE)
if final_numeric_grade >= 93 :
  final_letter_grade = "A"
elif final_numeric_grade >= 85 and final_numeric_grade < 93 :
  final_letter_grade = "B"
elif final_numeric_grade >= 78 and final_numeric_grade < 85 :
  final_letter_grade = "C"
elif final_numeric_grade >= 70 and final_numeric_grade < 78 :
  final_letter_grade = "D"
elif final_numeric_grade < 70 :
  final_letter_grade = "F"
print("\n*** ENGLISH STUDENT ***\n")
print("Midterm grade is : ", midterm)
print("Final Exam grade is : ", final_exam_grade)
print("Research grade is : ", research)
print("Presentation grade is: ", presentation)
print("\nFinal Numeric Grade is: ", final_numeric_grade)
print("Final Letter Grade is: ", final_letter_grade)
# 2 is a Math Student

if response == "2":
  midterm=int(input("\nEnter the Midterm Grade: "))
  final_exam_grade =  int(input("Enter the Final Examination Grade: "))
  final_numeric_grade = \
   (midterm * MATH_MIDTERM_PERCENTAGE) + \
   (final_exam_grade * MATH_FINAL_EXAM_PERCENTAGE)
  if final_numeric_grade >= 90 :
    final_letter_grade = "A"
  elif final_numeric_grade >= 83 and final_numeric_grade < 90 :
    final_letter_grade = "B"
  elif final_numeric_grade >= 76 and final_numeric_grade < 83 :
    final_letter_grade = "C"
  elif final_numeric_grade >= 65 and final_numeric_grade < 76 :
    final_letter_grade = "D"
  elif final_numeric_grade < 65 :
    final_letter_grade = "F'
  print("\n*** MATH STUDENT ***\n")
  print("Midterm grade is : ", midterm)
  print("Final Exam grade is : ", final_exam_grade)
  print("\nFinal Numeric Grade is: ", final_numeric_grade)
  print("Final Letter Grade is: ", final_letter_grade)
# 3 is a Science Student

if response == "3":
  midterm=int(input("\nEnter the Midterm Grade: "))
  final_exam_grade =  int(input("Enter the Final Examination Grade: "))
  research = int(input("Enter the Research Grade: "))
  final_numeric_grade = \
   (midterm * SCIENCE_MIDTERM_PERCENTAGE) + \
   (final_exam_grade * SCIENCE_FINAL_EXAM_PERCENTAGE) + \
   (research * SCIENCE_RESEARCH_PERCENTAGE)
```

```
if final_numeric_grade >= 90 :
    final_letter_grade = "A"
elif final_numeric_grade >= 80 and final_numeric_grade < 90 :
    final_letter_grade = "B"
elif final_numeric_grade >= 70 and final_numeric_grade < 80 :
    final_letter_grade = "C"
elif final_numeric_grade >= 60 and final_numeric_grade < 70 :
    final_letter_grade = "D"
elif final_numeric_grade < 60 :
    final_letter_grade = "F"
print("\n*** SCIENCE STUDENT ***\n")
print("Midterm grade is : ",  midterm)
print("Final Exam grade is : ",  final_exam_grade)
print("Research grade is : ",  research)
print("\nFinal Numeric Grade is: ",  final_numeric_grade)
print("Final Letter Grade is: ",  final_letter_grade)

print("\nTHANKS FOR USING THE GRADES CALCULATION PROGRAM!")
```

3. Save your source file as <u>Grades.py</u> in the \PythonFiles\Grades folder (select File | Save As from Notepad's menu bar). Be sure to save your source file with the filename extension py.

4. Execute your program and test it thoroughly. See what happens if you immediately hit the ENTER key without making a selection for the student type. What happens if you indicate a student type not equal to 1, 2 or 3, such as 4? What happens if you enter the letter 'a' instead of the number 1, 2 or 3?

5. Indicate that you wish to calculate the grade for an **English** student. Enter **70** for the midterm grade, **80** for the final examination grade, **90** for the research grade, and **100** for the presentation grade. A final numeric grade of **84.5** should be displayed with a letter grade of **C**.

6. Execute your program again. Indicate that you wish to calculate the grade for a **Math** student. Enter **70** for the midterm grade and **80** for the final examination grade. A final numeric grade of **75** should be displayed with a letter grade of **D**.

7. Execute your program again. Indicate that you wish to calculate the grade for a **Science** student. Enter **70** for the midterm grade, **80** for the final examination grade, and **90** for the research grade. A final numeric grade of **78** should be displayed with a letter grade of **C**.

Discussion

Completing this exercise took the class nearly 40 minutes to complete. It was very tedious to type, and the indentation of the If statements caused problems for some of my students. Ultimately, though, all of my students completed the exercise, and had a working Grades Calculation Program.

"This exercise was a lot of fun to code," Rhonda said, "but although I was able to complete it, I must confess I'm not absolutely sure about everything that's going on here."

"I suspect you're not the only one who feels that way, Rhonda," I said. "There's a great deal of code in this exercise, and it includes a Python function we haven't discussed in class yet. As we always do, let's examine the program one step at a time, beginning with the creation of our variables and Pseudo Constants at the top of the program. Some of these Pseudo Constants (the ones belonging to the English student) appeared in last week's version of the Grades Calculation program, and some (the ones belonging to the Math and Science students) are new to this version. Last week we calculated the grade for only the English student. In this version of the program, we're calculating the grades for Math and Science students also, so we also need to create Pseudo Constants for the component grade pieces for those student types. Remember, constants don't actually exist in Python, but by convention, we can simulate them by naming variables in all uppercase letters."

"Remind me again what these Pseudo Constants represent?" Blaine asked.

"The Pseudo Constants," I said, "have values equal to the relative percentage of the component grade for each one of the three student types we'll be calculating. If in the future we need to change the percentage of any one of the component grade pieces, all we need to do is change the value of the correct Pseudo Constant. Naming them in all CAPS makes them very easy to find in our program also."

```
ENGLISH_MIDTERM_PERCENTAGE = .25
ENGLISH_FINAL_EXAM_PERCENTAGE = .25
ENGLISH_RESEARCH_PERCENTAGE = .30
ENGLISH_PRESENTATION_PERCENTAGE = .20
MATH_MIDTERM_PERCENTAGE = .50
MATH_FINAL_EXAM_PERCENTAGE = .50
SCIENCE_MIDTERM_PERCENTAGE = .40
SCIENCE_FINAL_EXAM_PERCENTAGE = .40
SCIENCE_RESEARCH_PERCENTAGE = .20
```

"In the previous version of our program," I said, "we followed up the Pseudo Constant declarations by assigning values to variables in order to hard-code the grades for an English Student. We no longer need to hard code the grades since we'll be prompting for that information, and assigning those values to variables, within the If Statement blocks a little later on."

I paused before continuing.

"Following the creation of the Pseudo Constants," I said, "this line of code displays a Welcome message in the Python Console..."

```
print("WELCOME TO THE GRADES CALCULATION PROGRAM")
```

"...This line of code is a comment. As our programs get more complex, using comments to explain what is going on is a great idea."

```
# What type of student are we calculating?
```

"Now," I said, "we ask the user what type of student grade they wish to calculate. This is a crucial piece of information for our program. Rather than rely on the user to type in the type of student, we make things a little easier on them (and ourselves) by instead prompting the user to enter a number equating to the Student type—1 for an English student, 2 for a Math student, and 3 for a Science student."

"That's clever," Linda said. "That eliminates the possibility that the user will type the student type incorrectly, or enter a value for which we aren't checking."

"Exactly Linda," I answered. "We use the **input()** function to prompt for the number 1, 2 or 3, and then assign their answer to the *response* variable. Remember, even though the user is entering a number, the *response* variable is created as a String Data Type. "

```
response = input("\nEnter student type (1=English, 2=Math, 3=Science) :")
```

"I was wondering why we were asking for numbers," Peter said. "Tell me again: Why not just have the user type English, Math or Science?"

"We could have done that, Peter," I said, "but it's best to avoid requiring the user to do much typing when they interact with our program. Even if they manage to type the word English correctly, will you require that the E in English be capitalized? Suppose they spell English in all upper case letters? Or all lower case letters? In general, prompting the user for long strings will lead to typing errors, and typing errors cause program problems. If the user must type, and sometimes it's unavoidable, then minimize their typing by having them choose from preselected values, which is what we're doing here by having them enter a single number—1, 2, or 3—instead of typing out the words English, Math, or Science."

> **NOTE: Developing a Windows like interface in your Python program can eliminate typing almost entirely, and is something we'll explore in my next book (and University course), Developing Graphical User Interface (Window) programs with Python**

"This next section of code," I said, "determines whether the user has pressed the ENTER key without telling us the type of student for whom they wish to calculate a grade. We display a message to the user in the Python Console and immediately end the program by executing a function we haven't seen before, the **exit()** function. The **exit()** function immediately ends our program---something we need to do here since we don't have the information required to calculate a student grade. Without the Student type, we can't prompt for the appropriate component grade pieces, and because of the Falling Rock behavior of Python code, we must bypass the remaining lines of code in the program."

```
if response =="":
  print("You must select a Student Type")
  exit()
```

"Using the **exit()** function," I said, "is frowned upon by many in the Python User Community, and next week, after we learn about Loop processing, it will no longer be required, and we'll remove it from our Grades Program entirely."

I paused before continuing.

"By the way," I said, "most Python functions, such as **print()**, **input()**, and **int()** to name a few, are included in the <u>Default Namespace</u> of our Python program. The Default Namespace is where built-in Python functions are stored, and are readily accessible to our programs when we write and execute them. The **exit()** function is <u>usually</u> included in the Default Namespace of our Python program, but not always included."

"Why is that?" Steve asked.

"Python runs on a variety of devices and platforms," I said, "For instance, here at the University, we're running Python on a Windows PC. Python also runs on Apple Devices (iMacs, iBooks, iPhones, iPads) Linux Devices, Android Phones, and Microwave ovens, just to name a few. Some of those devices---particularly those without a great deal of memory---may have fewer Python functions included in their Default Namespace. One of the functions typically <u>excluded</u> is the **exit()** function. Trying to execute a function that is not included in the Default Namespace results in a Python syntax error."

"Does that mean we can't use the **exit()** function?" Blaine asked.

"Not at all," I said, "the **exit()** function is included in the Python <u>sys</u> module which is located in a folder included in the Python Device installation. . We just need to explicitly include the sys module in our program's own Namespace by using the import statement, like this…"

```
import sys
```

"Because of that," I said, "we then need to code the **exit()** function to include the name of the sys module, like this."

```
sys.exit()
```

> **NOTE: Python purists avoid coding an exit() function wherever possible. If you insist upon using it, include the sys module in your program's namespace by using the import statement.**

"To emphasize," I said, "you can always code the **exit()** function, but in some cases, you may need to use an import statement to tell Python where to find it. If you, you will need to code it as **sys.exit()**. But, as I said earlier, starting next week, we won't be using the **exit()** function anyway."

"It would be great," Ward said, "if instead of just ending the program here we could redisplay the prompt for the student type. It seems abrupt to just end the program the way we did."

"I totally agree, Ward," I said, "and that's what we'll be doing after we learn about the Python Loop Structure next week. For now though, we will just gracefully end the program using the **exit()** function."

I paused before discussing the remainder of the program.

"Provided the user hasn't immediately pressed the ENTER key," I said, "we now know that the user has entered a response of some kind. Now it's time to determine if their entry is the number 1, 2 or 3? As you should have noticed when completing the exercise, if the user enters a letter here instead of a number, the Python Interpreter will display a syntax error and immediately end the program. This is called an Unhandled Exception---we didn't write code to deal with this, Python did this on its own. Handling this condition, where the user enters a letter instead of a number, is something we will learn about in Week 8, when we learn about Exception Handling."

> **NOTE: If, while testing your program, you entered the letter 'a' instead of an Integer, the Python Interpreter will display a Syntax error and immediately end the execution of the program. This is something we will correct in Week 8, when we learn about Exception Handling.**

"If we've gotten this far in the program," I said, "let's assume that the user has entered a valid Integer. We now need to determine whether their entry is outside the range of valid numbers for which we are looking---in other words, if their entry is less than 1 or greater than 3---that means that their entry is not 1, 2, or 3. Using an If Statement, with the Python Or Operator, this section of code allows us to determine whether the number entered is outside the range of numbers for which we're checking."

```python
if int(response) < 1 or int(response) > 3 :
  print(response, "is not a valid Student Type")
  exit()
```

"If the number entered is either less than 1 or greater than 3 (the < operator means less than, and the > operator means greater than), we display a message to the user indicating that they have entered an invalid student type, and we end the program by executing the **exit()** function."

"Now we're in business!" Kathy said. "If the number entered isn't less than 1 and isn't greater than 3, then it must be 1, 2, or 3."

"You hit the nail right on the head, Kathy," I said. "If our program has gotten this far, we now know that the number the user has entered is a 1, 2, or 3, and that allows us to use a series of If statements to deal with each one of those cases, each of which equate to a different student type. First up, we check if the user has entered the number 1."

```python
#Student type is valid, now let's calculate the grade
#1 is an English Student
if response =="1":
```

" Notice," I said, "that the number 1 is sandwiched within quotation marks---since the *response* variable is a String Data Type. If the *response* variable is equal to 1, that means that the user wants to calculate the final numeric grade for an English student. With the Imperative Statements following the colon, we prompt the user, via the **input()** function, for the <u>four</u> component grades pieces that comprise the English student's final grade—midterm, final exam, research, and presentation grades. The user's response to each prompt is assigned to the *midterm*, f*inal_exam_grade*, *research*, and *presentation* variables. Because the return value of the **input()** function is a String Data type, and because we'll be performing Mathematical calculations using these component grade pieces, we need to use the **int()** function to convert or cast the String value returned from the **input()** function to an Integer prior to assigning it to these variables."

```python
midterm=int(input("\nEnter the Midterm Grade: "))
final_exam_grade =  int(input("Enter the Final Examination Grade: "))
research = int(input("Enter the Research Grade: "))
presentation = int(input("Enter the Presentation Grade: "))
```

"That's easy for you to say," Rhonda said, smiling. "But I think I follow you!"

"The next five lines of code," I said, "calculate the final numeric grade for an English student. This is essentially the same calculation we performed with last week's version of the program, although the names of the Pseudo Constants have changed. We multiply the value entered by the user for each component grade piece by the appropriate Pseudo Constant and then sum them to arrive at the final numeric grade which we then assign to the *final_numeric_grade* variable."

```
final_numeric_grade = \
(midterm * ENGLISH_MIDTERM_PERCENTAGE) + \
(final_exam_grade * ENGLISH_FINAL_EXAM_PERCENTAGE) + \
(research * ENGLISH_RESEARCH_PERCENTAGE) + \
(presentation * ENGLISH_PRESENTATION_PERCENTAGE)
```

"With the final numeric grade calculated," I said, "we then use a series of If...Elif statements to determine the final letter grade for the English Student. (This is an example of a Nested If Statement.) Using the greater than or equal to Operator, we can easily determine if the final_numeric_grade is <u>greater than or equal to</u> 93. If it is, the English student has earned an 'A' for the course..."

```
if final_numeric_grade >= 93 :
  final_letter_grade = "A"
```

"If the value of *final_numeric_grade* is not greater than or equal to 93," I said, "it must be less than 93. We then use the Python And Operator to determine if the value of *final_numeric_grade* is greater than or equal to 85 <u>and</u> also less than 93. In other words, between 85 and 92.9999. If it is, the English student has earned a 'B' for the course."

```
elif final_numeric_grade >= 85 and final_numeric_grade < 93 :
  final_letter_grade = "B"
```

"The Elif Clauses continue to evaluate the value of **final_numeric_grade** for a grade of 'C' or 'D' and finally 'F'..."

```
elif final_numeric_grade >= 78 and final_numeric_grade < 85 :
  final_letter_grade = "C"
elif final_numeric_grade >= 70 and final_numeric_grade < 78 :
  final_letter_grade = "D"
elif final_numeric_grade < 70 :
  final_letter_grade = "F"
```

"Notice," I said, "that *final_letter_grade* is a new String variable for this version of the program. We're using it to store the student's calculated letter grade."

> **NOTE: Sharp eyed readers might notice that we could write the last two lines of the If statement in a single line that reads 'else final_letter_grade= "F", much like in the retirement practice exercise earlier. You'd be correct in doing so, but I prefer this version of the program because it's more explicit and easier for beginner students to see and understand.**

"With the final numeric grade and the final letter grade calculated," I said, "it's time to display the results of the Grade Calculation in the Python Console. First, we display the type of student for whom we have calculated a grade."

```
print("\n*** ENGLISH STUDENT ***\n")
```

"...This is followed by the display of the component grade pieces, followed by the final numeric grade, and the final letter grade."

```
print("Midterm grade is : ", midterm)
print("Final Exam grade is : ", final_exam_grade)
print("Research grade is : ", research)
print("Presentation grade is: ", presentation)
print("\nFinal Numeric Grade is: ", final_numeric_grade)
print("Final Letter Grade is: ", final_letter_grade)
```

"All of this code," I said, "including the final six **print()** functions, is part of a very large If statement. All of this code will only execute if the Student Type entered is equal to 1. This is why indentation, and paying careful attention to it, is so crucial in a Python program."

Everyone seemed OK so far.

"Let's take a look at the If statement for the Math student," I continued. "It's similar to the If statement for the English student, with the difference being that Math Students do not have Research and Presentation grade components, and the component percentages for a Math Student are different from an English Student."

```
# 2 is a Math Student

if response == "2":
  midterm=int(input("\nEnter the Midterm Grade: "))
  final_exam_grade =  int(input("Enter the Final Examination Grade: "))
  final_numeric_grade = \
  (midterm * MATH_MIDTERM_PERCENTAGE) + \
  (final_exam_grade * MATH_FINAL_EXAM_PERCENTAGE)
  if final_numeric_grade >= 90 :
    final_letter_grade = "A"
  elif final_numeric_grade >= 83 and final_numeric_grade < 90 :
    final_letter_grade = "B"
  elif final_numeric_grade >= 76 and final_numeric_grade < 83 :
    final_letter_grade = "C"
  elif final_numeric_grade >= 65 and final_numeric_grade < 76 :
    final_letter_grade = "D"
  elif final_numeric_grade < 65 :
    final_letter_grade = "F"
  print("\n*** MATH STUDENT ***\n")
  print("Midterm grade is : ",  midterm)
  print("Final Exam grade is : ",  final_exam_grade)
  print("\nFinal Numeric Grade is: ",  final_numeric_grade)
  print("Final Letter Grade is: ",  final_letter_grade)
```

"Finally," I said, "here's the If statement for a Science student. Once again, it's similar to the code for the English Student, except that Science Students do not have a Presentation grade component, and the component percentages for a Science Student are different from an English Student."

```
# 3 is a Science Student

if response == "3":
  midterm=int(input("\nEnter the Midterm Grade: "))
  final_exam_grade =  int(input("Enter the Final Examination Grade: "))
  research = int(input("Enter the Research Grade: "))
  final_numeric_grade = \
  (midterm * SCIENCE_MIDTERM_PERCENTAGE) + \
  (final_exam_grade * SCIENCE_FINAL_EXAM_PERCENTAGE) + \
  (research * SCIENCE_RESEARCH_PERCENTAGE)
  if final_numeric_grade >= 90 :
    final_letter_grade = "A"
  elif final_numeric_grade >= 80 and final_numeric_grade < 90 :
    final_letter_grade = "B"
  elif final_numeric_grade >= 70 and final_numeric_grade < 80 :
    final_letter_grade = "C"
  elif final_numeric_grade >= 60 and final_numeric_grade < 70 :
    final_letter_grade = "D"
  elif final_numeric_grade < 60 :
    final_letter_grade = "F"
  print("\n*** SCIENCE STUDENT ***\n")
  print("Midterm grade is : ",  midterm)
  print("Final Exam grade is : ",  final_exam_grade)
  print("Research grade is : ",  research)
  print("\nFinal Numeric Grade is: ",  final_numeric_grade)
  print("Final Letter Grade is: ",  final_letter_grade)
```

"...Finally, this line of code thanks the user for using our program. It comes after the execution of the three If statements."

```python
print("THANKS FOR USING THE GRADES CALCULATION PROGRAM!")
```

"Wow," Ward said. "This is starting to be a lot of fun."

"Are we going to be able to handle the calculation of more than one grade?" Linda asked.

"We'll be able to do that after next week's class on Loops," I answered.

"I just realized," Dave said, "that we don't have any validation for the component grade values that the user enters. Is that a problem?"

"You're right Dave," I said. "this version of the program has no validation for the individual grade pieces that the user enters. For instance, there's nothing to prevent the user from entering a negative number as a midterm grade. This is something we will take care of in the future, but not until our Python Classes and Objects course. For now, we're going to rely on the user to enter a valid grade."

I waited for more questions, but there were none. I had expected my students to be pretty worn out at this point, but instead they were still experimenting with the programs they had written, genuinely proud of their work.

I dismissed class for the day, telling them that next week they would learn about a very powerful feature of Python programming, the Python Loop Structure.

Summary

In this chapter, we examined Selection Structures and how they are used to vary the way a program behaves based on conditions found at runtime.

Remember the falling rock?

You saw how you can use Selection Structures to change this behavior, starting with the plain If statement.

If a test expression evaluates to True, then the Imperative Statement or statements following the If statement are executed.

The If statement can be enhanced to include instructions for a False condition as well , using the Else clause, and even further with the Elif clause.

We also came to a significant point in our Grades Calculation project: a working prototype. This is a very important stage in the development process, because all the key working parts of the program are now in place.

From this point on, we'll be adding functionality to the Grades Calculation program turn our prototype into a professional-level Python program.

Chapter 5---Loops

In this chapter, we'll discuss the two types of Loop Structures available in Python, For Loops and While Loops. You'll learn that Loop processing can give your programs tremendous power.

Why Loops?

"Last week I mentioned the term Loop several times," I said, as I began our fifth class. "In today's class, we'll examine the two types of Python Loop Structures, the For Loop and the While Loop."

"What exactly is a Loop" Kathy wanted to know.

"A Loop," I said, "allows the programmer to repeatedly execute a line or lines of code without having to type those lines of code over and over again in the source file. A Loop---and the code within in---can be executed a definite number of times, called a Definite Loop. The code within a Loop can also be executed an indefinite number of times, the exact number of times based upon some a test condition. This is called an Indefinite Loop."

"So a Loop can save you a great deal of typing?" Bob asked.

"That's right Bob," I said, "But that's not the only benefit of a Loop. The Loop, and its ability to repeatedly execute code, gives your program enormous power, the power to perform many types of operations that would otherwise be impossible. Loops truly allow you (and your programs) to take advantage of the tremendous speed of modern computers."

"Can you give us an example where a Loop does that?" Mary asked.

"Here's one Mary," I said. " A common real world programming problem is one in which a computer program needs to read data, in the form of electronic records, from an external disk file or database. This is similar to using the input() function to seek data from a user, but a million times faster because there's no interaction with the user required. All that's required is that your program specifies the location and name of the file, open it, and start reading records. Reading a single electronic record from a disk file or database isn't difficult. The challenge is that you do not know, ahead of time, how many electronic records your program will need to read."

"I'm not sure I understand what you mean?" Peter asked.

"A file or database may contain ten electronic records, or it may contain five billion," I said. "When you write your Python program, you don't know how many times to execute the line of code that Python uses to read a single record. This is where the Loop Structure comes in handy. Using a Loop Structure, with just a few lines of code, we can write the code necessary to read every electronic record in a file or database, regardless of the number of records. In essence, we tell Python to execute the line of code to read the records until we have reached the end of the file.."

"Like reading a book," Dave said. "We read pages until the last page is encountered."

"Excellent Dave," I said. "That's exactly right."

"Will we be reading records from a file or database in this course?" Chuck asked.

"Not in this course Chuck," I said, "We'll do that in our Advanced Topics Python course. But even so, we can still find great uses the Python Loop Structure. As we saw last week, our Grades Calculation Program right now can calculate the grade for just a single student. By implementing a Loop Structure in the Grades Calculation Program, we can calculate student grades until the user tells us there are no more to calculate."

"Fantastic!," I heard Lou say.

"Are there different types of Loops in Python?" Dave asked. "I know there are in other languages such as Java and Visual Basic."

"Python has two types of Loop Structures, Dave," I replied. "One Loop Structure, the For Loop, executes one or more statements in a section of code, called the body of the Loop, a definite number of times. For that reason I call the For Loop a Definite Loop. The other Python Loop Structure, called the While Loop, is less definite in nature, which means that the number of times the body of the While Loop is executed is usually undetermined until the program runs. The number of times that the body of a While Loop is executed is dependent upon the evaluation of a test expression at runtime. Getting back to the example of reading electronic records from an external disk file or database, we do not know ahead of time how many records are in that file—the file could even be empty! This type of programming problem is a perfect application for the use of an Indefinite type of loop, the <u>While Loop</u>."

I suggested that we begin our examination of Python Loops with the For Loop.

The For Loop

I started by displaying the syntax for the For Loop Structure on my classroom projector…

```
for variable in sequence:
  execute the body of the For Loop containing a statement or statements
```

"This syntax," I said, "is the official syntax for the For Loop."

"What's a sequence?" Blaine asked.

"Good question Blaine," I said. "A Python sequence is essentially a List. The For Loop is very full featured, and can work with many types of sequences or Lists. In the examples we'll see today, we'll be working with Lists of numbers generated by the **range()** function. Two weeks from now, we'll use the For Loop to work with Lists that we create ourselves. Here's the syntax for the For Loop to work with a List of numbers created from the **range()** function."

```
for iteration variable in range(start,stop,step):
  execute the body of the For Loop containing a statement or statements
```

"We'll talk about the details of generating a List of numbers using the **range()** function in a minute," I said, "For now, you may prefer this translation, which I think is a little easier to deal with

```
for iteration variable in range(iterate through each of the numbers in the range):
  execute the body of the For Loop containing a statement or statements
```

"I like to say a picture is worth a thousand words. Here's the code for a Python For Loop in a program designed to display the numbers from 1 to 10 in the Python Console," I said, as I displayed this code on the classroom projector.

```
# Example5_1.py

for counter in range (1,11,1) :
 print (counter)
print("\nAll done!")
```

"The For Loop," I continued, "begins with the keyword <u>for</u>, in lowercase letters, followed by the name of a variable of our choosing. This variable is called the Iteration Variable, because the For Loop will 'iterate' or move through the items in a List of numbers generated by the **range()** function. For now, we'll use the variable name *counter* as the name of the Iteration Variable, although it can be anything we want. The Iteration Variable is followed by the word <u>in</u> followed by the **range()** function, with the parameters for the **range()** function included within parentheses---<u>start</u> value, <u>stop</u> value, <u>step</u> value. This line of code ends with a colon, much like the If statement that we examined last week, which should now trigger in your mind the need to indent the following line or lines of code that comprise the 'body' of the For Loop."

> **NOTE: You may have noticed that in Python, a colon indicates the need to indent the following line or lines of code. We've seen it with the If Statement, and here again with the For Loop.**

"You said the **range()** function generates a List of numbers?" Barbara asked, obviously puzzled. "I don't remember you mentioning that before."

"You're right Barbara," I said, "We haven't seen ranges before. The **range()** function is a Python function that generates a Python List object. This List object contains a List of Integers, or whole numbers. The Integers contained in the List are determined by the <u>start</u>, <u>stop</u> and <u>step</u> parameters of the **range()** function."

"What is the List used for?" Steve asked.

"The List of Integers," I said, "provides a value for the Iteration Variable *counter* within the body of Loop. Each time the body of the For Loop is executed, the List provides a new value for *counter*. The <u>first time</u> the body of the For Loop is executed, the value of *counter* is 1. The <u>second time</u>, 2, the <u>third time</u> 3 and so on until the end of the List is reached. This will allow us to easily display the List of Integers in the Python Console."

"What happens when we reach the end of the List?" Mary asked.

"When the For Loop recognizes that there are no more numbers in the List," I said, "the For Loop stops executing."

The Range() Function

"I'm still not sure about this notion of the range?" Rhonda said. "How does it create a List of numbers?"

"The **range()** function," I said, "creates a List of numbers using the first argument as the start value, the second argument as the stop value, and the third argument as the step value. Therefore, this statement..."

```
range (1,11,1)
```

"...will create a List of numbers starting at 1, followed by 2, 3, 4, etc up to, **but not including** 11."

"So just the numbers 1 through 10?" Dave said.

"That's right Dave," I answered. "Just like this..."

```
1
2
3
4
5
6
7
8
9
10
```

"...Notice that 11 is **NOT** included in the List."

"This List of numbers looks like a column in a spreadsheet," Barbara said.

> NOTE: In Python, the range() function generates a Python List. A List (as we will see in Chapter 7) contains items. In the case of the List created by the range() function, this List contains items that are Integers, or whole numbers.

"That's a good way to look at it," I answered. "By the way, the default value for the step value argument in the **range()** function is 1, so many Python programmers don't even bother to code it, like this. This syntax also creates a List containing the numbers from 1 through 10."

```
range (1,11)
```

"So now that we have a List of numbers" Rhonda asked "you said we can use that List with the For Loop?"

"That's right Rhonda," I said, "Using the Python For statement, we execute the body of the For Loop and 'iterate' through each item in the List, using its value for the value of the *counter* variable, then printing the value of the *counter* variable. We do this for each Integer item in the List, one by one."

```
for counter in range (1,11,1) :
    print (counter)
```

Is there anything special about the *counter* variable," Kate asked, "or is it just an ordinary variable?"

"*counter* is an ordinary variable," I said. "What may look strange to you is the way it appears in the first line of the For Loop, following the word 'for'. The variable that we specify here, sometimes called the Iteration Variable, is just an ordinary variable."

"We can name the Iteration Variable anything we want?" Bob asked.

"That's right Bob," I said. "Some Python programmers don't bother naming their Iteration Variables with meaningful names, since the variable is used only within the For Loop. Instead they prefer to name them with single-letter names, such as i, j, k or x, or begin them with the underscore character. Variable names like this are referred to as throwaway variable names because they are used once and never referenced anywhere else in the program. I prefer to give my Iteration Variables more meaningful names, so here I've named ours *counter*. One more thing. When we use a For Loop to iterate through a List that we create ourselves (as we'll do in Chapter 7,) typically the Iteration Variable will be the singular form of the name of the List. For instance, two weeks from now we'll create a list called *grades* and the Iteration Variable will be named *grade*."

Again I waited for questions.

"I mentioned it once already," I said, "but it bears repeating. Don't forget the colon at the end of the line containing the word For. This is similar to the colon we see at the end of the line containing an If statement. It tells Python to execute the indented line, or lines of code, for as long as there is an item in the List generated by the **range()** function remaining to be processed."

> **NOTE: In a For Loop, the statement or statements following the colon MUST be indented in order to be understood by Python**

"Based on what you're telling us," Peter asked, "does that mean this Loop will execute ten times?"

"That's right Peter" I said. "Because the **range()** function generated a List object containing the Integers 1 through 10, the line of code following the For statement will be executed 10 times---each time with a different value for the *counter* variable. Finally, when each item in the List generated by the range() function has been processed, the For Loop is complete, and the line of code following the body of the Loop will be executed. In this case, that is the display of "All done!" in the Python Console."

```
print("\nAll done!")
```

> **NOTE: You may remember that the \n character in the print() function tells Python to generate a new line before displaying "All done!"**

"Why did you include that line of code?" Steve asked. "Is it necessary."

"When introducing Loops to my students," I said, "I always like to include a line of code to let us know that Loop processing is complete."

I then saved the program as Example5_1.py, and ran it for the class. The following screenshot was displayed on the classroom projector:

"The numbers 1 through 10 are displayed (almost) at the speed of light," I said.

"That's pretty amazing," Kate said, "considering the fact that we displayed those 10 numbers in the Python Console with so little code."

"That's what I mean about the power of loops" I said. "As Kate pointed out, with just 2 lines of code we quickly and easily displayed 10 numbers. Furthermore, we could have displayed 1 through 1 million if we had chosen to---again with just 2 lines of code, by changing the parameters of the **range()** function. This illustrates how computers are excellent at performing repetitive tasks---and doing them very quickly."

"I think I understand everything that's going on," Blaine said, "except what eventually makes the For Loop end"

"The indented statement or statements following the 'for' line," I said, "comprise the body of the For Loop, and are executed once for each item in the List. As the For Loop processes, Python keeps track of each item in the List, and as we 'iterate' through each one, Python marks that item as complete. When Python has processed the last item in the List, the For Loop is notified that there are no more items in the List to process, and the For Loop ends."

That explanation seemed to satisfy Blaine.

"Can we see an example," Joe asked, "of a loop that executes more than one statement?"

"No problem Joe," I said. I displayed this code on the classroom projector.

```
# Example5_2.py

for counter in range (1,11,1) :
 print ("I love Python!")
 print (counter)
print("\nAll done!")
```

"This Loop has two lines of code in the body of the For Loop," I said. "Notice that both lines are indented. That's how Python determines what is within the body of the For Loop."

I then saved the program as Example5_2.py and ran it for the class. The following screenshot was displayed on the classroom projector.

```
C:\Windows\system32\cmd.exe

C:\PythonFiles\Examples>Example5_2
I love Python!
1
I love Python!
2
I love Python!
3
I love Python!
4
I love Python!
5
I love Python!
6
I love Python!
7
I love Python!
8
I love Python!
9
I love Python!
10

All done!

C:\PythonFiles\Examples>_
```

"As you can see," I said, "both statements in the body of the For Loop--the display of 'I love Python!' and the value of the variable counter---were both executed by Python. A total of 10 times each."

No one seemed to be having any problems following what was going on.

Variations on the For Loop Theme

"I didn't mention this earlier," I said, "but regarding the three arguments for the **range()** function, start, stop and step. Of the three arguments, only the second, the stop value, is required. Both start and step have default values that have presumed values if they aren't supplied. For the first argument, the default start value is 0, and for the third argument, the default step value is +1."

"So start and step are optional arguments?" Dave asked.

"That's right Dave," I said. "Some function arguments are defined with default values that in essence make the arguments optional. If they aren't supplied, Python supplies the value from the defined default value. That's the case with the range() function. In Week 6 of our class we'll create functions of our own called user-defined functions, and we'll learn how to specify optional function arguments using a default value."

"Why is the default for the start value 0?" Rhonda asked. "Shouldn't it be 1?"

"In the world of computers, Rhonda," I answered "zero is almost always the first number in any List. That's the case here. Here's an example of the range() function with just a single argument passed to it. See if you can guess what it might do."

```
# Example5_3.py
for counter in range (5) :
  print (counter)
print("\nAll done!")
```

"I'm guessing that the numbers 1 through 5 will be displayed in the Python Console," Rhonda volunteered.

"You're close Rhonda," I said, "You're correct that 5 numbers will be displayed in the Python Console, but the numbers displayed will be 0 through 4, not 1 through 5."

"I'm confused," Rhonda said.

"The number 5 in this example is the stop argument," I said. "The start value is presumed to be 0 and the step value is presumed to be +1. Think of this line of code…"

```
for counter in range (5) :
```

"…as this…"

```
for counter in range (0,5,1) :
```

I then saved the program as Example5_3.py and ran it for the class. The following screen shot was displayed on the classroom projector.

"Why wasn't the number 5 displayed?" Bob asked. "The stop value is 5."

"The List Object created from the **range()** function contains the numbers 0 through 4," I said. "The numbers beginning from the start value, up to but not including the stop value, are included in the List."

I paused before continuing.

"I don't recommend not providing all three arguments to the **range()** function," I said. "I prefer my code to be as explicit as possible. That makes it easier for me, and other programmers, to read and understand my code later. However, I must tell you that many experienced programmers prefer to make their code as 'lean' as they can by coding the fewest possible characters possible. Again, this isn't something I recommend."

"Are there any other variations possible with the For Loop?" Dave asked.

"What does Dave mean?" Rhonda asked.

"I think Rhonda, that Dave thinks displaying the numbers 1 through 10 is pretty boring," I said, seeing the two of them laughing together. "And it's a great question. By varying the three arguments of the **range()** function we can achieve some very interesting results. For instance, if instead of specifying +1 for the step value of the range, if we specify -1, the Integer items in the List will decrease in value by 1. This can enable our Loop to display our numbers backwards. And don't forget. The first Integer item in our List doesn't have to be 1. We can start with any number. In fact, the start value doesn't even have to be a positive number."

I explained that it's possible to simulate some interesting real-world situations if you get a little creative with the **range()** function arguments with a For Loop.

"Last week, we worked with some fictitious restaurants in New York City," I said. "Today, let's pretend we've expanded into the hotel business, and we own a Manhattan hotel in which the room floors are numbered from 2 to 20. Let's further pretend that the hotel has three elevators: Elevator #1 stops at all the floors of the hotel, Elevator #2 stops only at the even-numbered floors, and Elevator #3 stops only at the odd-numbered floors. For our first practice exercise of the day, let's write a Python program that displays, in the Python Console, the floor numbers at which Elevator 1 stops."

I then distributed this exercise for the class to complete.

Practice 5-1 Your first For Loop

In this exercise, you'll code a For Loop to display the floors at which Elevator #1 stops.
1. Using Notepad (or Notepad++), enter the following code.

```
# Practice5_1.py

print ("Elevator #1 stops at these floors...")

for floor in range (2,21,1) :
 print (floor)
print("\nAll done!")
```

2. Save your source file as Practice5_1.py in the \PythonFiles\Practice folder (select File | Save As from Notepad's menu bar). Be sure to save your source file with the filename extension py.
3. Execute your program. You should see the following output in the Python Console:

Discussion

There were only 5 lines of code, including 1 that was a comment. My students were careful to indent the line of code following the colon on the line of code containing the word 'for'.

One student, however, had forgotten to indent the line of code that displays "All done!" in the Python Console. As a result, "All done!" was displayed after each number in the Python Console in his version of the program.

"I notice that the variable name *room* seems to have taken the place of the *counter* variable?" Steve asked, referring to the absence of the *counter* variable in the code we had just written.

"Yes Steve," I said, "I decided to use a more meaningful name for the Iteration Variable in this program. Instead of using *counter*, I decided to use *floor*, which is what the Integer items in the range represent---floor numbers."

"Speaking of floors," Kathy asked, "Where's the first floor of the hotel? Why did the display start with the number 2?"

"Remember, Kathy, the floors are numbered from 2 to 20," I said. "That's why the **range()** function had a start value of 2."

"That's right," Kathy said. "I entirely forgot."

"This was a good exercise to get your feet wet with the For Loop," I said. "Now let's get to work on a more challenging problem—Elevator #2. Elevator #2 is the elevator that stops only at the even-numbered floors of the hotel. Does anyone have any ideas on how we should code a For Loop to display only the even-numbered floors of the hotel?"

After a few seconds, Dave suggested that we code a For Loop, initializing our **range()** function to 2 by setting the <u>start</u> value to 2, and most importantly, that we specify 2 as the <u>step</u> value of our range() function."

"Excellent suggestions, Dave," I said, as I distributed this exercise for the class to complete.

Practice 5-2 Modifying the For Loop to Handle Even-numbered Floors

In this exercise, you'll code a For Loop to display the even-numbered floors of the hotel at which Elevator #2 stops.
1. Using Notepad (or Notepad++), enter the following code.

```
# Practice5_2.py

print ("Elevator #2 stops at these floors...")

for floor in range (2,21,2) :
 print (floor)
print("\nAll done!")
```

2. Save your source file as <u>Practice5_2.py</u> in the \PythonFiles\Practice folder (select File | Save As from Notepad's menu bar). Be sure to save your source file with the filename extension py.
3. Execute your program. You should see the following output in the Python Console:

```
C:\Windows\system32\cmd.exe

C:\PythonFiles\Practice>Practice5_2
Elevator #2 stops at these floors...
2
4
6
8
10
12
14
16
18
20

All done!

C:\PythonFiles\Practice>
```

Discussion

No one had any problems completing the exercise, although it was obvious that my students were paying careful attention to indentation.

"As you can see," I said, "Dave's suggestions were right on the mark! By setting the **range()** function to start at 2 and increment by 2, we were able to display the even numbered floors from 2 through 20. Of course, to include 20 we needed to specify a stop value of 21. Remember, the stop value is not included when the Integer List of items is created."

"That was very clever of Dave," Rhonda said, obviously impressed. "I don't think I ever would have thought of incrementing the Iteration Variable by 2."

"Solving programming problems like this requires some imagination," I told Rhonda. "The more programs you write, the easier it will be to think of little tricks like this to solve these types of problems. Of course, you can always search the Internet if you need to. There aren't that many problems that haven't already been solved."

"I've been thinking about Elevator #3," Lou said, "the one that stops only at odd-numbered floors in the hotel. I know what you said about using your imagination to solve this problem, but so far, I haven't been able to get it to work. How should we code that loop?"

Linda suggested that a For Loop with a **range()** function initialized to 3, and once again incrementing the value of the Iteration Variable by 2 would be the way to go. Like this.

```
for floor in range (3,21,2):
```

"Of course," Lou said, "that was my mistake! I kept initializing the value of the range to 2 instead of 3."

"Shouldn't the initial value of the range be 1?" Rhonda asked.

"Don't forget, Rhonda," I said, "the hotel has no first floor. The first odd-numbered floor is 3, so initializing the **range()** function to 3 takes care of that. Why don't we code this problem as a practice exercise now?"

I then distributed this exercise for the class to complete.

Practice 5-3 Modifying the For Loop to Handle Odd-Numbered Floors

In this exercise, you'll code a For Loop to display the odd-numbered floors at which Elevator #3 stops.
1. Using Notepad (or Notepad++), enter the following code.

```
# Practice5_3.py

print ("Elevator #3 stops at these floors...")

for floor in range (3,21,2) :
 print (floor)
print("\nAll done!")
```

2. Save your source file as Practice5_3.py in the \PythonFiles\Practice folder (select File | Save As from Notepad's menu bar). Be sure to save your source file with the filename extension py.
3. Execute your program. You should see the following output in the Python Console:

Discussion

By this point, no one seemed to be having any major problems with our elevator exercises.

"Here are the odd numbered floors from 1 through 19 displayed," I said.

"Shouldn't the **range()** function have specified a <u>stop</u> value of 20 since the odd numbered floors stop at 19?" Kate asked

"That's a good question Kate," I said, as I displayed her suggestion on the classroom projector.

```
for floor in range (3,20,2) :
```

"Those parameters would have achieved the same results as the ones we used in the exercise," I said. "This illustrates what I frequently say---there's more than one way to paint a picture, and frequently more than one way to code a problem and still achieve the correct result. That's the case here. Of course, which alternative is the more 'correct' alternative is something we could debate for some time. Either way, no one could say we are wrong."

"I've got to say that writing these programs has been great fun," Joe said. "I figured there had to be some way to do this kind of thing. Now that we've done it, it seems pretty easy. I can't wait to use Python Loops to do something practical back at the work place."

"You'll get a chance to work with Loops in the Grades Calculation Program," I said. "But we still have some more work to do before we get to that point."

I continued by pointing out that all three of the **range()** function arguments (start, stop, and step) could be expressed not only as Numerical Literals (that is, numbers), as we had just done, but also as variables or constants.

I then distributed this exercise to demonstrate my point.

Practice 5-4 Modifying the For Loop to Work with Variables and Constants

In this exercise, you'll code a For Loop to display the floors at which Elevator #1 stops--but instead of using Numeric literals for the start, stop and step arguments of the **range()** function you'll use Pseudo Constant (variables).

1. Using Notepad (or Notepad++), enter the following code.

```
# Practice5_4.py

BOTTOM_FLOOR = 2
TOP_FLOOR = 21

print ("Elevator #1 stops at these floors...")

for floor in range (BOTTOM_FLOOR,TOP_FLOOR) :
 print (floor)
print("\nAll done!")
```

2. Save your source file as <u>Practice5_4.py</u> in the \PythonFiles\Practice folder (select File | Save As from Notepad's menu bar). Be sure to save your source file with the filename extension py.
3. Execute your program. You should see the following output in the Python Console:

Discussion

No one had any problems completing the exercise----working with the elevator practice exercise was now very familiar to the---and the changes required to the program were minimal.

"Does everyone see what we're doing here?" I asked.

"It looks like we've done two new things here," Linda said. "First, we created a variable called BOTTOM_FLOOR for the <u>start</u> argument of the **range()** Function. We also created a variable called *TOP_FLOOR* to use as the <u>stop</u> argument in the **range()** function."

"That's an excellent analysis, Linda," I said. "Using a variable (or a variable named in Capital Letters to denote it's a Pseudo Constant) like this doesn't impact the behavior of the For Loop, but it does make your code a lot more readable."

"I'll agree with that," Blaine said. "The variable names *BOTTOM_FLOOR* and *TOP_FLOOR* make it easy to visualize what's going on in the For Loop."

"How about this for a challenge?" I said. "Suppose we want to display the floors of our hotel backwards?"

"Can we do that with a For Loop" Rhonda asked.

"It can be done," I said, "but I have to warn you, we will have to be very careful the way we code the **range()** function. I don't ordinarily like to do this, but I'm going to ask you to complete an exercise that I know won't work. It will illustrate the problems that can occur when you set up the **range()** function to work with the For Loop."

I then distributed this exercise for the class to complete:

Practice 5-5 Displaying the Floors Backwards--but there's a problem

In this exercise, you'll code a For Loop to display the floors of the hotel--backwards. But beware---this code has a bug in it and won't behave properly.
1. Using Notepad (or Notepad++), enter the following code.

```
# Practice5_5.py

print ("Floors in the hotel, listed backwards are...")

for floor in range (20,1) :
 print (floor)
print("\nAll done!")
```

2. Save your source file as <u>Practice5_5.py</u> in the \PythonFiles\Practice folder (select File | Save As from Notepad's menu bar). Be sure to save your source file with the filename extension py.
3. Execute your program. You should see the following output in the Python Console:

Discussion

I noticed one or two students exchange knowing glances as they completed the exercise---I think they knew immediately what the problem with the program was.

"Nothing happened," Rhonda said. "No floor numbers were displayed--did the For Loop execute at all?"

Rhonda was correct. Nothing seemed to happen. Of course, the program did something, just not what we had hoped.

"You're right Rhonda," I said, "although technically speaking, the For Loop did execute. It executed the first line, executed the **range()** function to create a List of Integers, but then decided not to execute the body of the For Loop. Can anyone tell me why?"

Dave spoke up immediately. .

"I think I know what the problem is," Dave said. "We intended to have the For Loop count backwards, and display the floors from 20 to 2. Specifying a <u>start</u> value of 20, with a <u>stop</u> value of 1 intuitively sounds like we're counting backwards, but not to Python. We never specified a <u>step</u> argument for the **range()** function. Because of that, by default, we accepted a step value of +1. Python immediately knew that it could not reach the stop value of 1 by adding 1 to 20. Only a negative step value could do that. For that reason, I think Python just stopped, and created an empty List. Am I close?"

"Excellent, Dave," I said. "I don't think I could have said it any better. The only way to count backwards in a For Loop is to create a List with a step value that is a negative number."

"So how can we make this loop count backwards?" Rhonda asked. "What do we need to change?"

"Just change the step value," I said. "The correct syntax should read…"

```
for floor in range (20,1,-1) :
```

"By the way," I continued, "this is the reason I cautioned you earlier about accepting default values in the **range()** function. Let's work on the correct version now."

I then distributed this exercise for the class to complete.

Practice 5-6 Displaying the Floors Backwards Correctly

In this exercise, you'll correct the code from Practice 5-5, so that the floors of our hotel are correctly displayed backwards.

1. Using Notepad (or Notepad++), enter the following code.

```
# Practice5_6.py

print ("Floors in the hotel, listed backwards are...")

for floor in range (20,1,-1) :
 print (floor)

print("\nAll done!")
```

2. Save your source file as <u>Practice5_6.py</u> in the \PythonFiles\Practice folder (select File | Save As from Notepad's menu bar). Be sure to save your source file with the filename extension py.

3. Execute your program. You should see the following output in the Python Console:

Discussion

"That's better," I heard Mary say. "Now the floors are properly displayed---backwards."

"That's right Mary," I said, "All we needed to do was to execute the **range()** function with a negative step value. This creates a List of Integers in reverse order."

"Can we specify a negative number besides -1?" Joe asked.

"Yes, we can specify any negative value we want," I said. "We could write a program that displays the odd numbered floors in the hotel by specifying a step value of -2."

There were no more questions, so I suggested we take a 15-minute break.

"When we return from our break," I said, "we'll look at the indefinite kind of Python Loop I mentioned earlier---the While Loop."

The While Loop

Resuming after break, I began a discussion of what I call the Python Indefinite loops—the While Loop.

"I'm not sure if this will be true for our class," I said, "but most beginners find the While Loop a bit more confusing than the For Loop."

I paused before continuing.

"There are some differences," I said, "but there are also some similarities between the two. Just like the For Loop, the While Loop Structure permits us to execute a section of code---the body of the While Loop. The main difference is that when a While Loop ends is not nearly as definite as it is for a For Loop."

"How so?" Mary asked.

"With the For Loop," I continued, "you saw that we can specify a definite endpoint for our Loop by the way we specify our arguments for the **range()** function. The **range()** function creates a List Object containing Integers. When the For Loop has processed (or iterated through) each Integer in the List, it ends. However, with a While Loop, there is no built-in List through which the For Loop can iterate. Instead, with a While Loop, we need to specify a test expression that is evaluated before the body of the While Loop is executed. If the test expression evaluates to True, then the body of the While Loop is executed. If the test expression evaluates to False, the While Loop ends. Once the body of the While Loop is executed, the text expression is evaluated again. If the test expression evaluates to True, the body of the While Loop is executed. This process of evaluating the test expression continues until the test expression evaluates to False---or, could theoretically continue forever if the test expression never evaluates to False."

"An Endless Loop," Dave said.

"That's right Dave," I agreed, "an Endless Loop. An Endless Loop, one that continues to execute forever, is something that can't happen with a For Loop, but is easy to code with a While Loop. Shortly we'll intentionally create an Endless Loop so that you can learn to avoid them."

> Note: There were times early in my career when I intentionally created Endless Loops. In modern programming languages, they're almost always a mistake.

"Are these test expressions similar to the test expressions in an If statement?" Ward asked.

"They're exactly like them Ward," I said, "You can specify any test expression that evaluates to a True or False value."

"Can we see an example of the While Loop?" Mary asked.

"Good idea Mary," I said. "I think that will clear up any confusion you may have."

I then displayed the 'official' syntax for the While Loop on the classroom projector:

```
while (test expression is True):
   execute the body of the While Loop containing a statement or statements
```

"You're right," Joe said, "this does look a little confusing to me."

"I think this example program will help," I said. "This is the While Loop equivalent of the For Loop program I wrote as Example5_1 for you earlier this morning. Like Example5_1, this program will display the numbers 1 through 10 in the Python Console."

```
# Example5_4
counter = 1
while counter < 11:
  print (counter)
  counter += 1
print("\nAll Done!")
```

I then saved the program as Example5_4.py and ran it for the class. The following screenshot was displayed on the classroom projector:

"The results of both programs are identical," I said. "The numbers 1 through 10 are displayed in the Python Console."

"I notice that the For Loop version has 3 lines of code," Joe said, "whereas the While Loop version has 5 lines of code, not including comments and blank lines."

"That's right Joe," I said, "there's a bit more work involved in setting up the While Loop. The extra work is with what I call the Loop-Control Variable---initializing it and then updating it so that we don't end up with an Endless Loop."

"Loop-Control Variable?" Blaine asked. "Did you mean to say Iteration Variable. Isn't *counter* an Iteration Variable?"

"It's a matter of semantics," I said, "but I prefer the term Loop-Control Variable here instead of Iteration Variable. With the For Loop, the Iteration Variable is created for us as a byproduct of executing the **range()** function and producing a sequence or List of numbers, and the execution of the For Loop stops when there are no more items in the List to process. With the While Loop, the programmer has more responsibility to ensure that the While Loop executes the way we want it to and also that it will eventually stop. First, we have to initialize the value of the Loop Control Variable prior to executing the While Loop. Secondly, we have to test the value of the Loop Control Variable as part of the While statement. Finally, within the body of the While Loop, we have to modify the value of the Loop Control Variable in some way so that the Test Expression eventually evaluates to False, and the While Loop finally ends. I think calling the variable the Loop-Control Variable more properly describes what it does."

That explanation seemed to satisfy Blaine.

"That first line of code in the program?" Mary asked. "Is that where we initialize the Loop-Control Variable to 1."

```
counter = 1
```

"That's right Mary," I said, "It's just a simple assignment statement. "Because we want to be sure that the first number displayed is 1, we initialize *counter* to 1."

I paused before continuing to make sure I hadn't lost anyone.

"The Loop-Control Variable plays a vital role in determining how many times the body of the While Loop will be executed," I said, "and in providing a way for the While Loop to end. As is the case with the For Loop and its Iteration Variable, we can name the Loop-Control Variable anything we want."

"I noticed you initialized the *counter* variable outside the While Loop," Kate noted.

"That's right Kate," I said, "If we initialized the *counter* variable within the body of the While Loop, we would create an Endless Loop, and display an endless series of '1's' in the Python Console. I should warn you that just about every beginner programmer winds up coding an Endless Loop by accident. I know I did back in 1973 when I wrote my first Fortran program. Our Computer Operator wasn't happy with the ream of paper on which I printed 'Go Hawks'. By the way, I haven't unintentionally coded an Endless Loop since."

> **NOTE: The Fortran assignment called for us to print 'Go Hawks' (our college mascot) ten times. My failure to increment the Loop-Control Variable resulted in my program running indefinitely.**

I paused a moment before continuing.

"Let's take a look at the first line of the While Loop," I said. "Notice that it begins with the word 'while' followed by a test expression, followed by a colon."

```
while counter < 11:
```

"Is that the test expression?" Ward asked. "counter less than 11?"

"That's right Ward," I answered. "This test expression checks if the value of the Loop-Control Variable has reached our desired stop value, which is 11. I think it was you Ward who earlier asked if this test expression is like the test expression in an If statement. I think you can see that it is. Here, Python is basically asking this question: Is the value of the *counter* variable less than 11. If it is, that means counter is some number less than 11 (0 through 10, or even a negative number.) If so, the result of the test expression is True, and the body of the While Loop---the indented statement or statements following the colon are executed. If the result of the expression is False, the While Loop ends, and the statement following the last line in the body of the While Loop is executed."

> **NOTE: In a While Loop, the statement or statements following the colon MUST be indented in order to be understood by Python**

"Let's take a look at the body of our While Loop," I said, "It contains 2 statements. The first you are familiar with--- the **print()** function used to display the value of the *counter* variable in the Python Console."

```
print (counter)
```

"The second statement might look a bit confusing," I said, "It's the line of code that we use to increment the value of the *counter* variable by 1. With the For Loop, this is done for us automatically. With the While Loop, the responsibility for doing so is all ours. Here we use the Augmented Addition Operator to increment the value of the *counter* variable."

```
counter += 1
```

"We learned about the Augmented Addition Operator two weeks ago," I said. "Read it this way. Take the current value of *counter*---which is 1—and add 1 to it, giving us a result of 2. Now assign that result—2- to the value of *counter*. The new value of *counter* is now 2."

I paused before continuing.

"So each time the body of the While Loop executes," I said, "the value of the *counter* variable (our Loop-Control Variable) is incremented, until finally, after the **print()** function displays the number 10 in the Python Console, the value of *counter* is set to 11. As a result, the next time the test expression is tested, the value 11 is not less than or equal to 11 (it's equal to it), so the test expression evaluates to False, the body of the While Loop is bypassed, and the line following it is executed, which displays "All done!" in the Python Console."

```
print ("\nAll done!)
```

I gave my students a chance to digest what I had just said.

"So," Steve said after a minute, "the initialization of the *counter* variable is equivalent to what we did when we initialized the **range()** function to 1."

"That's beautifully stated Steve," I replied. "Likewise, the line of code where we add 1 to the current value of the *counter* variable is equivalent to setting the step argument of the **range()** function to a positive 1."

"And the test expression within the While Loop," Barbara said, "is equivalent to the stop value of the **range()** function being 11."

"Perfect Barbara," I said. "Because of their ability to handle indefinite kinds of conditions, While Loops are considered to be more powerful than For Loops. But, as you can see, we have a little more work to do to set up a While Loop to perform the way we intend it to work. If we forget to initialize the Loop-Control Variable, or to test it properly, or to provide a way for the While Loop to end, we will have some problems."

"Do Loop-Control Variables have to be numbers that can be incremented?" Joe asked.

"Not at all," I said. "Loop-Control Variables can also be Strings. In fact, the Loop-Control Variable for the Grades Calculation Program will be a String, the answer to the question, 'Do you have grades to calculate?'"

"Is it possible to code a While Loop whose body never executes, not even once?"

"Absolutely right," I said,

"Why would you want to do that?" Bob asked.

"Suppose you code a While Loop to read records from a disk file?" I suggested. "The body of the While Loop would contain instructions to read the records and do some processing. Suppose, however, that the file you anticipating reading is empty? Or the file isn't there at all ? In both cases, you wouldn't want to execute the body of the While Loop, not even once. If you did, you would attempt to read a record from a file with no records or a non-existent file. Both attempts would generate an error and cause your program to terminate. That's why the composition of the first line of the While Loop is so important. We need to create a test expression that is worded in such a way that the While Loop can terminate without the body of the While Loop executing even once."

At this point, there were no other questions, and I suggested that we complete an exercise to give everyone a chance to work with the While Loop.

Practice 5-7 Use the While Loop to Display the Floors of our Hotel

In this exercise, you'll code a While Loop to display the floors of our hotel in the Python Console.
1. Using Notepad (or Notepad++), enter the following code.

```
# Practice5_7.py

floor = 2

print ("The floors in the hotel are...")

while floor < 21:
  print (floor)
  floor += 1
print ("\nAll done!")
```

2. Save your source file as Practice5_7.py in the \PythonFiles\Practice folder (select File | Save As from Notepad's menu bar). Be sure to save your source file with the filename extension py.
3. Execute your program. You should see the following output in the Python Console: If for some reason your program won't stop executing---i.e. you have coded an Endless Loop---press the Control+C combination and your program will end.

```
C:\Windows\system32\cmd.exe

C:\PythonFiles\Practice>Practice5_7
The floors in the hotel are...
2
3
4
5
6
7
8
9
10
11
12
13
14
15
16
17
18
19
20

All done!

C:\PythonFiles\Practice>
```

Discussion

Unlike some of the previous exercises that my students completed with no problems, not unexpectedly, there were some problems completing this one. Most of the problems were Endless Loops. The combination of Control+C was a lifesaver to stop their programs from running indefinitely!

"As you can see," I said, starting the discussion of the exercise after getting everyone on track "we've successfully displayed the floors of our hotel, using a While Loop. I think once you get used to the format, you'll find that working with the While Loop—and, specifically, coding the test expression—won't be too difficult at all. Remember, though, as I said earlier, we need to do a little more work with the While Loop than with the For Loop. Specifically, because the While Loop does not utilize the **range()** function, there is no built-in start value. We need to take care of that ourselves, before the While Loop Structure, with this line of code which sets the initial value of the Loop -Control Variable. In this case, because the first floor in the hotel is 2, we initialize the Loop-Control Variable to 2. Notice how we have selected a meaningful variable name for the Loop-Control Variable..."

```
floor = 2
```

"As we did with our For Loop," I said, "we use the **print()** function to display a heading for what we are displaying in the Python Console..."

```
print ("The floors in the hotel are...")
```

"Here's the While Loop," I said, "and its test expression, in which we tell Python to execute the body of the While Loop as long as the value of the *floor* variable is less than 21. Notice the colon following the test expression, and the indented statement on the next line which is the first line of the body of our loop that displays the value of the *floor* variable in the Python Console:"

```
while floor < 21:
  print (floor)
```

I reminded the class that several students had made mistakes in this area of the exercise. One had spelled 'while' with an upper case 'W'. One student had forgotten the colon after the test expression, and more than one had forgotten to indent the code in the body of the While Loop.

"This next line of code," I said "the last line of code in the body of the While Loop may be the most important line of code in this program. Because the While Loop does not have a built-in increment argument of its own via the **range()** function, it's imperative that we take care of incrementing the Loop-Control Variable. We do that with this line of code using the Augmented Addition Operator."

```
floor += 1
```

I reminded my students how important it is that this line of code be included within the body of the While Loop.

"If it's not indented," I said, "this line of code is <u>not</u> part of the body of the While Loop, it's the first line of code <u>after</u> the body of the While Loop and we will be executed after the While Loop finishes. The problem is that without the incrementation of the Loop-Control Variable, the While Loop will never end. It will be an Endless Loop."

"I confess," Rhonda said, "that's exactly what I did. I indented the **print()** function, but didn't indent the incrementation of the floor variable. Thank goodness for Control + C!"

"Finally," I said, "we use the **print()** function to display a message in the Python Console saying we are all done displaying the floors in the hotel."

```
print ("\nAll done!")
```

"Notice," I said, "that this line of code indicating that the program has ended <u>isn't indented</u>. If you had indented it, it would have been executed each time the body of the While Loop was executed."

"I confess," Blaine said, smiling "I did exactly that. I can guarantee I'll be more careful in the future!"

"I always say we learn most from our mistakes," I said, "that's why I asked you to code the 'All done!' statement on our Loop programs, so you would get a flavor for how we write code beyond the body of the While Loop."

"Why didn't the number 21 display in the Python Console?" Joe asked. "Why did it stop at 20?"

"Our test expression told Python to execute the body of the While Loop while the value of the *floor* variable is less than 21." I said. "As soon as the value of *floor* is equal to 21, the test expression returns a False value, and the While Loop <u>immediately</u> terminates. Execution of the program then resumes with the line of code following the body of the While Loop."

"How important is it to increment the value of *floor* <u>inside</u> the While Loop?" Kathy asked.

"Vitally important," I said. "Beginners typically make two kinds of mistakes with the While Loop. Either they initialize the value of their Loop-Control Variable (the variable they evaluate within their test expression) <u>inside</u> the body of loop, or they increment the value of that Loop-Control Variable <u>outside</u> the While Loop. Either of these mistakes will generate an Endless Loop."

"And that will be a problem?" Rhonda said, "I know from experience!"

"That's right Rhonda," I said. "If we initialize the value of *floor* within the body of the While Loop, then each time the body of the While Loop is executed, the value of *floor* is reset to 2. This means that the While Loop will never terminate since the value of *floor* never increments and the test expression always evaluates to True. Similarly, if we increment the value of *floor* outside the body of the While Loop, the value of *floor* will always be 2, and once again, the test expression will always evaluate to True...."

```
while floor < 21:
```

"In both cases," I said, "we wind up with an Endless Loop."

"I confess!," Mary said, "that's exactly what I did the first time I attempted the exercise. I coded the initialization of the *floor* variable within the body of the While Loop and my display showed---and continued to show---all 2's. I didn't know how to stop the program, but then I re-read your instructions about pressing Control+C simultaneously, and the program stopped."

"I had a similar problem," Kate said. "I coded the incrementation of the *floor* variable within the body of the While Loop---or so I thought. As it turned out I didn't indent it. Python thought it was outside the body of the While Loop, and the *floor* variable was never incremented. I also saw nothing but an endless series of 2's in the Python Console. I had to use Control+C to end the program, before I could fix it."

"Could we see an Endless Loop in action?" Blaine asked. Obviously, Blaine hadn't accidentally generated one.

"Good idea Blaine," I said. "Let's reproduce the mistake that Kate made when she didn't indent the line of code where the *floor* variable is incremented by 1. She expected this line of code to execute each time the body of the While Loop was executed, but the lack of indentation meant that it wouldn't be executed until after the While Loop was finished. The problem: since the value of the *floor* variable never changed, it was always 2, always less than 21 when the test expression was executed, and the value 2 was always displayed in the Python Console."

"That's a lot of always," Kate said, smiling, "I know from experience!"

"Here's the code with the mistake," I said, "Because of the indentation required by Python for the body of the While Loop, this is a very easy mistake to make. As I mentioned earlier today, I made a similar mistake in a Fortran class I took in 1973."

```python
# Example5_5.py
# Let's intentionally generate an Endless Loop

floor = 2

print ("The floors in the hotel are...")

while floor < 21:
  print (floor)
floor += 1          #This line is not indented. It's outside the body of the loop
print ("\nAll done!")
```

I then saved the program as Example5_5.py and ran it for the class. The following screen shot was displayed on the classroom projector---a series of scrolling 2's.

"Here's our Endless Loop, Blaine" I said, as a series of 2's was infinitely displayed in the Python Console. "As you can see, Python is continuing to display the number 2 in the Python Console, and it's scrolling endlessly. If we left the program running at the end of today's class, it would still running when we arrived in the Computer Lab next week."

"And you say that pressing the Control and the letter C together will end the program?", Mary asked.

"That's right," I said, "let's do that now."

I pressed **Control+C** simultaneously. The following screenshot was displayed on the classroom projector.

"Python is telling us that we interrupted the program via a KeyboardInterrupt," I said. "That's what pressing the Control Key and the letter C is---a keyboard interrupt. Python also displays the line of code it was executing when we interrupted the program, which is the line of code executing the **print()** function with the current value of the *floor* variable. In case you're wondering, Python counts the blank lines in our program when it displays the line number."

"You said earlier that While Loops have an indefinite nature," Linda said, "but this loop seems pretty definite to me. The numbers 2 through 20 will always be displayed in the Python Console. Can you give us an example of a While Loop that's indefinite?"

"I sure can," I said. "One type of indefinite loop would be one in which we interact with the user and ask them a question. Let's code a While Loop that continues to execute until the user tells it to stop."

I then distributed this exercise for the class to complete.

Practice 5-8 An Indefinite Version of the While Loop

In this exercise, you'll create a While Loop that displays consecutive numbers in the Python Console. It will be up to the user to choose how many numbers to display.
1. Using Notepad (or Notepad++), enter the following code.

```
# Practice5_8.py

counter = 1

loop_response = input("Should I start counting? ")

while loop_response.upper() == "YES":
    print (counter)
    counter += 1
    loop_response = input("Should I continue? ")
print("\nThanks for counting with me!")
```

2. Save your source file as <u>Practice5_8.py</u> in the \PythonFiles\Practice folder (select File | Save As from Notepad's menu bar). Be sure to save your source file with the filename extension py.
3. Execute your program. The program will ask you if you wish to start counting. Type **Yes** at the Python prompt, as shown here:

4. Now press the ENTER key. The number 1 should appear in the Python Console, and the program will then ask you if you wish to continue counting, as shown here:

5. Type **Yes** once again. Don't worry if you type Yes as YES. The program code will handle that. Here's what the screen will look like:

6. Press the ENTER key. The number 2 will then be displayed in the Python Console, and once again you'll be asked if you wish to continue counting. Numbers will continue to be displayed in the Python Console for as long as you type **Yes**.

7. Type **No** in answer to the prompt to continue counting and press the ENTER key (if you want you can also type your name. Anything other than the word Yes will end the program. A thank you message will be displayed in the Python Console, and the program will end with a friendly message, as shown here:

8. Execute your program again. The program will ask you if you wish to start counting. Type **No** at the Python prompt. What happens? The program will immediately end, after displaying a friendly thank you message.

Discussion

There was a fair amount of confusion and problems with this exercise, and it took us about 15 minutes to get through it.

The code in the exercise was tedious to type. In addition, not everyone in the class was as attentive as they needed to be as to how they typed the word **YES** in their Python code. This caused some problems when they first ran their programs.

"This program." I said, "is a good example of the Indefinite capabilities of the While Loop. Unlike Practice5_7, the exact number of times that this Loop executes is not known by the programmer ahead of time---it's determined by the user of the program. The programmer has no idea how many numbers the user might want to display in the

Python Console. That's the beauty of the While Loop. It gives us a way for a loop to run indefinitely but most importantly, still with a way for it to end. As soon as the test expression evaluates to False, the While Loop ends. Let's take a look at the code now. The first thing we did was to initialize a variable called *counter* equal to 1."

```
counter = 1
```

"But the counter *variable* is not the Loop-Control Variable in this program, is it?" Kate asked.

"That's a great observation Kate," I said, "In this program, the Loop-Control Variable is a String variable called *loop_response. counter* is a variable that we use to display numbers in the Python Console. *loop_response* is a variable to which we assign the answer to the prompt from the execution of the **input()** function. We have two **input()** prompts for the user. The first is before the While Loop is executed, and asks the user if he or she wishes to start counting, and the second is within the body of the While Loop and asks the user if they wish to continue counting. Here's the first **input()** function, where we display a message to the user asking them if they wish to start counting, and then store their response in the *loop_response* variable."

```
loop_response = input("Should I start counting? ")
```

"If the user immediately answers anything other than Yes," I said, "because of the While statement that follows this line of code, the While Loop will immediately end, and no numbers will be displayed in the Python Console."

Rhonda had a question.

"I guess I'm just a little confused as to why we're not using the *counter* variable as the Loop-Control Variable the way we did in the previous exercise," Rhonda said. "Is that because of the Indefinite nature of this program?"

"That's exactly right Rhonda," I said. "Our Loop will end when the user tells us so. Asking the user to provide Yes or No to a prompt via the **input()** function is the ideal way to set up a While Loop. In the previous exercise, we used the value of *counter* in the test expression to determine if the While Loop should end. This program is different in that we let the user's response to the questions 'Should I start counting?' and 'Should I continue?' determine when the While Loop ends. That's the function of the *loop_response* variable here, a variable whose value is determined by the user's typed entry. The variable *counter*, as it was in Practice 5-7, is still the number we display in the Python Console."

I paused before continuing.

"As I said a minute ago," I continued, "this next line of code is crucial, and no doubt you may find it confusing at first. Two things are being done here. First, whatever the user entered via the **input()** function in the previous line of code that is currently stored in the *loop_response* variable is converted to upper case and then overlaid in the *loop_response* variable. In other words, if 'Yes' is stored in the *loop_response* variable, it will be re-written as 'YES'. Secondly, the value of the *loop_response* variable is then compared to the value 'YES'---in all capitals. A True or False result from the test expression is then generated."

```
while loop_response.upper() == "YES":
```

I didn't suspect that my students were confused---I knew it. I could see it in their faces.

"What is **upper()**?" Linda asked. "I presume it's a function?"

"You're close Linda" I said. "**upper()** is a method of the Python String object, and no one would argue with you if you called it a function. As I mentioned last week, methods are nothing more than functions that belong to a Python object. In this case, the **upper()** method 'belongs' to the Python String object, and is designed to take the value of a String variable and return its uppercase equivalent. If we take the String value that the user enters via the **input()** function and store it in a String variable, such as *loop_response*, we can then use the **upper()** method to return its 'upper case' value as a return value. Like other String methods that we'll learn about in two weeks, the **upper()** method does not operate directly on a String variable. The value of the String variable is not updated in any way. We are dealing with the return value of the upper() method here. In order to use it, all we need to do is code the String variable name, put a period at the end of it, and then follow that name with the word **upper** and a pair of parentheses."

"So whatever the user enters is converted, as a return value, to all Capital letters?" Ward asked.

"That's right, Ward," I said. "Just remember, store the user's entry in a String variable first. If the user enters the String j-o-h-n, the **upper()** method would replace it with J-O-H-N."

> **NOTE:** It's possible to upper-case the user's response to the input() function without storing the entry in a String variable, but their response won't be stored for further processing.

"By the way, if this code confuses you a bit, we could have written the code this way..."

```
loop_response = loop_response.upper()
while loop_response == "YES":
```

"Instead of 1 line of code," I said, "it's now 2 lines. However, the single line of code we wrote is more compact, and in the Python world, that's the name of the game."

"But why are we doing this?" Kate asked.

"Upper casing the user's response makes checking for the word 'Yes' simpler," I said. "Were you aware that with a 3 letter response, there are 8 possible ways to spell the word 'Yes'?"

"What do you mean eight different ways?" asked Barbara.

"Each letter of the word 'yes' can be entered by the user in either upper or lowercase letters," I explained. "Although it's nice to believe that the user would enter 'YES' in all capital letters or 'Yes' if we asked them to type it that way, in reality, some users mix and match case as they're entering values into an input box or a text field. If you consider all the possible combinations of the word yes, you'll see that there are eight different ways of writing it."

```
YES    yES
YEs    yEs
YeS    yeS
Yes    yes
```

"Wow," Kathy said, "I didn't realize there were that many ways to spell Yes. I guess the larger the String, the more ways there are to enter it?"

"That's right Kathy," I replied. "With a 3 letter word, there are 8 possible combinations. With a 4 letter word, 16. With a 5 letter word 32."

> **NOTE: The formula to calculate the possible combinations is this: Raise 2 to the power of letters in the String. For a 3 letter word, 2 raised to the power of 3 is 8 (2x2x2). For a 4 letter word, 2 raised to the power of 4 is 16 (2x2x2x2). For a 5 letter word, 2 raised to the power of 5 is 32 (2x2x2x2x2). You get the idea.**

"If we 'convert' the user's response to all uppercase characters, " I said, "we only need to perform the comparison in our test expression to just one word, the word we are looking for in all capital letters. Looking for the word 'yes,' the alternative would be to write code using a series of Or Operations with Python line continuation characters (the backslash) that would look like this."

```
while loop_response == "YES" or loop_response == "YEs" \
or loop_response == "YeS" or loop_response == "Yes" \
or loop_response == "yES" or loop_response == "yEs" \
or loop_response == "yeS" or loop_response == "yes":
```

"I see what you mean now," Ward said. "That makes a great deal of sense, and it makes even more sense if we ask the user a question whose answer requires 13 characters!"

"That's right, Ward," I said. "A word of 13 characters can be entered 8,192 different ways by the user—that's a comparison I wouldn't want to code using a series of Or operators."

I paused a moment before continuing.

"Let's get back to our program" I said, "and take a look again at that first line of the While Loop, in which we tell Python to execute the body of the While Loop provided the variable *loop_response* is equal to the uppercase value YES."

```
while loop_response.upper() == "YES":
```

"OK, that's the benefit of having converted the user's response to uppercase letters," Rhonda said. "The light bulb just went on!"

"And it's possible that the body of the While Loop will not execute even once?" Blaine asked.

"That's right, Blaine," I said. "Because the test expression in a While Loop is evaluated at the top of the While Loop Structure, the body of the While Loop will be executed only if the test expression evaluates to True, something that can only happen if the user answers 'yes' to the question, Should I start counting? Provided the user answers 'yes' using any of the eight variations of 'yes,' this next indented line of code in the body of the While Loop will then display the value of the ***counter*** variable in the Python Console."

```
print (counter)
```

"And this line of code will increment the value of the ***counter*** variable."

```
counter += 1
```

"Incrementing the value of ***counter*** is important," I said, "but it's not as important as it was in Practice 5-7."

"How so?" Lou asked.

"Because ***counter*** is not the Loop-Control Variable here," I said, "The ***loop_response*** variable is. If we fail to increment the value of the ***counter*** variable, the While Loop can still end if the user answers anything other than 'yes' to the prompt, Should I continue?"

"So what would happen if we forget to increment the counter variable?" Mary asked.

"We would just continue to display the number 1 in the Python Console," I replied. "The responsibility for ending the While Loop lies with the user and their response that is stored in the ***loop_response*** variable. We need to provide a way, within the body of the While Loop, to permit the user to change update the ***loop_response*** variable. We do that by coding another **input()** function, this time asking the user if they want to continue counting."

```
loop_response = input("Should I continue? ")
```

"Do we need to 'upper case' the user's response to this prompt?" Peter asked.

"Good question Peter," I said. "The answer is no. Whatever the user enters into the ***loop_response*** variable via the **input()** function will be 'upper cased' as part of the test expression of the While Loop."

```
while loop_response.upper() == "YES":
```

"So the While Loop will continue until the user answers 'no' to the prompt, Should I continue?" Ward asked.

"Not exactly, Ward," I said. "The While Loop will continue to execute as long as the user types any of the eight variations of the word 'yes' in answer to the prompt, Should I continue? If the user types anything else---the word 'no', their name, the letter 'x'---then the test expression will evaluate to False, and the While Loop will end, at which time the line following the last line of the body of the While Loop will be executed. In this case, that line is the display of a message thanking the user for counting with us. The program then ends."

```
print("\nThanks for counting with me!")
```

"Remind me again," Rhonda said, "what is the \n used for?"

"It generates a blank line," I said, "followed by the thank you message. I think it makes our display a little neater."

Before moving on, I repeated my earlier assertion that one of the biggest mistakes beginners make with the While Loop is to forget to include code within the body of the While Loop that enables the While Loop to end.

"Because the test expression we set up is to compare the value of the ***loop_response*** variable to YES," I said, "if we forget to give the user the opportunity to change the value of that variable, we'll create an Endless Loop condition."

I had one more thing to point out.

"It's a minor thing," I said, "but I just to emphasize that it's possible for this While Loop to never execute the body of the While Loop, not even once. If the user immediately answers no (as we did in Step 8 at the end of our exercise,) the body of our Loop will never execute, and the first line of code following the body of the While Loop will be executed. In our case, the thank you message will be immediately displayed."

"Is there ever a case where you would want the While Loop to execute at least once?" Kate asked.

"That's a good question Kate," I answered, "In Practice5_8, if we had initialized the ***loop_response*** variable to 'YES' and chosen not to ask the user if he or she wanted to start counting, the While Loop would have executed once, displayed the number 1, and then asked the user if they wished to continue counting. In Practice5_8, it made sense to first ask the user if they wanted to start counting. However, there are programs we will write where we are certain that the body of the While Loop should execute at least once, and in those, we'll structure the While Loop so that it executes at least once. In fact, that's exactly what we'll be doing with the Grades Calculation Program in just a few minutes."

Break and Continue Statements in For and While Loops

"We've seen both kinds of Loops," Ward said, "The For and the While Loop. What else is left to cover?"

"Just one more topic," I said. "Although I don't do it too often, it is possible to alter the 'normal' flow of both the For Loop and the While Loop using either the **break** or **continue** commands."

"What do you mean?" Kathy asked. "Alter the normal flow."

"When either statement is executed in either a For or a While Loop," I said, "the remaining lines of code in the body of the While Loop are bypassed. The difference between the two statements is that with the **break** statement, execution of the program begins with the first line of code <u>after</u> the body of the Loop. With the **continue** statement, execution of the program begins with the first line of code within the body of the Loop."

"I see what you mean about altering the natural flow of the loop," Barbara said.

"So essentially," Dave said, "with the **break** statement, the loop immediately ends. With the **continue** statement, the remaining lines of code in the body of the loop are bypassed, but execution resumes with the first line of code within the body of the loop? It's like a re-loop command."

"I couldn't have said it better myself Dave," Rhonda said, smiling.

"I should tell you," I said, "that there are some Python experts who would argue that using the **break** or **continue** statements is never necessary, and that you can write more elegant code to achieve the same results. However, the break and continue statements are part of the Python programming language, and we'll be using the **continue** statement shortly when we modify the Grades Calculation Program."

"An example or two would be great here," Joe suggested. .

"I agree Joe," I said. "Let me show you two examples that illustrate how each of these statements work. We'll start with the **break** statement. Here's <u>Example5_3</u> which I wrote earlier. When we run it, we display the numbers 0 to 4 in the Python Console…"

```
# Example5_3.py

for counter in range (5) :
  print (counter)
print("\nAll done!")
```

"As an illustration of the how the <u>break</u> statement works," I said, "let's modify Example5_3 to use an If statement to determine if the value of the *counter* variable is equal 2. If it is, we'll use the <u>break</u> statement to bypass the remainder of the code in the body of the loop, and exit the For Loop. As a result, only the numbers 0 and 1 will be displayed in the Python Console…"

```
# Example5_6.py

for counter in range (5) :
  if counter==2:
    break
  print (counter)
print("\nAll done!")
```

I then saved the program as <u>Example5_6.py</u> and ran it for the class. The following screen shot was displayed on the classroom projector. The numbers 0 and 1 were displayed in the Python Console, along with the message 'All done!'

"Does everyone see what happened?" I asked. "When the value of the *counter* value reached 2 within the body of the For Loop, the if statement evaluated to True, executed the <u>break</u> statement, and the remainder of the code in the body of the For Loop was bypassed. The number 2 was never displayed in the Python Console, and the For Loop also ended, resulting in the message 'All Done!' being displayed in the Python Console."

"I see," Barbara said. "This is a quick way to end a loop if you encounter a condition that warrants it. Will this also work for a While Loop?"

"Yes it works with the While Loop also," I said. "Both the <u>break</u> statement that we've seen here, and the <u>continue</u> statement that we're about to see, work equally well with While Loops."

"Let's modify <u>Example5_3</u>," I said, "to use an If statement to determine if the value of the *counter* variable is equal to 2. If it is, we'll use the **continue** statement to bypass the remaining lines of the code in the body of the For Loop, but this time we'll resume execution of the For Loop with the first line of the For Loop. As a result, the numbers 0 and 1 will be displayed, followed by 3 and 4 in the Python Console…"

```
# Example5_7.py

for counter in range (5) :
  if counter==2:
    continue
  print (counter)
print("\nAll done!")
```

I then saved the program as <u>Example5_7.py</u> and ran it for the class. The following screen shot was displayed on the classroom projector. The numbers 0,1,3 and 4 were displayed in the Python Console, along with the message 'All done!"

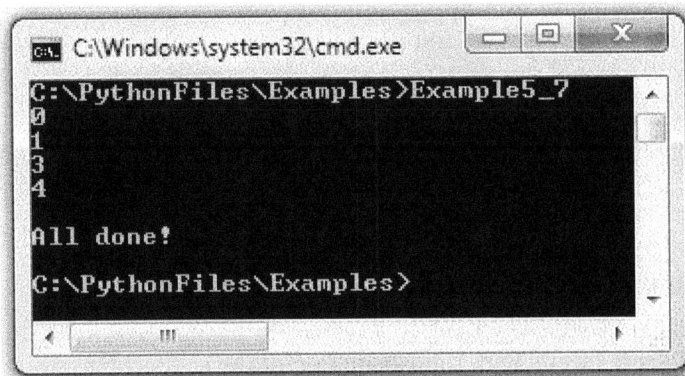

"Very cool," I heard Ward say. He was obviously impressed.

"Does everyone see what happened?" I asked. "When the value of the *counter* value reached 2 within the body of the For Loop, the if statement evaluated to True, executed the <u>continue</u> statement, and the remainder of the code in the body of the For Loop was bypassed. The number 2 was never displayed in the Python Console, but this time, instead of ending the For Loop, execution continue with the first line of code in the body of the For Loop. As a result, the numbers 0,1,3 and 4 were displayed in the Python Console."

> **NOTE: The break and continue statements work with both the For Loop and the While Loop Structures we have discussed in this chapter.**

I asked if there were any questions about the While Loops. No one had any questions. Either they were fine with what we had discussed, or they were in Loop fatigue. It can be a confusing subject.

I asked my students to take a 15-minute break.

"When we return from break," I said, "we'll be working on a modification to the Grades Calculation Program to include Loop processing."

Adding a Loop to the Grades Calculation Program

When my students returned from break, a couple of them immediately asked what we would be doing with the Grades Calculation Program that involved a loop.

"Right now," I said, "the Grades Calculation Program properly calculates the grade for an English, Math or Science student, but it only executes one grade calculation before ending."

"That's right," Blaine said. "One grade calculation, and the program ends. That's a definite issue, having to re-start the program to calculate another grade. By using loop processing, will the program be able to perform multiple calculations before it ends?"

"You hit the nail right on the head, Blaine" I said. "That's exactly what it will do."

"How will we do that?" Chuck asked. "Will the program need to change much?"

"Not much at all," I said. "We'll 'sandwich' the code that we wrote last week that performs the grade calculation within a Loop Structure so that we can calculate the grades for as many students as the user desires instead of just one. Can anyone suggest the kind of loop we should use to do that?"

"I suppose we could use a For Loop," Rhonda suggested, "but from what we've learned today, the For Loop is best when we know for certain the number of times we want the body of the While Loop to execute. That wouldn't be the case here because each time the program runs, there's likely to be a different number of grades to be calculated. For that reason, I think the While Loop is the way to go."

"Great thinking, Rhonda," I said, "and I agree, a While Loop makes the most sense to use here. We'll let the user determine when the While Loop ends."

"You say we can just sandwich the code we wrote last week within a loop?" Linda asked.

"That's basically it Linda," I said, "but we'll need to be extremely careful when we do so. Remember how 'picky' Python is about indenting the body of the While Loop? The code we wrote last week wasn't indented, so all of the code we wrote last week will need to be indented at least 2 spaces so that Python can identify it as being 'within' the body of a very large While Loop."

I saw some confusion in the eyes of my students, but I knew this would be cleared up when they started to code the modifications to the Grades Calculation Program. I then distributed this exercise for the class to complete.

Don't Forget: If typing these long examples and exercises isn't something you want to do, feel free to follow this link to find and download the completed solutions for all of the examples and exercises in the book. Just click on the Python book, then follow the link entitled exercises ☺

http://www.johnsmiley.com/main/books.htm

Practice 5-09 Add a loop to the Grades Calculation Program

In this exercise, you'll modify the Grades Calculation Program you last worked on last week by giving it the ability to calculate more than one student's grade before ending. Be very careful with the indentation of the code within the body of the While Loop, and also the If statements.

1. Using Notepad (or Notepad++), locate and open the Grades.py source file you worked on last week. (It should be in the \PythonFiles\Grades folder)
2. Modify your code so that it looks like this.

```python
# Grades.py
# After Chapter 5

ENGLISH_MIDTERM_PERCENTAGE = .25
ENGLISH_FINAL_EXAM_PERCENTAGE = .25
ENGLISH_RESEARCH_PERCENTAGE = .30
ENGLISH_PRESENTATION_PERCENTAGE = .20
MATH_MIDTERM_PERCENTAGE = .50
MATH_FINAL_EXAM_PERCENTAGE = .50
SCIENCE_MIDTERM_PERCENTAGE = .40
SCIENCE_FINAL_EXAM_PERCENTAGE = .40
SCIENCE_RESEARCH_PERCENTAGE = .20

print("WELCOME TO THE GRADES CALCULATION PROGRAM")

loop_response = "YES"

while loop_response.upper() == "YES":

    # What type of student are we calculating?
```

```
response = input("\nEnter student type (1=English, 2=Math, 3=Science ) ")

if response == "":
  print("You must select a Student Type")
  continue

if int(response) <1 or int(response) > 3 :
  print(response, "is not a valid Student Type")
  continue

#Student type is valid, now let's calculate the grade

#1 is an English Student

if response =="1":
  midterm=int(input("\nEnter the Midterm Grade: "))
  final_exam_grade =  int(input("Enter the Final Examination Grade: "))
  research = int(input("Enter the Research Grade: "))
  presentation = int(input("Enter the Presentation Grade: "))
  final_numeric_grade = \
   (midterm * ENGLISH_MIDTERM_PERCENTAGE) + \
   (final_exam_grade * ENGLISH_FINAL_EXAM_PERCENTAGE) + \
   (research * ENGLISH_RESEARCH_PERCENTAGE) + \
   (presentation * ENGLISH_PRESENTATION_PERCENTAGE)
  if final_numeric_grade >= 93 :
    final_letter_grade = "A"
  elif final_numeric_grade >= 85 and final_numeric_grade < 93 :
    final_letter_grade = "B"
  elif final_numeric_grade >= 78 and final_numeric_grade < 85 :
    final_letter_grade = "C"
  elif final_numeric_grade >= 70 and final_numeric_grade < 78 :
   final_letter_grade = "D"
  elif final_numeric_grade < 70 :
    final_letter_grade = "F"
  print ("\n*** ENGLISH STUDENT ***\n")
  print("Midterm grade is : ",midterm)
  print("Final Exam grade is : ",final_exam_grade)
  print("Research grade is : ",research)
  print("Presentation grade is: ",presentation)
  print("\nFinal Numeric Grade is: ",final_numeric_grade)
  print("Final Letter Grade is: ",final_letter_grade)

# 2 is a Math Student

if response == "2":
  midterm=int(input("\nEnter the Midterm Grade: "))
  final_exam_grade =  int(input("Enter the Final Examination Grade: "))
  final_numeric_grade = \
   (midterm * MATH_MIDTERM_PERCENTAGE) + \
   (final_exam_grade * MATH_FINAL_EXAM_PERCENTAGE)
  if final_numeric_grade >= 90 :
    final_letter_grade = "A"
  elif final_numeric_grade >= 83 and final_numeric_grade < 90 :
    final_letter_grade = "B"
  elif final_numeric_grade >= 76 and final_numeric_grade < 83 :
   final_letter_grade = "C"
  elif final_numeric_grade >= 65 and final_numeric_grade < 76 :
   final_letter_grade = "D"
  elif final_numeric_grade < 65 :
    final_letter_grade = "F"
  print ("\n*** MATH STUDENT ***\n")
```

```
    print("Midterm grade is : ",midterm)
    print("Final Exam grade is : ",final_exam_grade)
    print("Research grade is : ",research)
    print("Presentation grade is: ",presentation)
    print("\nFinal Numeric Grade is: ",final_numeric_grade)
    print("Final Letter Grade is: ",final_letter_grade)

# 3 is a Science Student

if response == "3":
  midterm=int(input("\nEnter the Midterm Grade: "))
  final_exam_grade =  int(input("Enter the Final Examination Grade: "))
  research = int(input("Enter the Research Grade: "))
  final_numeric_grade = \
   (midterm * SCIENCE_MIDTERM_PERCENTAGE) + \
   (final_exam_grade * SCIENCE_FINAL_EXAM_PERCENTAGE) + \
   (research * SCIENCE_RESEARCH_PERCENTAGE)
  if final_numeric_grade >= 90 :
    final_letter_grade = "A"
  elif final_numeric_grade >= 80 and final_numeric_grade < 90 :
    final_letter_grade = "B"
  elif final_numeric_grade >= 70 and final_numeric_grade < 80 :
    final_letter_grade = "C"
  elif final_numeric_grade >= 60 and final_numeric_grade < 70 :
    final_letter_grade = "D"
  elif final_numeric_grade < 60 :
    final_letter_grade = "F"
  print ("\n*** SCIENCE STUDENT ***\n")
  print("Midterm grade is : ",midterm)
  print("Final Exam grade is : ",final_exam_grade)
  print("Research grade is : ",research)
  print("Presentation grade is: ",presentation)
  print("\nFinal Numeric Grade is: ",final_numeric_grade)
  print("Final Letter Grade is: ",final_letter_grade)

 loop_response = input("Do you have another grade to calculate? ")
print("\nTHANKS FOR USING THE GRADES CALCULATION PROGRAM!")
```

3. Save your source file as Grades.py in the \PythonFiles\Grades folder (select File | Save As from Notepad's menu bar). Be sure to save your source file with the filename extension py.

4. Execute your program and test it thoroughly. We need to verify that the looping behavior of the program is working correctly.

5. See what happens if you immediately hit the ENTER key without making a selection for the student type. What happens if you indicate a student type not equal to 1, 2 or 3, such as 4?

6. Indicate that you wish to calculate the grade for an **English** student. Enter **70** for the midterm grade, **80** for the final examination grade, **90** for the research grade, and **100** for the presentation. A final numeric grade of **84.5** should be displayed with a letter grade of **C**.

7. After the grade is displayed, the program should ask you if you have more grades to calculate.

8. Answer **Yes** and calculate the grade for a Math student. Enter **70** for the midterm and **80** for the final examination. A final numeric grade of **75** should be displayed with a letter grade of **D**.

9. After the grade is displayed, the program should ask you if you have more grades to calculate.

10. Answer **Yes** and calculate the grade for a Science student. Enter **70** for the midterm, **80** for the final examination, and **90** for the research grade. A final numeric grade of **78** should be displayed with a letter grade of **C**. After the grade is displayed, the program should ask you if you have more grades to calculate.

11. Answer **No**. You should be thanked for using the program, and the program should end.

Discussion

Making the modifications to the code in the Grades program required careful attention to detail, and there were a few problems coding it.

Most of the problems dealt with 'sandwiching' the existing code within a While Loop.

A couple of students forgot to code the last line in the body of the While Loop asking the user if they had another grade to calculate. As a result, they wound up with Endless Loops.

In retrospect, I think the class might have been better off coding this version of the Grades program from scratch. It sounds easy to 'sandwich' the existing code within a While Loop, but Python's insistence on indentation can be a real problem if you miss indenting even a single line.

> **NOTE: If you are using Notepad++, you can indent one or more lines of code easily by selecting the line or lines of code to be indented, then pressing the tab key or selecting Edit-Indent from the menu.**

In the end, ultimately, everyone was able to complete the exercise, and seemed very happy that their program was now able to calculate more than one grade before ending.

"I have to say I'm very impressed with the practical use for this loop," Ward said. "I wasn't happy to have to start the previous version of the program again to calculate another grade."

"Me, too," Rhonda said. "In a way, this program kind of reminds me of an Automated Teller Machine in that once you are done withdrawing your money, it asks whether you have another transaction to complete before giving you your card back."

> **NOTE: Some Automated Teller Machines (ATM's) are now giving the card back after a single transaction because of the tendency of customers to leave their card in the machine.**

"Can you go over the code?" Mary asked. "I think I understand what's going on here, but I want to be absolutely sure."

"I'd be glad to do that, Mary," I said. "The only change we made to the program was to add a While Loop to our program so that we can now calculate more than one grade without having to start the program again. To do that, we placed the code that does the grade calculations within the While Loop. We first created a Loop-Control Variable called *loop_response*. Unlike Practice5_8, where we asked the user if they wished to start counting, here we have made the presumption that the user of our Grades Calculation program has at least one grade to calculate, and so we initialize the *loop_response* variable to 'YES'. Doing so will ensure that our Loop executes at least one time."

```
loop_response = "YES"
```

"For some reason," Barbara said, "I thought we were going to code the While Loop in such a way that it might not execute even one time."

"We could have done that Barbara," I said. "Just before the While Loop was executed for the first time, we could have asked the user, via the **input()** function, if he or she has any grades to calculate. If the user answers 'no,' the test expression in the While Loop would immediately evaluate to False, and the body of the While Loop would be bypassed. That's a design decision based on the likelihood of the user starting the program, and then immediately deciding that he or she had no grades to calculate. I didn't think that very likely here."

> **NOTE: My students seemed to agree with that design decision. If we believed that there was a chance that the user would start our program, and then immediately have no grades to calculate, just before the While Loop was executed for the first time, we could have asked the user if he or she has a grade to calculate, then set the value of the loop_response variable to 'No', causing the While Loop to immediately terminate. The choice is up to you.**

"This next line of code is very important," I said. "It is where we set up the While Loop Structure, using the value of the *loop_response* variable as the test expression."

```
while loop_response.upper() == "YES":
```

"The first time through the While Loop," I said, "the value of *loop_response* is equal to 'YES', and so we are sure the While Loop will execute at least once. Contained within the body of the While Loop is the code that we wrote last week to calculate the student's final numeric and letter grades."

"So really, not much has changed with the program," Joe said. "except for its indentation."

"That's right, Joe," I said. "The difficult code to calculate the various grades for English, Math and Science students was written last week. What we've done this week is to give our program the ability to calculate grades for more than one student without ending."

"And the important thing is to place the code within a Loop," Rhonda said emphatically. "I'm enjoying today's class. I'm seeing the true power of Python."

I paused before continuing.

"The last line of the body of the While Loop is crucial," I said, "It asks the user if he or she has another grade to calculate. If we forget to include this line of code, our While Loop will never end. In fact, one or two of you did exactly that while completing the exercise."

```python
loop_response = input("Do you have another grade to calculate? ")
```

I saw a few smiles in the classroom acknowledging how easy it is to make error.

"If the user answers anything other than 'yes' or its 8 variations," I said, "the test expression in the While Loop will evaluate to False, and the While Loop will terminate, executing the line of code immediately following the body of the While Loop that thanks the user for using our program."

```python
print("\nTHANKS FOR USING THE GRADES CALCULATION PROGRAM!")
```

"If the user answers 'yes,' or any of its 8 variations," I said, "the test expression in the While Loop will evaluate to True, and the body of the While Loop will execute again, permitting another grade to be calculated."

"I just noticed I have a problem," Rhonda said. "When I run my version of the program, it thanks me for using the program after each student's grade is calculated. Shouldn't my program do that only when I say I'm finished calculating grades?"

"That's right, Rhonda," I said, "The program should thank the user just once, when they indicate they have no more grades to calculate."

I took a walk over to Rhonda's workstation. I had a feeling I knew what the problem was and I was right. Rhonda had placed the message thanking the user within the body of the While Loop, not outside of it. As a result, it was executed every time the body of the While Loop was executing.

"By placing that line of code within the While Loop, Rhonda," I said, "you ensured that you thanked the user for using your program each time you calculated a student's grade. By design, that should only be done once at the end of the program."

"I see what you mean," Rhonda said, as she hurriedly corrected her program and gave me a 'thumbs up' to say she had fixed it.

"I think the While Loop isn't the only thing that's new in this program?" Dave said.

"Thanks for reminding me Dave," I said. "One other thing that's new in this code is the use of the continue statement that we discussed a few minutes ago. We used the continue statement twice in the program, when the user gave us what was <u>not</u> considered an acceptable response to the prompt of a type of student to calculate, either because they pressed the ENTER key without making a numeric entry or because they entered a number that was not 1, 2 or 3..."

```python
response = input("\nEnter student type (1=English, 2=Math, 3=Science )")

if response == "":
  print("You must select a Student Type")
  continue

if int(response) <1 or int(response) > 3 :
  print(response, "is not a valid Student Type")
  continue
```

"In both instances," I said, "we display a warning message to the user, then execute the continue statement. The continue statement tells Python to resume execution at the first line of the body of the While Loop."

> **NOTE:** Sharp eyed readers may notice that if the user enters a letter such as the letter 'a' as a Student Type, the program will end with a Python Exception. We'll handle this error in Chapter 8.

"In essence," Barbara said, "we're giving the user a chance to do it over?"

"That's right Barbara," I said. "Continue tells Python to immediately 'jump' to the first line of code in the body of the While Loop. As you observed, we're giving the user a chance to do it over, that is, to make a correct choice."

"This is quite an upgrade from last week's version of the Grades program where the program simply ended here if the user made an incorrect choice," Dave observed.

"I agree Dave," Kate said. "It's frustrating to have the program stop, if you make a silly data entry mistake, and then have to start it again."

Ward expressed some concern over the growing length and complexity of the code in the Grades Calculation Program.

"The size of the program just keeps growing and growing," Ward said. "I realize there isn't much we can do about its length. However, it's becoming so complex that I'm having a harder and harder time following it."

"We'll deal with that complexity in the next few weeks Ward," I said. "There are some enhancements we can make that will make it easier to follow and understand."

"Looking at the Requirements Statement," Rhonda said, "I think we've fulfilled all the requirements for the project, haven't we? What more can we do with it?"

"I think you're right Rhonda," I replied. "However, we do have three weeks left in the class, and we'll continue to modify the Grades Calculation Program each week. Next week, we'll address Ward's concerns about the complexity of the Grades Calculation Program by writing functions of our own. Doing so will make the program easier to follow, and most importantly, easier to modify. In Week 7, we'll learn how to create our own Lists, and add one to the Grades Calculation program. Finally, in Week 8, we'll add Exception Handling to our Grades Calculation program. So you see, we still have plenty to learn, and plenty of work to do with the program."

I looked around the classroom. I could see that everyone was feeling proud of the program they were producing week by week. I could also see that they were pretty worn out; it had been an intense session. I dismissed class for the day.

Summary

In this chapter, we discussed how loop processing can make our programming lives a lot easier, and make our programs extremely powerful. There are two types of loop statements in Python.

- **For Loops**: these loops execute a definite number of times. The number of times that the For Loop executes is determined by the Start, Stop and Step parameters of the **range()** function in the 'For' line of the For Loop.

- **While Loops**: these loops typically execute an indefinite number of times, determined by a test expression that evaluates to True or False. The While Loop continues to run while a specified test expression is True.

We also modified the Grades Calculation Program so that it calculates more than one student's grade.

In the next chapter, we'll take a look at creating functions of our own, and adding 'Modularity' to the programs we write.

Chapter 6---Creating Your Own Functions

In this chapter, we'll discuss how to make our programs more readable, more efficient and easier to modify by creating user-defined functions of our own. Sometimes called Custom Functions, like Python's built in functions, User-defined Functions are pieces of code that perform a single task, and promote a concept called *modularity*.

Modular programs are easier to maintain and understand

"In the previous five weeks of our class," I said, "we've been using Python's built in functions to write our programs. Today we're going to learn how to create functions of our own, called User-defined Functions (sometimes called Custom Functions.) Creating our own functions will make our programs more readable, more efficient, and easier to maintain. Good Functions are designed to do one thing, and one thing only. This is known as Modular Programming. The code that we write and place in functions can be 'reusable'---that is, used in more than one program, and used by more than one programmer.

"I'm not quite sure what you mean by 'reusable'?" Steve asked.

"We've been using reusable functions our entire class," I said. "Every built-in Python function was designed to be reusable. As an example, the **print()** function was written once by Guido van Rossum, the author of Python, in 1991, and has been used by millions of programmers in millions of programs since then."

"So can we do something like that ourselves?" Kate asked. "Write code that can be used by other Python programmers?"

"Exactly Kate," I said. "It's possible for you to create a function that is so fantastic, that Python incorporates it into the language and makes it available to Python programmers around the globe. More likely, though, it's a function that you may use yourself in the future, or perhaps other programmers in your company."

I gave my students a chance to think about that.

"I think I understand the concept of reusability now," Blaine said, "but what is this concept of Modular programming?"

"A Modular program," I said, "is one in which, as much as possible, code to perform one aspect of the program is self contained. For instance, right now, in the Grades Calculation program, the code to calculate all of the student grades appears in a single part of our program, called the main module---actually, it's the only module. Our program is not modular at all. By the end of today's class, however, the code to calculate the grade for an English Student will be separate from the code to calculate the grade for a Math Student. In a similar way, the code to calculate the grade for a Science Student will also be separated. We'll have placed the code in 3 distinct User-defined functions. This is Modular programming. Not only that, but if in the future we write another program for the University in which the grade for an English, Math or Science student needs to be calculated, we can incorporate those 3 User-defined functions into that program as well."

"And you said that other programmers could use our functions also?" Chuck asked.

"That's right Chuck," I answered.

"It's hard to believe," Mary said, "that some of the code we write will be so good that other programmers will want to use it."

"That can happen Mary," I said. "Just consider how often we've used the **print()** and **input()** functions in this class. These functions are used so often in Python that they are built-in functions, part of the intrinsic Python language. Python has a number of other libraries containing functions that we haven't even discussed. Believe it or not, some of those functions were written by programmers who were once students just like you. You'll learn how to do that today."

> **NOTE: In my Python Classes and Objects course (book,) you'll learn how to create Classes and Objects that expand upon this notion of Function reusability.**

"Did you say that writing our own functions will make our programs more efficient?" Mary asked. "What exactly is an efficient program?"

"I'm sure you've heard the term 'reinventing the wheel?'" I replied. "An efficient program is one that utilizes, as much as possible, existing functions in Python libraries, and where functions don't exist to perform the task you need to do, only then do you write the code yourself, and ideally, incorporate it into your own User-defined functions.

"Will that mean less lines of code in our program?"

"That depends upon what you mean by your program," I said. "So far, all of the programs we've written have been written in a single Python file. When we execute a built-in Python function, we are executing hundreds of lines of code that are invisible to us in a Standard Python Library. When we create modular programs, with functions of our own, we'll place the functions in an external file or module. So, in answer to your question, the size of our main program file will shrink because much of the code will be in an external file or module."

I paused before continuing.

"As an example," I said, "the current version of our Grades program we worked on last week has 125 lines of code in it. The modified version of the Grades program we'll create today will have the same functionality, but we'll place a great deal of that functionality in User-defined functions, which we'll store in an external file (module) called util.py. Overall, the number of lines of code in Grades.py and util.py won't be less, in fact there will be a few more. However, the size of Grades.py file itself will be much smaller."

"Speaking of size," Kate asked, "is there a limit to the number of lines of code in a Python program?"

"There's no limit to the number of lines of code in a Python program," I said. "Just remember, the more lines of code in your program, the more difficult the program is to read, understand and maintain."

"What do you mean by maintain?" Rhonda asked. "Is that anything like car maintenance?"

"That's a good analogy Rhonda," I said. "Maintenance means to change or update your program. Programs don't 'wear out' in the sense that a car does. A program we write today in theory will run 20 years from now (in fact, some of mine are,) but sometimes changes to programs are required by external factors. For instance, the Operating System on the user's PC may have been upgraded, requiring an update to the program or one of the program libraries that it uses. Programs may need to be modified because of a change in the business environment for which the program was written. Perhaps we wrote a program to track in-store sales and now the company is selling on the Internet. Programs may need to be modified due to changes in Governmental Regulations, such as a new tax or a change in a tax rate. Programs may need to be modified (maybe upgrade is a better word here) because of requests from the users who are working with it every day. Regardless of the reason, you can be almost certain that the program you write today, if it is at all popular, will eventually need to be changed---if not by you, then by another programmer."

"Is changing or updating a program a big deal?" Linda asked.

"That depends a great deal," I said, "on whether the person making the change is the original programmer, and also to some degree how long it's been since the original program was written. Obviously, modifying a program that you wrote yourself just a few weeks ago isn't nearly as hard as modifying a program someone else (perhaps no longer with the company) wrote 5 years ago. It also depends on how well written the program is---how the original author chose their variable names (or Pseudo Constants), the names of their functions (as we'll see today), whether they self-documented their code with good comments. Even if the program is well written, even if all that needs to be changed in the program is a single line of code, finding that exact line of code in a program with hundreds or even thousands of lines of code isn't as easy as it sounds. Our topic today is modular programming---if the program was written in a modular fashion, it's much easier."

"There's that word modular again," Lou said. "Can you give us an example of modular programming?"

"Here's one Lou," I said, "Suppose a change in State law changes the State Sales tax rate to change---and a program you are responsible for that calculates State Sales Tax needs to be changed. If the calculation for the State Sales tax appears in a User-defined function that you or another programmer wrote called **calculate_sales_tax()**, it will be much easier to make the appropriate change. Most likely it's a single line of code, ideally appearing in just one place in the program, or perhaps an external file or module. Modular programs are programs that are written in distinct, logical units---all of the code pertaining to calculating the sales tax should appear in a function of its own---and only in that function."

"Do programs change that often that we need to worry about this?" Blaine asked.

"Most programs that are written for commercial purposes will at one time or other need to be changed." I answered. "Even the programs I've written myself for home use need to be changed from time to time. It's been estimated that the programming staff in a large corporation may spend up to 85 percent of its time modifying the code in already existing programs."

"That's incredible," Chuck said. "Now I see why making programs easier to read and maintain is so important."

"Absolutely," I said. "In fact, it's likely that the Grades Calculation program we're writing for Frank Olley will need to be changed some time in the future. If the English, Math, or Science departments change their formulas for the way a student's final grade is calculated, we'll need to change the Grades Calculation Program."

"And having functions in the Grades Calculation Program will make that process easier?" Valerie asked.

"Much easier," I said. "If we need to change the formula for the calculation of the Math grade in the Grades Calculation Program, won't it be easier if the code for that calculation appears in just one place, ideally in a function called **calculate_math_grade()**?"

What is a Function?

"I'll agree with that," Bob said, "So in theory, a function is code that performs a single task, and ideally, that task is not performed anywhere else in the program?"

"That's fantastic, Bob," I said. "In the Grades Calculation Program, all of the code we've written so far is in the main body of a single python file---Grades.py. By the end of today's class, we'll have taken that code and redistributed much of it into separate functions. For instance, all the code that executes the calculation for the final grade of an English student will be placed in a function of its own called **calculate_english_grade()**. In a similar way, the code to perform the calculation for the final grade of a math student will be placed in a function of its own called **calculate_math_grade()**, and the code to perform the calculation for the final grade of a science student will be placed in a function of its own called **calculate_science_grade()**."

"I'm beginning to see what you're getting at now," Ward said. "If the code to calculate the final grade for a math student is in a function of its own, finding it and making changes to it should be much easier."

"Should we write our functions from scratch right from the beginning," Dave asked, "or place all of our code in the main body our program and then at some point move the code out of there into separate functions as we're doing today with the Grades Calculation Program?"

"That's a great question Dave," I said. "I think you'll find that with a little experience under your belt, you'll create functions of your own right from the very start of your program. In fact, you'll probably gravitate towards writing a program that is mainly functions, with just a little code in the main body of the program."

I paused before continuing.

"I know it seems strange to you now," I said, "because for the last five weeks all of the code that we've written has been in the main body of a single Python file, but the more programs you write, the more natural the process of creating functions will become. You'll identify processes that perform a single task and intuitively place the code for it into a User-defined function."

"Why didn't we do that with the Grades Calculation Program?" Rhonda asked.

"We needed to concentrate on learning the fundamentals of the Python language first," I said, "before worrying about making our programs modular. Making our programs modular through the creation of User-defined functions is what we will spend the remainder of today's class learning about."

> **NOTE:** The natural extension of creating functions of our own is to create a Class, in which the function code becomes a Class method. This is a topic for a future course---a course on Classes and Objects. You'll need to check out my book, Learn to Program with Python Classes and Objects, for more information on that topic.

"I can imagine having other programmers use your functions is quite an ego trip," Ward said, "That's quite an incentive for me to learn this great language."

"I have just one question," Mary said. "If we take all of the code out of the main body of our program and place it in functions, what will be left in the main body of our program?"

"We won't be taking all of the code out of the main body of the program," I answered. "The main body of the program will shrink in size, but it will contain the code that 'calls' or requests the execution of the code contained in our functions."

Creating your own Functions...

"This all sounds very exciting," Rhonda said. "I can't wait to get started. How do we create functions of our own, and what do we name them?"

"Let's start with <u>naming</u> first," I said, "You can name your functions virtually anything you want, Rhonda, but be sure to pick a meaningful name. Stylistically, function names follow the same rules as for variable names. By convention, function names (like variables) are all lowercase letters. If a function name consists of more than one word, as some of ours will do, the words should be separated with an underscore. As far as how to <u>create</u> functions, Function Definitions are designated with a special keyword **<u>def</u>**, followed by the function name and a colon. After that, comes the function code, and not surprisingly, it is indented. Functions can be placed in the main body of the program (as we'll do in our early examples) or in a separate module or file (which we'll do later.) When functions are placed in the main body of our program, they must be defined before they are 'called' in the program. When functions are placed in a separate module or file, we need to include an 'import' statement at the top of our program to tell Python where to 'find' our functions."

"This is different from using the built-in functions like **print()** or **input()**," Dave said.

"That's right Dave," I said, "**print()** and **input()** are built-in Python functions, and no special reference needs to be made in our program to use them. User-defined functions are different, and we either need to include the Function Definition within our program, or use an <u>import</u> statement to let Python know where the function and its definition are found."

"I remember we used an import statement earlier in the class," Valerie said. "Didn't we use it to tell Python we wanted to use the *datetime* object?"

"That's right Valerie," I said, obviously impressed with her recall. "We also used it to specify the location of the **exit()** function back in week 4."

I then displayed this code on the classroom projector:

```
# Example6_1.py

print("I love Python!")
```

"Does this code look familiar?" I asked. "This is the first Python program we wrote a few weeks ago. As you know, it displays the message 'I love Python!' in the Python Console. Let's see how we can take the code to display that message and place it in a function that we will call **display_message()**."

I modified the code in <u>Example6_1.py</u> to look like this and displayed it on the classroom projector:

```
# Example6_2.py

def display_message():       #Function Definition
    print("I love Python!")

display_message()            #Call of User-defined function
```

I then saved the program as <u>Example6_2.py</u>, and ran it for the class. The message "I love Python!" was displayed in the Python Console.

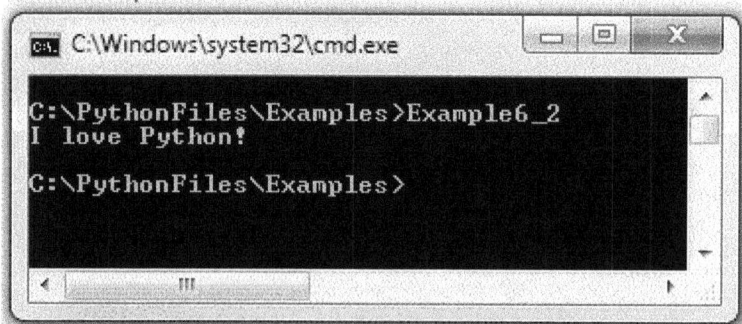

"As you can see," I said, "we displayed 'I love Python!' in the Python Console. This program--<u>Example6_2</u>--- behaves in the same manner as the previous version <u>Example6_1</u> did, but in this version of the program, the Python instruction to display the message 'I love Python!' is no longer being executed directly from the main body of the program. Instead, the instruction is executed from within a function called **display_message()**. Python requires that we define the function using the **def** keyword prior to using the function. and as I warned you, the Function

Definition must appear at the 'top' of our code to ensure that Python sees the definition before we attempt to execute it."

"Where's the import statement?" Rhonda asked. "Shouldn't we have one?"

"No import statement is required in this example," I answered. "because the Function Definition is included in the main body of the program itself. Only when the function is defined in another module or file do we need an import statement."

"Can we look at that first line of the function a little closer?" Kate asked.

"Sure thing Kate," I said. "The first line of the function is called the Function Header. It starts with the def keyword, followed by the name of the function and the name of any arguments that it accepts, identical to the arguments that we've seen with Python's built in functions, such as **input()**, **print()** and **range()**. We'll look at creating functions with one or more arguments a little later on. The Function Header ends with a colon, followed by a line or lines of indented code that comprise the body of the function. The body of a function needs to be indented, and in this way, it very much resembles the body of an If statement or the body of a loop."

```
def display_message():          #Function Definition
```

"Why did we place an empty pair of parentheses after the function name?," Mary asked.

"The empty pair of parentheses," I explained, "tells Python that we are defining our function with no parameters(see note below). That means we will not be passing our function any 'extra' information when we call it. We just want to execute the code within it."

> **NOTE #1: The terms parameter and argument are sometimes used interchangeably. The designer of the function defines the parameter (or parameters) in the Function Header, and the user of the function supplies the argument for the parameter when he or she calls the function. The argument is the actual value passed to the function when it is called.**

> **NOTE #2: Those of you who know other languages such as Java and C++ know that in those languages, you explicitly define, in the Function Header, whether the function returns a value and the Data Type of its return value. Python doesn't do that.**

"Can you give us an example of a function that accepts arguments?" Kate asked.

"Sure thing Kate," I replied, "we've been using one since the first day of class---the **print()** function. The **print()** function accepts, as an argument, what we want it to print---either the value of a variable, or a String, like this..."

```
print("I love Python!")
```

"I see now," Bob said. "I suppose the **input()** function is also an example of a function that accepts an argument."

"That's right Bob," I replied. "There are also functions and methods that accept more than one argument, and as we saw with our own User-defined function **display_message()**, there are functions that accept no arguments. It's up to the designer of the function or method to decide that."

"Did you use the phrase call a function?" Rhonda asked.

"That's right Rhonda," I said, "Call is another name for execute. You will frequently hear the term 'call' in reference to executing a function."

I paused before continuing.

"After the Function Header," I said, "comes the body of the function, indented. The body of the function contains the code to execute when the function is called. In this simple example, the body of the function is a single line of code. Notice that aside from indenting the body of the Function Definition, there's nothing special about it. Whatever is indented is considered to be the body of the function."

```
print("I love Python!")
```

"After skipping a line to make our code more readable," I said, "we then call (execute) our User-defined function the way we would any built-in Python function..."

```
display_message()          #Call of User-defined function
```

"Notice," I continued, "that the code to call or execute the **display_message()** function references the name of the function exactly, and also includes the empty pair of parentheses. Function names, like variable names, are case sensitive."

"You said that the function needs to be defined before it is called in the program? Linda asked.

"That's right Linda," I said. "Watch what happens if we try to call a function before defining it, like this..."

I copied Example6_2.py, modified it and displayed it on the classroom projector.

```
# Example6_2bad.py
# Calling a function before you define it will generate an error
# This code will not execute!!!

display_message()              #Call of User-defined function

def display_message:           #Function Definition
  print("I love Python!")
```

"See how the call of **display_message()** takes place before it is defined?" I said. "That will be a problem when we run this program."

I then saved the program as Example6_2bad.py, and ran it for the class. The following screen shot was displayed on the classroom projector:

```
C:\Windows\system32\cmd.exe

C:\PythonFiles\Examples>Example6_2bad
Traceback (most recent call last):
  File "C:\PythonFiles\Examples\Example6_2bad.py", line 5, in <module>
    display_message()              #Call of Custom Function
NameError: name 'display_message' is not defined

C:\PythonFiles\Examples>
```

> **NOTE: Functions must be defined before they can be called in your code. For this reason, Function Definitions appear first in the main body of your code---unless they are stored in an external file or module, in which case an import statement to 'include' them in the program must appear before the function is called.**

"The Python Interpreter has displayed a NameError Exception," I said. "We'll discuss NameError Exceptions in Week 8 of our class. Basically, Python is saying that it doesn't know what **display_message()** is, even though it's pretty obvious to us that it's a function that we defined in the program."

"But after we call it," Rhonda said. "That's the problem. We defined it on line 7, but called it on line 5."

"That's right Rhonda," I replied.

"I don't think we've ever called a function that accepts no arguments," Peter said. "In that case, do we need to include an empty pair of parentheses? I know we did here, but are they required?"

"I think we do, Peter" Kate interrupted. "In fact, I accidentally coded this example program without them, and although there were no errors when the program executed, nothing seemed to happen."

"That's a good question Peter," I said, "and a good observation Kate. Python is pretty intelligent, but it turns out that if you don't include the parentheses when you call a function, Python thinks that you are defining a variable called **display_message,** not executing a function by that name."

"As you said earlier," Kathy noted, "the use of the colon at the end of the Function Header does remind me of the body of a loop in an If statement or a While Loop."

"That's right Kathy," I retorted. "The code that follows the colon in a Function Header is the body of the function. In this simple example, the body of the function is a single line of code, but it can be as many lines of code as are necessary to do the job. Our Function Headers, and definitions, can get even more complex when we start creating functions that accept arguments and return values."

"Return values?" Blaine asked.

"Yes Blaine," I said, "We can user-defined function that returns a value back to the code that calls it. These are called Return values, and we'll cover Return values in more detail in just a few minutes."

A Function defined with a Single Mandatory Parameter

I suggested that we modify the **display_message()** function we defined in Example6_2.py to accept a single argument.

"The **display_message()** function from Example6_2.py is pretty bland," I said. "It always does the same thing, displays 'I love Python!' in the Python Console."

"But of course!," Rhonda said smiling. "What else would we want to display? I know it's my favorite programming language!"

"I know it's hard to believe Rhonda," I said, "but that may not be true for everyone. Why don't we modify the **display_message()** function to allow the programmer to pass an argument specifying his or her favorite programming language to the function, and then display that in the Python Console. To do that, we'll need to modify our Function Definition to accept a single argument, the user's favorite programming language, and we'll also need to modify the Function Definition to do 'something' with that argument once it is passed to the function."

I thought for a moment and then displayed this code on the classroom projector:

```
# Example6_3.py

def display_message(language):          #Function Definition
  print("I love " + language + "!")

display_message("Java")                 #Call of User-defined function
display_message("C++")                  #Call of User-defined function
display_message("Python")               #Call of User-defined function
```

"We've modified the Function Definition," I said. "We will then call the function three times with a different favorite programming language each time."

I then saved the program as Example6_3.py, executed it, and the following screenshot was displayed on the classroom projector.

"Three calls of the **display_message()** function," I said, "with three different passed arguments results in three different languages displayed in the Python Console."

"The Function Definition isn't all that much different from the previous version," Steve said.

"That's right Steve," I said. "Our Function Header is almost the same as it was with the previous version of the function, except instead of an empty pair of parentheses, this one has the name of a single parameter (argument) called language within the parentheses."

```
def display_message(language)          #Function Definition
```

"Within the body of the function," I said, "Python gives us access to the argument that is passed to the function, and we use the name of the parameter (argument) within in the body of the function to display its value in the Python Console."

```
print("I love " + language + "!")
```

"So the word *language* in the **display_message()** function is the name of the parameter?" Mary asked.

"That's right, Mary," I said. "Parameters are named in the Function Header, and *language* is my choice for a meaningful parameter name. The parameter name can be virtually anything you want---of course, my preference is to select something meaningful. Notice we then use the parameter name *language*, like a variable, within the body of the function."

"I'm a little confused here with terminology," Kate said. "Are parameters and arguments the same thing?"

"That's a great question Kate," I said. "Many programmers use the terms arguments and parameters interchangeably, and probably only a Computer Scientist would argue with you over the difference. The difference between the two terms is slight: Parameters are the names that appear in a Function Header, and Arguments are the actual values that are passed to the function by the code that calls it. For each parameter specified in the function's header, there must be a corresponding argument passed to it, unless we define the parameter as an optional parameter. More on that in a few minutes."

> **NOTE: The terms parameter and argument are sometimes used interchangeably. The designer of the function defines the parameter (or parameters) in the Function Header, and the user of the function supplies the argument for the parameter when he or she calls the function. The argument is the actual value passed to the function when it is called.**

"So parameters appear in the Function Header, and arguments are the actual values passed to the function when it is called. Is that correct?" Dave asked.

"Perfect, Dave," I said. "I—"

"I know," Rhonda said, laughing. "You couldn't have said it any better yourself!"

"Let's look at the code to call the **display_message()** function." I said. "Calling a function that requires a parameter is easy, provided you know the Function's Signature."

"Function Signature?" Joe asked.

"The Function's Signature is the function name, along with the number of arguments required," I said. "In order to be able to call a function, at a minimum we need that information, which is usually provided to us in some form of documentation. It's no different from calling a built-in Python function, such as **input()**, **print()** or **range()**. We need to know the function name, along with the number and order of parameters required. Of course, it also helps to know what the function will do with those parameters, and if it will return a value to the calling program."

> **NOTE: In the real world of programming, information about user-defined functions, their purpose, their usage, and their signatures will be communicated to programmers wishing to use these functions in a variety of ways. In a small company, it could be via email. In the case of a new Python library, it would be via the official Python Website.**

I paused before continuing.

"Since we wrote **display_message()** ourselves," I said, "the function signature is no problem. We know that we need to pass the **display_message()** function just a single argument."

"Do parameters have a Data Type?" Mary asked.

"That's an excellent question Mary," I said. "When we define parameters within a Function Header, we specify the name, but not a Data Type. When a value is passed as an argument to the called function, within the function the parameter assumes the data type of the data that is passed to it. Since we know that **display_message()** is expecting a String value to be used with the **print()** function, we pass it a String within quotation marks when we call it. As you can see, we execute **display_message()** three times, each time specifying a different String value as its argument."

```
display_message("Java")          #Call of User-defined function
display_message("C++")           #Call of User-defined function
display_message("Python")        #Call of User-defined function
```

"Again," I said, "it's important that we enclose the argument within quotation marks when we call the function. Why? Within the **display_message()** function the passed argument is itself used as an argument to the **print()** function, which is expecting a String value."

"I'm a little confused as to what the **display_message()** function does with the argument once it receives it from the calling program," Barbara said. "Can you clear that up?"

"I'll try, Barbara," I answered. "Let's look at the code from the body of the **display_message()** function in Example6_2, which was hard-coded to display 'I love Python!' in the Python Console."

```
print("I love Python!")
```

"Here's the modified code from Example6_3, in which we use the value of the passed parameter *language* as an argument to the **print()** function (sandwiched, using concatenation, between 'I love' and an exclamation point). If we pass 'Java' as the value of the *language* parameter, 'I love Java' is then displayed in the Python Console."

```
print("I love " + language + "!")
```

"Is *language* a variable?" Lou asked. "And if so, why isn't it defined or initialized within the body of the function?"

"Parameters are a lot like variables," I said, "but they don't need to be defined within the body of the function because they are defined in the Function Header itself."

"Getting back to passing a String value to the **display_message()** function," Ward said. "What would happen if we forgot the quotation marks?"

"Good question Ward," I answered. "What if our call to the **display_message()** function looked like this without the word 'Java' being enclosed within quotation marks?"

I displayed this alternative code on the classroom projector.

```
display_message(Java)        #Call of User-defined function
```

"Without the quotation marks, Python would think we were passing the value of a variable called *Java* to the **display_message()** function. Passing a variable as an argument to a function is something we can do. However, since we haven't defined or initialized a variable called *Java*, when we execute the program, we would receive a NameError Exception indicating that the name 'Java' is not defined."

I modified the code with the incorrect function call, saved it as Example6_3bad.py, and executed the program. The following screen shot was displayed on the classroom projector.

```
C:\Windows\system32\cmd.exe

C:\PythonFiles\Examples>Example6_3bad
Traceback (most recent call last):
  File "C:\PythonFiles\Examples\Example6_3bad.py", line 6, in <module>
    display_message(Java)                #Call of Custom Function
NameError: name 'Java' is not defined

C:\PythonFiles\Examples>_
```

> NOTE: We'll discuss the NameError Exception, how it occurs, and how to prevent it, in more detail in Chapter 8.

"We'll learn how to pass the value of a variable as an argument to a function in a few minutes," I said.

A Function Defined with two or more Mandatory parameters

"I assume it's possible," Barbara said, "to create a function that accepts more than one argument, along the lines of the **range()** function. If that's the case, how does Python know which parameter is which when the code that calls the function passes the arguments?"

"Yes Barbara," I said, "it's very common to design functions that accept more than one argument. How does Python know which passed argument refers to which parameter in the Function Header? One way is to pass arguments to the function using the parameter name. This is commonly called calling a function using Named Arguments. We'll take a look at that technique in a few minutes. However, it's not necessary to use Named Arguments. In Python, arguments are passed positionally, which means that if the Function Header specifies two parameters, Python assumes that the first passed argument to the function is the first parameter and that the second passed argument to the function is the second parameter. Make sense?"

"I think so," Rhonda said. "An example would help."

"I agree Rhonda," I said, "Let me show you exactly what I mean by modifying the **display_message()** function we just wrote in Example6_3 to accept two arguments, not one."

I then modified the code from Example6_3.py to look like this and displayed it on the classroom projector:

```
# Example6_4.py

def display_message(language,how_much):          #Function Definition
  print("I love " + language + " " + how_much)

display_message("Java","a lot!")                 #Call of User-defined function
display_message("C++", "a little bit.")          #Call of User-defined function
display_message("Python", "more than any other!")  #Call of User-defined function
```

"We've modified the **display_message()** function to accept two arguments," I said. "Doing so allows us to display not only our favorite programming language, but also an assessment as to how much we like it."

I then saved the program as Example6_4.py, and ran it for the class. The following screen shot was displayed on the classroom projector:

```
C:\Windows\system32\cmd.exe

C:\PythonFiles\Examples>Example6_4
I love Java a lot!
I love C++ a little bit.
I love Python more than any other!

C:\PythonFiles\Examples>
```

Don't Forget: If typing these long examples and exercises isn't something you want to do, feel free to follow this link to find and download the completed solutions for all of the examples and exercises in the book. Just click on the Python book, then follow the link entitled exercises ☺

http://www.johnsmiley.com/main/books.htm

"Before we look at the function calls in detail," I said. "let's take a look at the differences in both the Function Header and the body of the function for **display_message()**. The Function Header is now defined with two parameters: *language* and *how_much*. Modifying the function to accept a second parameter would be useless if we didn't use it in the body of the function. We do that by modifying the line of code with the **print()** function to use both arguments as arguments to the **print() function**."

```
def display_message(language,how_much):          #Function Definition
  print("I love " + language + " " + how_much)
```

I gave my students a change to absorb the change to the **print()** function before continuing.

"Now that the Function Header for **display_message()** specifies two parameters," I said, "the call to the function must also specify two arguments. Since the **print()** function within the body of our function requires String values to be passed to it, as was the case in our previous example, all of the passed arguments are also enclosed within quotation marks."

```
display_message("Java","a lot!")                 #Call of User-defined function
display_message("C++", "a little bit.")          #Call of User-defined function
display_message("Python", "more than any other!")  #Call of User-defined function
```

"Using two parameters makes this function even more powerful and flexible," Ward said. "This stuff is pretty neat."

"You're right, Ward," I said. "The more arguments a function accepts, the more flexible the function can be when executed. Of course, that also means that the code in the function will be more complex as well."

"Suppose we had forgotten to supply the function call with the correct number of arguments." Lou said. "What would happen? Would the program bomb when we ran it?"

"What's that?" Rhonda asked.

"Lou is asking what happens if a function requires two arguments, and we pass it only one," I said.

I gave my students a chance to think about that.

"Let's modify our code to see what would happen," I said.

I copied Example6_4.py, modified it, and displayed it on the classroom projector:

```
# Example6_4bad.py
# Function requires 2 arguments, we pass only 1
# This code will not execute!!!

def display_message(language,how_much):         #Function Definition
  print("I love " + language + " " + how_much)

display_message("Python")                        #Call of User-defined function
```

"Notice that we are now calling the **display_message()** function and passing it just one argument," I said. "The Function Header, however, still specifies that two arguments are required."

I then saved the program as Example6_4bad.py, and ran it for the class. The following screen shot was displayed on the classroom projector:

```
C:\Windows\system32\cmd.exe

C:\PythonFiles\Examples>Example6_4bad
Traceback (most recent call last):
  File "C:\PythonFiles\Examples\Example6_4bad.py", line 7, in <module>
    display_message("Python")                    #Call of Custom Function
TypeError: display_message() missing 1 required positional argument: 'how_much'

C:\PythonFiles\Examples>
```

"This TypeError message is pretty clear," I said. "Python is telling us we are missing a required positional argument on line 7. Python even tells us the name of the missing argument---*how_much*."

"That's a pretty clear error message," Mary said.

"That's right Mary," I said. "Not all Python error messages are as explicit as this one, but this one is pretty clear."

"What do you mean by positional arguments?" Steve asked.

"Python determines the arguments you are passing to a function by using their position in the function call," I said. "If you pass a function requiring two arguments only one, Python assumes that you provided the first argument and that the second argument is 'missing'."

"What happens if you provide both arguments but accidentally reverse them?" Blaine asked.

"That's an excellent question Blaine," I said. "Let's see what happens if we pass the *how_much* argument first and the *language* argument second like this..."

I displayed this line of code on the classroom projector.

```
display_message("more than any other!","Python")
```

I quickly modified the program and executed it. The following screenshot was displayed on the classroom projector.

```
C:\Windows\system32\cmd.exe

C:\PythonFiles\Examples>Example6_4
I love more than any other! Python

C:\PythonFiles\Examples>
```

"Oops, that's not right," Rhonda said. "Something's not correct. The phrase doesn't make sense."

"That's right Rhonda," I said, "Python expected two arguments, and that's we provided, but Python has no way of knowing that we reversed them. Because both arguments were String values, the program executed with no errors, but it didn't execute the way we intended."

Calling a Function Using Named Arguments

"Didn't we learn something about Named Arguments in our C++ class?" Dave asked. "Does Python have Named Arguments? If so, that could be something useful to guard against confusing the arguments in a function call."

"Python does support Named Arguments," I said.

"What is a Named Argument?" Rhonda said.

"With Named Arguments," I said, "you provide the name of the parameter in the function call, along with its value. It's a bit more code, but it is more explicit and very definitive. Let me show you by modifying our function call from Example6_4.py to pass our two String Literals as Named Arguments. It's very simple."

I copied Example6_4.py, modified it to include Named Arguments in the function call, and then displayed it on the classroom projector:

```python
# Example6_5.py
# Call a function using Named Arguments

def display_message(language,how_much):              #Function Definition
    print("I love " +  language + " " + how_much)

display_message(language="Python",how_much="A lot!")   #Call of Function with Named Arguments
```

I then saved the program as Example6_5.py, and ran it for the class. The following screenshot was displayed on the classroom projector:

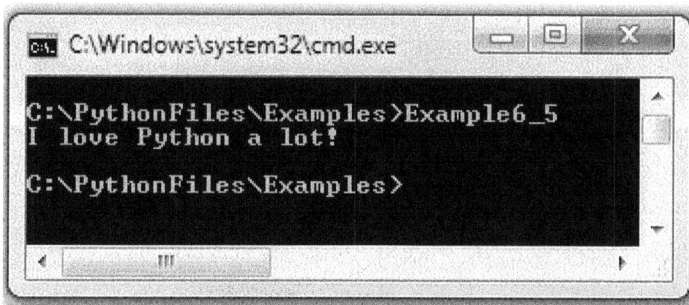

```
C:\Windows\system32\cmd.exe

C:\PythonFiles\Examples>Example6_5
I love Python a lot!

C:\PythonFiles\Examples>
```

"The results are the same," I said. "Does everyone see the difference? Named Arguments are specified in the function call by using the name of the parameter, followed by an equal to sign, followed by the value for the argument."

```python
display_message(language="Python",how_much="A lot!")   #Call of User-defined function
```

"Whether you use Named Arguments in your function calls is entirely up to you," I said. "Using them does add a few more keystrokes to your code, but there are many benefits to using them. First, Named Arguments make your function call virtually error proof. There's no (or very little) chance of confusing the arguments in a function call if all if the arguments you pass to the function are named. Secondly, Named Arguments also make great documentation. It's easier for the original programmer, or another programmer, to understand what the function call is/was attempting to do. Finally, one other reason to use Named Arguments is very compelling. There will be times when you are calling a function defined with a large number of arguments, perhaps some or all of them optional arguments with default values (as we learned the **range()** function has back in Week 4 of our class.) Using Named Arguments allows us to easily specify only the argument we wish to specify a value for, accepting the default value for the others."

"Is that such a big deal?" Ward asked.

"It can be Ward," I said. "In the University's Python GUI programming class (that I hope all of you take) we will work with a Python library called tkinter. The tkinter library has a number of functions used to create Windows, Buttons, Checkboxes, List boxes and other window like elements. Many of these functions are defined with a large number of optional arguments with default values that impact the size, placement, and look of these elements. You can accept the default values, but some of them you might want to change---for instance, the size and name of a button to place within a window. Without Named Arguments, you would need to make the function call and pass the argument you want to pass positionally. That would require that you specify <u>all</u> of the arguments in the function call until you reach, positionally, the one you intended to set. With Named Arguments, all you need to do is specify the argument and value you want to change."

A Function Defined with Optional Parameters

"Let's create a user-defined function of our own with optional parameters," I said. "To create an optional parameter in a Function, all we need to do is specify a default value for the parameter. Creating optional parameters for a user-defined function call makes a great deal of sense if you know that most times the default value is the value the user of the function would choose anyway."

"Can we specify a combination of Optional and Mandatory parameters in our Function Signature?" Kate asked. "Like we did with the **range()** function, where the start and step parameters were optional, but the stop parameter was required."

"Yes you can Kate," I said, "However, mandatory Parameters (those with no default value) must appear first in the Function Header. If a parameter with no default value (that is, a mandatory parameter) follows a parameter in the Function Header with a default value (an optional parameter), the Python Interpreter will flag this as an error when you try to execute your program."

"When we used the **range()** function," Dave asked, "didn't a mandatory parameter, the second (<u>stop</u>), follow an optional parameter, the first (<u>start</u>), and itself was followed by another optional parameter, <u>step</u>?"

"Good point Dave," I said, "Python is written in the C programming language, and built-in functions have different rules than those for user-defined functions. With user-defined functions, mandatory parameters must come first in the Function Header, followed by any optional parameters."

> **NOTE: There's another type of Python parameter that we don't discuss in this class called the variable parameter. With variable parameters, you tell Python that you don't know before hand how many arguments may be passed to your function by the user. As a result, any number of arguments can be passed to a function, however since the designer has no idea what arguments will be passed, he or she also cannot set default values for them. In essence, every argument passed to the function is optional. If this sounds a bit chaotic, it is. It's a topic for an advanced class, and we won't be covering it in this class.**

"Let's modify <u>Example6_4</u>," I said, "to include a third parameter called *how_long*. *how_long* will be an optional parameter that will allow the user of our function to specify how long he or she has been using the programming language they are specifying, in addition to how much they enjoy it. Python knows *how_long* is optional because of the default value of 'Not specified' that is defined for it. Notice that in the Function Header, both mandatory parameters appear first, followed by the single optional parameter."

I then modified the code from <u>Example6_4.py</u> to look like this, and displayed it on the classroom projector:

```
# Example6_6.py
# Function defined with optional how_long parameter with a default value

def display_message(language,how_much,how_long="Not specified"):        #Function Definition
  print("I love " + language + " " + how_much + ". I've used it for: " + how_long)

display_message("Java","A lot","2 years")                        #Call of User-defined function
display_message("C++","A little bit","6 months")                 #Call of User-defined function
display_message("Python","More than any other")                  #Call of User-defined function
```

I then saved the program as <u>Example6_6.py</u>, and ran it for the class. The following screen shot was displayed on the classroom projector:

```
C:\Windows\system32\cmd.exe

C:\PythonFiles\Examples>Example6_6
I love Java A lot. I've used it for: 2 years
I love C++ A little bit. I've used it for: 6 months
I love Python More than any other. I've used it for: Not specified

C:\PythonFiles\Examples>_
```

"We executed the function call three times," I said. "As a result, we have three messages displayed in the Python Console. Let's take a look at this code now, to be sure we understand what happened here. The difference between Example6_4 and Example6_6 is the number of parameters that are defined in the Function Header. Example6_6 has 3 parameters---with two required, and one--the last parameter---optional."

```
def display_message(language,how_much,how_long="Not specified"):       #Function Definition
```

"And Python knows that *how_long* is optional because of the default value 'Not specified' that appears after the equal to sign?" Valerie asked.

"That's excellent Valerie," I said.

I paused before turning my attention to the body of the function.

"Having changed the Function Header," I said, "we need to modify the body of our function to work with the new *how_long* parameter. (It doesn't make sense to add the parameter to the Function Header and then not use it in the body of the function.) All we've done is include the value of the passed parameter *how_long* within the **print()** function, thereby enhancing what we display in the Python Console."

```
print("I love " + language + " " + how_much + ". I've used it for: " + how_long)
```

"Nothing needs to be done in the body of the function to account for the user not providing a value for *how_long*?" Steve asked.

"No it doesn't Steve," I said, "If the function call doesn't provide a value for *how_long*, Python will assign a value of 'Not specified' to it, and this value will then be used in the body of the function wherever *how_long* appears."

I paused before continuing.

"Let's look at the function calls now," I said. "The first two times we call **display_message()** in the main body of our program, we provide an argument for the optional **how_long** parameter and that value is then displayed in the Python Console..."

```
display_message("Java","A lot","2 years")                    #Call of User-defined function
display_message("C++","A little bit","6 months")             #Call of User-defined function
```

"However," I said, "the third time we call the **display_message()** function, we provide only the two mandatory arguments, not the optional argument..."

```
display_message("Python","More than any other")              #Call of User-defined function
```

"Because of that," I said, "Python uses the default value 'Not specified' when displaying the user's response in the Python Console."

"That's pretty impressive," Ward said.

"I'm growing fond of Named Arguments," Kate said. "I suppose we could use Named Arguments to call **display_message()** with optional parameters as well?"

"That's right Kate." I said, "In this example, calling **display_message()** with Named Arguments would look like this..."

```
display_message(language="Java",how_much="A lot",how_long="2 years")
display_message(language="C++",how_much="A little bit",how_long="6 months")
display_message(language="Python",how_much="More than any other")
```

"Like you Kate," I said, "many programmers love the self documenting nature of using Named Arguments like this. It leaves no doubt as to exactly what the caller of the function intends. Using Named Arguments also allows you to pass your arguments in any order, like this, although I don't recommend it."

```
display_message(how_much="A lot",language="Java", how_long="2 years")
```

A Function that returns a value

"Our next topic deals with writing a user-defined function that returns a value," I said.

I could see some puzzled looks in the class.

"Some Python functions," I said, "return a value of some kind to the program that calls them. This is called a Return Value. The **input()** function, which we've executed many times in this class, is a perfect example of a function that returns a value---in this case, the keystrokes that the user enters in response to a prompt. When we've executed the **input()** function, we've assigned its return value to a variable. We've also executed the **range()** function in this class. Its return value is a List object, which we then used in a For Loop. Designers of functions use the return value in a variety of ways, subject only to their imagination."

"And we can return a value of some kind in our user-defined functions?" Linda asked.

"That's right Linda," I said. "To return a value from our own function to the calling program, all we need to do is code a return statement in our function, like this..."

```
return "Function Complete"
```

"So functions always do something," Kate said, "but sometimes they return a value, and sometimes they return nothing at all."

> **NOTE: Python purists will point out that when a function appears to return no value, it actually returns the 'None' Object. More on that shortly.**

"That's right, Kate," I said, "It's entirely up to the designer of the function to decide if it will return a value or not, and also the type of return value they wish to return---for instance, a String or a number. In the case of the **display_message()** function we wrote in Example6_2, we chose NOT to return a value. If we had chosen to return a value, we would code the return statement in the body of the function---and the caller of our function would then have to deal with the return value."

"Deal with it?" Blaine asked.

"By that," I answered, "to either store the return value in a variable, use the return value in another function of some kind, or just choose to ignore it, which defeats the purpose of having the function return a value in the first place. If the architect of the function designs their function to return a value, it's probably important that the caller of the function do something with the return value."

"Can we return more than one return value from a function?" Bob asked.

"The answer is no, Bob," I said, "A function can return just a single value, although as we saw with the **range()** function, it is possible to return a List of values from a function. This effectively allows you to return more than one value from the function."

I paused before continuing.

"The return statement should be the last line of code in your user-defined function," I said.

"Why is that?" Joe asked.

"When Python encounters a return statement in the body of the function," I said, "the execution of the function ends, the return value is passed back to the calling program, and execution of the program resumes with the next line of code following the function call. If the return statement appears in the middle of the body of a function, the rest of the function code will be bypassed."

"Suppose you accidentally code more than one return statement in a function," Rhonda asked.

"Only the return value from the first return statement will be passed back to the calling program," I said. "This is a mistake that I've seen many beginners make. Remember. Only one return statement per function!"

> **NOTE: When Python encounters a return statement in the body of a function, the execution of the function ends, the return value is passed back to the calling program, and the execution**

of the resumes with the next line of code following the function call

"Can we see an example of how to write a function of our own that returns a value?" Barbara asked.

"Great idea, Barbara," I said. "Let's write a function that accepts two numbers as arguments, multiplies them, and then returns the result to the calling program via the return statement. We'll then store the return value in a variable, and then use the value of that variable as an argument to the Python **print()** function to display the answer in the Python Console."

I then displayed this code on the classroom projector.

```
# Example6_7.py
# Call function and store the return value in a variable---then print it

def lets_multiply(x,y):               #Function Definition
    return x*y                        #Return the result of the multiplication

retval = lets_multiply(3,5)           #Call of User-defined function
print("The result is " + str(retval))
```

I saved the program as Example6_7.py, and ran it for the class. The following screenshot was displayed on the classroom projector:

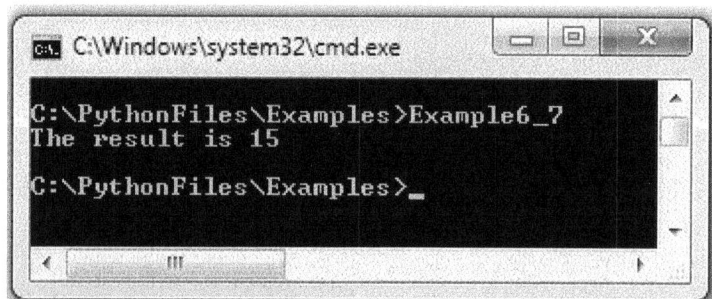

```
C:\Windows\system32\cmd.exe

C:\PythonFiles\Examples>Example6_7
The result is 15

C:\PythonFiles\Examples>_
```

The result of the multiplication, using a function call, was displayed.

"That's pretty impressive," I heard Ward say. "All of the hard work of multiplication was done by the **lets_multiply()** function."

"That's right Ward," I said. "Let's take a look at the code, beginning with the Function Definition for the **lets_multiply()** function. Nothing new here. As we did in Example6_6.py, we defined a function with 2 mandatory parameters, which we called x and y."

```
def lets_multiply(x,y):               #Function Definition
```

"Every line of code that is indented following the Function Header," I said, "is the body of the function. In this case, the body of the function is a single line of code, where we return the result of x multiplied by y."

```
    return x*y                        #Return the result of the multiplication
```

"That confused me at first," Valerie said, "but once I realized that we were multiplying x by y and then returning that result, I was OK with it."

"I can understand your initial confusion Valerie," I said. "We could have executed the multiplication on a line of its own, assigned the result to a variable, and then returned the value of that variable back to the calling program, like this..."

```
    result = x*y
    return result
```

"...but as I've mentioned before, most Python programmers like their code to be as short and concise as possible."

I waited before continuing.

"Let's see how we call the **lets_multiply()** function," I said. "Since **lets_multiply()** returns a value, we should do 'something' with the return value. Some choices are: store the return value in a variable, evaluate the return value directly in an If statement, or use the return value in another function, such as the Python built-in **print()** function. For this version of the program, we store the return value in a variable called *retval*..."

```
retval = lets_multiply(3,5)           #Call of User-defined function
```

"...then display the value of the *retval* variable in the Python Console using the built in Python **print()** function."

```
print("The result is " + str(retval))
```

"What's the purpose of the **str()** function we're using here?" Ward asked. "Is that similar to the **int()** function we used last week? Are we converting the number to a String here for some reason?"

"That's exactly what we're doing Ward," I said. "We want to concatenate the return value from our function to the String 'The result is '. But there's a problem. **lets_multiply()** is returning a number from the result of the multiplication it performs. Python will not permit us to directly concatenate a number to a String, so we must first convert the number to a String before we concatenate it. That's what the **str()** function does. As you pointed out, like the **int()** function we learned about last week, **str()** is a function that converts one Python data type to another."

"Did you say we could have used the return value from **lets_multiply()** directly in the **print()** function?" Linda asked.

"That's right Linda," I said. "Instead of storing the return value of **lets_multiply()** in a variable, we could have used the return value directly as an argument to the **print()** function, like this."

I displayed this code on the classroom projector.

```
# Example6_8.py
# Call function and use the return value directly in the print() function

def lets_multiply(x,y):                 #Function Definition
    return x*y

print(lets_multiply(3,5))               #Call of User-defined function
```

I then saved the program as Example6_8.py, and ran it for the class. The following screenshot was displayed on the classroom projector:

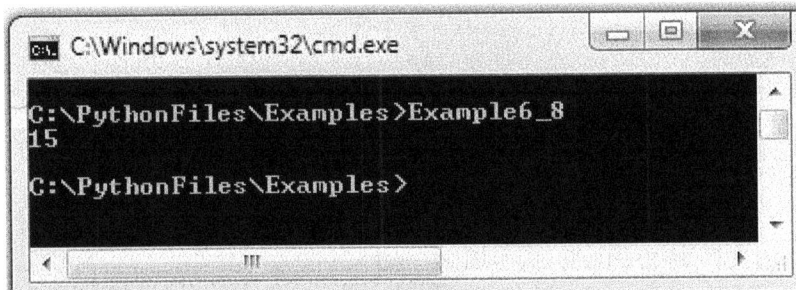

"The answer is the same," I said, "although for simplicity's sake, this time I chose not to display 'The result is' in the Python Console. Instead of two lines of code to call the function and display its results, we combine all of that functionality into a single line of code that includes the call to the function as part of the passed argument to the **print()** function. Experienced Python programmers love the compact nature of this style of code."

```
print(lets_multiply(3,5))               #Call of User-defined function
```

I gave my students a chance to absorb what I was saying.

"I'm surprised," Rhonda said. "that I think I actually understand what's going on here."

"Can we see what happens if we forget to code a return statement within the body of the **lets_multiply()** function?" Kate asked. "What happens if the user of the calling program attempts to work with a return value that is never returned."

"Now that's a very interesting question Kate," I said. " Let's take Example6_8.py, and modify it by 'forgetting' to code a return statement."

I displayed this code on the classroom projector.

```
# Example6_8bad.py
# Oops---we forgot the return statement in the function
# A function without a return statement actually returns the None Object

def lets_multiply(x,y):                 #Function Definition
    x*y                                 #Perform the multiplication but forget to return the result

print(lets_multiply(3,5))               #Call of User-defined function.
```

"Does everyone see," I asked, "that we performed the multiplication in the body of the **lets_multiply()** Function Definition but we didn't code a return statement. The user of our function is expecting the result of the multiplication as a return value and is going to use it directly as an argument to the **print()** function."

I then saved the program as Example6_8bad.py, and ran it for the class. The following screenshot was displayed on the classroom projector:

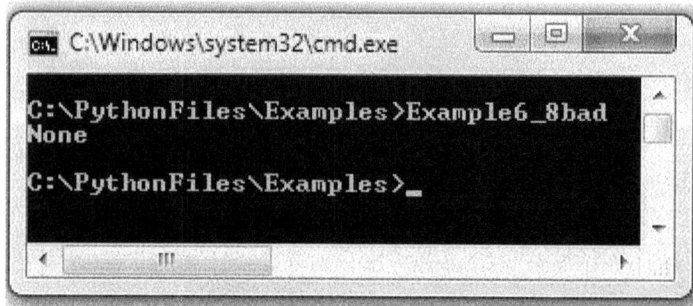

```
C:\Windows\system32\cmd.exe

C:\PythonFiles\Examples>Example6_8bad
None

C:\PythonFiles\Examples>_
```

"None?" I heard Mary say, referring to the display in the Python Console. "What does that mean?"

"Every Python function," I said, "even a function with no explicitly coded return statement returns something back to the calling program. A Python function with no return statement coded returns a Python Object called None. When we used None as an argument to the **print()** function, the word None was then displayed in the Python Console."

"You told us Python was very Object-Oriented," Ward said. "To return an object called None is very thorough on the part of its designers."

"So if the user of our function," Linda said, "discovers that None is being returned from the function call, the user will know something is wrong and needs to contact the author/designer of the function?"

"Exactly Linda," I said.

Passing Variables As Arguments to a Function

"So far," I said, "we've passed with String Literals or numbers to the user-defined functions we write. Let's code up an example where we pass variables as arguments."

"Will that be a problem?" Rhonda asked. "Haven't we already done that?"

"We've passed variables to built-in Python functions," I said, "but we've only passed Numeric and String Literals to the two functions we wrote this morning----**display_message()** and **lets_multiply()**."

"Is there anything special we need to do with our own user-defined functions to accept variables?" Blaine asked.

"Nothing special Blaine," I said. "As I sometimes say, a picture is worth a thousand words. Let's create a simple example by modifying Example6_8.py so that we pass two variables to the **lets_multiply()** function instead of two numbers."

I then displayed this code on the classroom projector.

```
# Example6_9.py
# Call function using variables and use the return value in the print() function

def lets_multiply(x,y):                  #Function Definition
  return x*y

number1 = 3
number2 = 5

print(lets_multiply(number1,number2))    #Call of User-defined function
```

"Notice that instead of passing the numbers 3 and 5 to the **lets_multiply()** function," I said, "we assign the value 3 to the variable *number1* and the value 5 to the variable *number2*. We then pass those two variables as arguments to **lets_multiply()** function."

I saved the program as Example6_9.py, and ran it for the class. The following screenshot was displayed on the classroom projector:

"The result is still 15," Barbara said.

"That's correct Barbara," I said, "This version of the program behaves in the same manner as the other version did by displaying the result of the multiplication in the Python Console. All that changed in the program was that we first created two numeric variables called *number1* and *number2* by assigning values to each one."

```
number1 = 3
number2 = 5
```

"Then," I said, "instead of passing numbers as arguments to the **lets_multiply()** function, we passed the names of the variables instead."

```
print(lets_multiply(number1,number2))        #Call of User-defined function
```

I gave my students a chance to absorb that.

"Passing variables as arguments to **lets_multiply()**," I said, "has no impact on the execution of the function. We didn't need to change the Function Header nor did we need to write special code in the Function body to handle the variable values. Python does everything for us by using the value of the passed variables wherever the argument name appears in the function body."

Variables Defined within Functions are Local Variables

"So far, all of our user-defined functions have been pretty simple," Mary said. "I presume user-defined functions can become pretty complex? Is that right?"

"User-defined functions," I answered, "can be as complex as the code that is contained in the main part of any program. We use the same coding techniques in functions that we use in the main body of the program. That includes If statements and all kinds of Loops"

"Can we create a variable within a user-defined function?" Blaine asked.

"I'm glad you asked that question Blaine," I said. "The answer is yes. Your question leads us nicely into our next topic, Local Variables."

I paused before continuing.

"Local variables," I continued "are variables created within a user-defined function. Back in Week 2, when we first learned how to work with variables, I told you there were Global Variables and Local Variables. All of the variables we've worked with so far in the class have been Global Variables, but I promised you back then we would talk about Local Variables when we learned how to create user-defined Function. It's time to learn about Local variables now, and also to learn how Global variables are handled in user-defined functions."

"Let me make sure I understand," Steve said. "Global variables are the variables we've been creating in the class. Variables created in the main part of our program. Local variables are variables created in a function?"

"Perfect Steve," I said. "Global variables are variables created in the main body of our program. Global variables can be seen or accessed anywhere within our program, including within the user-defined functions that we write. As we've seen, we don't need to do anything special to create a Global variable. We simply create a variable in the main body of our program, and Python creates the variable with Global Scope."

"Scope?" Kate asked.

"Scope refers to where, in our program, a variable can be seen. A Global variable can be seen everywhere. A Local variable can be seen only in the function where it is created. Unlike some other programming languages, there is no need to tell Python whether a variable is Local or Global. Python determines the scope based on where the variable is created."

I paused before continuing.

"Let's write a program," I said, "that displays the value of a Global variable, defined in the main body of our Python program, from within a function."

I then displayed this code on the classroom projector

```
# Example6_10.py
# A function can read a Global variable with no problem

def simple():                                    #Function Definition
  print("Execution of simple function")
  print("Full Name within function is " + full_name)

full_name = "John Smiley"
print("Full Name outside function is " + full_name)
simple()
print("Full Name outside function is " + full_name)
```

"This is the 3rd user defined function we've written this morning," I said. "**simple()** accepts no arguments and uses the **print()** function to display an informational message in the Python Console, and also displays the value of a Global variable called *full_name* in the Python Console. At no time do we attempt to change the value of the *full_name* variable---but we will try that in the next exercise."

```
def simple():                                    #Function Definition
  print("Execution of simple function")
  print("Full Name within function is " + full_name)
```

"Here's the code in the main body of the program," I continued, "We define a variable called *full_name* and assign it a value of my name, use the **print()** function to display its value, execute the **simple()** function to display its value a second time, then use the **print()** function to display the value of *full_name* once again."

```
name = "John Smiley"
print("Full Name outside function is " + full_name)
simple()
print("Full Name outside function is " + full_name)
```

"Why are we executing the **print()** function to display the value of *full_name* twice in the main body of the program?" Barbara asked.

"I wanted to prove to you," I answered, "that executing the **simple()** function has no impact on the value of the *full_name* variable. Of course, there's no code in the simple() function that attempts to change the value of *full_name*. We'll do that in the next example."

I then saved the program as <u>Example6_10.py</u>, and ran it for the class. The following screenshot was displayed on the classroom projector:

```
C:\Windows\system32\cmd.exe

C:\PythonFiles\Examples>Example6_10
Full Name outside function is John Smiley
Execution of simple function
Full Name within function is John Smiley
Full Name outside function is John Smiley

C:\PythonFiles\Examples>
```

"I'm a little confused as to what I'm seeing," Rhonda said.

"Basically," I said, "we displayed the value of the *full_name* variable three times. Once before we called the **simple()** function, once from within the **simple()** function, and then once more after calling the **simple()** function. In all three cases, the value of *full_name* was the same."

"So the main point to take away from this," Dave said, "is that the code within the **simple()** function had no problem accessing the value of the Global *full_name* variable?"

NOTE: Code within a function can access Global variables defined in the main portion of the program.

"That's perfect Dave," I said.

"In addition to reading or accessing the value of a Global variable," Kate asked. "can we also change the value of a Global variable within a function as well?"

"It's possible Kate," I said, "but changing the value of a Global variable is not as straightforward as you might believe it would be. I should mention that Python purists greatly frown upon changing the value of a Global variable (defined in the main body of a program) from within a function. In fact, Python purists don't like Global variables much at all."

NOTE: Who are these Python purists anyway? You can find them on stackoverflow.com. They are a group of very talented and knowledgeable Python programmers who give free advice to anyone who asks (as long as it's not a question about completing a homework assignment.)

"How can you avoid that?" Mary asked.

"Python purists," I said, "believe that just about everything in the main body of the program (code and variables) should reside in functions (or classes which we'll learn about in our Classes and Objects course). As much as possible, we'll do that in the final version of our Grades Calculation Program. However, some code will still remain in the main body of our program, along with two Global variables. However, we will never attempt to update the values of those Global variables directly from the functions we will write for the Grades Calculation Program."

I paused before continuing.

"We've been using only Global variables in this course for the last six weeks," I said, "and most Python programmers don't see a big issue in using them. Creating Global variables is faster when you're teaching Python in front of a class like I am, or just writing a quick test program. It's far easier to write code in the main body of a program than it is to create a function with that code, and then execute the function. Still, you're likely to run into a Python programmer who insists that's exactly what you should do. Regardless, just about every experienced Python programmer would agree that it's a bad idea to change the value of a Global variable within a function. Having said that, I'm about to show you how to do it---changing the value of a Global variable from within a function. But please, please, please don't ever do this yourself!"

I then modified Example6_10.py to look like this, and displayed the code on the classroom projector

```
# Example6_11.py
# Can a function update the value of a global variable?

def simple():                                    #Function Definition
    print("Execution of simple function")
    full_name = "Babe Ruth"                      #Attempt to update the Global variable full_name
    print("Full Name within function is " + full_name)

full_name = "John Smiley"
print("Full Name outside function is " + full_name)
simple()
print("Full Name outside function is " + full_name)
```

"The code in this program," I said "is nearly identical to Example6_10.py, with the exception of the body of the **simple()** function. We've added an additional line of code in the **simple()** function that assigns the value of one of my favorite baseball players to the *full_name* variable. Of course, *full_name* is the name of a Global variable that is defined in the main body of our program. Our intention is to change the initial value of 'John Smiley' with 'Babe Ruth'. Once we update the value of the *full_name* variable within the **simple()** function, we will then display its value in the Python Console."

```
def simple():                                    #Function Definition
    print("Execution of simple function")
    full_name = "Babe Ruth"
    print("Full Name within function is " + full_name)
```

"That looks like it should work," Rhonda said. "All of the other code is the same?"

"That's right Rhonda," I replied. "The main body of the program is identical to that in the previous example. We define a variable called *full_name* in the main body of our program and assign it a value of 'John Smiley', use the **print()** function to display its value, execute the **simple()** function to update and display its value, then use the **print()** function to display the value of *full_name* once again. As we did in the previous example, we execute the **print() function** both before and after executing the **simple()** function to determine if the **simple()** function has actually changed the value of the *full_name* variable. "

```
full_name = "John Smiley"
print("Full Name outside function is " + full_name)
simple()
print("Full Name outside function is " + full_name)
```

"Knowing what you know about Python," I said, "what do you think this program will do?"

Rhonda volunteered:

"I would expect to see 4 lines displayed in the Python Console," Rhonda said, "The first would say 'Full Name outside function is John Smiley', the second 'Execution of a simple function," the third 'Full Name within function is Babe Ruth', and finally 'Full Name outside function is Babe Ruth.'"

"So you're expecting." I replied, "that the **simple()** function will update the value of the Global *full_name* variable that is defined in the main body of our program?"

Rhonda (and most of the other students) nodded her head affirmatively.

"I'm not so sure," Ward said. "I think you're hitting us with a trick question. Didn't you just say that updating Global variables within a function isn't as straightforward as you might think? Will we generate an error message when we try to execute this program?"

"Let's see," I said.

I then saved the program as Example6_11.py, and ran it for the class. The following screenshot was displayed on the classroom projector:

"That looks good to me," Rhonda started to say.

But then she quickly changed her mind, and said "Wait a minute. 'John Smiley' was displayed on the last line. Shouldn't it have been 'Babe Ruth'?"

"That's what we were all expecting," I said.

"I was also," Kate said. "There was no error message displayed, but it appears that the value of the Global *full_name* variable in the main body of the program is still the same---'John Smiley'. I'm puzzled because when we changed the value of *full_name* within the **simple()** function, it appeared to change to 'Babe Ruth'. We know that because we displayed it in the Python Console. But when the **simple()** function ended, and we displayed the value of *full_name* again within the main body of the program, it still had its original value. Did the value of the *full_name* variable change back when the **simple()** function finished executing?"

"No it didn't change back, Kate" I said. "What happened is that it was never updated."

"How does that explain the display of 'Babe Ruth' in the Python Console?" Steve asked.

"Within the **simple()** function," I said, "when Python saw the assignment of 'Babe Ruth' to the variable called *full_name*, instead of updating the value of the Global *full_name* variable, Python instead created a new variable, a local variable called *full_name*. That's the variable that was displayed in the Python Console."

"Two variables with the same name?" Mary said. "Python can do that without getting confused?"

"Yes it can Mary," I said, "Python is smart enough to keep track of variables having the same name that appear in separate functions and in the main body of the program. It's like a postman who delivers to two people on the same street having the same name. Their physical addresses are different. Likewise, the Local *full_name* variable has the same name as the Global *full_name* variable, but each is stored in distinct addresses in the computer's memory. As a result, when the **simple()** function ended, and we displayed the value of the *full_name* variable within the main body of our program, we displayed the value of the Global variable, not the Local variable created in the **simple()** function. In fact, when the **simple()** function ended, the local variable *full_name* died and was removed from our computer's memory."

> NOTE: The confusion that can occur with Global and Local variables having the same name can easily be remedied by not giving Global variables the same names as Local variables defined in functions. For this reason, some of my programmer friends name their Global variables beginning with a prefix of g_ to avoid this confusion. i.e. The Global version of full_name would be g_full_name

"If the Local variable dies when the function stops executing," Kate asked, "Does that mean that Local variables defined within a function can't be accessed by code in the main body of the program?"

"That's right Kate," I said. "Not only that, but Local variables in a function can't be accessed by code in other functions either. Local variables created in a function die when that function completes execution---so naturally, code outside of the function can't access variables that no longer exist. Global variables, on the other hand (variables defined within the main body of our Python program) live for as long as the program itself is running. That doesn't mean, however, that the data stored in Local variables can't be shared with the main body of the program or other functions. We've seen this morning that it's possible to pass data from a function to the calling program via a return value."

> NOTE: Local variables defined within a function can't be accessed by code in the main body of the program or other functions. However, their values can be passed back to the calling program via a Return value.

"Getting back to Example6_11.py," Bob said. "We were unable to change the value of the Global variable *full_name* from within the **simple()** function, but you implied earlier that it is possible, just that it isn't straightforward. Can you show us how?"

"I can show you Bob," I said, "but remember, updating Global variables from within a function is considered poor programming practice. However, it can be done. All we need to do is tell Python that we are working with a Global variable within our function. We do that with the global keyword."

I displayed this code on the classroom projector.

```
# Example6_12.py
# Can a function update the value of a global variable?

def simple():                                    #Function Definition
    global full_name                             #Tell Python we are working with the Global full_name
    print("Execution of simple function")
    full_name = "Babe Ruth"                      #Attempt to update the Global variable full_name
    print("Full Name within function is " + full_name)

full_name = "John Smiley"
print("Full Name outside function is " + full_name)
simple()
print("Full Name outside function is " + full_name)
```

"This code looks identical to the code in the previous version of the program," Rhonda said, "except for the line right after the Function Header."

"That's right Rhonda," I replied. "What's important here is the use of the global keyword."

```
global full_name                    #Tell Python we are working with the Global name
```

"The global keyword," I continued, "tells Python that whenever it sees *full_name* within the **simple()** function, we are referring to the Global *full_name*, in the main body of our Python program. Although we could always access the Global variable within the function, we found that an assignment statement created a new full_name variable. With the global keyword, the assignment statement updates the Global full_name variable. By the way, it doesn't matter where the global keyword appears---as long as it appears before we modify the Global variable. That's all there is to it. Let's see if this works..."

I then saved the program as Example6_12.py, and ran it for the class. The following screenshot was displayed on the classroom projector:

```
C:\Windows\system32\cmd.exe

C:\PythonFiles\Examples>Example6_12
Full Name outside function is John Smiley
Execution of simple function
Full Name within function is Babe Ruth
Full Name outside function is Babe Ruth

C:\PythonFiles\Examples>
```

"This time," I said, "we see the results we were expecting before. The value of the Global variable *full_name* in the main body of our Python program has been updated from 'John Smiley' to 'Babe Ruth', unlike Example6_11 where the **simple()** function actually created a local variable with the same name, but never updated the Global variable."

"Cool," Joe said. "And I promise I'll never do this :)"

"I presume we can update numeric Global variables as well as String Global variables using the global keyword?" Steve asked.

"We can update the value of any type of Global variable from within a function," I said, "as long as we use the global keyword. Once again, I emphasize that doing so is poor programming practice. I recognize that sometimes you will want to update the value of a Global variable with using the code found in the function. However, instead of updating a Global variable directly from within a function, it is better to pass the value of the Global variable as an argument to a function, execute the function, and then return a value back to the calling program which then updates the value of the Global variable. Another reason to use that technique? Later on today, we'll learn that we can place functions in external files called modules. When we do that, there is no way for the function in a module to access Global variables defined in the main body of our program---even if we use the global keyword. So working with arguments and return values is the way to go. I'll show you that technique shortly."

"I heed your warning," Kate said smiling, "but can we see an example of how we can update a numeric Global variable from within a function?"

After thinking for a bit, I reluctantly displayed this code on the classroom projector.

```
# Example6_13.py
# Update the value of a numeric Global variable from within a function

def simple2():                          #Function Definition
    global counter
    counter += 1

counter = 0
print("The value of counter is " + str(counter))
simple2()
print("The value of counter is " + str(counter))
simple2()
print("The value of counter is " + str(counter))
simple2()
print("The value of counter is " + str(counter))
simple2()
print("The value of counter is " + str(counter))
```

I then saved the program as Example6_13.py, and ran it for the class. The following screenshot was displayed on the classroom projector:

I gave my students a chance to think about what they were seeing in the Python Console.

"What we've done here," I said "is define a new function called **simple2()**. It accesses the value of the Global variable *counter*, defined in the main portion of our program, and increments it by 1. To do that, as we did in Example6_12.py, we use the global keyword, followed by the name of the Global variable *counter* with which we wish to work. We then use the augmented operator += to increment the value of the Global variable *counter*..."

```
def simple2():                          #Function Definition
  global counter
  counter += 1
```

"Within the main body of our program" I continued, "we initialize the value of our Global variable *counter* to 0 and then immediately use the **print()** function to display its value, which is 0, in the Python Console... "

```
counter = 0
print("The value of counter is " + str(counter))
```

"...We then execute the **simple(2)** function, which increments the value of the *counter*, then once again we display its value, which is now 1, in the Python Console..."

```
simple2()
print("The value of counter is " + str(counter))
```

"...At this point we execute the **simple(2)** function again, display the value of the *counter* variable, which is now 2, in the Python Console..."

```
simple2()
print("The value of counter is " + str(counter))
```

"...and then repeat that process two more times..."

```
simple2()
print("The value of counter is " + str(counter))
simple2()
print("The value of counter is " + str(counter))
```

"...The end result is that we display the values 0,1,2, 3 and 4 in the Python Console."

"That's cool," Linda said. "What would happen if we forgot to code the global keyword with the *counter* variable? Would Python create a Local variable called *counter*, the way it did with *full_name* in the previous example."

"What we'll see Linda," I said, "is utter confusion on Python's part. Let me show you."

I then modified Example6_13.py, 'forgetting' to code the global keyword in the **simple2()** Function Definition, like this...

```
# Example6_14.py
# Oops, we forgot the global keyword

def simple2():                          #Function Definition
  counter += 1

counter = 0
print("The value of counter is " + str(counter))
simple2()
print("The value of counter is " + str(counter))
```

```
simple2()
print("The value of counter is " + str(counter))
simple2()
print("The value of counter is " + str(counter))
simple2()
print("The value of counter is " + str(counter))
```

I then saved the program as Example6_14.py, and ran it for the class. The following screenshot was displayed on the classroom projector:

```
C:\Windows\system32\CMD.exe

C:\PythonFiles\Examples>Example6_14
The value of counter is 0
Traceback (most recent call last):
  File "C:\PythonFiles\Examples\Example6_14.py", line 9, in <module>
    simple2()
  File "C:\PythonFiles\Examples\Example6_14.py", line 5, in simple2
    counter += 1
UnboundLocalError: local variable 'counter' referenced before assignment

C:\PythonFiles\Examples>
```

"What happened?" Rhonda asked.

"Python tried to run the program" I said. "It first displayed the value of the Global variable *counter* in the main body of the program, which is zero. However, when Python executed the **simple2()** function, and tried to increment the value of the *counter* variable, it produced an UnboundLocalError Exception. As Linda surmised, without the global keyword, when Python saw the incrementation of the *counter* variable, Python presumed it was working with a Local variable with that name. The problem is that no Local variable with the name **counter** had been previously created. You can't add 1 to something that doesn't exist."

"I would have thought that adding 1 to the *counter* variable would create a local copy of the *counter* variable," Blaine said. "I guess that's not the case?"

"That's right Blaine," I said. "In Python, a variable must first be created before we can start performing operations on it. Adding 1 to the value of a variable that hasn't yet been created will generate the UnboundLocalError we see here. This is an error we will look at in more detail in Week 8 of our class."

I paused before continuing.

"Of course," I said, "if we initialized the value of a Local variable called *counter* to 0 within the function, the program would run, but we would be defeating the purpose of the **simple2()** function which was to add 1 to the value of the global variable *counter* in the main module. If we did that, we would display a series of 0's in the Python Console."

"All of these problems might be why Python purists suggest it's a bad idea to work with Global variables," Dave said smiling.

"Exactly Dave," I said. "By the way, what we're attempting to do here, increment the value of a global variable is a pretty common programming application. The way we chose to implement it is the problem."

"You said that there is a better way to do this," Kate said. "By passing an argument and returning a value? Can you show us what that code would look like?"

"I'd be happy to show you the 'approved' method Kate," I said, smiling.

I then modified Example6_13.py to look like this...

```
# Example6_15.py


def simple3(x):                    #Function Definition
  x+= 1
  return x
```

```
counter = 0
print("The value of counter is " + str(counter))
counter=simple3(counter)
print("The value of counter is " + str(counter))
counter=simple3(counter)
print("The value of counter is " + str(counter))
counter=simple3(counter)
print("The value of counter is " + str(counter))
counter=simple3()
print("The value of counter is " + str(counter))
```

I then saved the program as Example6_15.py, and ran it for the class. The following screenshot was displayed on the classroom projector:

```
C:\Windows\system32\CMD.exe

C:\PythonFiles\Examples>Example6_15
The value of counter is 0
The value of counter is 1
The value of counter is 2
The value of counter is 3
The value of counter is 4

C:\PythonFiles\Examples>_
```

"As you can see," I said, "this program produces the same results as Example6_13, but without directly updating the Global variable *counter.*"

"That will make those Python purists you're always speaking of happy, won't it?" Rhonda said smiling.

"Yes it will Rhonda," I said. "What we've done here, is define a new function called **simple3()**. Unlike **simple2()**, **simple3()** accepts a single argument (for the sake of simplicity, we called it x). The calling program will pass us the value of *counter,* **simple3()** will increment it by 1, then return the incremented value back to the calling program as a return value. This return value will then be assigned to the *counter* variable, thereby overwriting it. In this way, we avoid directly updating the Global variable *counter* from within the **simple3()** function, but achieve the same results."

I paused before continuing.

"Let's take a look at the code in **simple3()**," I said. "An argument is passed as *x* to the **simple3()** function, *x* is incremented by 1, and the value of *x* is then returned back to the calling program."

```
def simple3(x):                    #Function Definition
  x+= 1
  return x
```

> **NOTE: In case you're wondering, we could have named the parameter in simple(3) counter with no ill effects. We would have produced the same results. However, I wanted to avoid confusing the parameter with the Global variable. It's perfectly acceptable to create a function with single letter parameter names (sometimes called throwaway parameters)**

"As we did with Example6_13.py," I continued, "within the main body of our program we initialize the value of our Global variable *counter* to 0 and then immediately used the **print()** function to display its value, 0, in the Python Console... "

```
counter = 0
print("The value of counter is " + str(counter))
```

"...We then execute the **simple(3)** function, passing the current value of *counter.* The **simple(3)** function, instead of directly updating the value of the Global variable *counter,* increments the value of the passed argument by 1, then returns the incremented value back to the calling program as a return value. The return value is then assigned to the Global variable *counter.* We then display the value of *counter,* which is now 1, in the Python Console..."

```
counter=simple3(counter)
print("The value of counter is " + str(counter))
```

"At this point," I continued, "we then execute the **simple(3)** function again, passing it the current value of *counter* (which is now 1), assign the return value (which is 2) to the *counter* variable, display its value in the Python Console..."

```
counter=simple3(counter)
print("The value of counter is " + str(counter))
```

"...and then repeat that process two more times..."

```
counter=simple3(counter)
print("The value of counter is " + str(counter))
counter=simple3(counter)
print("The value of counter is " + str(counter))
```

"...The end result is that we display the values 0,1,2, 3 and 4 in the Python Console."

"I'm glad you showed us the 'approved' technique for updating a Global variable," Rhonda said. "I think I prefer it. It seems more professional than declaring a Global variable within the function."

"I'm glad you agree with the Python purists Rhonda," I said. "Some day, perhaps sooner than you think, you'll be a professional Python programmer, and you may even turn out to be one of those Python purists!"

Placing Functions in an External Module

"I have one more thing to discuss before we take a break," I said, "I want to show you how to move functions out of the main body of your program into a separate file, called a module. A module is a file that contains functions. This is a step toward achieving the modularity that we discussed at the beginning of the class. One function can be used in multiple programs, without having to be copied into the main body of the program that wants to use it. Once functions are moved into a module, they can easily be called from that module within the main body of any program. And if for some reason the code in the function needs to be 'tweaked' or improved, it only needs to be changed once in the module---not in every program that uses it."

I waited to see if there were any questions before moving on. My students seemed to understand what I was getting at.

"Example6_8.py," I said "contains a function called **lets_multiply()** that accepts two arguments and returns a value. Let's move the **lets_multiply()** function out of the main body of the program and place it in a module called util.py."

```
# util.py

def lets_multiply(x,y):          #Function Definition
  return x*y
```

"That's all the code that is in util.py?" Ward asked. "Just the definition of the **lets_multiply()** function?"

"That's right Ward," I said. "A module can contain just a single function, or multiple functions. There's no need to include special code to tell Python that it's a function. Python will know that it's a module."

I paused before continuing.

"Now let's modify Example 6_8.py so that it looks like this," I said. "We've removed the Function Definition of **lets_multiply()** from our main program (although we're still executing it,) and because of that, we have included a new line of code in the body of our main program. See if you can identify it?"

```
# Example6_16.py
# Call a function located in a module called util.py

from util import *          #Tell Python to import every function from util.py

print(lets_multiply(3,5))          #Call of User-defined function in util.py
```

I then saved the program as Example6_16.py, and ran it for the class. The following screenshot was displayed on the classroom projector:

```
C:\Windows\system32\CMD.exe

C:\PythonFiles\Examples>Example6_16
15

C:\PythonFiles\Examples>
```

"We achieved the same results as Example6_8," I said. "The only difference between Example6_8.py and Example6_16.py is that we no longer have the Function Definition for **lets_multiply()** within the body of our main program. As a result, our main program has less lines of code, so we can that we have certainly streamlined our program. Furthermore, if we have multiple User-defined functions defined in the main body of our program, moving them to a separate module will substantially reduce the number of lines of code in our main program. Did anyone notice the new line of code we wrote in our main program?"

"Was it the import statement?" Rhonda asked.

"Very good Rhonda," I said. "Because we removed the Function Definition of **lets_multiply()** from the main body of our program, we need to tell Python where to find it. We do that with the import statement..."

```
from util import *                          #Instruct Python to import every function from util.py
```

"The import statement," I said, "tells Python the name of the module where our function is located. In actuality, it does a little more. Once found, Python includes the function in the memory space of our program, as if the function was included in the main body of our program."

"Haven't we seen an import statement elsewhere in the course?", Kate asked.

"Yes we have Kate," I said, "back in week 4, in Practice4_3, we imported the *datetime* module in order to be able to perform date arithmetic in the program. We used this syntax..."

```
import datetime
```

"This syntax is a little different," Kate said. "What's the purpose of the asterisk(*) following the word import here?"

"Good observation Kate," I said. "The import statement with the asterisk(*) tells Python to import **every** function that is located in the util.py module. Since that means that every function in util.py is included in the memory space of our program, for a module containing a large number of functions that can make the size of our program's memory space much larger than it needs to be. Alternatively, we can write the import statement specifying only the function or functions we wish to import using this syntax."

```
from util import lets_multiply            #Instruct Python to import just the simple() function from util.py
```

> NOTE: You can specify more than one function to import using this syntax by separating the function names with a comma

"Another option," I said, "of the import statement that doesn't inflate the size of our program's memory space more than it needs to be is this one without the word from..."

```
import util
```

"...Although we don't specify the name of the particular function we want included in our program's namespace with the import statement, we do so later when we reference it in our code by qualifying the name of the **lets_multiply()** function in the main body of our program when we call it, like this..."

```
print(util.lets_multiply(3,5))
```

"Many programmers," I continued, "find it a nuisance to have to qualify the name of their imported functions with the module name, particularly if there are a large number of functions being called in the main program."

"It seems that from util import * is the easiest and quickest to code," Bob said.

"That's right Bob" I said, "But Python purists would no doubt object to importing every function into the memory space of our program. Using this style of import statement would label you as a rank amateur. You should avoid it."

> NOTE: Python purists object to the use of the * in any import statement, arguing that it

inflates the size of your runtime Namespace, which can impact the performance (speed) of your program. You should avoid doing so whenever possible

"One more thing," I said. "I warned you about the dangers of Global Variables and here's another reason to avoid them. If we place a function into an external module that attempts to access a Global variable in the main part of the calling program, the function in the external module is not going to be able to find it."

"Even with the global keyword?" Steve asked.

"That's right Steve" I said. "With the import statement in the calling program, the calling program can find the function, but the function in the external module has no way of gaining access to the Global variable in the calling program. For that reason, it's best to design your functions to accept any Global variables they may need as a passed argument, and then use the return statement of a function to return any value or values as necessary."

NOTE: You could create an external module called config.py, create the Global variable in it, and then place an import statement in both the calling program and the external module. However, this is considered extremely poor programming practice. Better to design your function to accept any Global Variables it needs as a passed argument, and use the return statement to return values as necessary.

"Will we get a chance to practice any of the things we've learned this morning?" Rhonda asked.

"Yes we will Rhonda," I said. "Quite a bit of practice in fact. I have several exercises in mind for you to complete."

I glanced up at the clock on the wall. We had been working for quite some time, so I suggested we take a 15-minute break before completing our first exercise of the day.

Practice Using Functions to Fine-tune Your Code

Fifteen minutes later, I resumed class by reminding my students that the chief benefit in creating functions of our own—User-defined Functions---is that doing so promotes program modularity.

"Modularity," I said, "means that, as much as possible, you should create functions that perform one basic task and one task only, and place these functions in a module. In the long run, this makes your programs easier to read, understand, and modify in the future. Creating User-defined functions and placing them in modules allows our code to be easily used by other programmers. Plus, as I mentioned before, if the code in the custom needs to be 'tweaked', improved or corrected, it only needs to be changed in one place---the module."

I paused before continuing.

"Today," I said, "I have a pretty extensive first exercise for you to complete. There's a great deal of code in it, and as you write it, you'll see that, for now anyway, all of the code is being placed within the main body of our Python program. As you complete this exercise, try to think of ways you could use User-defined functions to make the program modular, because that's exactly what we'll be doing in the next exercise after this one."

I then distributed the first exercise of the day for the class to complete.

Don't Forget: If typing these long examples and exercises isn't something you want to do, feel free to follow this link to find and download the completed solutions for all of the examples and exercises in the book. Just click on the Python book, then follow the link entitled exercises ☺

http://www.johnsmiley.com/main/books.htm

Practice 6-1---The Smiley National Bank Program with All of the Code in the Main Body of our Python Program

In this exercise, you'll write a program that allows the user of the program to display their bank balance and to make deposits and withdrawals from their bank account.
1. Using Notepad (or Notepad++), enter the following code.

```
#Practice6_1.py

balance = 0.0
new_balance = 0.0
adjustment = 0.0

loop_response = input("Do you want to do some banking? ")
```

```
while loop_response.upper() == "YES":
  # What type of business are we doing?
  response = input("What would you like to do? (1=Deposit, 2=Withdraw, 3=Get Balance ): ")

  if response == "":
    print("You must make a selection")
    continue

  if int(response) <1 or int(response) > 3 :
    print(response, " is not a valid banking function")
    continue

  #1 is a Deposit
  if response =="1":
    adjustment=float(input("Enter the Deposit Amount: "))
    new_balance=balance + adjustment
    print ("\n*** SMILEY NATIONAL BANK ***\n")
    print("Old Balance is        : ",balance)
    print("Deposit is            : ",adjustment)
    print("New Balance is        : ",new_balance)

  #2 is a Withdrawal
  if response == "2":
    adjustment=float(input("Enter the Withdrawal Amount: "))
    new_balance=balance – adjustment
    print ("\n*** SMILEY NATIONAL BANK ***\n")
    print("Old Balance is        : ",balance)
    print("Withdrawal is         : ",adjustment)
    print("New Balance is        :",new_balance)

  #3 is a Balance Inquiry
  if response == "3":
    print("\n*** SMILEY NATIONAL BANK ***\n")
    print("Your current Balance is:",new_balance)

  balance=new_balance
  loop_response = input("\nDo you have more banking business? ")
print("\nThanks for banking with us!")
```

2. Save your source file as <u>Practice6_1.py</u> in the \PythonFiles\Practice folder (select File | Save As from Notepad's menu bar). Be sure to save your source file with the filename extension py.

3. Execute your program. The program will ask whether you wish to do some banking. Type **Yes** at the Python prompt.

```
C:\Windows\system32\cmd.exe - Practice6_1

C:\PythonFiles\Practice>Practice6_1
Do you want to do some banking? _
```

4. You will then be asked what you wish to do: make a deposit, make a withdrawal, or get a balance. Type **1** at the Python prompt to indicate you wish to make a deposit.

5. The program will then ask you how much you wish to deposit into your bank account. Type **50.11** at the Python prompt to indicate your deposit amount.

6. The program will display a confirmation message, indicating the amount of your deposit along with your old and new balances.

7. Notice that the program is asking whether you have more banking business. Type **Yes** at the Python prompt.

8. Once again, the program will ask you what you wish to do: make a deposit, make a withdrawal, or get a balance. Type **2** at the Python prompt to indicate you wish to make a withdrawal.

9. The program will then ask you how much you wish to withdraw. Type **20.22** at the Python prompt to indicate your withdrawal amount.

10. The program will display a confirmation message, indicating the amount of your withdrawal along with your old and new balances.

```
C:\Windows\system32\cmd.exe - Practice6_1

C:\PythonFiles\Practice>Practice6_1
Do you want to do some banking? Yes

What would you like to do? (1=Deposit, 2=Withdraw, 3=Get Balance): 1

Enter the Deposit Amount: 50.11

*** SMILEY NATIONAL BANK ***

Old Balance is  :  0.0
Deposit is:     :  50.11
New Balance is  :  50.11

Do you have more banking business? Yes

What would you like to do? (1=Deposit, 2=Withdraw, 3=Get Balance): 2

Enter the Withdrawal Amount: 20.22

*** SMILEY NATIONAL BANK ***

Old Balance is  :  50.11
Withdrawal is   :  20.22
New Balance is  :  29.89

Do you have more banking business? _
```

11. Once again, the program will ask you whether you have more banking business. Type **Yes** at the Python prompt.

12. The program will then ask you what you wish to do: make a deposit, make a withdrawal, or get a balance. Type **3** at the Python prompt to indicate you wish to display the current balance of your bank account.

13. The program will then display the current balance of your bank account.

```
C:\Windows\system32\cmd.exe - Practice6_1

C:\PythonFiles\Practice>Practice6_1
Do you want to do some banking? Yes

What would you like to do? (1=Deposit, 2=Withdraw, 3=Get Balance): 1

Enter the Deposit Amount: 50.11

*** SMILEY NATIONAL BANK ***

Old Balance is :   0.0
Deposit is:     :  50.11
New Balance is :  50.11

Do you have more banking business? Yes

What would you like to do? (1=Deposit, 2=Withdraw, 3=Get Balance): 2

Enter the Withdrawal Amount: 20.22

*** SMILEY NATIONAL BANK ***

Old Balance is :   50.11
Withdrawal is  :   20.22
New Balance is :   29.89

Do you have more banking business? Yes

What would you like to do? (1=Deposit, 2=Withdraw, 3=Get Balance): 3

*** SMILEY NATIONAL BANK ***

Your current Balance is:   29.89

Do you have more banking business?
```

14. Once again, the program will ask if you have more banking business to conduct. Type **No** at the Python prompt.

15. The program will then display a message thanking you for using it and then end.

```
C:\Windows\system32\cmd.exe

C:\PythonFiles\Practice>Practice6_1
Do you want to do some banking? Yes

What would you like to do? (1=Deposit, 2=Withdraw, 3=Get Balance): 1

Enter the Deposit Amount: 50.11

*** SMILEY NATIONAL BANK ***

Old Balance is :   0.0
Deposit is:     :   50.11
New Balance is :   50.11

Do you have more banking business? Yes

What would you like to do? (1=Deposit, 2=Withdraw, 3=Get Balance): 2

Enter the Withdrawal Amount: 20.22

*** SMILEY NATIONAL BANK ***

Old Balance is :   50.11
Withdrawal is  :   20.22
New Balance is :   29.89

Do you have more banking business? Yes

What would you like to do? (1=Deposit, 2=Withdraw, 3=Get Balance): 3

*** SMILEY NATIONAL BANK ***

Your current Balance is:   29.89

Do you have more banking business? No

Thanks for banking with us!

C:\PythonFiles\Practice>
```

Discussion

Although the program was very tedious to type, just about everyone seemed pretty comfortable with the code in it. There wasn't anything new in the program that we hadn't covered, and in about 15 minutes, all of my students had successfully coded the exercise.

"This program," I said, "is one we'll be working with for the next few exercises and is a good example of the type of program you may be asked to develop in the future on your own. It's also a good example of the type of program that can be enhanced significantly by writing User-defined functions. As you undoubtedly noticed while you composed the program, there's a great deal of code in it, and all of the code is contained in the main body of our program. As I mentioned several times today, having all of your code in the main body of the program makes reading and understanding it more difficult, and it also makes the task of modifying the program, if changes are ever required in the future, even more difficult."

I paused before continuing.

"Let's take a look at the program now," I said. "We began by creating and initializing 3 variables. *balance*, *new_balance* and *adjustment* are variables that will be used to enable us to keep track of the old balance, the new balance, and any deposit or withdrawal amounts in our simulated bank account. Notice that we have created our variables as floating point variables by assigning a number (0.0) with a fractional part to them. As we saw while completing the exercise, our customer may not be making deposits or withdrawals in whole numbers..."

```
balance = 0.0
new_balance = 0.0
adjustment = 0.0
```

> NOTE: Sharp eyed readers may experiment and discover that our program would have worked fine even if we had initialized the value of the three variables to an Integer value of 0.

When an assignment of a floating point value to a variable previously created as an Integer variable is made, Python actually creates a new variable with the same name with the new Data Type. However, for documentation purposes, I like to tell the readers of my program that I expect the variable to accept Floating Point values. Thus, the assignment of 0.0 to it up front in the program.

"...Now we ask the user if they have any banking business to do. We store their response in the *loop_response* variable..."

```
loop_response = input("Do you want to do some banking? ")
```

"...Now we create a While Loop structure that will allow us to perform some banking business. If the user has entered 'YES' (or any of the other 7 variants of 'YES',) the indented code within the While Loop will process---otherwise the While Loop will end, and a thank you message will be displayed. Provided the user has indicated a desire to do some banking business, we now ask him or her exactly what they would like to do, prompting them to enter 1, 2 or 3. We store their entered value into a variable called *response. response* and **loop_response** are not the same variable, and you must be careful not to store the user's entered value for a deposit, withdrawal, or get balance in the *loop_response* variable. *loop_response* is used to determine if use has more banking business to perform. *response* is used to indicate the type of banking business they wish to perform.."

```
loop_response = input("Do you want to do some banking? ")
while loop_response.upper() == "YES":
  # What type of business are we doing?
  response = input("What would you like to do? (1=Deposit, 2=Withdraw, 3=Get Balance ): ")
```

"...We're expecting the user to enter 1, 2 or 3, but suppose they don't? We need to check that he user has entered a valid response. If the user immediately hits the enter key without typing a number, we indicate that they need to make some sort of selection, and start the While Loop processing again by executing the continue statement as we did last week in our Grades Calculation program.."

```
if response == "":
  print("You must make a selection")
  continue
```

"...Remember, you can code a continue statement wherever you like within the body of a loop. Continue tells Python to 'jump' to the first line of code in the body of the While Loop. By coding continue here, we're giving the user an opportunity to make a valid choice without forcing them to start the program all over again."

I paused before continuing.

"...In the same way, if the user enters a number, but it is not 1, 2 or 3, we display their incorrect entry, tell them it's not a valid banking function, and we give them a chance to enter it again by coding the continue statement, beginning again with the first line of code in the body of the While Loop. Again, this is very similar to the code we used last week in the Grades Calculation program..."

```
if int(response) <1 or int(response) > 3 :
  print(response, " is not a valid banking function")
  continue
```

"...Provided we've gotten this far in the While Loop that means the user has entered a value of 1, 2 or 3. Now it's a matter of determining exactly what their response is. We do that with an If statement. If the user entered a value of 1 (for a deposit), we then prompt them for the deposit amount using the **input()** function. Because the return value of the **input()** function is a String, we use the **float()** function to convert their String response to a floating point number. We then store that value in the *adjustment* variable we created at the top of our program..."

```
#1 is a Deposit
if response =="1":
  adjustment=float(input("Enter the Deposit Amount: "))
```

"...With the deposit amount safely stored in the *adjustment* variable, we then calculate the value of the *new_balance* variable. It is equal to the current value of the *balance* variable plus the value of the *adjustment* variable..."

```
new_balance=balance + adjustment
```

"...We then summarize the transaction neatly in the Python Console..."

```
print ("\n*** SMILEY NATIONAL BANK ***\n")
print("Old Balance is          : ",balance)
print("Deposit is              : ",adjustment)
print("New Balance is          :",new_balance)
```

"...The If statement ends, and the final two lines of the While Loop are executed. The first one is crucial to allowing the program to calculate more than one transaction. It takes the value of the *new_balance* variable, and assigns it to the *balance* variable. At this point, the values of *balance* and *new_balance* are identical. In this way, if the user elects to perform more banking business, the balance variable now contains an up to date balance.."

```
balance=new_balance
```

> NOTE: Sharp eyed readers may wonder why we have a balance and a new_balance variable. If we had elected NOT to display both the old balance and the new balance, we simply could have made the adjustment of a deposit or withdrawal amount directly to the balance variable, and negated completely the need for a new_balance variable.

"...Finally, the last line of code in the While Loop asks the user if they have more banking business to conduct. This allows us to conduct more than one transaction of banking business when the program runs."

```
loop_response = input("\nDo you have more banking business? ")
```

"...We store the user's answer in the *loop_response* variable. If it's 'YES', or any of its other 7 variants, the While Loop will process one more time. If it's anything other than 'YES' or any of its other 7 variants, the While Loop will end, and we then thank the user for banking with us..."

```
print("\nThanks for banking with us!")
```

"...The code for the Withdrawal transaction is similar to that of the Deposit transaction, except we <u>subtract</u> the value of the *adjustment* variable from the value of the *balance* variable and then assign that result to the *new_balance* variable...

```
#2 is a Withdrawal
if response == "2":
  adjustment=float(input("Enter the Withdrawal Amount: "))
  new_balance=balance - adjustment
  print ("\n*** SMILEY NATIONAL BANK ***\n")
  print("Old Balance is          : ",balance)
  print("Withdrawal is           : ",adjustment)
  print("New Balance is          :",new_balance)
```

"...The code for a Balance Inquiry (if the user enters a value of 3 as their response,) is pretty simple---we just display the current value of the *new_balance* variable..."

```
#3 is a Balance Inquiry
if response == "3":
  print("\n*** SMILEY NATIONAL BANK ***\n")
  print("Your current Balance is:",new_balance)
```

"I made a mistake or two while coding this exercise," Kate said, "and trying to find those mistakes was certainly compounded by the length of the code and the fact that it's all in the main body of the program. I can't wait to break up the code we wrote into functions. I already have some ideas on how to do that."

"I'm glad you're thinking ahead Kate," I said. "That's exactly what we'll be doing with the next exercise. As you probably noted yourself, by carefully examining our code, we'll find that we're performing three distinct tasks: making a deposit, making a withdrawal, and displaying a balance. From what we've learned today about program modularity, those three tasks should be placed in three separate User-defined functions, exactly what we'll be doing in the next exercise. Before we start working on those modifications, does anyone have any questions about anything in this code?"

"I think just about everything in this program is something we've done before," Steve said, "but I was a little confused about the use of the two variables, *balance* and *new_balance*. Was the reason that we needed these two variables because we chose to display both the old balance and the new balance whenever the user made a transaction?"

"That's exactly right, Steve," I answered. "Because we chose to display both the old balance and the new balance in the Python Console, we needed to keep both the old and the new balance in our program's memory. Displaying the old balance is no problem—it's stored in the *balance* variable. To calculate the new balance, we execute alternative lines of code, depending on the transaction type. If a **deposit** is made, we execute this calculation."

```
new_balance = balance + adjustment
```

"And if the user makes a **withdrawal**, we perform this calculation."

```
new_balance = balance - adjustment
```

"Regardless of the type of transaction, just *before* asking the user if they have more banking business to do, we must set the value of the *balance* variable equal to the value of the *new_balance* variable, so that we the balance variable has the correct value for the beginning of the next transaction---if the user elects to make another transaction, that is."

```
balance = new_balance
```

"Makes sense to me," Steve answered. "Thanks for the explanation."

I waited to see if there were more questions before continuing.

"Okay," I said, "let's make an attempt at modifying this program to use three User-defined functions: one function for a deposit, one function for a withdrawal, and one function to display a balance. There will still be some code in the main body of our program—we're not moving all of it into User-defined functions—but the main body of our program will certainly be smaller this time around. When we have finished the exercise, this new version of the program should behave identically to the one we wrote in Practice 6-1, but this version will be easier to read and much easier to modify in the future if necessary."

I then distributed this exercise for the class to complete.

Don't Forget: If typing these long examples and exercises isn't something you want to do, feel free to follow this link to find and download the completed solutions for all of the examples and exercises in the book. Just click on the Python book, then follow the link entitled exercises ☺

http://www.johnsmiley.com/main/books.htm

Practice 6-2--The Smiley National Bank Program with Three User-defined functions

In this exercise, you'll modify the program you wrote in Practice 6-1, taking much of the code now found in the main body of the program and placing it in one of three User-defined functions you'll create.

1. Using Notepad (or Notepad++), enter the following code.

```
#Practice6_2.py
def make_deposit(balance):
 new_balance = 0.0
 adjustment=float(input("\nEnter the Deposit Amount: "))
 new_balance=balance + adjustment
 print ("\n*** SMILEY NATIONAL BANK ***\n")
 print("Old Balance is   : ",balance)
 print("Deposit is       : ",adjustment)
 print("New Balance is   :",new_balance)
 return new_balance

def make_withdrawal(balance):
 new_balance = 0.0
 adjustment=float(input("\nEnter the Withdrawal Amount: "))
 new_balance=balance - adjustment
 print ("\n*** SMILEY NATIONAL BANK ***\n")
 print("Old Balance is   : ",balance)
 print("Withdrawal is    : ",adjustment)
 print("New Balance is   :",new_balance)
 return new_balance
```

```
def display_balance(balance):
 print("\n*** SMILEY NATIONAL BANK ***\n")
 print("Your current Balance is:",balance)


balance = 0.0

loop_response = input("Do you want to do some banking? ")

while loop_response.upper() == "YES":
  # What type of business are we doing?
 response = input("\nWhat would you like to do? (1=Deposit, 2=Withdraw, 3=Get Balance ): ")

 if response == "":
   print("You must make a selection")
   continue

 if int(response) <1 or int(response) > 3 :
   print(response, " is not a valid banking function")
   continue

 #1 is a Deposit
 if response =="1":
   balance=make_deposit(balance)

 #2 is a Withdrawal
 if response == "2":
   balance=make_withdrawal(balance)

 #3 is a Balance Inquiry
 if response == "3":
   display_balance(balance)

 loop_response = input("\nDo you have more banking business? ")

print("\nThanks for banking with us!")
```

2. Save your source file as <u>Practice6_2.py</u> in the \PythonFiles\Practice folder (select File | Save As from Notepad's menu bar). Be sure to save your source file with the filename extension py.

3. Execute your program. The program will ask whether you wish to do some banking. Type **Yes** at the Python prompt.

4. You will then be asked what you wish to do: make a deposit, make a withdrawal, or get a balance. Type **1** at the Python prompt.

5. The program will then ask you how much you wish to deposit into your bank account. Type **50.11** at the Python prompt to indicate your deposit amount.

6. The program will display a confirmation message, indicating your deposit amount and your old and new balance.

7. Notice that the program is asking whether you have more banking business. Type **Yes** at the Python prompt.

8. Once again, the program will ask you what you wish to do: make a deposit, make a withdrawal, or get a balance. Type **2** at the Python prompt to indicate you wish to make a withdrawal.

9. The program will then ask you how much you wish to withdraw. Type **20.22** at the Python prompt to indicate your withdrawal amount.

10. The program will display a confirmation message, indicating your withdrawal amount and your old and new balances.

11. Once again, the program will ask whether you have more banking business. Type **Yes** at the Python prompt.

12. The program will then ask you what you wish to do: make a deposit, make a withdrawal, or get a balance. Type **3** at the Python prompt to indicate you wish to display the current balance.

13. The program will then display the current balance of your bank account.

14. Once again, the program will ask whether you have more banking business. Type **No** at the Python prompt.

15. The program will then display a message thanking you for using it and end.

Discussion

During the completion of this exercise (which took about 10 minutes for my students to complete,) the question as to how best complete this exercise came up. Most of the class coded a new source file from scratch. However, several students with Practice6_1.py open in Notepad or Notepad++, performed a File-SaveAs to Practice6_2.py, then modified the code for the new exercise. This technique was quicker than coding the new program from scratch, but sometimes can be confusing. The choice is up to you.

"As you can see," I said, "the behavior of the program hasn't changed. All we've done here is to take the code to make a deposit, a withdrawal, and display a balance out of the main body of our program and move that code into three User-defined functions called **make_deposit()**, **make_withdrawal()**, and **get_balance(),** respectively. Because the value of the *balance* variable in the main portion of our program is essential to how our program works, its creation and initialization to 0.0 remains in the main portion of our program."

```
balance = 0.0
```

"Does that mean that *balance* is one of those dreaded Global variables?" Rhonda asked. "Aren't we supposed to avoid using Global variables?"

"You're right Rhonda," I replied. "*balance* is a Global variable, but we haven't violated any major Python rules since we didn't update it from within any of our three functions. As we'll see shortly, we update *balance* in the main body of the program using the return value from **make_deposit()** or **make_withdrawal()**, and that's perfectly fine."

I paused before continuing.

"Let's move onto our functions now," I said. "Notice how all three functions are passed, as a single argument, the value of the Global variable *balance*, which reflects the current balance of our bank account. Again, passing the value of a Global variable to a function using it as an argument is the proper way to design your functions. In addition, after **make_deposit()** and **make_withdrawal()** have calculated a new bank account balance, we then pass back to the calling program, via a return value, the calculated *new_balance*, which is then assigned to the Global variable *balance* in the calling program. Here's the code for the **make_deposit()** function. Notice the *balance* parameter in the Function Header, and the return of the local *new_balance* variable via the return statement as the last line of code in the Function Definition..."

```
def make_deposit(balance):
  new_balance = 0.0
  adjustment=float(input("\nEnter the Deposit Amount: "))
  new_balance=balance + adjustment
  print ("\n*** SMILEY NATIONAL BANK ***\n")
  print("Old Balance is        : ",balance)
  print("Deposit is            : ",adjustment)
  print("New Balance is        :",new_balance)
  return new_balance
```

"*balance* in the Function Header and the Global variable *balance* have the same name," Dave said, "Is that required in the Function Header?"

"Good observation Dave," I said, "No it's not required. We could have called the parameter in the **make_deposit()** header anything we want----the letter x if we wanted, in which case the Function Definition would look like this..."

```
def make_deposit(x):
  new_balance = 0.0
  adjustment=float(input("\nEnter the Deposit Amount: "))
  new_balance=x + adjustment
  print ("\n*** SMILEY NATIONAL BANK ***\n")
  print("Old Balance is        : ",x)
  print("Deposit is            : ",adjustment)
  print("New Balance is        :",new_balance)
  return new_balance
```

"I preferred to name the parameter what it is that we are working on," I said. "But as you see, we can call it anything we want."

I paused before continuing to make sure I hadn't lost anyone.

"Here are the lines of code in the main body our program which calls the **make_deposit()** function," I said. "Notice how we pass, as an argument, the value of the *balance* variable, and then assign the return value of the **make_deposit()** function to the value of the *balance* variable..."

```
if response =="1";
  balance=make_deposit(balance)
```

"So that's what's happening there," Blaine said. "I was confused at first with this code. There's a lot happening in just a single line of code. I see what you mean when you say that using functions can make your code compact."

"That's right Blaine," I said. "That single line of code is marvelously compact. All of the hard work is being done by the function, and the calculated result--the new balance---is then returned back to the calling program."

"That's pretty clever," Rhonda said. "We send the value of the *balance* variable to the function, then assign the return value of the function back to it, all in a single line of code."

"That's a great summary of what's happening Rhonda," I said.

"And the **make_withdrawal()** function works the same way?" Linda asked.

"That's right Linda," I said. "Here's the code for the **make_withdrawal()** function. Once again, notice the *balance* parameter in its header, and the return of the local *new_balance* variable via the return statement as the last line of code in the Function Definition..."

```
def make_withdrawal(balance):
  new_balance = 0.0
  adjustment=float(input("\nEnter the Withdrawal Amount: "))
  new_balance=balance - adjustment
  print ("\n*** SMILEY NATIONAL BANK ***\n")
  print("Old Balance is   : ",balance)
  print("Withdrawal is    : ",adjustment)
  print("New Balance is   :",new_balance)
  return new_balance
```

"Here's the line of code which calls the **make_withdrawal()** function," I said. "As we did with the call to the **make_deposit()** function, we pass, as an argument, the value of the *balance* variable, and then assign the return value of the **make_withdrawal()** function to the value of the *balance* variable..."

```
balance=make_withdrawal(balance)
```

"That's how the old balance becomes the new balance?" Rhonda asked.

"Exactly Rhonda," I said, "Through the use of the return value. That's a much better method than trying to directly update the Global variable *balance*."

I gave my students a chance to process what was going on before continuing.

"Here's the code," I said, "for the **display_balance()** function. It too is passed, as an argument, the value of the *balance* variable from the calling program. **display_balance()** doesn't perform any calculations, it just displays the current value of our bank account balance."

```
def display_balance(balance):
  print("\n*** SMILEY NATIONAL BANK ***\n")
  print("Your current Balance is:",balance)
```

"I notice that there's no return statement as the last line of code in the **display_balance()** function," Rhonda said.

"That's right Rhonda," I said. "Since the **display_balance()** function doesn't change the balance of our bank account, there's no need to return a value back to the calling program. The value of the *balance* variable in the calling program doesn't need to change."

"I just noticed that the *adjustment* and *new_balance* variables are no longer created within the main body of our program," Kate said. "They went from being Global variables to Local variables."

"That's a great observation Kate, "*adjustment* and *new_balanace* are no longer created and initialized in the main part of our program, but instead are now created and updated in both the **make_deposit()** and **make_withdrawal()** functions. As such, as you astutely pointed out, they are now local variables. By the way, this is a wonderful illustration of the concept of encapsulation."

"Encapsulation?" Blaine asked.

"Encapsulation means that all of the data (i.e. variables) and code to adjust the balance of our bank account now resides in the **make_deposit()** and **make_withdrawal()** functions. The user of the function doesn't need to know about the inner workings of these functions. All the programmer wishing to use them needs to know is how to call the function, and how to work with the return value."

> NOTE: Encapsulation is typically seen in reference to classes and objects, but since functions are the precursors of classes, it fits perfectly here also. Encapsulation means that data and code (that is the inner workings of a function) are hidden or protected from the user of the function. We'll see this even more when we learn about Classes and Objects in my Python Classes and Objects book

"Did you say that we were going to move these functions into an external file?" Steve asked. "I'd like the practice of doing that."

"Yes we are Steve," I said, "And I agree. It will be great practice for us."

I then distributed this exercise for the class to complete.

Don't Forget: If typing these long examples and exercises isn't something you want to do, feel free to follow this link to find and download the completed solutions for all of the examples and exercises in the book. Just click on the Python book, then follow the link entitled exercises ☺

http://www.johnsmiley.com/main/books.htm

Practice 6-3--The Smiley National Bank Program with Functions in an external module

In this exercise, you'll take the three functions that you wrote in Practice 6-2.py and place them in an external module called util.py. You will then modify the main body of your program to include an import statement to tell Python where to 'find' these functions.

1. Using Notepad (or Notepad++), enter the following code into a file you will call util.py. Instead of coding the three functions from scratch, you may also copy and paste them from Practice6_2.py if you like.

```
#util.py

def make_deposit(balance):
  new_balance = 0.0
  adjustment=float(input("\nEnter the Deposit Amount: "))
  new_balance=balance + adjustment
  print ("\n*** SMILEY NATIONAL BANK ***\n")
  print("Old Balance is        : ",balance)
  print("Deposit is            : ",adjustment)
  print("New Balance is       :",new_balance)
  return new_balance

def make_withdrawal(balance):
  new_balance = 0.0
  adjustment=float(input("\nEnter the Withdrawal Amount: "))
  new_balance=balance - adjustment
  print ("\n*** SMILEY NATIONAL BANK ***\n")
  print("Old Balance is        : ",balance)
  print("Withdrawal is          : ",adjustment)
  print("New Balance is       :",new_balance)
  return new_balance

def get_balance(balance):
  print("\n*** SMILEY NATIONAL BANK ***\n")
  print("Your current Balance is:",balance)
```

2. Save your source file as util.py in the \PythonFiles\Practice folder (select File | Save As from Notepad's menu bar). Be sure to save your source file with the filename extension py.
3. Using Notepad (or Notepad++), enter the following code.

```
#Practice6_3.py

from util import make_deposit,make_withdrawal,get_balance

balance = 0.0
```

```
loop_response = input("Do you want to do some banking? ")

while loop_response.upper() == "YES":
 # What type of business are we doing?
 response = input("\nWhat would you like to do? (1=Deposit, 2=Withdraw, 3=Get Balance ): ")

 if response == "":
   print("You must make a selection")
   continue

 if int(response) <1 or int(response) > 3 :
   print(response, " is not a valid banking function")
   continue

 #1 is a Deposit
 if response =="1":
   balance = make_deposit(balance)

 #2 is a Withdrawal
 if response == "2":
   balance = make_withdrawal(balance)

 #3 is a Balance Inquiry
 if response == "3":
   get_balance(balance)

 loop_response = input("\nDo you have more banking business? ")

print("\nThanks for banking with us!")
```

4. Save your source file as Practice6_3.py in the \PythonFiles\Practice folder (select File | Save As from Notepad's menu bar). Be sure to save your source file with the filename extension py.
5. Execute your program. The program will ask whether you wish to do some banking. Type **Yes** at the Python prompt.
6. You will then be asked what you wish to do: make a deposit, make a withdrawal, or get a balance. Type **1** at the Python prompt.
7. The program will then ask you how much you wish to deposit into your bank account. Type **50.11** at the Python prompt to indicate your deposit amount.
8. The program will display a confirmation message, indicating your deposit amount and your old and new balance.
9. Notice that the program is asking whether you have more banking business. Type **Yes** at the Python prompt.
10. Once again, the program will ask you what you wish to do: make a deposit, make a withdrawal, or get a balance. Type **2** at the Python prompt to indicate you wish to make a withdrawal.
11. The program will then ask you how much you wish to withdraw. Type **20.22** at the Python prompt to indicate your withdrawal amount.
12. The program will display a confirmation message, indicating your withdrawal amount and your old and new balances.
13. Once again, the program will ask whether you have more banking business. Type **Yes** at the Python prompt.
14. The program will then ask you what you wish to do: make a deposit, make a withdrawal, or get a balance. Type **3** at the Python prompt to indicate you wish to display the current balance.
15. The program will then display the current balance of your bank account.
16. Once again, the program will ask whether you have more banking business. Type **No** at the Python prompt.
17. The program will then display a message thanking you for using it and end.

Discussion

As was the case when my students completed Practice6_2.py, the question as to how best complete this exercise came up. This exercise was a bit more complicated than the previous one, in that we were splitting Practcie6_2.py into 2 files, util.py and Practice6_3.py. One or two students coded both files from scratch. However, most of the class, with Practice6_2.py open in Notepad or Notepad++, performed a Cut-Paste operation into util.py, then performed a File-SaveAs to Practice6_3.py, then made the single modification of the code for this exercise. This technique was much quicker than coding the new files from scratch. Ultimately, 15 minutes later, everyone in the class had successfully completed the exercise.

"There's just one new line of code here," I said, after my students had finished the exercise successfully. "The majority of our work was in rearranging code by placing the functions we wrote in the Practice6_2.py into an external file called util.py. Having done that, we then needed to tell Python where to find our functions. We did that using the from import statement…"

```
from util import make_deposit,make_withdrawal,get_balance
```

"That's the only change we made?" Rhonda asked. "It seemed like a lot more than just one line of code."

"All of the work we did was in moving the functions out of the main body of our program into a separate file," I said. "Once we did that, nothing in the main body of the program had to change except for the inclusion of the import statement."

"We certainly have streamlined the main body of our program," Kate said. "It's so much shorter now."

"Yes we have Kate," I said, "Writing functions and then including them in an external module like we did here can dramatically shorten the length of our main program. In addition, future modifications will be much easier to make. For instance, if sometime in the future we find that the three functions we've written here are being used by hundreds of programs in our company, and the SMILEY NATIONAL BANK changes its name, none of the hundreds of programs will need to be changed. Only the three functions in util.py will need to be updated to reflect the new bank name."

"I love that!" Ward said. "That's a great advertisement for encapsulation."

"It certainly is Ward," I agreed.

"That line of code importing the three functions can get very long, can't it?" Blaine asked.

"Yes it can Blaine," I said, "If the number of functions to be imported causes the line of code with the import statement to get very long, you can break it up into multiple lines, like this…"

```
from util import make_deposit
from util import make_withdrawal
form util import get_balance
```

"Some programmers," I continued, "would simply code it like this…"

```
from util import *
```

"However," I continued, "as I mentioned earlier in the class, Python purists frown upon the use of the asterisk, because it inflates the size of our program's namespace or memory space. If at all possible, resist the temptation, and specify just those functions that you wish to import."

> NOTE: As I mentioned earlier, Python purists object to the use of the * in any import statement, arguing that it inflates the size of your runtime Namespace, which can impact the performance (speed) of your program. This may not seem like a big deal, but if the util.py module contains thousands of functions, and if the memory of the device running your program is limited, such as a phone or camera, then your program can run very slowly or simply not run at all.

"Is there any magic to the naming of the external module?" Mary asked. "Is util.py a standard naming convention?"

"That's a good question Mary," I said, "There is no real standard. Some programmers name their external modules based on the code that appears in the module. For instance, based on the type of functions we placed in it, we could have named our module Banking.py. Other programmers might choose to name their module based on the name of the project they are working on, for instance CorporateBanking.py. Some programmers, like me, name the module util.py to denote the fact that it's doing some utility or helper type work."

I waited for more questions, but my students seemed comfortable with their knowledge of functions---it was time to run our attention to the Grades Calculation Program.

Adding Functions to the Grades Calculation Program

"With the remaining time we have left today," I said, as I glanced at the classroom clock, "I'd like to make changes to the version of the Grades Calculation program we worked on last week by adding several User-defined functions to it."

I then distributed this exercise for the class to complete.

Don't Forget: If typing these long examples and exercises isn't something you want to do, feel free to follow this link to find and download the completed solutions for all of the examples and exercises in the book. Just click on the Python book, then follow the link entitled exercises ☺

http://www.johnsmiley.com/main/books.htm

Practice 6-4---The Grades Calculation Program with User-defined functions

In this exercise, you'll modify the Grades Calculation program by taking some of the code currently residing in main body of the program and creating three User-defined functions: **calculate_english_grade()**, **calculate_math_grade()**, and **calculate_science_grade()**.

1. Using Notepad (or Notepad++), locate and open the Grades.py source file you worked on last week. (It should be in the \PythonFiles\Grades folder)

2. Modify your code so that it looks like this.

```python
# Grades.py
# After Chapter 6

def calculate_english_grade():
    ENGLISH_MIDTERM_PERCENTAGE = .25
    ENGLISH_FINAL_EXAM_PERCENTAGE = .25
    ENGLISH_RESEARCH_PERCENTAGE = .30
    ENGLISH_PRESENTATION_PERCENTAGE = .20

    midterm=int(input("\nEnter the Midterm Grade: "))
    final_exam_grade =  int(input("Enter the Final Examination Grade: "))
    research = int(input("Enter the Research Grade: "))
    presentation = int(input("Enter the Presentation Grade: "))
    final_numeric_grade = \
     (midterm * ENGLISH_MIDTERM_PERCENTAGE) + \
     (final_exam_grade * ENGLISH_FINAL_EXAM_PERCENTAGE) + \
     (research * ENGLISH_RESEARCH_PERCENTAGE) + \
     (presentation * ENGLISH_PRESENTATION_PERCENTAGE)
    if final_numeric_grade >= 93 :
      final_letter_grade = "A"
    elif final_numeric_grade >= 85 and final_numeric_grade < 93 :
      final_letter_grade = "B"
    elif final_numeric_grade >= 78 and final_numeric_grade < 85 :
      final_letter_grade = "C"
    elif final_numeric_grade >= 70 and final_numeric_grade < 78 :
      final_letter_grade = "D"
    elif final_numeric_grade < 70 :
      final_letter_grade = "F"
    print ("\n*** ENGLISH STUDENT ***\n")
    print("Midterm grade is : ",midterm)
    print("Final Exam grade is : ",final_exam_grade)
    print("Research grade is : ",research)
    print("Presentation grade is: ",presentation)
    print("\nFinal Numeric Grade is: ",final_numeric_grade)
    print("Final Letter Grade is: ",final_letter_grade)

def calculate_math_grade():
    MATH_MIDTERM_PERCENTAGE = .50
    MATH_FINAL_EXAM_PERCENTAGE = .50

    midterm=int(input("\nEnter the Midterm Grade: "))
    final_exam_grade =  int(input("Enter the Final Examination Grade: "))
    final_numeric_grade = \
     (midterm * MATH_MIDTERM_PERCENTAGE) + \
     (final_exam_grade * MATH_FINAL_EXAM_PERCENTAGE)
```

```python
        if final_numeric_grade >= 90 :
          final_letter_grade = "A"
        elif final_numeric_grade >= 83 and final_numeric_grade < 90 :
          final_letter_grade = "B"
        elif final_numeric_grade >= 76 and final_numeric_grade < 83 :
          final_letter_grade = "C"
        elif final_numeric_grade >= 65 and final_numeric_grade < 76 :
          final_letter_grade = "D"
        elif final_numeric_grade < 65 :
          final_letter_grade = "F"
        print ("\n*** MATH STUDENT ***\n")
        print("Midterm grade is : ",midterm)
        print("Final Exam grade is : ",final_exam_grade)
        print("\nFinal Numeric Grade is: ",final_numeric_grade)
        print("Final Letter Grade is: ",final_letter_grade)

def calculate_science_grade():
        SCIENCE_MIDTERM_PERCENTAGE = .40
        SCIENCE_FINAL_EXAM_PERCENTAGE = .40
        SCIENCE_RESEARCH_PERCENTAGE = .20

        midterm=int(input("\nEnter the Midterm Grade: "))
        final_exam_grade =  int(input("Enter the Final Examination Grade: "))
        research = int(input("Enter the Research Grade: "))
        final_numeric_grade = \
         (midterm * SCIENCE_MIDTERM_PERCENTAGE) + \
         (final_exam_grade * SCIENCE_FINAL_EXAM_PERCENTAGE) + \
         (research * SCIENCE_RESEARCH_PERCENTAGE)
        if final_numeric_grade >= 90 :
          final_letter_grade = "A"
        elif final_numeric_grade >= 80 and final_numeric_grade < 90 :
          final_letter_grade = "B"
        elif final_numeric_grade >= 70 and final_numeric_grade < 80 :
          final_letter_grade = "C"
        elif final_numeric_grade >= 60 and final_numeric_grade < 70 :
          final_letter_grade = "D"
        elif final_numeric_grade < 60 :
          final_letter_grade = "F"
        print ("\n*** SCIENCE STUDENT ***\n")
        print("Midterm grade is : ",midterm)
        print("Final Exam grade is : ",final_exam_grade)
        print("Research grade is : ",research)
        print("\nFinal Numeric Grade is: ",final_numeric_grade)
        print("Final Letter Grade is: ",final_letter_grade)

print("WELCOME TO THE GRADES CALCULATION PROGRAM")

loop_response = "YES"

while loop_response.upper() == "YES":
  # What type of student are we calculating?
  response = input("\nEnter student type (1=English, 2=Math, 3=Science) : ")

  if response == "":
    print("You must select a Student Type")
    continue

  if int(response) <1 or int(response) > 3 :
    print(response, "is not a valid Student Type")
    continue

  #Student type is valid, now let's calculate the grade
```

```
#1 is an English Student
if response == "1":
  calculate_english_grade()

# 2 is a Math Student
if response == "2":
  calculate_math_grade()

# 3 is a Science Student
if response == "3":
  calculate_science_grade()

loop_response = input("\nDo you have another grade to calculate? ")
print("\nTHANKS FOR USING THE GRADES CALCULATION PROGRAM!")
```

3. Save your source file as <u>Grades.py</u> in the \PythonFiles\Grades folder (select File |Save As from Notepad's menu bar). Be sure to save your source file with the filename extension py.

4. Execute your program and test it thoroughly. We need to verify that the looping behavior of the program is working correctly.

5. See what happens if you immediately hit the ENTER key without making a selection for the student type. What happens if you indicate a student type not equal to 1, 2 or 3, such as 4?

6. Indicate that you wish to calculate the grade for an **<u>English</u>** student. Enter **70** for the midterm grade, **80** for the final examination grade, **90** for the research grade, and **100** for the presentation. A final numeric grade of **84.5** should be displayed with a letter grade of **C**.

7. After the grade is displayed, the program should ask you if you have more grades to calculate.

8. Answer **Yes** and calculate the grade for a Math student. Enter **70** for the midterm and **80** for the final examination. A final numeric grade of **75** should be displayed with a letter grade of **D**.

9. After the grade is displayed, the program should ask you if you have more grades to calculate.

10. Answer **Yes** and calculate the grade for a Science student. Enter **70** for the midterm, **80** for the final examination, and **90** for the research grade. A final numeric grade of **78** should be displayed with a letter grade of **C**. After the message box is displayed with the calculated grade, the program should ask you if you have more grades to calculate.

11. Answer **No**. You should be thanked for using the program, and the program should end.

Discussion

This was a very tedious exercise to complete. We weren't introducing any new code into the Grades Calculation Program, just placing as much of the code as possible within 3 User-defined functions. As my students were completing the project, I emphasized the need to be very careful with whatever approach they were using. Some students coded the new version from scratch. Others attempted to work with the previous version, creating Function Headers, and then cutting and pasting the code into the function. It took us approximately 30 minutes until everyone in the class had coded the new version of the Grades Calculation Program, and was able to successfully complete it.

"Wow, that was extremely intense," Rhonda said. "My program works, and amazingly, I think I understand what we did here. We've taken a great deal of code out of the main body of our program and put it into one of three User-defined functions."

"That's exactly right, Rhonda," I said. "We created three User-defined functions—**calculate_english_grade()**, **calculate_math_grade()**, and **calculate_science_grade()**. Did you notice, that unlike our practice banking program, we didn't pass any parameters to these functions, neither did we return a value from them---although that may change next week. As much as possible, I think the program is now modular, although I'm sure some of you might have done things differently if you were designing the program yourselves."

> NOTE: The design of a good, modular program doesn't mean that there's just a single workable solution. There may be many ways to write your code and still achieve the goals of your program, and still adhere to good design principles. As I often say, there's more than one way to paint a picture.

I paused before continuing.

"Because we have created three User-defined functions," I said, "the number of lines of code in the main body of the program has been significantly reduced. You may have noticed that we moved the creation of our constants out of the main body of the program and placed them in the User-defined function to which they properly belong. That is, constants required to calculate the grade for an English student are now <u>local</u> constants in the **calculate_english_grade()** function. Constants related to a Math student are now <u>local</u> constants in the **calculate_math_grade()** function, and constants related to a Science student are now <u>local</u> constants in the **calculate_science_grade()** function. Here is the header, along with the four constant definitions, for the **calculate_english_grade()** function. Again, notice that this function, as well as the other three functions, accept no arguments and return no value..."

```python
def calculate_english_grade():
    ENGLISH_MIDTERM_PERCENTAGE = .25
    ENGLISH_FINAL_EXAM_PERCENTAGE = .25
    ENGLISH_RESEARCH_PERCENTAGE = .30
    ENGLISH_PRESENTATION_PERCENTAGE = .20
```

"The rest of the **calculate_english_grade()** function is very straightforward," I said, "We took the code directly out of the main body of the previous version of the program."

```python
    midterm=int(input("\nEnter the Midterm Grade: "))
    final_exam_grade = int(input("Enter the Final Examination Grade: "))
    research = int(input("Enter the Research Grade: "))
    presentation = int(input("Enter the Presentation Grade: "))
    final_numeric_grade = \
    (midterm * ENGLISH_MIDTERM_PERCENTAGE) + \
    (final_exam_grade * ENGLISH_FINAL_EXAM_PERCENTAGE) + \
    (research * ENGLISH_RESEARCH_PERCENTAGE) + \
    (presentation * ENGLISH_PRESENTATION_PERCENTAGE)
    if final_numeric_grade >= 93 :
      final_letter_grade = "A"
    elif final_numeric_grade >= 85 and final_numeric_grade < 93 :
      final_letter_grade = "B"
    elif final_numeric_grade >= 78 and final_numeric_grade < 85 :
      final_letter_grade = "C"
    elif final_numeric_grade >= 70 and final_numeric_grade < 78 :
      final_letter_grade = "D"
    elif final_numeric_grade < 70 :
      final_letter_grade = "F"
    print ("\n*** ENGLISH STUDENT ***\n")
    print("Midterm grade is : ",midterm)
    print("Final Exam grade is : ",final_exam_grade)
    print("Research grade is : ",research)
    print("Presentation grade is: ",presentation)
    print("\nFinal Numeric Grade is: ",final_numeric_grade)
    print("Final Letter Grade is: ",final_letter_grade)
```

"Here's the code for the **calculate_Math_grade()** function," I said. "Notice that the two constants required for the calculation of the Math grade are included in the function...."

```python
def calculate_math_grade():
    MATH_MIDTERM_PERCENTAGE = .50
    MATH_FINAL_EXAM_PERCENTAGE = .50

    midterm=int(input("\nEnter the Midterm Grade: "))
    final_exam_grade = int(input("Enter the Final Examination Grade: "))
    final_numeric_grade = \
    (midterm * MATH_MIDTERM_PERCENTAGE) + \
    (final_exam_grade * MATH_FINAL_EXAM_PERCENTAGE)
    if final_numeric_grade >= 90 :
      final_letter_grade = "A"
    elif final_numeric_grade >= 83 and final_numeric_grade < 90 :
```

```
    final_letter_grade = "B"
  elif final_numeric_grade >= 76 and final_numeric_grade < 83 :
    final_letter_grade = "C"
  elif final_numeric_grade >= 65 and final_numeric_grade < 76 :
    final_letter_grade = "D"
  elif final_numeric_grade < 65 :
    final_letter_grade = "F"
  print ("\n*** MATH STUDENT ***\n")
  print("Midterm grade is : ",midterm)
  print("Final Exam grade is : ",final_exam_grade)
  print("\nFinal Numeric Grade is: ",final_numeric_grade)
  print("Final Letter Grade is: ",final_letter_grade)
```

"...and finally the **calculate_science_grade()** function, along with the three constants required for the calculation of the Science grade..."

```
def calculate_science_grade():
  SCIENCE_MIDTERM_PERCENTAGE = .40
  SCIENCE_FINAL_EXAM_PERCENTAGE = .40
  SCIENCE_RESEARCH_PERCENTAGE = .20

  midterm=int(input("\nEnter the Midterm Grade: "))
  final_exam_grade = int(input("Enter the Final Examination Grade: "))
  research = int(input("Enter the Research Grade: "))
  final_numeric_grade = \
  (midterm * SCIENCE_MIDTERM_PERCENTAGE) + \
  (final_exam_grade * SCIENCE_FINAL_EXAM_PERCENTAGE) + \
  (research * SCIENCE_RESEARCH_PERCENTAGE)
  if final_numeric_grade >= 90 :
    final_letter_grade = "A"
  elif final_numeric_grade >= 80 and final_numeric_grade < 90 :
    final_letter_grade = "B"
  elif final_numeric_grade >= 70 and final_numeric_grade < 80 :
    final_letter_grade = "C"
  elif final_numeric_grade >= 60 and final_numeric_grade < 70 :
    final_letter_grade = "D"
  elif final_numeric_grade < 60 :
    final_letter_grade = "F"
  print ("\n*** SCIENCE STUDENT ***\n")
  print("Midterm grade is : ",midterm)
  print("Final Exam grade is : ",final_exam_grade)
  print("Research grade is : ",research)
  print("\nFinal Numeric Grade is: ",final_numeric_grade)
  print("Final Letter Grade is: ",final_letter_grade)
```

"Notice that all input and output operations are done from within each of the three functions," I said. "For that reason, we would say that they are nicely encapsulated."

"Encapsulated?" Kathy asked.

"Encapsulated," I said, "means that everything that is needed to perform the calculations, including prompting the user for the component pieces of the grade, is included within the function. I should tell you that not every programmer would write these functions exactly like this."

"Why is that?" Ward asked. "Is there something wrong with the way we've done it?"

"There's an art to designing functions," I said. "And because it's an art, no two people are likely to design their functions in the exact same way, which is one of the things I very much love about teaching programming. For instance, some programmers, instead of displaying the final grade from within the function, might have chosen to return the calculated grade to the calling program, and have the calling program take care of displaying the result. My preference is to have the function do as much as possible."

"I guess you could also argue," Dave said, "that calculating a grade and displaying a grade are different tasks, and that these tasks should reside in different functions."

"That's true Dave," I said, "How 'deeply' you want to break down the 'subtasks' in your functions is up to you. Right now, I'm satisfied that each function is performing a single major task that meets the requirements for our program."

"Can we take a look at the main body of the program now?" Rhonda said, "It's been shortened quite a bit, but it's by no means empty."

"That's right Rhonda," I said, "there's still plenty of code in the main body of the program, all of it (with the exception of the code in the three User-defined functions) identical to what was there before, and most of it contained within the body of our While Loop. By the way, you probably guessed this, but we'll be moving our three User-defined functions into a separate module in the last exercise of today's class. Back to the main body of the program. All of the constants have been moved to one of our three User-defined functions. We first display our 'Welcome' banner, then initialize the value of the *loop_response* variable to 'YES'..."

```python
print("WELCOME TO THE GRADES CALCULATION PROGRAM")
loop_response = "YES"
```

"...followed by our While Loop and its test expression. Because we initialized the *loop_response* variable to 'YES', the test expression will always evaluate to True the first time we execute it, ensuring that our loop executes at least once..."

```python
while loop_response.upper() == "YES":
  # What type of student are we calculating?
  response = input("\nEnter student type (1=English, 2=Math, 3=Science) : ")
```

"...If the user's response is invalid, we display a friendly warning message and using the continue statement, start the While Loop from the beginning..."

```python
if response == "":
  print("You must select a Student Type")
  continue

if int(response) <1 or int(response) > 3 :
  print(response, "is not a valid Student Type")
  continue
```

"...Provided the user's response is 1, 2 or 3, we then call one of the three User-defined functions we wrote to calculate the student's grade. Which User-defined function we call is dependent upon the user's response. With no return value to worry about, all we need to do is call the function..."

```python
#Student type is valid, now let's calculate the grade

#1 is an English Student
if response == "1":
  calculate_english_grade()

# 2 is a Math Student
if response == "2":
  calculate_math_grade()

# 3 is a Science Student
if response == "3":
  calculate_science_grade()
```

"The final two lines of code in the main body of our program," I said, "is the final line of code in our While Loop that asks the user if he or she has another grade to calculate. If the answer is 'YES' (or any of its other 7 variants), the While Loop continues, and execution resumes with the first line of code in the body of the While Loop. If the answer is not 'YES' (or any one of its other 7 variants), the next line of code is executed. It thanks the user for using the Grades Calculation program."

```python
loop_response = input("\nDo you have another grade to calculate? ")
print("\nTHANKS FOR USING THE GRADES CALCULATION PROGRAM!")
```

NOTE: The user isn't required to enter 'NO' to stop the Grades Calculation Program. Any entry other than 'YES' (or its 8 variants) will end the program :)

Everyone seemed very happy with what they had done.

"I guess it's time we placed our three User-defined functions into a module, the way we did with our banking practice exercise?" Ward asked.

"You're right Ward," I said. I then distributed the final exercise of the day for the class to complete.

Don't Forget: If typing these long examples and exercises isn't something you want to do, feel free to follow this link to find and download the completed solutions for all of the examples and exercises in the book. Just click on the Python book, then follow the link entitled exercises ☺

http://www.johnsmiley.com/main/books.htm

Practice 6-5---The Grades Calculation Program with User-defined functions placed in an external module

In this exercise, you'll take the User-defined functions you created in Practice 6-4, and place them in a module called util.py. You will then modify the main body of your Grades.py program to include an import statement to tell Python where to 'find' these functions.

1. Using Notepad (or Notepad++), enter the following code into a file you will call util.py that you will save in the \PythonFiles\Grades folder. Instead of coding the three functions from scratch, you may also copy and paste them from the current versions of Grades.py if you like.

```python
# util.py
def calculate_english_grade():
    ENGLISH_MIDTERM_PERCENTAGE = .25
    ENGLISH_FINAL_EXAM_PERCENTAGE = .25
    ENGLISH_RESEARCH_PERCENTAGE = .30
    ENGLISH_PRESENTATION_PERCENTAGE = .20

    midterm=int(input("\nEnter the Midterm Grade: "))
    final_exam_grade =  int(input("Enter the Final Examination Grade: "))
    research = int(input("Enter the Research Grade: "))
    presentation = int(input("Enter the Presentation Grade: "))
    final_numeric_grade = \
     (midterm * ENGLISH_MIDTERM_PERCENTAGE) + \
     (final_exam_grade * ENGLISH_FINAL_EXAM_PERCENTAGE) + \
     (research * ENGLISH_RESEARCH_PERCENTAGE) + \
     (presentation * ENGLISH_PRESENTATION_PERCENTAGE)
    if final_numeric_grade >= 93 :
      final_letter_grade = "A"
    elif final_numeric_grade >= 85 and final_numeric_grade < 93 :
      final_letter_grade = "B"
    elif final_numeric_grade >= 78 and final_numeric_grade < 85 :
      final_letter_grade = "C"
    elif final_numeric_grade >= 70 and final_numeric_grade < 78 :
     final_letter_grade = "D"
    elif final_numeric_grade < 70 :
      final_letter_grade = "F"
    print ("\n*** ENGLISH STUDENT ***\n")
    print("Midterm grade is : ",midterm)
    print("Final Exam grade is : ",final_exam_grade)
    print("Research grade is : ",research)
    print("Presentation grade is: ",presentation)
    print("\nFinal Numeric Grade is: ",final_numeric_grade)
    print("Final Letter Grade is: ",final_letter_grade)

def calculate_math_grade():
    MATH_MIDTERM_PERCENTAGE = .50
    MATH_FINAL_EXAM_PERCENTAGE = .50
```

```
  midterm=int(input("\nEnter the Midterm Grade: "))
  final_exam_grade =  int(input("Enter the Final Examination Grade: "))
  final_numeric_grade = \
   (midterm * MATH_MIDTERM_PERCENTAGE) + \
   (final_exam_grade * MATH_FINAL_EXAM_PERCENTAGE)
  if final_numeric_grade >= 90 :
    final_letter_grade = "A"
  elif final_numeric_grade >= 83 and final_numeric_grade < 90 :
    final_letter_grade = "B"
  elif final_numeric_grade >= 76 and final_numeric_grade < 83 :
    final_letter_grade = "C"
  elif final_numeric_grade >= 65 and final_numeric_grade < 76 :
    final_letter_grade = "D"
  elif final_numeric_grade < 65 :
    final_letter_grade = "F"
  print ("\n*** MATH STUDENT ***\n")
  print("Midterm grade is : ",midterm)
  print("Final Exam grade is : ",final_exam_grade)
  print("\nFinal Numeric Grade is: ",final_numeric_grade)
  print("Final Letter Grade is: ",final_letter_grade)

def calculate_science_grade():
  SCIENCE_MIDTERM_PERCENTAGE = .40
  SCIENCE_FINAL_EXAM_PERCENTAGE = .40
  SCIENCE_RESEARCH_PERCENTAGE = .20

  midterm=int(input("\nEnter the Midterm Grade: "))
  final_exam_grade =  int(input("Enter the Final Examination Grade: "))
  research = int(input("Enter the Research Grade: "))
  final_numeric_grade = \
   (midterm * SCIENCE_MIDTERM_PERCENTAGE) + \
   (final_exam_grade * SCIENCE_FINAL_EXAM_PERCENTAGE) + \
   (research * SCIENCE_RESEARCH_PERCENTAGE)
  if final_numeric_grade >= 90 :
    final_letter_grade = "A"
  elif final_numeric_grade >= 80 and final_numeric_grade < 90 :
    final_letter_grade = "B"
  elif final_numeric_grade >= 70 and final_numeric_grade < 80 :
    final_letter_grade = "C"
  elif final_numeric_grade >= 60 and final_numeric_grade < 70 :
    final_letter_grade = "D"
  elif final_numeric_grade < 60 :
    final_letter_grade = "F"
  print ("\n*** SCIENCE STUDENT ***\n")
  print("Midterm grade is : ",midterm)
  print("Final Exam grade is : ",final_exam_grade)
  print("Research grade is : ",research)
  print("\nFinal Numeric Grade is: ",final_numeric_grade)
  print("Final Letter Grade is: ",final_letter_grade)
```

2. Be sure to save the file as <u>util.py</u> in the \PythonFiles\Grades folder (select File-Save As from Notepad's Menu Bar). Be sure to save your source file with the file name extension 'py'.

3. Using Notepad (or Notepad++), locate and open the Grades.py source file you worked on in Practice 6-4. (It should be in the \PythonFiles\Grades folder)

4. Modify your code so that it looks like this. Pay particular attention to the <u>from statement</u> right after the comments.

```
# Grades.py
# After Chapter 6
```

```
from util import calculate_english_grade, calculate_math_grade, calculate_science_grade
print("WELCOME TO THE GRADES CALCULATION PROGRAM")
loop_response = "YES"
while loop_response.upper() == "YES":
  # What type of student are we calculating?
  response = input("\nEnter student type (1=English, 2=Math, 3=Science): ")
  if response == "":
    print("You must select a Student Type")
    continue
  if int(response) <1 or int(response) > 3 :
    print(response, "is not a valid Student Type")
    continue
  #Student type is valid, now let's calculate the grade
  #1 is an English Student
  if response == "1":
    calculate_english_grade()
  # 2 is a Math Student
  if response == "2":
    calculate_math_grade()
  # 3 is a Science Student
  if response == "3":
    calculate_science_grade()
  loop_response = input("\nDo you have another grade to calculate? ")
print("\nTHANKS FOR USING THE GRADES CALCULATION PROGRAM!")
```

5. Save your source file as <u>Grades.py</u> in the \PythonFiles\Grades folder (select File | Save As from Notepad's menu bar). Be sure to save your source file with the filename extension py.

6. Execute your program and test it thoroughly. We need to verify that the looping behavior of the program is working correctly.

7. Calculate the grade for an English student. Enter **70** for the midterm, **80** for the final examination, **90** for the research grade, and **100** for the presentation. A final numeric grade of **84.5** should be displayed with a letter grade of **C**.

8. After the grade is displayed, the program should ask you if you have more grades to calculate.

9. Answer **Yes** and calculate the grade for a Math student. Enter **70** for the midterm and **80** for the final examination. A final numeric grade of **75** should be displayed with a letter grade of **D**.

10. After the grade is displayed, the program should ask you if you have more grades to calculate.

11. Answer **Yes** and calculate the grade for a Science student. Enter **70** for the midterm, **80** for the final examination, and **90** for the research grade. A final numeric grade of **78** should be displayed with a letter grade of **C**. After the message box is displayed with the calculated grade, the program should ask you if you have more grades to calculate.

12. Answer **No**. You should be thanked for using the program, and the program should end.

Discussion

No one had any major problems completing the exercise---although it took some time.

"There's just one new line of code here," I said, after my students had finished the exercise successfully. "The majority of our work was in rearranging code by placing the functions we wrote in the previous version of the Grades.py program into an external file called <u>util.py</u>. Having done that, we then needed to tell Python where to find our functions. We did that using the <u>from import statement</u>..."

```
from util import calculate_english_grade, calculate_math_grade, calculate_science_grade
```

"As was the case with our Banking exercise," I said, "all of the work we did was in moving the three functions out of the main body of our program into a separate file. Once we did that, nothing in the main body of the program had to change except for the inclusion of the import statement."

Everyone had to agree. In theory, this was a pretty simple exercise, but you can never underestimate how tricky and error prone it can be to cut and paste."

"Incredible," Kate said, "I love what we've done here. Look how concise the Grades.py program is now. Most of its code is now in util.py."

"That's right Kate," I said, "Grades.py is now very modular and easy to read, with three encapsulated functions included in an external module. Just about anyone could look at the code in the main body of the program and quickly figure out what the program does. That's the beauty of Python."

My students seemed very pleased with their efforts for the day. With no further questions, I dismissed class for the day.

Summary

In this chapter, we learned about the concept of program modularity and the benefits of creating User-defined functions in our Python programs.

We discussed details of creating our own functions, how to define functions to accept one or more parameters, and how to return a value from the function.

You also learned how to place functions in an external module.

We finished the chapter by modifying the Grades Calculation Program to include three User-defined functions and placed them in a module of their own.

Chapter 7---Lists and Strings

In this chapter, you'll learn about one of the most fundamental data structures in the world of Python programming: Lists. Lists are collections of variables, each having the same name but possessing a unique number called an Index. Lists permit a programmer to easily solve certain types of problems that would otherwise be extremely tedious to code. We'll also learn about Strings, which in essence, are Lists of characters. Programmers frequently need to work with Strings, and their similarities to Lists make then a natural fit in this chapter.

Lists

I began our seventh class by telling my students that we would spend most of the class discussing the topic of Lists, and finish it off by discussing Strings.

"Is a List similar to a regular variable?" Dave asked.

Dave had been reading ahead again.

"Yes it is, Dave," I said. "A variable is a single piece of data stored in the computer's memory and given a name. A List is similar, except that instead of a single piece of data, a List is a collection of data stored in the computer's memory, collectively given a name. Individual elements in the List are called items. Each item has the same name, but can be individually accessed by a number called an Index. Just like variables, items in a List can be created to store a value, updated with a new value, and simply read to obtain the current value of the item. Performing any of these operations on an item in the List requires that you specify its Index value.

> NOTE: You will sometime see the term subscript used in a description of a List Index. For our purposes, they are the same thing.

"Is a List a distinct Data Type, like an Integer or a float?" Peter asked.

"Lists are a collection of the other Python Data Types," I said. "and Lists don't have to be the same Data Type. In Python, a List can consist of items of any Data Type, such as an Integer, a Float, or a String. A List can have some items that are Integers, some Floats, and some Strings. In fact, a List can even have items that are themselves other Lists. However, Lists may not be the best choice for mixed Data Types (we'll see why a little later on.) A Dictionary is a better choice, but unfortunately, we won't learn about Dictionaries until our Classes and Objects Course."

> NOTE: In addition to Lists, Python has other types of Collections, such as Tuples, Sets and Dictionaries. Dictionaries, in particular, lend themselves to storing items of different Data Types. We will cover these more in my Classes/Objects book.

"Why would we want to create a List?" Joe asked. "So far, we've created only ordinary variables, and those have met our requirements just fine."

"Certain types of programming problems can more easily be solved using Lists," I said. "In fact, it's probably safe to say that there are certain types of programming problems that could not be solved without the use of Lists. Lists are very useful where is a need to work with large amounts of data---something we haven't needed to do so far."

"Could you give us an example of a problem like that?" Kate asked.

"Let's pretend Kate," I said, "that you are a meteorologist and, using the knowledge of Python that you have acquired in this class, you decide to write a program to keep track of 365 days worth of daily high temperature readings."

"That sounds interesting," Ward said. "365 days worth? That's a great deal of data—at least more than we're used to working with."

"Let's also pretend," I said, "that Kate would also like to calculate the average high temperature for the year. In terms of variables, how do you think we should proceed?"

Rhonda had an idea.

"We could create 365 distinct variables," Rhonda said, "called *high_temperature1, high_temperature2, high_temperature3*, and so on through *high_temperature365*, and then store the daily high temperature values in the individual variables."

"I agree that would work," Dave said, "but that means we would have to code to assign values to 365 distinct statements to create and assign a high temperature value for each day of the year. And suppose our program prompts the user for those values. That might mean having to execute the **input()** function 365 times as well."

"And what about the calculation for the average high temperature?" Kathy said. "That could be a real nightmare. The average would be the total of all the high temperatures divided by 365. That would be a very long line of code. Is this where a List could help us?"

"Exactly Kathy," I said. "A List containing high temperature readings is a much better way to solve this problem than creating 365 variables with different names. Not only does a List eliminate the need to create distinct variables, but once the high temperature values for a year are stored in the List, it's a simple process to use a For Loop to access each individual item of the List, retrieve the value, add it to an *accumulator* variable, and then calculate an average temperature. Believe it or not, the average calculation can all be done with about five lines of code. And as far as Dave's concern about multiple input() function calculations? That can be streamlined also."

"I can't wait to see this in action," Steve said.

"Let me give you another example," I said. "On Wednesday evenings, I teach a Database Administration class here at the University. Last Wednesday, I gave a quiz to the six students in my class. What would you say if I asked you to write a Python program to calculate the overall class average for that quiz? Based on what you've learned in the first six weeks of this course, but excluding what we've discussed so far today about Lists, do you have any idea as to how we could calculate the class average?"

"I guess," Ward suggested, "that one way would be to borrow the functionality that we are currently using with the Grades Calculation Program."

"Can you elaborate on that for me Ward?" I asked.

"We could prompt the user of the program to enter quiz grades for each one of the six students," he replied. "You told us to discount today's discussion of Lists, so the best I can suggest is to create six variables, one each to represent the quiz grades for each of the six students, and to assign the user's response to a prompt to enter a grade to one of those six variables. Once the user has entered all six student grades, we can then sum the values of the six variables and divide by six in order to calculate an overall class average."

"Based on what you've learned so far during the course Ward, and discounting today's discussion of Lists, that's an excellent approach," I said. "However, I'm sure that once you learn more about Lists, you'll come to the conclusion that this technique, as effective as it is, is what I call a 'brute force' method."

I gave my students a chance to ponder that statement.

"If I haven't made it clear," I said, "programs written using Lists are much easier to modify than the brute force method. For instance, suppose the number of students taking my Database quiz next week is seven instead of six?"

"That would require a change to the program," Linda said.

"You're right Linda," I said, "it would be a minor change, but a change nonetheless. Now suppose the program becomes so popular that the University's Biology Department with 500 freshman students wants to use it to calculate an overall class average. Would that change your approach to solving the problem?"

"I think we would need to find a better approach to solving the problem than this," Rhonda replied. "I don't want to have to create 500 variables! There must be a better way, and from you're telling us, it must be to use a List. Can you show us how to write the program?"

"Absolutely correct, Rhonda," I said, "I think it would be a great idea to write the overall class average calculation program using a List. But before we do that, with our first practice exercise of the day, let's write the program using the brute force method. That will allow you to see how tedious programming the solution would be without Lists. Then we'll modify it to use List processing in the next exercise."

I then distributed this exercise for the class to complete.

Don't Forget: If typing these long examples and exercises isn't something you want to do, feel free to follow this link to find and download the completed solutions for all of the examples and exercises in the book. Just click on the Python book, then follow the link entitled exercises ☺

http://www.johnsmiley.com/main/books.htm

Practice 7-1 Brute Force---Life without Lists

In this exercise, you'll write a program that prompts the user for six quiz grades and then calculates and displays the overall class average in the Python Console.

1. Using Notepad (or Notepad++), enter the following code.

```
#Practice7_1.py

counter = 6

grade1 = int(input("What is the first grade? "))
grade2 = int(input("What is the second grade? "))
grade3 = int(input("What is the third grade? "))
grade4 = int(input("What is the fourth grade? "))
grade5 = int(input("What is the fifth grade? "))
grade6 = int(input("What is the sixth grade? "))

accumulator=grade1+grade2+grade3+grade4+grade5+grade6

average = accumulator/counter

print()
print(grade1)
print(grade2)
print(grade3)
print(grade4)
print(grade5)
print(grade6)

print("\nThe class average is " + str(average))
```

2. Save your source file as <u>Practice7_1.py</u> in the \PythonFiles\Practice folder (select File-Save As from Notepad's Menu Bar). Be sure to save your source file with the file name extension 'py'.

3. Execute your program. The program will prompt you for six grades. Enter **82** for the first grade, **90** for the second, **64** for the third, **80** for the fourth, **95** for the fifth, and **75** for the sixth.

4. The program will then display the grades, plus the calculated overall class average, which is **81.0**

```
C:\Windows\system32\cmd.exe

C:\PythonFiles\Practice>Practice7_1
What is the first grade? 82
What is the second grade? 90
What is the third grade? 64
What is the fourth grade? 80
What is the fifth grade? 95
What is the sixth grade? 75

82
90
64
80
95
75

The class average is 81.0

C:\PythonFiles\Practice>_
```

Discussion

This was a very simple program for my students to code. No one had any problems with it, and my students agreed that the code in this exercise did what every good program must do: It worked! The calculation for the class average was correct.

"Brute force is right," Peter said. "What a boring program to write! Even with only six students. I can't wait to see how a List can improve upon this."

"Before we do that Peter," I said, "let's take a look at the code. Just about all of it will be familiar to you, because as Ward suggested earlier, we're using the same technique that we use in the Grades Calculation Program in terms of prompting the user to enter a grade. One thing that is new in this program that doesn't appear in the Grades Calculation Program is the creation of a variable called *counter*, to which we assign the value 6, the number of grades to be entered by the user of our program..."

```python
counter = 6
```

"We then prompt the user for each one of the 6 grades to be used in the overall class average calculation," I said, "using six **input()** function statements, and assigning the value of the user's response to each one of them to a distinct variable. You can see how tedious this code would be to write if there were 150 students in the class, not the six that we have here. That would cause the program to balloon in size."

```python
grade1 = int(input("What is the first grade? "))
grade2 = int(input("What is the second grade? "))
grade3 = int(input("What is the third grade? "))
grade4 = int(input("What is the fourth grade? "))
grade5 = int(input("What is the fifth grade? "))
grade6 = int(input("What is the sixth grade? "))
```

"Here's the code." I said, "that sums the values of each one of the six grade variables, and then assigns that sum to the *accumulator* variable. As we progress through today's class, the code to work with the *accumulator* variable will become a little more elegant. For now, it's very much brute force."

```python
accumulator=grade1+grade2+grade3+grade4+grade5+grade6
```

"This next line of code," I said, "is probably the most important one in the program. "It calculates the overall class average by dividing the value of the *accumulator* variable by the value of the *counter* variable, and then assigns that value to the *average* variable."

```python
average = accumulator/counter
```

"Is there anything magical about the names of those two variables, the *accumulator* and *counter* variables?" Joe asked. "I know we've used *counter* before, but I don't recall using *accumulator* before."

"We can name them anything we want Joe," I said. "And you're right, we haven't used an *accumulator* variable before. In fact, we didn't need to have either variable in this program. We could have used this syntax, although I prefer the one we used instead. I'd rather not use Numeric Literals, such as 6, in a calculation..."

```python
average = (grade1 + grade2 + grade3+ grade4 + grade5 + grade6)/6
```

"That follows your theory that there is more than one way to paint a picture," Dave said smiling.

"You're right about that Dave," I said, pausing before continuing.

"This next section of code displays the values of the individually entered grades," I said. "This would be another problematic section of our code if the number of students taking the quiz increases. We would need to add an additional line of code to display each additional student's grade."

```python
print()
print(grade1)
print(grade2)
print(grade3)
print(grade4)
print(grade5)
print(grade6)
```

"What does the **print()** function with an empty pair of parentheses do?", Kate asked.

"That's just for formatting purposes," I said, "It displays a blank line between the user's entries and the display of the individual grades."

"Couldn't we have used a Backslash+n here the way we've done with some of the other code we wrote?" Lou asked.

"The Backslash+n escape sequence only works if it's included within a String," I said. "Using it here, like this, would generate a syntax error.."

```python
print(\ngrade1)          'This will generate a Python syntax error
```

"You'll see in a few moments," I continued, "when we convert this program to use a Python List that this section of code will much simpler, and automatically adjust to the number of students who have taken the quiz. In fact, no changes to the code will be necessary, regardless of the number of students taking the quiz."

"Wow, I can't wait to see that," Steve said.

"Finally," I said, "this line of code displays the class average using the value contained in the average variable. Of course, since the **print()** function is expecting a String Data type, we must first use the **str()** function to convert the average variable (which will either be an Integer or Float Data Type) to a String Data Type."

```
print("\nThe class average is " + str(average))
```

I checked the room for signs of confusion, but no one seemed to be having any trouble understanding what we had just done.

"Now that you've seen the brute force method of programming this solution," I said, "try to imagine the effort required to use this technique to calculate the class average for a class with 500 students."

My students agreed that modifying this program to calculate the class average for 500 students would be a real nightmare.

"We would need 500 prompts to the user," Kate said. "Plus, multiple lines of code to sum the values of the 500 variables and assign the result to the *accumulator* variable. And 500 lines of code to display all of the entered grades."

"Excellent points Kate," I said. "Examining the brute force method, even with just the six students we had here, gives us a chance to see the type of problem that can be more easily solved using List processing."

"I'm still a little confused as to exactly what a List is," Rhonda said. "I know you said it's a collection of items. What would a collection of grades look like?"

"In the past," I said, "many of my students have found my comparison of a List to a hotel to be pretty useful. Particularly if each floor of the hotel has just one room."

"A hotel with just one room on each floor?" Rhonda asked.

"That's right, Rhonda," I said. "And the first floor of the hotel is floor number 0."

I gave my students a chance to think about that.

"As you know," I said, "a Python variable is a storage location in the computer's memory. Getting back to the hotel analogy, think of an ordinary variable as a storage location consisting of just a single floor, with just one room. A List, on the other hand, is a storage location having more than one floor---like our hotel---with each floor having just one room on it, with its own unique floor number."

"Like a hotel," Joe said. "I see what you mean."

"Or a column in a spreadsheet," Dave suggested.

"Perhaps that's an even better comparison Dave," I said. "I'm not much of an artist, but here's a drawing of what I mean, comparing an ordinary variable called *grade* with a List called *grades.*"

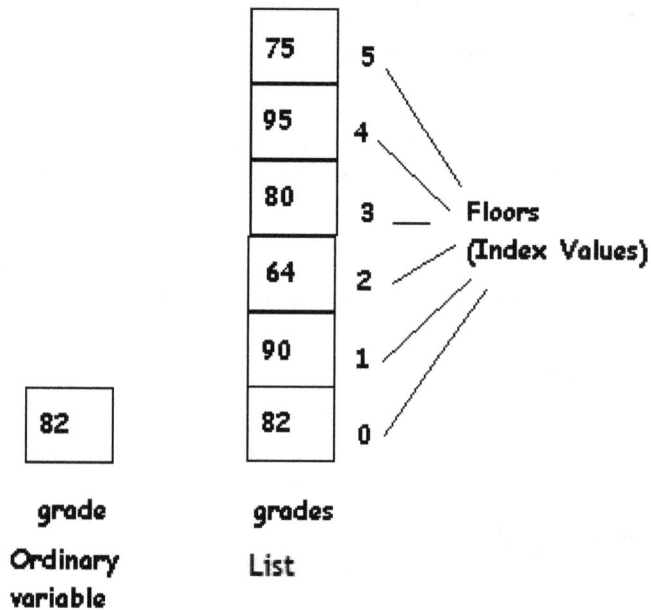

"Again," I said, "this drawing is an attempt to show the difference between an ordinary variable and a List. On the left-hand side of the drawing, we have an ordinary Integer variable called *grade* with an assigned value of 82. On the right-hand side of the drawing, we have a List called *grades*, containing six items, each item having its own value. As you can see, the ordinary variable *grade* can hold store only one grade value at a time. On the other hand, the List called *grades* can store six grades."

"What are those numbers to the right of the values in the *grades* List?" Barbara asked.

"Those are List Index values or indices," I said, "The plural form of Index is Indices. You can think of Indices as the floor numbers of the hotel. An Index uniquely identifies the item within the List. Each Item has an Index value, and Index values cannot be duplicated. This ensures that once a value is entered into an item of the List, you'll later be able to retrieve the value by using its Index."

"I know you said that the Index for the first item of the List begins with zero?" Ward asked. "Why doesn't it begin with one?"

"Let me guess, that's the basement!" Rhonda said, obviously joking.

"In a way, Rhonda, you're right," I replied. "In the computer world, many things begin with the number zero instead of one, and List item numbers are one of them. In Python, the first item of a List begins with the number zero—it's just something that you'll need to get used to."

Creating a List

"I'm anxious to see how to create a List?" Steve asked. "Is creating a List much different from creating an ordinary variable?"

"There are a couple of different ways to create a List," I said. "Here's some code that creates a Python List called *grades*, assigns 6 items to the List, then displays the List in the Python Console..."

```
# Example7_1.py
grades = [82,90,64,80,95,75]
print (grades)
```

I then saved the program as Example7_1.py, and ran it for the class. The following screenshot was displayed on the classroom projector:

```
C:\Windows\system32\cmd.exe

C:\PythonFiles\Examples>Example7_1
[82, 90, 64, 80, 95, 75]

C:\PythonFiles\Examples>_
```

"As you can see," I said, "creating a List is very similar to creating an ordinary variable. We come up with a name for the List---typically one that ends with the letter 's', and then assign to it the items in our List. These items are enclosed within square brackets (not parentheses), separated by commas. If the List item is a number, as they are here, no quotation marks are required. If the List item is a String, then the item must be enclosed within quotation marks, something we'll see in just a few minutes..."

```
grades = [82,90,64,80,95,75]
```

"Displaying the List in the Python Console is easy enough," I said, "just use the **print()** function, and supply as its argument, the name of the List."

```
print (grades)
```

"Supplying the name of the List," I said, "displays every item in the List, including the brackets."

"I'm not sure I like that," Valerie said.

"I agree Valerie," I said, "This may not be the best way to display the items in your List, but it can be pretty useful when you are first developing your program. There are ways to display the individual items in your List without the brackets. For instance, this code will display the <u>first</u> element in your List, whose Index value is 0, and whose value is 82..."

```
print (grades[0])
```

"...This code will display the item in the List whose Index is 1, and whose value is 90..."

```
print (grades[1])
```

"So it's the brackets that follow the variable name—I mean the List name—that tells Python we're creating a List?" Chuck asked.

"That's right, Chuck," I said. "Python knows we are creating a List because of the brackets. I think I mentioned Tuples earlier. Tuples are similar to Lists, and are created in a similar manner using Parentheses instead of brackets. In this class, we'll concern ourselves only with Lists."

"So the number 82 is found in Index Position 0?"Kate asked.

"That's right Kate" I said. "This List, which we have called *grades*, contains six items, each one of them an Integer, with its indices numbered from 0 through 5. In Python, all List items begin with the index number zero, which is why Lists are said to be 'zero based'. Many beginners have difficulty remembering this, believing that the first item of a List is 1, but it's actually 0. This also means that the highest index value in the List is one less than the number of items, so the highest index value in a six item List is 5."

"Did you say there is more than one way to create a List?" Linda asked.

"That's right Linda," I said. "We can also create a List by using this syntax. This is a List that contains no items..."

```
grades = []
```

"What good is that?" Mary pondered. "An Empty List?"

"That's exactly what it is Mary," I said, "an Empty List. A List that contains no items."

"But why would we want to do that?" Mary persisted.

"There are times," I said, "when we are writing a program that we know we want to create a List of items, but we don't know exactly how many items the List will contain."

"How is that possible?" Peter wondered.

"It may be the user of the program," I said, "who determines at run time the exact number of items our List will contain. For instance, the number of grades to be entered to be used in a calculation. For this reason, it's quite common to see an Empty List created in the beginning of a Python program for exactly this reason---the ultimate number of items in the List is unknown when the program is being written."

"I see what you're getting at," Dave said. "Something like the program we just wrote in Practice6_1 that calculated the overall class average for 6 quiz grades. An Empty List might be useful in modifying that program to handle a variable number of quiz grades."

"That's right Dave," I said. "An Empty List is exactly what we'll create when we modify Practice6_1 to use List processing in just a few moments."

> NOTE: Python Lists are said to be 'Mutable', that is, once created, they can be changed by adding, modifying, or deleting items. This may seem obvious, but later on, you'll learn that other Python objects, such as Tuples and Strings, are Immutable. They cannot be changed, although you can create a new Tuple or a new String with the same name.

"Does Python care how many items will be contained in the List?" Dave asked. "I know in some other programming languages, we need to tell the program in advance how many items we will be storing."

"That's not the case with Python Dave," I said. "We can store as many items in a List as we want---and there's no need to let Python know ahead of time how many items there will be."

"I presume that once we have created a List, we can add new items to it?" Kate asked.

"That's right Kate," I said, "We can add new items to a List that already contains items and also to an Empty. Because the List is a Python object, there are quite a few built-in methods to allow us to work with the List. One of these methods, the **append()** method, allows us to easily add a new item to the end of a List.:

"Is that all we can do to a List?" Steve asked. "Add new items to it?"

"Oh no Steve," I said. "In addition to adding new items to the List using the **append()** method, we can delete items from a List using the **delete()** method, insert new items between items using the **insert()** method, and replace items in the List with new values as I'm about to show you shortly. We can also completely overlay the List. And of course, once we have items in a List, we can easily retrieve the value from one or more of those items."

"I would think that would be tricky because of the Index numbers?" Ward asked.

"The List methods make working with Lists easy," I said. "but you're right Ward, we need to pay careful attention to our Index numbers."

Common Errors when working with Lists

"As Ward pointed out," I said, "working with the items in a List can be tricky because in order to do so, we have to use the Index associated with the item. Let's take a look at some common errors that beginners make with Lists when working with the Index. This code, which is designed to assign the value 82 to the first item in the *grades List* (whose Index is 0) appears to be fine, but watch what happens when we execute it.."

I then displayed this code on the classroom projector:

```
# Example7_2.py

grades = []                  #Create an empty List
grades[0] = 82               #Assign the value 82 to the element whose Index is 0

print (grades)
```

I saved the program as Example7_2.py, and ran it for the class. The following screenshot was displayed on the classroom projector:

"What happened?" I asked the class.

"Python is complaining that the index is out of range," Dave said. "Is that because we initially created an empty *grades* List and that there is no item whose Index value is 0?"

"That's excellent Dave," I said. "The code we used here would have worked fine if the *grades* List already contained an item with an Index of 0, which is a List with at least one item in it. However, since the *grades* List is empty, there are no items in it, and therefore no item with an Index of 0. Because of that, Python complains that the index value we are specifying is out of range."

"Perhaps a better message would have been that the Index simply doesn't exist?" Kate asked.

"I agree Kate," I replied.

"Did you say that code would have been OK if there was at least one item in the List?" Ward asked.

"Yes Ward," I answered, "the code would have executed fine if there had been one item in the *grades* List. In that case, we would have updated the item having an Index of 0 with the value of 82."

I paused before continuing.

"Here's another example of a problem that is bit more subtle," I said. "See if you can see what the problem will be with this code."

I then displayed this code on the classroom projector:

```
# Example7_3.py

grades = [82,90]          #Create a List with 2 items
grades[2] = 64            #Assign the value 64 to the element whose Index is 2

print (grades)
```

I saved the program as Example7_3.py, and ran it for the class. The following screenshot was displayed on the classroom projector:

"We received the same error as when we ran the other program" Rhonda said. "IndexError: list assignment index out of range Exception. But this time we don't have an empty List. We have 2 items in it, and we are trying to update the item whose Index is 2."

"I think I see what the problem is," Blaine said. "There is no item with an Index of 2."

"But there are 2 items in the *grades* List," Rhonda interjected.

"Blaine's right Rhonda," I said, "It's true that there are 2 items in the *grades* List, but you're forgetting that Index values in a List begin with 0. The first item in a List has an Index of 0, the second item has an Index of 1, and a third item would have an Index of 2---if it existed. Since the *grades* List contains only 2 items, there is no item in the List whose Index is 2. The code to update the second item in the *grades* List would look like this..."

```
grades[1] = 64
```

> NOTE: With Lists, Index numbers begin with zero, and the Index of an item is always 1 less than the Item's position in the List. That is, if a List contains 3 items, the Index of the last item in the List is 2, not 3.

"Tripped up again," Rhonda said smiling. "I'll be sure to remember that!"

Updating Items in a List using its Index

"I want to emphasize," I continued, "that the code we attempted to use to update the value of an item in a List is perfectly fine---provided an item exists with the Index that we specify. Look at this program that successfully updates an item in the *grades* List whose Index is 2."

"In other words, the third item in the List!," Rhonda said proudly.

"Perfect Rhonda," I said. "The third item in the *grades* List has an Index of 2."

I then displayed this code on the classroom projector:

```
# Example7_4.py

grades = [82,90,66]            #Create a List with 3 items

print (grades[0])
print (grades[1])
print (grades[2])

grades[2] = 64            #Assign the value 64 to the element whose Index is 2 and value is currently 66

print()
print (grades[0])
print (grades[1])
print (grades[2])
```

I saved the program as Example7_4.py, and ran it for the class. The following screenshot was displayed on the classroom projector:

"There are no errors this time," Rhonda said, "and it appears that the value for the third item in the List has been updated. Can you go over the code?"

"I'd be glad to Rhonda," I said, "The first thing we did was to create a List called *grades*, containing 3 items, where the items have Indices of 0, 1 and 2. The values for the items are placed within brackets, separated by commas. The first item in the List, with an Index of 0, is assigned the value 82. The second item in the List, with an Index of 1, is assigned the value of 90. The third item in the List, with an Index of 2, is assigned a value of 66. "

```
grades = [82,90,66]            #Create a List with 3 items
```

"And we didn't need to do anything to create the Indices?" Kate asked.

"That's right Kate," I said. "The indices for the items in a Python List are created automatically for us, based on the position of the values within the brackets. The first value is added as an item with an Index of 0, the second value as an item with an Index of 1, and so on."

I paused before continuing.

"This next section of code," I said, "enables us to display the three items in the *grades* List. In Example7_1.py we displayed the entire *grades* List (including the brackets) with a single execution of the **print()** function. Here, I wanted to show you how we can display individual items in the List using the Item's Index. Notice that we pass the **print()** function an argument containing the name of the *grades* List with the Index of the item we wish to display within brackets."

```
print (grades[0])
print (grades[1])
print (grades[2])
```

"This code," I said, "updates the value of the third item in the List with the number 64. to do that, we use what appears to be a variable assignment statement, but in addition to the name of the *grades* List, we also specify the Index of the item we wish to update..."

```
grades[2] = 64                #Assign the value 64 to the element whose Index is 2 and value is now 66
```

"Once again," I said, "we display the values of the three items in the *grades* List. This proves that the statement to update the third item worked."

```
print()
print (grades[0])
print (grades[1])
print (grades[2])
```

"I think you've told us before," Rhonda said, "but what does the **print()** function with an empty pair of parentheses do?"

"That's just for formatting purposes," I said, "It ensures that there's a blank line between the original values in the List, and the value of the items in the List after we have modified the 3rd item. You see this quite a bit in Python programs. We could have written the code like this instead..."

```
print (\ngrades[0])
print (grades[1])
print (grades[2])
```

Displaying Items in a List the Fast Way

"What would happen if you wanted to display the value of every item in the List on a line of its own," Chuck asked. "I know we can display the entire List by using the **print()** function with the name of the List as an argument, but all of the values are on a single line. Using the technique you just showed us can be pretty tedious---a line of code for each item in the List. There must be an easier way."

"You read my mind Chuck," I said. "I was just about to show you that easier way."

I displayed this modified code on the classroom projector....

```
# Example7_5.py

grades = [82,90,66]          #Create a List with 3 items
for grade in grades:
  print(grade)

grades[2] = 64               #Assign the value 64 to the item whose Index is 2

print()
for grade in grades:
  print(grade)
```

I then saved the program as Example7_5.py, and ran it for the class. The following screenshot was displayed on the classroom projector:

"The results are the same," I said, "although the code is a bit different. Let's take a look at the code now. As we did in Example7_4.py, we created a 3 item List called *grades*..."

```
grades = [82,90,66]
```

"Instead of using three distinct executions of the **print()** function to display each item in the *grades* List as we did in Example7_4.py," I said, "we're using a For Loop with a single line of code in the body of its loop to do it. As we iterate through the *grades* List, we execute the **print()** function, passing it, as an argument, the current item in the List via the *grade* variable..."

```
for grade in grades:
  print(grade)
```

"We can use a For Loop to display all of the items in a List?" Kate asked.

"Yes we can Kate," I said, "Two weeks ago, in Example5_3.py, we used a For Loop to iterate through a List of numbers generated by the **range()** function. This is similar, only this time we're using the For Loop to iterate through a List we created ourselves. Here's the code from Example5_3.py."

```
# Example5_3.py

for counter in range (5) :
  print (counter)
print("\nAll done!")
```

"I can see the similarities," Kate said, "Instead of iterating through a List of Integers generated by the range() function, we're iterating through the items of the List we created ourselves. So *grade* is the Iteration Variable for the For Loop in Example7_5.py?"

"That's right Kate," I said. "In Example5_3.py, we named the Iteration Variable *counter*, here I named it *grade*, which more accurately describes what it is. As we iterate through the items in the *grades* List, the item is assigned to the *grade* variable. We could just as easily named *grade* the letter x if we had wanted to---and you may see that in other programmers code. Typically, however, the Iteration Variable for the items in a List is the singular form of the name of the List. Thus, *grade* for the *grades* List."

> NOTE: When you use a For Loop to iterate through the items of a List, the Iteration Variable is typically the singular form of the name of the List. Thus, grade for grades.

"At this point," I continued, "we update the value of the third item in the *grades List* (the one with an Index of 2) to 64, then once again use a For Loop to display the value of each of the items in the *grades* List."

```
grades[2] = 64
print()
for grade in grades:
  print(grade)
```

"This would pay dividends," Dave said, "if the List had 1,000 grades in it. Instead of using 1,000 lines of code to display each grade value on a separate line in the Python Console, two lines of code will do the trick."

"You're right Dave," I said. "That's the beauty of Loop processing and the beauty of Lists. Try to incorporate both whenever you can."

"I love what we've done here with Lists," Ward said, "Once we got past that out of range error, that is. And you say there's more we can do with Lists?"

"Much, much more," I said.

"I was about to say," Kathy said, "List processing isn't bad at all, as long as we remember that Index values begin with 0."

"I agree, Kathy," I said. "The fact that the items of a List are numbered starting with zero can be confusing. Just remember that the last item in a List has an Index value that is always one less than the total number of items in the List. In other words, if a List contains 10 items, the last item has an Index of 9."

Displaying Items in a List using Negative Indices

"I almost hate to bring this up," Ward said, "but last week at work I was looking over the shoulder of one of our programmers, and I noticed that she was using what appeared to be a negative Index number while working with a List. Was I seeing things?"

"You weren't imaging things Ward," I said. "Negative Index numbers are valid in Python. With Positive Index numbers, which start with 0, you are starting with the first item in the List (or as we'll see later, the left-hand side of a String.) If you use a Negative Index number, you are starting with the last item in the List (or, as we'll see later, the right-hand side of a String.) For instance, -1 is always the Index number of the last item added to the List, or as we'll see later, the right most character in a String. -2 is the next to last item in a List, and so on. I don't see Negative Indices used that often, and when I do it's almost always a programmer who wants to update the last item in a List, and not knowing the exact Positive Index number, it's very easy to use -1 as the Index since it's always the last item in the List. We can modify the code we used in Example 7_5 to update the value of the last grade in the *grades* List using a Negative Index numbers. As a reminder, here's the code to update the third item in the List to 64…"

```
grades[2] = 64
```

"The code to do the update using a Negative Index number," I said, "would look like this. Since the third item in the *grades* List is also the last item in the *grades* List, we use -1 as the value of the Index."

```
grades[-1] = 64
```

"I'm having a hard enough time understanding Positive Indices," Rhonda said, "I don't think I want to deal with Negative Indices."

"As Ward discovered," I said, "it's good to know that Python supports Negative Indices in case you see them somewhere in your Python career."

Plus, if a List contains a large number of items, -1 allows you to easily access the last item in the List without having to come up with an exact number matching the last item."

> **NOTE: Not many programming languages use Negative Indices, but they can be quite useful with a very large List, particularly using -1 to access the last item in a List. Positive Indices, Negative Indices. The choice is yours!**

Creating a List of Strings

"In addition to a List of Integers," I said, "We can also create a List of Strings. The process is the same---except that Strings, as we've already seen in this class, must be enclosed within quotation marks. Here's a program that creates a List containing the seven days of the week, then uses a For Loop to display the seven items in the List."

I then displayed this code on the classroom projector....

```
# Example7_6.py

days_of_the_week = ["Monday","Tuesday","Wednesday","Thursday","Friday","Saturday","Sunday"]
for day in days_of_the_week:
    print(day)
```

I saved the program as Example7_6.py, and ran it for the class. The following screenshot was displayed on the classroom projector:

"As you can see," I said, "we have successfully created a List containing the seven days of the week and displayed each item in the List in the Python Console. This program is much like the previous example, except that this time, instead of creating a List of numbers, we have created a List containing the days of the week. The process is the same---enclose the items within a set of quotation marks, separate the items by commas, then enclose all of them within a set of brackets."

```python
days_of_the_week = ["Monday","Tuesday","Wednesday","Thursday","Friday","Saturday","Sunday"]
```

"As we did in Example7_5.py," I said, "we use a For Loop to display each of the items in the *days_of_the_week* List."

```python
for day in days_of_the_week:
  print(day)
```

"I didn't show you here," I said, "but we can easily modify a String item in the List like we did in Example7_5.py. This code would modify the first item in the List from 'Monday' to 'Mon'..."

```python
days_of_the_week[0] = "Mon"
```

"I've been trying to follow along on my own," Rhonda said, "but I'm not seeing the same results you produced. I'm seeing an error message that says: name 'Sunday' is not defined."

Without even walking over to Rhonda's workstation I sensed what was wrong.

"Do you have quotation marks around the items in your List Assignment statement?" I asked.

"Oops," I heard Rhonda say.

She had forgotten the quotation marks. Remember, String Literals such as this must be enclosed within quotation marks (or single quotes or triple quotes as we discussed a bit earlier.)

Rhonda corrected the program and gave me a thumbs up to indicate success with her version of it.

Creating a List with mixed Data Types

"In addition to a List of numbers and a List of Strings," I continued, "we can also create a List that has a mixture of Data Types, for instance numbers and Strings. Here's some code that creates a List with items of baseball player names and the number of Home Runs they hit in their career. For those of you who are not baseball fans, Hank Aaron hit 755 Home Runs in his career, Babe Ruth 714 Home Runs, and Willie Mays 660 Home Runs."

I then displayed this code on the classroom projector.

```python
# Example7_7.py

baseball_greats = ["Hank Aaron",755, "Babe Ruth",714,"Willie Mays",660]
for player in baseball_greats:
  print(player)
```

I saved the program as Example7_7.py, and ran it for the class. The following screenshot was displayed on the classroom projector:

```
C:\Windows\system32\cmd.exe                      _  □  X

C:\PythonFiles\Examples>Example7_7
Hank Aaron
755
Babe Ruth
714
Willie Mays
660

C:\PythonFiles\Examples>_
```

"As you can see," I said, "we have successfully created a List containing three baseball players and the number of Home Runs each hit during their careers. We also displayed each item in the List in the Python Console."

I paused before continuing.

"This program is much like the previous examples," I said, "except that this time, instead of creating a List of the same Data Type, we have created a List containing a mixture of Strings and Numbers. The process is the same--- enclose the String items within a set of quotation marks, the numbers without quotation marks, separate the items by commas, then enclose all of them within a set of brackets."

baseball_greats = ["Hank Aaron",755, "Babe Ruth",714,"Willie Mays",660]

"As we did in the previous examples," I said, "we then use a For Loop to display each of the items in the *baseball_greats* List."

for player in baseball_greats:
  print(player)

"In the assignment statement for the List," Rhonda said, "Why aren't the Home Runs placed within quotation marks?"

"That's an excellent question Rhonda," I said. "We could have placed quotation marks around the number of Home Runs, which would have told Python to store the item in the List as a String, but I wanted the number of Home Runs in the *baseball_greats* List to be stored as Integers. Storing the number of Home Runs as an Integer Data Type allows us to more easily execute Mathematical Operations on it than if it was stored as a String."

"I don't mean to be overly critical," Ward said, "but shouldn't we display the number of Home Runs next to the player's name on the same line?"

"That would make our display look better," I said. "I mentioned a few minutes ago that a List may not be the best way to represent mixed Data Types like this. The problem is that the player's name and the number of Home Runs the player hit are logically related, however they appear as different items in the List. Every other item is the name of the player, and every other item is the number of Home Runs associated with that player."

I thought for a moment.

"One way to display the items in a more user friendly way," I said, "would be to write the program like this..."

I displayed this code on the classroom projector.

Example7_8.py

baseball_greats = ["Hank Aaron",755, "Babe Ruth",714,"Willie Mays",660]

print (baseball_greats[0], baseball_greats[1])
print (baseball_greats[2], baseball_greats[3])
print (baseball_greats[4], baseball_greats[5])

I then saved the program as Example7_8.py, and ran it for the class. The following screenshot was displayed on the classroom projector:

This time the Python Console displayed a much neater display of players and their home runs.

"What we've done here is to display each item in the List individually," I said, "using the **print()** function to display both logically related items on the same line. Items with Index 0 and 1, Items with Index 2 and 3, Items with 4 and 5."

```
print (baseball_greats[0], baseball_greats[1])
print (baseball_greats[2], baseball_greats[3])
print (baseball_greats[4], baseball_greats[5])
```

"The display looks nicer," Ward said, "although I would imagine this can get very tedious for a List that contains more than two logically related items the way this does."

"And also for a List that contains more than a few items the way this one does," Barbara added.

"You're both right," I said. "If we were to create a List that contains a person's contact information, for instance, their name, their street number, city, state, zip code and phone number, and use that List to store contact information for thousands of people, it would be impractical to write code like this to display the logically related items in our List on the same line. There would be thousands of lines of code required to do it. For that reason, as we'll see in our Classes and Objects course, another type of Python object, the Dictionary, is a much better choice for logically related items. However there is another way around this problem, and that is to create a List that contains items that are also Lists."

Creating a List of Lists

"A List of Lists?" Rhonda said, obviously confused.

I knew this would take a minute to two to sink in, and so I paused before continuing.

"Don't panic Rhonda," I said, "It's not as bad as it sounds. Take a look at this code."

I displayed this program on the classroom projector.

```
# Example7_9.py

baseball_greats = [["Hank Aaron",755],["Babe Ruth",714],["Willie Mays",660]]
for player in baseball_greats:
  print(*player)
```

I then saved the program as Example7_9.py, and ran it for the class. The following screenshot was displayed on the classroom projector:

"As you can see," I said, "our display is properly formatted, but instead of the three lines of code it took to do that in Example7_8.py, with this program it only took two lines of code to do it. Even better, even if the List contains thousands of baseball players, it would still take just two lines of code to display it. The key is that the List we are working with contains items that are themselves Lists. Can everyone see that in this example, we have 3 items in the List, each of which is itself a List..."

```
baseball_greats = [["Hank Aaron",755],["Babe Ruth",714],["Willie Mays",660]]
```

"Is that why we have so many brackets?" Rhonda asked.

"That's right Rhonda," I answered. "The first left-hand bracket, and the final right-hand bracket mark the beginning and end of the *baseball_greats* List. Within the brackets, we have 3 pairs of left-hand and right-hand brackets, each of which sandwiches another List that contains the name of the baseball player and the number of Home Runs he hit during his career."

"So *baseball_greats* contains three Lists," Kate said, "each one of which contains 2 items—a String and a number?"

"That's perfect Kate," I said.

"We don't need to name those Lists that are items of the *baseball_greats List*" Bob asked.

"No we don't Bob," I answered. "Those unnamed Lists are called List Literals, much like we have seen numeric and String Literals during the class. Using List Literals, we can create a List of Lists like this very quickly, and because we don't need to first create the List and give it a name, that can save us a few lines of code. However, if you wanted to, you could code this example by first creating and naming the Lists to be added as items and then adding the named Lists as items to the *baseball_greats* List. It will produce the same result. Let me show you."

I then displayed this code on the classroom projector.

```
# Example7_10.py

hank_aaron = ["Hank Aaron",755]
babe_ruth = ["Babe Ruth",714]
willie_mays = ["Willie Mays",660]

baseball_greats = [hank_aaron,babe_ruth,willie_mays]

for player in baseball_greats:
  print(*player)
```

I saved the program as Example7_10.py, and ran it for the class. The following screenshot was displayed on the classroom projector:

"Once again," I said, "our display is neatly formatted. The results are the same. But this time we first created and named the three Lists that will be added to the baseball_greats List."

```
hank_aaron = ["Hank Aaron",755]
babe_ruth = ["Babe Ruth",714]
willie_mays = ["Willie Mays",660]
```

"The assignment statement for the *baseball_greats* List now looks like this," I said.

```
baseball_greats = [hank_aaron,babe_ruth,willie_mays]
```

"I never got around to explaining why this display is so neat and orderly" I said. "All that's required is a single **print()** function within a For Loop"

```
for player in baseball_greats:
  print(*player)
```

"That's looks different than the code from Example7_7.py," Mary said.

"You're right Mary," I said. "It is slightly different. As a reminder, here's the code from Example7_7.py that we used to display the items in the *baseball_greats* List."

```
for player in baseball_greats:
  print(player)
```

"Do you notice the difference?" I asked.

"There's an asterisk in front of the Iteration variable in Example7_8.py and Example7_9.py," Linda said.

"That's right Linda," I said, "The asterisk, called the *args Operator, when used with the **print()** function, tells Python to 'unpack' the List passed to it as an argument into its individual items and to display those. In other words, if a List is passed as an argument to the **print()** function with the asterisk, Python breaks down that List into its individual items and then displays those items."

> NOTE: The asterisk (called the *args Operator) can be used wherever there is a List, or any other type of Python sequence (for instance a Tuple.) It's not restricted to the print() function. A User-defined function requiring a List as an argument, could also use the *args Operator.

"That's about all the information I have to give you as far as creating Lists in Python," I said. "We also saw how easy it is to update the value of an existing item in a List. Does anyone have any questions?"

"I think I'm OK with everything we've covered so far," Rhonda said, "but I'll be sure to keep this page of notes about Lists of List specially marked for future reference."

Using the append() method to add one item to a List

"What about adding items to a List," Steve said, "Are you going to show us how to do that?"

"Yes I am Steve," I said, "We can easily add items one at a time to any List---either an empty List or a List that already has items---by using the built in **append()** method of the Python List object. Take a look at this code..."

```
# Example7_11.py

days_of_the_week = ["Monday","Tuesday","Wednesday","Thursday"]

print(days_of_the_week)

days_of_the_week.append("Friday")
days_of_the_week.append("Saturday")
days_of_the_week.append("Sunday")

print(days_of_the_week)
```

I then saved the program as Example7_11.py, and ran it for the class. The following screenshot was displayed on the classroom projector:

As predicted, we added three items to the *days_of_the_week* List.

"As you can see," I said, "we started out by creating a List called *days_of_the_week* containing 4 days of the week, then displayed them in the Python Console.."

```
days_of_the_week = ["Monday","Tuesday","Wednesday","Thursday"]
print(days_of_the_week)
```

"We then executed the **append()** method of the List object," I said, "to add the three remaining days of the week, one at a time, to the *days_of_the_week* List. To execute a method of a Python object, you type the name of the object, followed by a period, followed by the name of the method, followed by any mandatory arguments. With the **append()** method, the argument is the value of the item we wish to append to our List. Since the day of the week is a String, the argument is enclosed within quotation marks."

```
days_of_the_week.append("Friday")
```

"The **append()** method," I said, "permits us to add only one item at one time to the end of a List. Because of that, we need to execute the **append()** method two more times to add the remaining days of the week to our List."

```
days_of_the_week.append("Saturday")
days_of_the_week.append("Sunday")
```

"Finally," I said, "we execute the **print()** function again to prove to ourselves that the three items have been added to our List."

```
print(days_of_the_week)
```

"Alternatively," I said, "as we saw just a few minutes ago, we could have executed this code to display each item of the List on a separate line in the Python Console."

```
for day in days_of_the_week:
    print(day)
```

"Using the **append()** method, we can add items only to the end of a List, and only one item at a time, is that right?" Joe asked.

"That's right Joe," I said. "The **append()** method permits us to add just one item to the end of a List. Shortly, we'll see that we can use the **insert()** method to specify exactly where in a List items are to be added, but using the **append()** method, the item will be added to the end of a List. The **append()** method of the List object is perfect for dealing with user input, where the user is entering data that is to be added to a List one item at a time."

> NOTE: The append() method of the List object is perfect for dealing with user input, where the user is entering data that is to be added to a List one item at a time."

"Adding one item at a time to a List seems pretty inefficient," Barbara said. "especially if you have a great deal of items to add to the List. Is there a way to add more than one item to a List?"

Adding multiple items to a List using the extend() method

"Yes there is Barbara," I said. "There are two ways to do that. One way is to use the **extend()** method of the List object. That allows us to add more than one item to a List. Another way is to concatenate one list to another. I'll show you both methods. Let's start with the **extend()** method of the List object. Take a look at this code..."

```
# Example7_12.py
days_of_the_week = ["Monday","Tuesday","Wednesday","Thursday"]
print(days_of_the_week)
days_of_the_week.extend(["Friday","Saturday","Sunday"])
print(days_of_the_week)
```

I then saved the program as Example7_12.py, and ran it for the class. The following screenshot was displayed on the classroom projector:

```
C:\Windows\system32\cmd.exe

C:\PythonFiles\Examples>Example7_12
['Monday', 'Tuesday', 'Wednesday', 'Thursday']
['Monday', 'Tuesday', 'Wednesday', 'Thursday', 'Friday', 'Saturday', 'Sunday']

C:\PythonFiles\Examples>_
```

"As you can see," I said, "we successfully added three items to the end of the *days_of_the_week* List. As we did with Example7_11.py, we began by creating a List called *days_of_the_week* containing four days of the week, then displayed them in the Python Console.."

```
days_of_the_week = ["Monday","Tuesday","Wednesday","Thursday"]

print(days_of_the_week)
```

"We then executed the **extend()** method of the List object," I said, "to add the three remaining days of the week to the *days_of_the_week* List. Using the **extend()** method, we can add multiple items to the end of the List with a single line of code. The **extend()** method accepts just one argument, which must be a Python sequence. Python has several types of sequences, one of which is a range, another is a String, and another is a List. Here we're passing the **extend()** method what is known as a List Literal. Notice that we use the same bracket syntax that we use to create a List."

```
days_of_the_week.extend(["Friday","Saturday","Sunday"])
```

"I can verify that those brackets are important," Rhonda said. "I followed along and tried to extend the List without them, and Python complained that the **extend()** method expects just one argument, not three."

"Sometime we learn best by the mistakes we make Rhonda," I said smiling. "And it's better to make those mistakes here in class rather than back at the workplace."

I paused before continuing.

"Finally," I said, "we execute the **print()** function again to prove to ourselves that the three items have been added to our List."

```
print(days_of_the_week)
```

Adding multiple Items to a List using List Concatenation

"Another way to add items to a List," I said, "is to concatenate one List to another. We've worked with concatenation a bit during the course, in terms of concatenating Strings with the **print()** function. Concatenating one List to the end of another List is as simple as using the plus sign. Let's take a look at two ways we can perform List concatenation. In this example, we'll create two Lists, then append the second List to the first List using the Addition Operator (+)..."

I displayed this code on the classroom projector.

```
# Example7_13.py

days_of_the_week = ["Monday","Tuesday","Wednesday","Thursday"]

print(days_of_the_week)

more_days = ["Friday","Saturday","Sunday"]

days_of_the_week = days_of_the_week + more_days

print(days_of_the_week)
```

I then saved the program as Example7_13.py, and ran it for the class. The following screenshot was displayed on the classroom projector:

```
C:\Windows\system32\cmd.exe                                    _  □  x

C:\PythonFiles\Examples>Example7_13
['Monday', 'Tuesday', 'Wednesday', 'Thursday']
['Monday', 'Tuesday', 'Wednesday', 'Thursday', 'Friday', 'Saturday', 'Sunday']

C:\PythonFiles\Examples>
```

"Once again," I said, "we successfully added three items to the end of the *days_of_the_week* List. As we did in the previous examples, we began by creating a List called *days_of_the_week* containing four days of the week, then displayed them in the Python Console.."

```
days_of_the_week = ["Monday","Tuesday","Wednesday","Thursday"]

print(days_of_the_week)
```

"We then created another List, the *more_days* List, consisting of three days of the week..."

```
more_days = ["Friday","Saturday","Sunday"]
```

"Concatenating the *more_days* List to the end of the *days_of_the_week* List," I said, "is as easy as using the Addition Operator, but notice that we must then assign the result of the concatenation to the *days_of_the_week* List, thereby overlaying the previous value of the List..."

```
days_of_the_week = days_of_the_week + more_days
```

"We could also have used this code using the Augmented Addition Operator to concatenate the *more_days* List to the *days_of_the_week* List. As you can see, this is quick and concise..."

```
days_of_the_week += more_days
```

"Here's a variation in which we concatenate a List Literal to the end of the *days_of_the_week* List..."

```
days_of_the_week = days_of_the_week + ["Saturday","Sunday"]
```

"The Augmented Addition Operator can also be used to concatenate a List Literal to the end of the *days_of_the_week* List..."

```
days_of_the_week += ["Saturday","Sunday"]
```

"Finally," I said, "we can also concatenate two Lists together to create a third List, like this..."

```
# Example7_14.py

week_day = ["Monday","Tuesday","Wednesday","Thursday","Friday"]
week_end = ["Saturday","Sunday"]

days_of_the_week = week_day + week_end

print(days_of_the_week)
```

I saved the program as Example7_14.py, and ran it for the class. The following screenshot was displayed on the classroom projector:

```
C:\Windows\system32\cmd.exe                                    _  □  x

C:\PythonFiles\Examples>Example7_14
['Monday', 'Tuesday', 'Wednesday', 'Thursday', 'Friday', 'Saturday', 'Sunday']

C:\PythonFiles\Examples>
```

As predicted, the concatenated *days_of_the_week* List contained seven items.

"In this example," I said, "we first create two Lists called *week_day* and *week_end*."

```
week_day = ["Monday","Tuesday","Wednesday","Thursday","Friday"]
week_end = ["Saturday","Sunday"]
```

"...then concatenate the two Lists together and assign the result to a new List called days_of_the_week..."

```
days_of_the_week = week_day + week_end
```

"...then we display the days_of_the_week to prove that the concatenation was successful."

```
print(days_of_the_week)
```

"Wow, there are so many ways to add items to a List," Valerie said. "Is there anything else we can do to a List besides appending items to the end of an existing List

Inserting Items in a List using the insert() method

"Yes we can, Valerie" I answered, "We can insert items anywhere within a List, delete items from a List, sort items in a List, and also create a new List based on a 'Slice' of an existing List, something we'll look at a little later. For now, let's take a look at inserting items in a List using the **insert()** method of the List object. Take a look at this code in which we'll create a List called *days_of_the_week* that is missing Tuesday. We could use any number of methods to add Tuesday to end of the List, but of course, we want to add Tuesday after Monday but before Wednesday."

I then displayed this code on the classroom projector.

```
# Example7_15.py

days_of_the_week = ["Monday","Wednesday","Thursday","Friday","Saturday","Sunday"]
print(days_of_the_week)

days_of_the_week.insert(1,"Tuesday")
print(days_of_the_week)
```

I saved the program as Example7_15.py, and ran it for the class. The following screenshot was displayed on the classroom projector:

```
C:\Windows\system32\cmd.exe

C:\PythonFiles\Examples>Example7_15
['Monday', 'Wednesday', 'Thursday', 'Friday', 'Saturday', 'Sunday']
['Monday', 'Tuesday', 'Wednesday', 'Thursday', 'Friday', 'Saturday', 'Sunday']

C:\PythonFiles\Examples>
```

"Does everyone see what happened?", I asked. "We displayed the *days_of_the_week* List, containing only 6 days of the week, then executed the **insert()** method of the List object to properly position Tuesday in the List, then displayed the List again to show that our insertion worked correctly."

"That's pretty impressive," Ward said, smiling. "Now can you explain exactly how we did that?"

"I'd be happy to Ward," I said. "We began by creating a List called *days_of_the_week* that contains only six days of the week---we're missing Tuesday. Tuesday should be the 2nd item in the List, at Index Position 1..."

```
days_of_the_week = ["Monday","Wednesday","Thursday","Friday","Saturday","Sunday"]
```

"To insert Tuesday between Monday and Wednesday," I said. "we execute the **insert()** method of the List object. The **insert()** method expects two arguments. The first argument is the Index Position where the new item is to be inserted, and the second argument is the value for the new item. Since we want to insert Tuesday as the second item in the List, we specify 1 as the Index Position, and Tuesday as the value to be inserted. All of the items to the 'right' of the inserted item will automatically have their Indices adjusted..."

```
days_of_the_week.insert(1,"Tuesday")
```

"Displaying the items in the *days_of_the_week* List before and after the insert," I said, "proves that the code worked."

```
print(days_of_the_week)
```

"In case you are wondering," I said, "you can insert only one item at a time using the **insert()** method."

"If we wanted to insert an item at the beginning of the List, would we specify an Index value of 0?" Linda asked.

"That's right Linda," I said. "Inserting an item and specifying an Index value of 0 would place the new item as the first in the List."

> NOTE: Technically, you can insert an item at the end of the List by specifying an Index value greater than the last Index value in the List. Of course, you can also use append() method to do this, and you don't need to worry about calculating the correct Index value.

"Oops," I heard Rhonda say, "When I ran the code, I generated an error message, <u>TypeError: 'list; object is not callable</u>."

I took a walk to Rhonda's work station, and sure enough, this screen shot appeared on her workstation's monitor.

```
C:\Windows\system32\cmd.exe

C:\PythonFiles\Examples>Example7_15
['Monday', 'Wednesday', 'Thursday', 'Friday', 'Saturday', 'Sunday']
Traceback (most recent call last):
  File "C:\PythonFiles\Examples\Example7_15.py", line 6, in <module>
    days_of_the_week(1,"Tuesday")
TypeError: 'list' object is not callable

C:\PythonFiles\Examples>
```

Examining Rhonda's code, I saw that she had made the mistake that I've seen some other beginners make. This is how she attempted to code the **insert()** method---can you see what the problem is?

```
days_of_the_week(1,"Tuesday")        #Rhonda's incorrect code
```

"You forgot to code the name of the method after the name of the List," I said, "As a result, Python thought you were trying to call a function called **days_of_the_week()**, and Python knew that *days_of_the_week* is not a function but a List."

"In other words," Rhonda said, "I really confused Python."

"Don't feel bad Rhonda," I said. "This is the kind of mistake beginners make, particularly when they are rushing to practice new material. Next week, we'll be reviewing a number of common Python programming errors, including this one."

Rhonda took a minute to correct her code and it ran fine.

Deleting an Item in a List using the Delete (del) Statement

"I think you would agree that inserting an item within a List is pretty simple," I said. "Let's see if deleting items from a List is as easy. Python gives us two ways to delete an item from a List. One way is to use the Delete statement---the word <u>del</u>---which can be used not only with Lists but with Dictionaries as well. (We will learn about Dictionaries in our Classes and Objects course). The second way is to use the **remove()** method of the List object to delete items in a List. Let's work with the Delete statement first. Take a look at this code in which we create a List of the days of the week in which we accidentally include a month of the year. We'll then use the Delete (del) statement to remove it."

I then displayed this code on the classroom projector.

```
# Example7_16.py

days_of_the_week = ["Mon","Tue","Wed","February","Thu","Fri","Sat","Sun"]
print(days_of_the_week)

del days_of_the_week[3]
print(days_of_the_week)
```

I then saved the program as <u>Example7_16.py</u>, and ran it for the class. The following screenshot was displayed on the classroom projector:

```
C:\Windows\system32\cmd.exe

C:\PythonFiles\Examples>Example7_16
['Mon', 'Tue', 'Wed', 'February', 'Thu', 'Fri', 'Sat', 'Sun']
['Mon', 'Tue', 'Wed', 'Thu', 'Fri', 'Sat', 'Sun']

C:\PythonFiles\Examples>
```

"February is gone from the *days_of_the_week* List," Ward said. "That's great news, since it didn't belong there."

"That's right Ward," I said. "We've successfully deleted a single item from the List of the days of the week. Let's take a look at code now. As you can see, we 'accidentally' added the month of February to our List of the days of the week..."

days_of_the_week = ["Mon","Tue","Wed","February","Thu","Fri","Sat","Sun"]

"A month obviously doesn't belong in a List with the days of the week." I said, "Deleting an item using the Delete statement (del) is simple, we just type del, followed by the name of the List, and within brackets, the Index value corresponding to the item we wish to delete. Since we want to delete the 4th item in the List, February, and because Lists are zero based, we specify an Index value of 3..."

del days_of_the_week[3]

"That is easy, isn't it?" Rhonda said. "We just need to remember that the Index number is one less than the position of the item in the List. So if we want to delete the first item in the List, we need to specify an Index value of 0. The last item in this List would be Index value 7."

"I couldn't have said it better myself Rhonda," I said.

Deleting an Item in a List using the remove() method

"Bear in mind," I continued, "that the Delete statement is a generic type of tool that can be used on not just a List, but also on a Dictionary. Python also provides us a specific List method to use if we want to delete an item from a List. It's the **remove()** method and if using Index values is still confusing you, the **remove()** method allows us to remove an item from a List by specifying the item's value."

"So no Index?" Joe asked. "I think I prefer that. How does that work?"

"Let me show you Joe," I said. "Take a look at this code in which, similar to the previous example, we create a List of the days of the week in which we accidentally include a month of the year. This time we'll include March in the days_of_the_week List twice. We'll then use the **remove()** method to delete it."

I then displayed this code on the classroom projector.

Example7_17.py

days_of_the_week = ["Mon","Tue","Wed","March","Thu","Fri","Sat","Sun","March"]
print(days_of_the_week)

days_of_the_week.remove("March")
print(days_of_the_week)

I saved the program as Example7_17.py, and ran it for the class. The following screenshot was displayed on the classroom projector:

```
C:\Windows\system32\cmd.exe

C:\PythonFiles\Examples>Example7_17
['Mon', 'Tue', 'Wed', 'March', 'Thu', 'Fri', 'Sat', 'Sun', 'March']
['Mon', 'Tue', 'Wed', 'Thu', 'Fri', 'Sat', 'Sun', 'March']

C:\PythonFiles\Examples>
```

Although the program executed as I expected, I suspect some of the students didn't agree. We'd get around to discussing that in just a minute.

"As you can see," I said, "the *days_of_the_week* List starts out with two occurrences of the month of March..."

```
days_of_the_week = ["Mon","Tue","Wed","March","Thu","Fri","Sat","Sun","March"]
```

"Wanting to remove March from the List," I said, "we executed the **remove()** method of the List object, specifying the value of 'March' as its single argument. Notice, thought, that the **remove()** method removes only the first occurrence of the item specified."

```
days_of_the_week.remove("March")
```

"I just noticed that," Ward said. "We still have an item named March at the end of our List. Only the first instance of March was removed."

"That's right Ward," I said, "The **remove()** method of the List object removes the <u>first</u> occurrence of the specified item that it finds. If there is more than one item in the List with the value specified, that item or items remain in the List. Of course, there are ways around this. For instance, we could use this code to delete both occurrences of the month of March from our *days_of_the_week* List by executing the **remove()** method twice..."

I displayed this code on the classroom projector.

```
# Example7_18.py

days_of_the_week = ["Mon","Tue","Wed","March","Thu","Fri","Sat","Sun","March"]
print(days_of_the_week)

days_of_the_week.remove("March")
days_of_the_week.remove("March")
print(days_of_the_week)
```

I then saved the program as <u>Example7_18.py</u>, and ran it for the class. The following screenshot was displayed on the classroom projector:

This time the program behaved as my students were expecting---both instances of the month of March were removed.

"Executing the **remove()** method twice did the job," I said. "Both months of March have now been deleted."

```
days_of_the_week.remove("March")
days_of_the_week.remove("March")
```

"But, it's cumbersome," I said. "and as we've often pondered during the course of this class, what if there are hundreds of instances of the month of March in our List that we wish to delete? We don't want to be executing the **remove()** method hundreds of times, do we?"

"What can we do?" Rhonda asked. "There must be a better way."

"I bet we can use a Loop of some kind?" Kate asked.

Using the in operator to determine if an item exists in a List

"You're on the right track Kate," I said, "Anytime the need for multiple processing arises, you can almost be sure that there's a way to solve the problem using a Loop of some kind. Wait until you see just how easy it is to remove multiple items from a List using a For Loop. However, before I can show you that, we first need to learn about the 'in' Operator and how it can be used with a List."

"The 'in' Operator?" Bob asked. "We haven't seen that before have we?"

"No we haven't Bob," I said, "The 'in' operator, along with the 'not in' operator, are called the Python Membership Operators (there are only 2), and they allow us to determine if an item exists in a List. Used with an If statement, we the Membership Operators allow us to take some kind of action depending upon whether an item is or isn't found in the List. Here's a very simple example where we use an If statement, along with the 'in' Operator to determine if an item with the value 'March' exists in the *days_of_the_week* List..."

I displayed this code on the classroom projector.

```
# Example7_19.py

days_of_the_week = ["Mon","Tue","Wed","March","Thu","Fri","Sat","Sun","March"]
print(days_of_the_week)

if "March" in days_of_the_week:
  print("Found March in the List")
```

I then saved the program as Example7_19.py, and ran it for the class. The following screenshot was displayed on the classroom projector:

"As you can see," I said, "our program is reporting that March was found in the List. To use the 'in' Operator, we specify a value to search for, follow it with the 'in' Operator, followed by the name of the List..."

```
if "March" in days_of_the_week:
  print("Found March in the List")
```

"The 'in' Operator," I said, "is case sensitive. 'March' is found in the List, but 'march' would not be found. There is also a 'not in' Operator, which allows you to determine if an item doesn't exist in a List. The 'not in' Membership Operator works in a similar manner. We could use this code to verify that the month of February <u>does not</u> appear in the *days_of_the_week* List."

```
if "February" not in days_of_the_week:
  print("February not found in the List")
```

> NOTE: The 'in' Operator, along with the 'not in' Operator are called Python Membership Operators. These are the only two Membership Operators. In addition to determining if an item exists in a List, they can be used to determine if an item exists in a Tuple or a character or characters exist in a String.

Deleting Multiple Items in a List

"That worked great," Steve said. "Besides the If statement, can we use the 'in' and 'not in' Operators anywhere else?"

"You read my mind Steve," I said. "I was about to say that in addition to using the two Membership Operators with an If statement, we can also use them in a While Loop. Take a look at this code in which we use the 'in' Operator in a While Loop to remove every occurrence of the month of March from our *days_of_the_week* List..."

I displayed this code on the classroom projector.

```
# Example7_20.py

days_of_the_week = ["Mon","Tue","Wed","March","Thu","Fri","Sat","Sun","March"]
print(days_of_the_week)

while "March" in days_of_the_week:
  days_of_the_week.remove("March")

print(days_of_the_week)
```

I then saved the program as Example7_20.py, and ran it for the class. The following screenshot was displayed on the classroom projector:

```
C:\Windows\system32\cmd.exe

C:\PythonFiles\Examples>Example7_20
['Mon', 'Tue', 'Wed', 'March', 'Thu', 'Fri', 'Sat', 'Sun', 'March']
['Mon', 'Tue', 'Wed', 'Thu', 'Fri', 'Sat', 'Sun']

C:\PythonFiles\Examples>
```

"As you can see," I said, "unlike Example7_17.py, in which only the first occurrence of the month of March was deleted from the *days_of_the_week* List, here all occurrences of the month of 'March' have been deleted from the List. To do that, we coded a While Loop and used the 'in' Operation as its test expression. We're telling Python to execute the body of the While Loop as long as the *days_of_the_week* List contains an item whose value is equal to March. Within the body of the While Loop, we have just a single statement---the execution of the **remove()** method of the List object to delete the item whose value is equal to March."

```
while "March" in days_of_the_week:
  days_of_the_week.remove("March")
```

"That's marvelous," Ward said. "So this code will successfully remove every item whose value is equal to March, regardless of the number of items."

"That's right Ward," I said. "There could be just one, there could be hundreds. Every item whose value is equal to March will be removed from the List. In fact, even if there are no items in the List equal to March, the code will execute just fine."

Slicing Lists

"Right now," I said, "I want to introduce you to a Python feature called Slicing. Unlike the Index notation that we've been using this morning, that only allows us to work with one item in a List at a time, Slicing allows us to work with multiple items in one operation. For instance, we can display a 'Slice' of a List containing more than one item in the list. We can also update a 'Slice' of multiple items in a List. We can delete more than one item from a List at a time by using Slice Notation. These are just a few examples of the ways that Slicing can be used in Python. There are other things that Slicing can be used for that are beyond the scope of this class. Slicing, as we'll see later, can be used with Strings as well."

> NOTE: Any Python sequence object (a List, a String or a Tuple) can be Sliced.

Using Slices to delete items in a List

"Let's take our first look at Slicing by using Slice notation to delete a portion of a List (multiple items) with a single execution of the Delete Operation. Although we just learned that we can use the **remove()** method of the List object to delete multiple items from a List, using the Delete Operator will give us a great introduction to Slice Notation, which is how we specify the portion of the List with which we wish to work. In Example7_16.py, we used the Delete Operator to delete a single item from a List. As a reminder, here's the code...."

```
# Example7_16.py

days_of_the_week = ["Mon","Tue","Wed","February","Thu","Fri","Sat","Sun"]
print(days_of_the_week)

del days_of_the_week[3]
print(days_of_the_week)
```

"Take a look at the difference between that code, in which we delete a single item from a List, and this code in which we use Slice notation to tell Python we wish to delete more than one item from a List..."

I displayed this code on the classroom projector.

```
# Example7_21.py
```

```
days_of_the_week = ["Mon","Tue","Wed","February","March","April","Thu","Fri","Sat","Sun"]
print(days_of_the_week)

del days_of_the_week[3:6]
print(days_of_the_week)
```

I then saved the program as Example7_21.py, and ran it for the class. The following screenshot was displayed on the classroom projector:

"As you can see," I said, "February, March and April have been successfully deleted from our List."

I could see that a number of students immediately picked out the difference in code between Example7_16.py and Example7_21.py.

"Let's take a look at the code now," I said, "We began by 'accidentally' adding not only the month of February to our List of the days of the week, but March and April as well...."

```
days_of_the_week = ["Mon","Tue","Wed","February","March","April","Thu","Fri","Sat","Sun"]
```

"We know," I said, "that with a single line of code we can delete these three erroneous items from our List by executing the **remove()** method of the List, specifying values for the three months. We could also execute the Delete Operation three times, each time specifying an Index value for the item we wish to delete. However, by using Slice notation, we can delete all 3 items with a single execution of the Delete Operator (del)."

I paused before continuing.

"A Slice is created using Slice notation," I said, "Slice Notation uses a pair of brackets. Within the brackets, we specify the starting Index value of the first item in the Slice, in this case 3. We follow that with a colon, and then a value which is 1 greater than the Index value of the last item we want included in the Slice. We then pass the Slice as an argument to the Delete Operator."

```
del days_of_the_week[3:6]
```

"What do you mean by 1 greater than the Index value of the last item we want included in the Slice?" Rhonda asked.

"Since we want to delete the months of February, March and April," I said, "those are the items whose Index values are 3, 4, and 5. That means we need to specify a Slice of the *days_of_the_week* List where the start value for the Slice is 3, but the end value is 6. 6 is 1 more than the last item—5---we want included in the Slice."

"This Slice notation looks similar to the notation used to create a range that we learned about two weeks ago," Dave said, "The difference seems to be that Range notation uses commas, but Slice notation uses colons."

"That's a great observation Dave," I replied.

"I think I'm still confused," Rhonda said, "Why doesn't the Slice specify [3:5]?"

"[3:5] would create a Slice with only two items," I said. "having Index values of 3 and 4. The start value is included in the Slice, but the end value is not. As Dave pointed, out, that's the way the **range()** function works as well."

Rhonda consulted her notes from two weeks prior regarding the **range()** function and gave me a 'thumbs up'.

"Slice notation can be tricky," I said. "but it's also very powerful. As is the case with the **range()** function, the start and end values in Slice notation are optional. Also, like the **range()** function, we can optionally specify a step value for the Slice. Omitting the end value in the Slice tells Python to create a Slice that contains everything from the starting Index value to the end of the List. If we pass that Slice to the Delete Operator as an argument, everything from the starting Index value to the end of the List will be deleted. Let me show you."

I then displayed this code on the classroom projector.

Example7_22.py

```
numbers = [1,2,3,4,5,6,7,8,9,10,11,12]
print(numbers)

del numbers[3:]
print(numbers)
```

I saved the program as Example7_22.py, and ran it for the class. The following screenshot was displayed on the classroom projector:

"The numbers 4 through 12 have been deleted from the *numbers* List," I said. "Let's take a look at the code to see how we accomplished that. We started out by creating a List of Integers called *numbers*, assigning it the values 1 through 12…"

```
numbers = [1,2,3,4,5,6,7,8,9,10,11,12]
```

"Now it's time," I continued, "to create a Slice that will be passed as an argument to the Delete Operator. By specifying a Slice with a start value of 3 and no end value, we create a Slice that starts with the number 4 and continues to the end of the List which is 12. When this code is executed, only the numbers 1, 2 and 3 remain in the *numbers* List."

```
del numbers[3:]
```

I paused before continuing to make sure I hadn't lost anyone..

"I mentioned a minute ago," I continued, "that there is an optional step value we can use when we specify the Slice. It's optional because, as is the case with the **range()** function, the default value for the Slice step value is 1. Ca you guess that using a step value of 2 would do when creating a Slice?"

Dave ventured a guess: "I would think that Python would create a Slice based on every other item in the List, starting from the start value. "

"Excellent Dave," I said.

"Can we see an example?" Steve asked. "I'm having a hard time visualizing what you're saying."

"Here's one, Steve" I said, after thinking for a minute. "What do you think will happen?"

I then displayed this code on the classroom projector.

```
# Example7_23.py

numbers = [1,2,3,4,5,6,7,8,9,10,11,12]
print(numbers)

del numbers[1::2]
print(numbers)
```

I saved the program as Example7_23.py, and ran it for the class. The following screenshot was displayed on the classroom projector:

"It appears," Blaine said, "that every even number in the List was deleted."

"That's right Blaine," Rhonda said affirmatively. "All of the even numbers are gone from the List."

"You're both correct," I said. "Let's take a look at the code now. As we did in Example7_22.py, we started out by creating a List of Integers called *numbers*, assigning it the values 1 through 12…"

```
numbers = [1,2,3,4,5,6,7,8,9,10,11,12]
```

"Next," I said, "we created a Slice that will be passed as an argument to the Delete Operator."

```
del numbers[1::2]
```

"By specifying a Slice," I continued, "with a start value of 1 (which is the second item in our List,) no end value, and a step value of 2, we tell Python to create a Slice starting with the first even number, and every other number from that point until it reaches the end of the List. In other words, this code will create a Slice containing the numbers 2,4,6,8,10 and 12. When passed as an argument to the Delete Operator, every even number in the List will be deleted, leaving us with a List containing only odd numbers. We then proved that by displaying the *numbers* List in the Python Console."

```
print (numbers)
```

Using a Slice to display a portion of a List

"Using a Slice to delete items in a List is not the only use for Python Slices," I said. "A Slice can be used to easily display a portion of a List in the Python Console. This example is pretty simplistic, but later on we'll find this technique is very useful when we're working with Strings."

I displayed this code on the classroom projector.

```
# Example7_24.py

days_of_the_week = ["Monday","Tuesday","Wednesday","Thursday","Friday","Saturday","Sunday"]
print(days_of_the_week[2:5])
```

I then saved the program as Example7_24.py, and ran it for the class. The following screenshot was displayed on the classroom projector:

"As you can see," I said, "we displayed the list items Wednesday, Thursday and Friday in the Python Console. To do that, we first created a List called *days_of_the_week* containing the seven days of the week…"

```
days_of_the_week = ["Monday","Tuesday","Wednesday","Thursday","Friday","Saturday","Sunday"]
```

"We then created a Slice, with a start value of 2, and an end value of 5. This three item Slice was then passed as an argument to the **print()** function."

```
print(days_of_the_week[2:5])
```

"I think I'm beginning to understand," Rhonda said. "Once you understand the syntax for creating a Slice, it's a matter of finding an application to use it. Is there anything else we can do with a Slice?"

Updating Multiple Items in a List using a Slice

"Yes there is Rhonda," I said. "One of the first things we learned this morning in terms of Lists was how to update a single item in a List. We did that in Example7_4.py when we updated a single item in a List..."

```
# Example7_4.py

grades = [82,90,66]          #Create a List with 3 items
print(grades)

grades[2] = 64          #Assign the value 64 to the element whose Index is 2 and value is currently 66
print(grades)
```

"Using a Slice," I said, "we can update multiple items in a List with a single line of code. Some programmers like to think of this multiple update process as a two step delete-insert process, where first the referenced Index values are deleted, and then replaced with the specified items. Regardless of how you think about it, using Slice notation, we can easily update many items at one time. Take a look at this code."

I then displayed this code on the classroom projector.

```
# Example7_25.py

numbers = [1,2,3,4,5,6,7]
print(numbers)

numbers[2:4] = [91,99]
print(numbers)
```

I saved the program as Example7_25.py, and ran it for the class. The following screenshot was displayed on the classroom projector:

"As you can see," I said, "our original list, consisting of Integers with values 1 through 7, had the items whose values were 3 and 4 replaced by items with values of 91 and 99. Neither the items before 3 and 4, nor those after 3 and 4 , were updated. Let's take a closer look at the code that performed these multiple updates. It appears very much like an ordinary List assignment statement, except for the Slice notation on the left-hand side of the equal to sign. Notice that the Slice specified is 2 items long (Index values 2 and 3), and there are also two list items, representing the values that we wish to replace or update, on the right side of the equal to sign."

```
numbers[2:4] = [91,99]
```

"I'm impressed," Ward said. "That's a lot quicker than updating items one at a time. I presume we could update a List containing String values in the same way?"

"That's right Ward," I said. "Updating multiple String items using Slice notation is no problem either."

Inserting Items in a List using a Slice

"I would think it's important to make sure that if we specify two items for the Slice, we also specify two items for the assignment.," Joe said.

"Well Joe," I said, "that's where things can get interesting. Suppose we specify more items in the assignment statement than appear in the Slice notation."

"I'm not quite sure what you mean," Barbara said. "More items than specified in the Slice notation?"

"That's right Barbara," I said. "Suppose the size of our Slice is 2 items, but we specify an assignment statement that contains 3 items. Take a look at this code."

I then displayed this code on the classroom projector.

```
# Example7_26.py

numbers = [1,2,3,4,5,6,7]
print(numbers)

numbers[2:4] = [91,99,101]
print(numbers)
```

I then saved the program as Example7_26.py, and ran it for the class. The following screenshot was displayed on the classroom projector:

```
C:\Windows\system32\cmd.exe

C:\PythonFiles\Examples>Example7_26
[1, 2, 3, 4, 5, 6, 7]
[1, 2, 91, 99, 101, 5, 6, 7]

C:\PythonFiles\Examples>
```

"As you can see," I said, "our original list, consisting of Integers with values 1 through 7, had the items whose values were 3 and 4 replaced by items with values of 91 and 99. However, because there were 3 items specified in the assignment statement, 101 was inserted in the list after the value 99, but before the value 5."

"So the size of the *numbers* List grew from 7 to 8 items," Dave said. "We wound up inserting an additional item."

"That's right Dave," I said. "Look at the assignment statement. The Slice specified is 2 items long (Index values 2 and 3), but there are three items in the assignment statement, 91, 99 and 101. 91 and 99 replace 3 and 4, respectively, but 101 was inserted between 99 and 5."

```
numbers[2:4] = [91,99,101]
```

Deleting Items in a List using a Slice

"Suppose there are fewer items in the assignment than there are items in the Slice?" Kate asked. "Will the size of the List decrease?"

"Great question Kate," I answered, "let's see."

I then displayed this code on the classroom projector.

```
# Example7_27.py

numbers = [1,2,3,4,5,6,7]
print(numbers)

numbers[2:4] = [91]
print(numbers)
```

I then saved the program as Example7_27.py, and ran it for the class. The following screenshot was displayed on the classroom projector:

```
C:\Windows\system32\cmd.exe

C:\PythonFiles\Examples>Example7_27
[1, 2, 3, 4, 5, 6, 7]
[1, 2, 91, 5, 6, 7]

C:\PythonFiles\Examples>
```

"Can everyone see," I asked, "that our original list, consisting of Integers with values 1 through 7, had the item whose value was 3 replaced by an item with the value of 91. However, the item whose value was 4 was not replaced with anything---it's simply been deleted. Because the size of our Slice was two items, but there was only 1 item specified in the assignment statement, we lost one item from the List. As Kate suspected, the size of the *numbers* List shrunk from 7 to 6 items. Take a look at the assignment statement."

```
numbers[2:4] = [91]
```

"Wow," Steve said, "I can see how important it is to match the number of items in the assignment statement with the size of the Slice."

"Unless," Dave interjected, "you want to get fancy and either quickly insert or delete items in your List. I can see myself using this."

"Do you have any other tricks to show us with Slices?" Rhonda asked.

"Just a couple of more," I said, smiling. "You can also specify a Slice of nothing on the left-hand side and insert items starting at the position you specify. For instance, this code will insert items at position 0 of the List, which is the very left-hand side of the List."

I displayed this code on the classroom projector

```
# Example7_28.py

numbers = [1,2,3,4,5,6,7]
print(numbers)

numbers[0:0] = [91,99]
print(numbers)
```

I then saved the program as Example7_28.py, and ran it for the class. The following screenshot was displayed on the classroom projector:

"Can everyone see," I asked, "that our original list, consisting of Integers with values 1 through 7, had the items 91 and 99 inserted at the beginning of the List? Although the size of our Slice was zero items, the starting point for the Slice was specified as Index value 0---the beginning of the List."

```
numbers[0:0] = [91,99]
```

"Whatever items," I said, "that appear in the assignment statement will then be inserted at the location specified by the Slice. Because the size of the Slice is zero items, no items were replaced, although Python used the Slice location to determine where to insert the items. Ultimately, this is a pure insertion Operation."

Creating a new List using a Slice

I could sense that my students were starting to grow a bit weary. We had covered a great deal of material, and they were due for a break. I wanted to finish covering Lists before taking a break and resuming with coverage of Strings.

"Before we take a break," I said, "we have just a few more List topics to cover, and one final thing to say about Slices. What I'd like to do now is show you how we can use a List Slice to create an entirely new List. This action will have no impact on the original List. Take a look at this code."

```
# Example7_29.py

numbers = [1,2,3,4,5,6,7,8,9,10,11,12]
print("Numbers List",numbers)
```

```
odd_numbers=numbers[0::2]
even_numbers=numbers[1::2]


print ("\nOdd numbers", odd_numbers)
print ("Even numbers", even_numbers)
print("\nNumbers List",numbers)
```

I then saved the program as <u>Example7_29.py</u>, and ran it for the class. The following screenshot was displayed on the classroom projector:

```
C:\Windows\system32\cmd.exe

C:\PythonFiles\Examples>Example7_29
Numbers List [1, 2, 3, 4, 5, 6, 7, 8, 9, 10, 11, 12]

Odd numbers [1, 3, 5, 7, 9, 11]
Even numbers [2, 4, 6, 8, 10, 12]

Numbers List [1, 2, 3, 4, 5, 6, 7, 8, 9, 10, 11, 12]

C:\PythonFiles\Examples>
```

"As you can see," I said, "In the Python Console, we displayed the original *numbers* List, then a List of odd numbers, followed by a List of even numbers, followed by the *numbers* List after the two Slice Operations were performed. I wanted to prove that executing the Slice Operations had no affect on the original numbers List."

"I see what happened," Rhonda said, "but how did you manage to create those Lists? Can you explain what you did?"

"I'd be glad to Rhonda," I said. "As we did in the previous examples, we first created a List called *numbers* containing the numbers 1 through 12 and then displayed them in the Python Console...."

```
numbers = [1,2,3,4,5,6,7,8,9,10,11,12]
print("Numbers List",numbers)
```

"This next line of code," I said, "does two things. First, it creates a Slice of odd numbers and then assigns the Slice, which is a List itself, to a variable called *odd_numbers.*"

```
odd_numbers=numbers[0::2]
```

"What makes the *odd_numbers* List consist of just odd numbers?" Blaine asked.

"The key is the <u>step</u> parameter of the Slice," I said. "which is 2. If you think about it, if you start with the number 1, every other number is an odd number. Therefore, if you specify a Slice with a Starting Index of 0, which is the Integer 1 in the *numbers* List, with a step value of 2, we are creating a List of every other number starting with the Integer 1. In other words, odd numbers."

"Why is there no <u>end</u> value for the Slice?" Dave asked.

"We could have specified a value of 11 for the <u>end</u> value for the Slice," I said, "which is the last item in the *numbers* List. However, specifying no <u>end</u> value is a better way to code this. This way, if the amount of items in the *numbers* List changes, we don't need to change this line of code in any way. It will still work fine---regardless of the number of items in the *numbers* List."

"What about the code that creates the List of even numbers?" Joe asked. "That code looks similar."

"It is Joe," I said. "Once again, the <u>step</u> value of the Slice is 2, but this time, the <u>start</u> value is 1, which is the second item in the list, and happens to be an even number. With a <u>start</u> value of 1, and a <u>step</u> value of 2, we are creating a Slice of every other Integer in the *numbers* List starting with the Integer 2. In other words, even numbers. We then assign that Slice to the variable *even_numbers.*"

```
even_numbers=numbers[1::2]
```

"We then display the items in the *odd_numbers* List and the *even_numbers* List in the Python Console, and to prove that Slicing had no effect on the original *numbers* List, we also display its items in the Python Console."

```
print ("\nOdd numbers", odd_numbers)
print ("Even numbers", even_numbers)
print("\nNumbers List",numbers)
```

"Notice that the display of the *numbers* List both before and after the creation of the other two Lists from the Slicing Operation is identical," I said.

"I'm getting an idea that Slicing is a very powerful Python feature," Rhonda said. "We've seen it used in so many ways.?

"Yes we have Rhonda," I said, "That's just about it for List Slicing, although later on, we'll see that we can also Slice Strings."

Sorting Items in a List

"One of the very useful things you can do with a List is to sort the items in it," I said. "You can sort the items in a List either alphabetically (if the List contains Strings) or numerically (if it contains numbers.) Python gives us two ways to sort a List. One way is to use the generic **sorted()** function and the other way is to use the **sort()** method of the List object."

"There are two says to sort items in a List?" Rhonda asked. "I can see that this is going to be confusing. The **sorted()** function and the **sort()** method look and sound so much alike. Yet they seem to act very differently."

"That's right Rhonda," I said. "I agree. They are very close in spelling. The function ends with the letters 'ed', the method does not."

> NOTE: Seems like an accident waiting to happen, the sorted() function and the sort() method. But they are spelled differently! You just have to be careful when you use them to be sure you intend to use either the function or the method.

"In addition to the differences in the way the two are spelled," I said, "there are also differences between the ways they both work. The **sorted()** function does not modify the List itself. Instead, as is the case with many of the functions we've learned about, the **sorted()** function returns a return value which is itself a sorted List. You can then either display the sorted List, use it as an argument to another function or method, or assign it to another List variable. Another thing to note. The **sorted()** function works on any Python iterable, such as Strings, Lists, Tuples, and Dictionaries."

> NOTE: A Python iterable is a Python Object that contains groups of items. More about that in my Python Classes and Objects book

"What about the **sort()** method?" Steve asked.

"The **sort()** method, since it is a method of the List object, works only with Lists. Unlike the **sorted()** function, which does not modify the List itself, the **sort()** method of the List object does modify the original List."

"Is that what you meant by generic when you described the **sorted()** function?" Kate asked. "That it works with more than one type of object?"

"That's exactly right Kate," I said. "Much like the Delete statement that we examined earlier today, that can be used not only with a List object but with a Dictionary object as well."

> NOTE: For a list of all the built-in Python functions, follow this link.
> http://docs.python.org/3/library/functions.html

"Let's examine the **sorted()** function first," I said. "We'll create a List containing names, display it in the Python Console, and then execute the **sorted()** function and display the return value in the Python Console. We'll then display the List once more in the Python Console to prove that the original List has not been updated. We'll then do the same thing to a List containing numbers."

I then displayed this code on the classroom projector.

```
# Example7_30.py
# Using the sorted() function to display a List sorted alphabetically or numerically

names = ["John","Linda","Tom","Kevin","Rita","Gil","Melissa"]
print(names)
```

```
print(sorted(names))
print(names)


numbers = [11,26,3,12,8,18]
print()
print(numbers)
print(sorted(numbers))
print(numbers)
```

I saved the program as Example7_30.py, and ran it for the class. The following screenshot was displayed on the classroom projector:

```
C:\Windows\system32\cmd.exe

C:\PythonFiles\Examples>Example7_30
['John', 'Linda', 'Tom', 'Kevin', 'Rita', 'Gil', 'Melissa']
['Gil', 'John', 'Kevin', 'Linda', 'Melissa', 'Rita', 'Tom']
['John', 'Linda', 'Tom', 'Kevin', 'Rita', 'Gil', 'Melissa']

[11, 26, 3, 12, 8, 18]
[3, 8, 11, 12, 18, 26]
[11, 26, 3, 12, 8, 18]

C:\PythonFiles\Examples>
```

"Can everyone see that we displayed a sorted version of each of our Lists without updating the original Lists?" I asked. First we displayed the original List, then displayed the return value of the **sorted()** function, then displayed the original List again. In both cases, the original List was unchanged."

"That's pretty cool," Ward said, "although I can't wait to see how we can update the original List as well."

"We'll get to that shortly Ward," I said, "Let's take a look at the code now. The first thing we did was to create a List called *names* containing seven first names, and then displayed the List in the Python Console. Notice that the first names in the List are not in alphabetical order..."

```
names = ["John","Linda","Tom","Kevin","Rita","Gil","Melissa"]
print(names)
```

"We then executed the **sorted()** function," I said, "passing the **sorted()** function the *names* List as a single argument, and then used its return value as an argument to the **print()** function, thereby displaying the sorted List in the Python Console. Then, to prove that the original *names* List had not been modified in any way, we then displayed the original *names* List in the Python Console using the **print()** function with the *names* List as an argument."

```
print(sorted(names))
print(names)
```

"To prove that the **sorted()** function works with numbers as well as Strings," I said, "we then created a List called *numbers*, executed the **sorted()** function, passing it the *numbers* List as a single argument, then used its return value as an argument to the **print()** function, thereby displaying the sorted List in the Python Console. And then, again, to prove that the original *numbers* List had not been modified in any way, we displayed the original *numbers* List in the Python Console."

```
numbers = [11,26,3,12,8,18]
print()
print(numbers)
print(sorted(numbers))
print(numbers)
```

I paused to be sure I hadn't lost anyone---I expected to lose one or two students..

"I just want to be sure I understand what's going on here," Rhonda said, "The **sorted()** function does not alter the original List."

"That's right Rhonda," I said. "The **sorted()** function makes a copy of the items in the original List, sorts them, then returns the sorted List as a return value. The original List is left unchanged. If we have the need to update the original List, we need to use the **sort()** method of the List object. Let me show you how to do that using the **sort()** method now."

I displayed this code on the classroom projector.

```
# Example7_31.py
# Use the sort() method to sort the original List

names = ["John","Linda","Tom","Kevin","Rita","Gil","Melissa"]
print(names)
names.sort()
print(names)

numbers = [11,26,3,12,8,18]
print()
print(numbers)
numbers.sort()
print(numbers)
```

I then saved the program as Example7_31.py, and ran it for the class. The following screenshot was displayed on the classroom projector:

"Once again we have sorted the two Lists," I said, "but this time the original List was updated. Here we have displayed the List before, and after, executing the sort() method of the List Object."

> Note: In Example7_30.py, we displayed three lines for each List in the Python console. In Example7_31.py, we displayed just two lines---the before and after version of the List.

"Let's take a look at the code now," I said. "As we did in Example 7.30, the first thing we did here was to create a List called *names* containing seven first names, and then displayed the List in the Python Console. Notice that the first names in the List are not in alphabetical order..."

```
names = ["John","Linda","Tom","Kevin","Rita","Gil","Melissa"]
print(names)
```

"We then executed the **sort()** method of the List object," I said, "To execute the **sort()** method, we type the name of the List we wish to sort, followed by a period, followed by the name of the method. The **sort()** method will sort the List in place---that means the List itself is modified."

```
names.sort()
```

"To prove that the original *names* List has been modified by the **sort()** method, we then displayed the *names* List in the Python Console."

```
print(names)
```

"We then execute the same operation on the *numbers* List," I said. "Again, to sort the List, all we need to do is execute the **sort()** method on it..."

```
numbers.sort()
```

Rhonda had a problem.

"I just noticed that my *names* List hasn't been sorted," Rhonda said, "although my *numbers* List was."

I love a good mystery and so I hurried over to Rhonda's workstation.

I noticed that Rhonda had forgotten to code an empty pair of parentheses following the **sort()** method of the *names* List---although she had correctly done so for the **sort()** method of the *numbers* List. Perhaps she had hurriedly typed the code.

Rhonda's <u>incorrect</u> code for the sort of the *names* List looked like this..."

```
names = ["John","Linda","Tom","Kevin","Rita","Gil","Melissa"]
print(names)
names.sort                              #Rhonda's incorrect code!!!!
print(names)
```

"Rhonda, you forgot you code the empty pair of parentheses following the name of the **sort()** method," I explained. "This is a pretty common error for beginners to make. When you forget to include the parentheses after a function or method call, the function or method is not executed. A function or method name without the parentheses means something else entirely to Python. Even worse, Python doesn't flag the missing parentheses as an error."

"Why is that?" Kate asked.

"Coding a function or method name without parentheses is a technique that an advanced Python programmer might use." I said. "Unfortunately, doing so is well beyond the scope of this Introductory class. The bottom line: remember those parentheses!"

"Is it possible to do a reverse sort of the items in a List?" Chuck asked.

"Yes it is," I said. "Both the **sorted()** function and the **sort()** method have the ability to reverse sort a List. Once again, the s**orted()** function <u>will not</u> modify the original List, but the **sort()** method will. For both the **sorted()** function and the **sort()** method, all we need to do to reverse sort is to include the 'reverse = True' parameter with the function or method call. Be sure to spell the word True with a capital T."

I paused before continuing.

"Let's write a program." I said, "to reverse sort the *names* and *numbers* Lists we've been working with this morning. We'll combine both operations in the same program, using the **sort()** method to reverse sort the items in the *names* List, and the **sorted()** function to reverse sort the items in the *numbers* List. Remember, the **sorted()** function will not modify the original List, but the **sort()** method will..."

I displayed this code on the classroom projector.

```
# Example7_32.py
# Reverse sorts using the sorted() function or sort() method

names = ["John","Linda","Tom","Kevin","Rita","Gil","Melissa"]
print(names)
names.sort(reverse=True)
print(names)

numbers = [11,26,3,12,8,18]
print()
print(numbers)
print(sorted(numbers,reverse=True))
print(numbers)
```

I then saved the program as <u>Example7_32.py</u>, and ran it for the class. The following screenshot was displayed on the classroom projector:

```
C:\Windows\system32\cmd.exe

C:\PythonFiles\Examples>Example7_32
['John', 'Linda', 'Tom', 'Kevin', 'Rita', 'Gil', 'Melissa']
['Tom', 'Rita', 'Melissa', 'Linda', 'Kevin', 'John', 'Gil']

[11, 26, 3, 12, 8, 18]
[26, 18, 12, 11, 8, 3]
[11, 26, 3, 12, 8, 18]

C:\PythonFiles\Examples>
```

"Can everyone see that the items in the *names* and *numbers* Lists are displayed in reverse order?" I asked. "Here's the execution of the **sort()** method for the *names* List with the 'reverse=True' parameter...."

```
names.sort(reverse=True)
```

"And here's the **sorted()** function with the 'reverse=True' parameter for the numbers List," I said. "Since the **sorted()** function doesn't modify the original List, to display the sorted items we needed to pass the return value of the **sorted()** function as an argument to the **print()** function."

```
print(sorted(numbers,reverse=True))
```

I waited to see if any of my students had any questions, but everyone seemed to be OK with the concept of sorting items (and reverse sorting items) in a List.

Reversing Items in a List

"One final thing about Lists that I want to show you this morning," I said, "is how to reverse the items in a List using the **reverse()** method of the List object."

"Didn't you just show us how to do that?" Rhonda asked. "We reverse sorted items in a List using the **sorted()** function and the **sort()** method."

"Reversing items in a List is not the same as reverse sorting items," I said, "When you reverse the items in a List, you don't sort them---you reverse their position in the List. In other words, the first item in the List becomes the last item in the List, the second item in the List becomes the second from the last item in the List, and so on."

> NOTE: Reversing items in a List is not the same as reverse sorting items

I could see some confusion on the faces of my students.

"Take a look at this," I said, as I displayed this list of letters on the classroom projector.

```
S F I A C O
```

"If we reverse this list of letters," I said, "it looks like this. It's not sorted, but the items have been reversed."

```
O C A I F S
```

"Does everyone see the difference between the two Lists?" I asked. "The letter S was switched with the letter O, the letter F was switched with the letter C, and the letter I was switched with the letter S."

"I see what you mean now," Steve said.

"Like the **sort()** method of the List object," I said, "the **reverse()** method of the List object also modifies the original List."

I paused before continuing.

"Let's continue working with the *names* and *numbers* Lists," I said, "and write a program in which the seven names in the *names* List are reversed and the six numbers in the *numbers* List are also reversed."

I displayed this code on the classroom projector.

```
# Example7_33.py
names = ["John","Linda","Tom","Kevin","Rita","Gil","Melissa"]
print(names)
```

```
names.reverse()
print(names)

numbers = [11,26,3,12,8,18]
print()
print(numbers)

numbers.reverse()
print(numbers)
```

I then saved the program as Example7_33.py, and ran it for the class. The following screenshot was displayed on the classroom projector:

```
C:\Windows\system32\cmd.exe

C:\PythonFiles\Examples>Example7_33
['John', 'Linda', 'Tom', 'Kevin', 'Rita', 'Gil', 'Melissa']
['Melissa', 'Gil', 'Rita', 'Kevin', 'Tom', 'Linda', 'John']

[11, 26, 3, 12, 8, 18]
[18, 8, 12, 3, 26, 11]

C:\PythonFiles\Examples>
```

"Can everyone see what happened?" I asked. "In the *names* List, 'John' was the first item in the List and 'Melissa' was last. After we executed the **reverse()** method of the List object, 'Melissa' is now first, and 'John' is now last. All of the other items have also been reversed.."

names.reverse()

"Similarly, in the *numbers* List, " I said, "the number 11 was the first item in the List, and the number 18 was the last. After we executed the **reverse()** method of the List object, the number 18 was the first item in the List and the number 11 was the last. All of the other items have also been reversed."

numbers.reverse()

"For both Lists," I said, "we displayed the List before and after we executed the **reverse()** method. As you can see, the **reverse()** method modifies the original List."

"I understand how the **reverse()** method works," Blaine said, "but why would we want to reverse the items in a List?"

"Advanced Python programmers might do this for many reasons," I said. "One reason might be that they want to display the items in a List in the order in which they were added to the List. In that case, the last item in the List would be the one most recently added to the List. To do so would require displaying the last item in the List first, the next to last item second, and so forth. Using the **reverse()** method of the List object, this would be simple to do."

"I've heard some of the programmers at work talking about doing that exact operation," Ward said.

We were finished with our discussion of Lists, and it seemed like a sensible place to take a 15-minute break before continuing on with a discussion of Strings.

Strings

"Much of what we just learned about Lists this morning," I said, resuming class after our break "is applicable to Strings as well. One distinction between Lists and Strings that generally means little to beginner programmers is the notion that Strings, unlike Lists, are Immutable."

"What does that mean?" Kathy asked. "Immutable?"

"String Immutability," I answered, "means that once a String has been created, the String cannot be changed. Lists, on the other hand, are Mutable. As we saw with the sort() and reverse() methods of the List object, we were able to update a List. Many of the actions we took with Lists are applicable to Strings also, but some---appending, inserting, deleting, overwriting items---are not available to Strings because Strings are Immutable. But we still have a great deal of functionality with Strings as we'll soon see."

"I've heard the programmers at work discussing the Immutability of Strings," Ward said, "But I've done a little experimentation on my own, and I'm almost certain that I've changed the value of String variables. Doesn't immutability mean that the String can't be changed?"

"It's tricky Ward," I said. "You can change the value of a String variable in Python, but when you do, you create a new String Object, and Python then points your String variable to the new String Object. The original String Object that was created when you created the String variable is unchanged, and basically orphaned in your program's memory space."

"I'm not sure I understand what you mean," Ward said. "String Object? Orphaned"

"Python," I said, "as I think you have discovered during this course, is very much Object Oriented. Not surprisingly, whenever you create a variable and assign it a value, Python creates an Object to store its value. The type of Object Python creates is determined by the value that you assign to the variable. For instance, if the value is a String, Python creates a String Object. If the value is an Integer, Python creates an Integer Object. If the value is a Float, Python creates a Float Object. If you assign items to a variable, Python creates a List Object. Once created, these Objects reside in your program's memory space. If you later change the value associated with a variable, if the Object is Mutable, the value is changed within the Object that resides in your program's memory space. If the Object is Immutable, no change can be made to the Object, so a new Object of the same Data type is created with the new value. Of the Objects I've mentioned this morning, only List Objects and Dictionary Objects are Mutable. The others (Strings, Integers, Floats and Tuples) are Immutable."

"This is all so complicated," Rhonda said, "Is this important for us to know?"

"Not at all Rhonda," I said, "All of this occurs behind the scenes and is done automatically for you. I only mentioned that Strings are Immutable because you may be wondering why some of the functionality of the List Object is not available with the String Object."

> **NOTE: Python represents all data as objects. Most objects, like the String Object we are discussing now, are Immutable. This includes Integers and Floats and Tuples. Lists and Dictionaries are an exception to this rule, as they are Mutable. Again, all of this goes on behind the scenes and is of little concern to the beginner Python programmer. I only mention it here because you may be wondering why some of the functionality of the List Object is not available to the String Object.**

"When Python creates a new String Object," Joe asked, "What happens to the old String Object?"

"The old String Object stays 'alive' as long as your program has a reference to it," I answered. "Usually once you assign a new value to a variable, the reference to the old Data Object is terminated, and eventually the memory space is reused."

"You say usually the reference is terminated?" Joe asked. "Not always?"

"That's right Joe," I said, "Some Advanced Python programmers might write code in which more than one variable references the same String object. In that case, merely changing the value of one of the variables (and creating a new String Object) means that other variables are still referencing the old String Object, and expecting it to be there with its original value. As I said, this isn't something that a typical beginner programmer would do."

"I'd love to see an example of that code," Dave said.

I hesitated, because theoretical discussions of this type usually don't go over too well in a beginners class---but Dave persisted.

"Take a look at this code," I said, "in which we create a variable called *string1*, assign it a String value of 'John', set a second variable called *string2* equal to *string1*, then change the value of *string1* to 'Mary'. When we display the values of *string1* and *string2* in the Python Console, you'll see that although we have changed the value of the variable *string1* to 'Mary', the value of *string2* is still equal to the original String object 'John'. *string2* is referencing the old *string1* variable. Strings are Immutable just for this reason. Variables that refer to the original String object need to be guaranteed that it won't change. Python does that for us."

I displayed this code on the classroom projector.

```
# Example7_34.py
# Strings are Immutable

string1 = "John"

string2 = string1

print("string1 is",string1)
print("string2 is",string2)

string1 = "Mary"

print()
print("string1 is now",string1)
print("string2 is still",string2)
```

I then saved the program as <u>Example7_34.py</u>, and ran it for the class. The following screenshot was displayed on the classroom projector:

"Can everyone see what I mean by String Immutability?" I said. "The String object with the value 'John' that was originally assigned to the variable *string1* was not changed because string2 had been assigned a reference to it. A new String object with the value 'Mary' was created and assigned to the variable *string1*, while the original String object with the value of 'John' is still pointed to by *string2*."

"You assigned one String variable the value of another?" Valerie asked. "I never would have thought to do that."

```
string2 = string1
```

"More precisely Valerie," I said, "I assigned a String variable a reference to another String variable. Behind the scenes, Python assigned the variable *string2* the memory address of the original *string1* variable. That's what Python does with variable assignments. As you might imagine, this is not a line of code that a beginner programmer likely would write, but you won't be a beginner programmer for long."

> NOTE: If you find all of this talk about Objects, references, addresses and pointing confusing, enroll in the **Python Classes and Objects** course that follows this one.

"String, Integer and Float Objects all work in the same way," I said. "If you change the value of a String, Integer or Float Object, the old Object continues to exist in memory, but a new one Object will be created and then assigned to the variable."

"Python keeps track of Objects in memory through the use of a reference counter," I said. "When an Object no longer is being referenced by any part of your program, the Object is destroyed and the memory used by that object is made available for your program to use. The process whereby all of this happens automatically for you in the background is known as <u>Python Garbage Collection</u>."

"Did you say that Lists and Dictionaries don't behave in this fashion?" Linda asked.

"That's right Linda," I said. "Lists and Dictionary Objects are Mutable. Their Objects can be changed without Python have to create a new Object. To prove the point, let's modify the code from <u>Example3_34</u> where we assigned one String variable to another, and assign one List variable to another instead."

I then displayed this code on the classroom projector.

```
# Example7_35.py
```

```
list1 = [1,2,3]
list2 = list1

print("list1 is",list1)
print("list2 is",list2)

list1.append(33)

print()
print("list1 is now",list1)
print("list2 is now",list2)
```

I then saved the program as Example7_35.py, and ran it for the class. The following screenshot was displayed on the classroom projector:

```
C:\Windows\system32\cmd.exe

C:\PythonFiles\Examples>example7_35
list1 is [1, 2, 3]
list2 is [1, 2, 3]

list1 is now [1, 2, 3, 33]
list2 is now [1, 2, 3, 33]

C:\PythonFiles\Examples>
```

"Can everyone see that the original List Object referred to by the variables *list1* and *list2* has been updated," I said. "The values for *list1* and *list2* are now identical. This is the opposite behavior we encountered with Example7_34."

I paused before resuming with a discussion of the code.

"We started off by creating a variable called **list1**, then assigned the List the items 1, 2 and 3..."

list1 = [1,2,3]

"Then," I said, "as we did in Example3_34, we assigned one variable the value of another, this time a variable pointing to a List Object..."

list2 = list1

"We then updated the value of the *list1* variable," I said, "using one of the built-in List methods, **append()**."

list1.append(33)

"Even though both *list1* and *list2* pointed to the original List object," I said, "because Lists are Mutable, the List Object referenced by both *list1* and *list2* was changed in place. No new Object was created. As a result, the values of both *list1* and *list2* were changed, and they are now identical."

> NOTE: Experiment yourself with this code using Integer and Float Data Types. You'll see that Integer and Float objects are also Immutable.

"Why is the behavior of Lists and Strings different?" Kate asked. "Why aren't Lists Immutable as well?"

"It's a common design feature." I said, "of major programming languages for Lists (and Dictionaries) to be Mutable. Lists and Dictionaries are Objects that when used in a program typically have their values changed quite often within the program. (hundreds, thousands, even millions of times.) If Lists and Dictionaries were Immutable, each update to its value would mean a new Object was created in the program's memory space. This would cause the program to run slower, and potentially impact your program's memory resources."

I paused before continuing.

"The Mutability or Immutability of Python objects may not mean much to you now," I said, "but it's something to tuck into the back of your mental database. Some day (or night) you may be working on a Python program that isn't giving you the results you expect, and all of a sudden, you'll realize it because of the Mutability or Immutability of the Object with which you are working.

Strings are made up of characters

"Let's move on," I said, "from the theoretical Immutability of Strings, and discuss some of the fun things we can do with Strings. Like a List that is made up of individual items, Strings are also comprised of items which we generally call characters. Here's some code that allows us to isolate the characters in a String and display them in the Python Console."

I displayed this code on the classroom projector.

```
# Example7_34.py

my_name = "John Smiley"

for character in my_name:
  print(character)
```

I then saved the program as Example7_36.py, and ran it for the class. The following screenshot was displayed on the classroom projector:

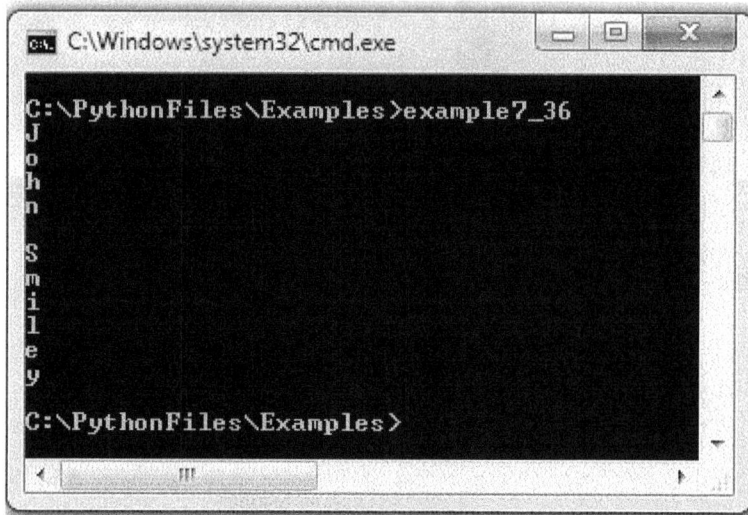

```
C:\Windows\system32\cmd.exe

C:\PythonFiles\Examples>example7_36
J
o
h
n

S
m
i
l
e
y

C:\PythonFiles\Examples>
```

"As you can see," I said, "we have displayed each character in the String on a separate line in the Python Console. This code is very similar to the code from Example7_6 where we iterated through the items in a List. Here, instead of iterating through the items of a List, we use a For Loop to iterate through the characters in a String."

```
for character in my_name:
  print(character)
```

"By the way," I said, "we could have used any variable name in our For Loop. Many Python programmers would use the character x which is shorter to type..."

```
for x in my_name:
  print(x)
```

"...but using the variable name *character* in our For Loop emphasizes that each item in the String is a character..."

I paused before continuing.

"Not surprisingly," I said, "just like a List, each item or character in a String can also be referred to using its Zero-based Index, like this."

I displayed this code on the classroom projector.

```
# Example7_37.py

my_name = "John Smiley"
print (my_name[0])
```

I then saved the program as Example7_37.py, and ran it for the class. The following screenshot was displayed on the classroom projector:

"As you can see," I said, "we displayed the character in the String whose Index is 0---the letter J. Referring to characters in a String is very much like referring to items in a List. Let's check out the code that displays the character whose Index is 0. As is the case with Lists, we include the index value within brackets."

```
print (my_name[0])
```

"Does that mean we can also Slice Strings," Kate asked, "the way we can Slice Lists?"

Slicing Strings

"That's exactly where I was headed Kate," I said. "As you sensed, Strings can be Sliced just like a List. As is the case with Lists, Slicing a String has no impact on the original String. Using String Slicing, we can display a portion of a String, and we can also create a new String from the Slice of another String. However, since Strings are Immutable, we can't use the Slice Operations we saw with Lists to insert, delete, or update characters in a String."

I paused to see if I lost anyone.

"Let me show you Slice notation for a String," I said. "It's identical to that of a List, except instead of working with items, with Strings we're working with characters. Let's create a String that consists of my first name and last name, then create a Slice that contains just my first name, and display both the Slice and the original String in the Python Console..."

I displayed this code on the classroom projector.

```
# Example7_38.py
my_name = "John Smiley"
print (my_name[0:4])
print (my_name)
```

I then saved the program as Example7_38.py, and ran it for the class. The following screenshot was displayed on the classroom projector:

"As you can see," I said, "we displayed both our Slice and the original String. Let's look at the code. First, we created a String consisting of my first and last name..."

```
my_name = "John Smiley"
```

"As we did when we created a Slice from a List earlier," I said, "to create a String Slice, once again we use Index values within a pair of brackets to specify the start and end position of the Slice within the String. In this case, my first name is in Index Positions 0, 1, 2 and 3, so we specify [0:4] for the Slice, and then use the Slice as an argument to the **print()** function.."

```
print (my_name[0:4])
```

"I know we covered this with Lists," I said, but if you are wondering why the Slice doesn't specify [0:3], it's because the end position in a Python Slice is up to, **but not including**, the last item to be included in the Slice. All Slices are the same, whether the Slice is used in a range the way we learned two weeks ago or a List Slice that we learned about earlier in the class. One thing is for sure. If your results are not what you're expecting, it's most likely your ending value."

I paused before continuing.

"...Finally, in order to prove that the String itself hasn't been modified, we display the original String in the Python Console..."

```
print (my_name)
```

"We could just have easily assigned the Slice to another String variable," I said. "like this..."

```
first_name = my_name[0:4]
```

Using the in operator to determine if a character exists in a String

"As we did when we used the 'in' operator to determine if an item exists in a List," I said, "we can use the 'in' operator to determine if one or more characters exist in a String. This is slightly different than with a List in that we can use the 'in' operator for only one List item, but can use it for more than one character in a String."

"I'm beginning to see a lot of similarities between Lists and Strings," Barbara said.

"There are a great deal of similarities between them Barbara," I replied, "and also some differences as we've already seen. That why I like to cover Lists and Strings back to back in the same class. Let's take a look at this code where we can use the in operator to determine if the letters 'mi' appear in a String. Once again, let's use a String that consists of my first and last name."

I displayed this code on the classroom projector.

```
# Example7_39.py

my_name = "John Smiley"

if "mi" in my_name:
  print("Found mi...")
```

I then saved the program as Example7_39.py, and ran it for the class. The following screenshot was displayed on the classroom projector:

"As you can see," I said, "our program is reporting that the characters 'mi' were found in the String. To use the 'in' Operator, we specify a value to search for, follow it with the 'in' Operator, followed by the name of the String..."

```
if "mi" in my_name:
```

"Notice," I said, "how we are able to look for more than a single character in a String using the 'in' operator. This is a little different from the way the 'in' operator works with Lists, where we are restricted to searching for just one item."

The replace() method of the String object

"I mentioned a bit earlier," I said, "that we can't use Slices to insert, delete or update characters in a String. However, there is a String method that allows us to take a String and seemingly replace **one or more** characters in the String with other characters. However, because Strings are Immutable, the String itself isn't modified. The **replace()** method takes the original String, and returns a String as the return value of the method. The original String remains unchanged. Take a look at this code in which we will create a String called **ocean_liner**, assign it a String with the name of the most famous ocean liner ever built (or sunk) and then seemingly replace every occurrence of the letter 'i' in it with an asterisk..."

I displayed this code on the classroom projector.

```
# Example7_40.py

ocean_liner = "Titanic"

print("ocean_liner",ocean_liner)
new_ocean_liner = ocean_liner.replace("i","*")


print("new_ocean_liner",new_ocean_liner)
print("ocean_liner",ocean_liner)
```

I then saved the program as Example7_40.py, and ran it for the class. The following screenshot was displayed on the classroom projector:

```
C:\Windows\system32\cmd.exe

C:\PythonFiles\Examples>Example7_40
ocean_liner: Titanic
new_ocean_liner: T*tan*c
ocean_liner: Titanic

C:\PythonFiles\Examples>
```

"As you can see," I said, "both instances of the letter 'i' in the String 'Titanic' have been replaced with an asterisk. We assigned that modified String to a new variable. The original String, as we would expect, hasn't been changed."

"That's cool," Ward said, "I can see a lot of application for a search and replace method like this."

"I agree Ward," I said, "It's a very powerful feature. Let's take a look at the code now. We started by creating a String with the name of the most famous passenger liner ever built and then displayed its value in the Python Console..."

```
ocean_liner = "Titanic"
print("ocean_liner",ocean_liner)
```

"We then seemingly replaced," I said, "the letter 'i' in the String with an asterisk using the **replace()** method. I say seemingly because the **replace()** method doesn't update the original String, it generates a return value which is a String with the updates performed."

I paused before continuing.

"The **replace()** method," I said, "requires two arguments. The first argument is the character or characters to search for, and the second argument is the character or characters to replace if the first argument is found in the String. We then assigned the return value to a new variable called *new_ocean_liner* and displayed its value in the Python Console."

```
new_ocean_liner = ocean_liner.replace("i","*")
print("new_ocean_liner",new_ocean_liner)
```

"Finally," I said, "to prove that the original String hasn't been updated, we display it in the Python Console."

```
print(ocean_liner)
```

"Do you need to have the same number of characters for both arguments?" Linda asked.

"It's not required, but be careful that the results you are seeing is what you wanted." I said. "If the replace argument has more characters than the search for argument, the size of the return value String will be greater than the original String. For example, this code will replace the character 'i' with two asterisks..."

```
new_ocean_liner = ocean_liner.replace("i","**")
```

"The returned String," I said, "will be..."

```
T**tan**c
```

"The size of the String," I said, "will grow from 7 characters to 9. On the hand, if the <u>replace</u> argument has fewer characters than the <u>search for</u> argument, the size of the return value String will be <u>less</u> than the original String. This is where I see the most errors among beginners. For example, you might think that this code will replace the characters 'it' with two asterisks. It won't. 'it' will be replaced with a single asterisk."

```
new_ocean_liner = ocean_liner.replace("it","*")                    #Not likely what you intended
```

"The returned String," I said, "will be..."

```
T*anic
```

"The size of the String," I said, "will shrink from 7 characters to 6."

I looked for signs of confusion, but it appeared that everyone was OK with the **replace()** method of the String object. It was now time to talk about String Concatenation.

String Concatenation

"Let's talk a bit about String Concatenation," I said. "To concatenate means to join one String to another, and we use the Plus (+) Operator to do so. We've been concatenating Strings since week 4 when we wrote this line of code in <u>Example4_1</u>..."

```
print("You have great taste. " + response + " is a great language.")
```

"In that example," I said, "we concatenated the value of a String variable onto a String Literal, and then concatenated a String Literal onto that combination. There's no limit to the number of Strings you can concatenate, but the important thing to remember is that you can only Concatenate Strings. If you wish to concatenate a Data Type other than a String to another String, you must first convert (or in Python terms cast) the other Data Type to a String, using the **str()** function, as we did in a similar fashion like this in <u>Example6_7.py</u>..."

```
print("The result of 3 multiplied by 5 is " + str(retval))
```

"Just to review," I said, "let's concatenate two Strings containing my first name and last name together to create a third String. For formatting purposes, we'll concatenate a String Literal containing a space between the two of them..."

I displayed this code on the classroom projector.

```
# Example7_41.py

first_name = "John"
last_name = "Smiley"

full_name = first_name + " " + last_name

print(full_name)
```

I then saved the program as <u>Example7_41.py</u>, and ran it for the class. The following screenshot was displayed on the classroom projector:

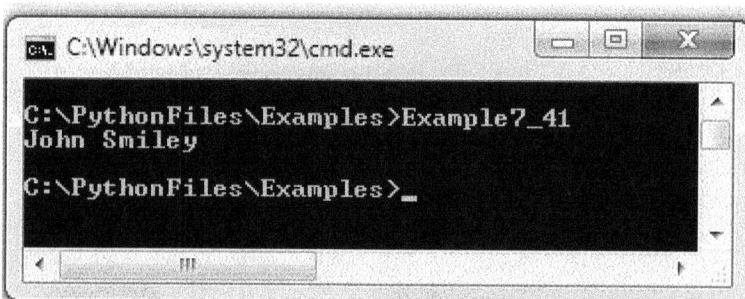

"As you can see," I said, "we displayed the value of the String variable *full_name* in the Python Console. Probably the most difficult part of this code was determining how to insert a space between the first and last names..."

```
full_name = first_name + " " + last_name
```

"As you can see," I said, "a String Literal of a space works quite nicely. I've also seen students create a variable called space, assign it a single space, and concatenate the three String variables like this..."

```
first_name = "John"
last_name = "Smiley"
space = " "

full_name = first_name + space + last_name
```

"That will also work," I said.

"This was a pretty simple example," Rhonda said, "but I think that trick with the space between the first and last name is pretty neat. I'm not sure I would have thought of either of those tricks. I guess this proves what you always say: there's more than one way to paint a picture."

"Programming tricks like that Rhonda," I said, "are tricks of the trade. You pick them up as you go along."

The upper() method of the String object

"We've already seen and used this method in the class," I said, "Back in week 5, we introduced the upper() method. The **upper()** method 'upper cases' a String and returns the result also as a String. Because Strings are Immutable, the original String is not modified. Here's a simple example where we have a String consisting of the lower case letters a,b,c,d and e. Let's use the **upper()** method to return a String which has those letters capitalized..."

I displayed this code on the classroom projector.

```
# Example7_42.py

letters = "abcde"

print("letters:", letters)

new_letters =letters.upper()
print("new_letters:", new_letters)
print("letters:", letters)
```

I then saved the program as Example7_42.py, and ran it for the class. The following screenshot was displayed on the classroom projector:

```
C:\Windows\system32\cmd.exe

C:\PythonFiles\Examples>Example7_42
letters: abcde
new_letters: ABCDE
letters: abcde

C:\PythonFiles\Examples>_
```

"As you can see," I said, "the lower case letters in the variable *letters* were converted to upper case, then assigned to the variable *new_letters*. Once again, we see that the value of the variable *letters* has not been changed. Let's take a look at the code now. We started by creating a String called *letters* that contains the lowercase letters a,b,c,d and e, and displaying it in the Python Console..."

```
letters = "abcde"
print("letters:", letters)
```

"This is the code that takes the value of the *letters* variable," I said, "converts (casts) it to upper case and then assigns the return value of the **upper()** method to the variable *new_letters*. To execute the **upper()** method of a String object, just type the name of the String variable, followed by a period, followed by the method name. Don't forget the empty pair of parentheses!"

```
new_letters =letters.upper()
```

"We then display the value of *new_letters* in the Python Console," I said, "and to prove that the original String hasn't been modified, we also display it in the Python Consol."

```
print("new_letters:", new_letters)
print("letters:", letters)
```

The lower() method of the String object

"Similar to the **upper()** method of the String object," I said, "the **lower()** method of the String object returns the lower case value of a String as a return value. Once again, because Strings are Immutable, the original String is not modified."

I displayed this code on the classroom projector.

```
# Example7_43.py

letters = "ABCDE"

print("letters:", letters)

new_letters = letters.lower()
print("new_letters", new_letters)
print("letters:", letters)
```

I then saved the program as Example7_43.py, and ran it for the class. The following screenshot was displayed on the classroom projector:

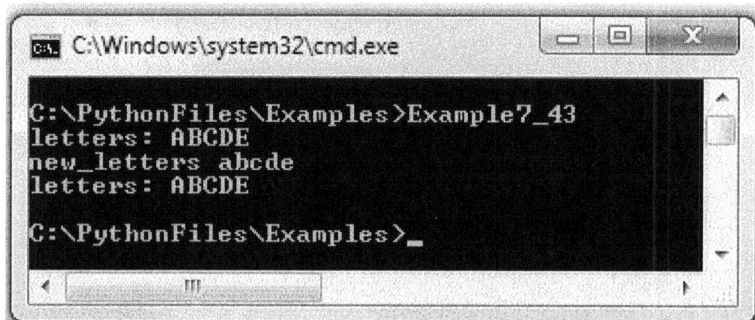

```
C:\Windows\system32\cmd.exe

C:\PythonFiles\Examples>Example7_43
letters: ABCDE
new_letters abcde
letters: ABCDE

C:\PythonFiles\Examples>_
```

"As you can see," I said, "the upper case letters in the variable *letters* were converted to lower case, then assigned to the variable *new_letters*. The value of the variable *letters* has not been changed. Let's take a look at the code now. We started by creating a String called *letters* that contains the uppercase letters A,B,C,D and E, and displaying its value in the Python Console..."

```
letters = "ABCDE"
print("letters:", letters)
```

"This is the code that takes the value of the *letters* variable," I said, "converts it to all lower case letters and then assigns the return value of the **upper()** method to the variable *new_letters*. To execute the **lower()** method of a String object, just type the name of the String variable, followed by a period, followed by the method name. Don't forget the empty pair of parentheses!"

```
new_letters =letters.lower()
```

"We then display the value of *new_letters* in the Python Console," I said, "and to prove that the original String hasn't been modified, we display it in the Python Console also."

```
print("new_letters:", new_letters)
print("letters:", letters)
```

The capitalize() method of the String object

"The **capitalize()** method," I said, "returns a String in which only the first character in a String has been capitalized. For instance, if you have a String that looks like this..."

```
john smiley
```

"...The **capitalize()** method will return this String."

```
John smiley
```

"Notice," I said, "that the letter 's' in 'smiley' has not been capitalized. Only the first letter in the String will be capitalized. You must be careful though. If there are already capital letters in the String, the **capitalize()** method strangely enough will lower case them, most likely not what you intend to happen. Take a look at this code, where I create two String variables, one called *string1* where my entire name is in lower case, and **string2** where my last name in the String is capitalized. See what the **capitalize()** method does with each one..."

I displayed this code on the classroom projector.

```
# Example7_44.py

string1 = "john smiley"

print("string1:",string1)

new_string1 = string1.capitalize()
print("new_string1:", new_string1)
print("string1", string1)

string2 = "john Smiley"
print()
print("string2:",string2)

new_string2 = string2.capitalize()
print("new_string2:", new_string2)
print("string2", string2)
```

I then saved the program as Example7_44.py, and ran it for the class. The following screenshot was displayed on the classroom projector:

```
C:\Windows\system32\cmd.exe

C:\PythonFiles\Examples>Example7_44
string1: john smiley
new_string1: John smiley
string1: john smiley

string2: john Smiley
new_string2: John smiley
string2: john Smiley

C:\PythonFiles\Examples>
```

"Do you see what happened when we executed the **capitalize()** method with the first String?" I asked. "The lower case 'j' was capitalized, as expected. And to prove our point that Strings are Immutable, we also displayed the Original String in the Python Console---it was unchanged."

```
string1 = "john smiley"
print("string1",string1)
new_string1 = string1.capitalize()
print("new_string1", new_string1)
print("string1", string1)
```

"With the second String, however, the lower case 'j' was also capitalized, however the upper case 'S' in my last name was lower cased. This is behavior that you need to be aware of if you use the **capitalize()** method of the String object. Once again, to prove that the Original String was unchanged, we displayed it in the Python Console..."

```
string2 = "john Smiley"
print()
print("string2",string2)
new_string2 = string2.capitalize()
print("new_string2", new_string2)
print("string2", string2)
```

The title() method of the String object

"Is there a way to capitalize each word in the String?" Bob asked.

"You must have read my mind Bob," I said. "The next method of the String object we'll examine, the **title()** method, does exactly that. "The **title()** method returns a String in which the first character of <u>each word</u> in the String is capitalized. Take a look at this code in which we use the **title()** method to deal with two Strings, one containing my name and the other containing a longer, popular phrase."

I displayed this code on the classroom projector.

```
# Example7_45.py
string1 = "john smiley"

print("string1:",string1)

new_string1 = string1.title()
print("new_string1",new_string1)
print("string1",string1)

string2 = "the quick brown fox jumped over the lazy dog."
print()
print("string2:",string2)

new_string2 = string2.title()
print("new_string2:",new_string2)
print("string2:",string2)
```

I then saved the program as <u>Example7_45.py</u>, and ran it for the class. The following screenshot was displayed on the classroom projector:

```
C:\Windows\system32\cmd.exe

C:\PythonFiles\Examples>Example7_45
string1: john smiley
new_string1: John Smiley
string1: john smiley

string2: the quick brown fox jumped over the lazy dog.
new_string2: The Quick Brown Fox Jumped Over The Lazy Dog.
string2: the quick brown fox jumped over the lazy dog.

C:\PythonFiles\Examples>
```

"Do you see what happened when we executed the title() method with the first String?" I asked. "The first letters of both words in the String, both the lower case 'j' and the lower case 's' were capitalized. And to prove our point that Strings in Python are Immutable, we also displayed the Original String in the Python Console---it was unchanged."

```
string1 = "john smiley"
new_string1 = string1.title()
print("string1",string1)
print("new_string1",new_string1)
print("string1",string1)
```

"With the second String, we see the same behavior, it's just a String with 9 words, and all 9 words are uppercased..."

```
string2 = "the quick brown fox jumped over the lazy dog."
print()
print("string2",string2)
new_string2 = string2.title()
print("new_string2",new_string2)
print("string2",string2)
```

"Suppose the String contains capital letters?" Barbara asked.

"Good question Barbara," I said. "With the **title()** method there are no surprises. If your String already contains capital letters, they won't be lowercased as they are with the **capitalize()** method."

The len() function

"Our last String topic of the day is the **len()** function," I said. "It allows you to determine the length of a String, which can come in quite handy in advanced applications."

"**len()** is a function, but not a method of the String object?" Dave asked.

"That's right Dave," I said. "There is no specific String method to determine its length. Like the **sorted()** function, the **len()** function can be used with several types of Python Objects, including Strings and Lists. Here's a very simple illustration where we execute the **len()** function against a String containing my first and last names, and display the result in the Python Console."

I displayed this code on the classroom projector.

```
# Example7_46.py

my_name = "John Smiley"
print("The length of the string is",len(my_name))
```

> NOTE: For a list of all of the functions available in Python, check out this link
>
> https://docs.python.org/3.6/library/functions.html

I then saved the program as Example7_46.py, and ran it for the class. The following screenshot was displayed on the classroom projector:

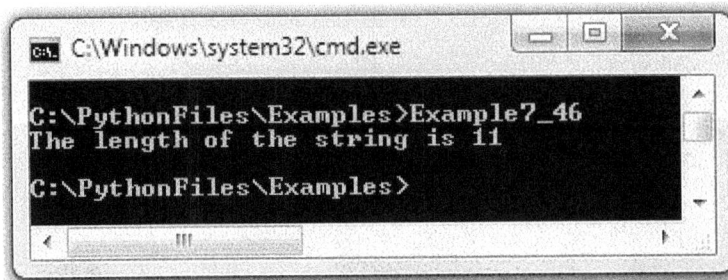

"As you can see," I said, "we displayed the length of the string *my_name* in the Python Console. Using the **len()** function is simple, just pass, as an argument, the name of the String for which you wish to obtain the length."

```
my_name = "John Smiley"
print("The length of the string is",len(my_name))
```

"You said the **len()** function is something that might be used in advanced applications?" Chuck asked.

"That's right Chuck," I answered. "Advanced programmers do a great deal of work with Strings, and it's often quite useful to know the length of the String you are working on. In a minute, you'll see that we can also use the **len()** function to determine the number of items in a List. That will be valuable in our next practice exercise."

"Wow, there are so many things you can do with Strings," Rhonda exclaimed. "I'm not sure I'll be able to remember them all."

"You're right Rhonda," I said, "but there's no need to memorize them, or anything else in Python. You can always check the Python online documentation and learn more about them on your own."

> NOTE: For more on Strings, check out this link
>
> https://docs.python.org/3.6/library/stdtypes.html#text-sequence-type-str

I waited for questions, but there were none. I think my students, for the moment anyway, felt comfortable creating and working with Lists and Strings.

"I have an exercise for you to complete that will give you a chance to use a List to perform the same average calculation we did earlier in Practice 7-1 using the brute force method---but I think you'll enjoy this method a whole lot more."

I then distributed this exercise for the class to complete.

Practice 7-2 Our First Look at Lists

In this exercise, you'll create your first Python List.
1. Using Notepad (or Notepad++), enter the following code.

```
#Practice7_2.py

grades = [82,90,64,80,95,75]

accumulator=grades[0]+grades[1]+grades[2]+grades[3]+grades[4]+grades[5]
average = accumulator/len(grades)

print(grades[0])
print(grades[1])
print(grades[2])
print(grades[3])
print(grades[4])
print(grades[5])

print("\nThe class average is " + str(average))
```

2. Save your source file as Practice7_2.py in the \PythonFiles\Practice folder (select File | Save As from Notepad's menu bar). Be sure to save your source file with the filename extension py.
3. Execute the program. The program will then display each of the six grades, plus the calculated overall class average, which is **81.0**

```
C:\Windows\system32\cmd.exe

C:\PythonFiles\Practice>Practice7_2
82
90
64
80
95
75

The class average is 81.0

C:\PythonFiles\Practice>_
```

Discussion

Except for a student or two who confused parentheses and square brackets, no one had any real trouble completing this exercise.

"As you can see," I said, "the results of this program are identical to those in Practice7_1: the display of six grades, plus the calculated overall class average. Of course, instead of prompting the user for 6 grades, this version used a List. Don't worry---we'll get back to allowing the user to enter grades in Practice7_4. For now, let's take a closer look at the code. As I just mentioned, the previous version of this program used user input to assign values to variables named *grade1* through *grade6.* We no longer have 6 variables. Instead we have a single List called *grades*, and within our program, we assign values to the individual items of the *grades* List, with this single line of code. Notice that the values for the List items are contained within the brackets, separated by commas..."

```
grades = [82,90,64,80,95,75]
```

"Using a List here," I said, "we've reduced the number of lines of code necessary to create the variables to store our six grades from six to one. As I think you know by now, the first item in the *grades* List has an index of 0 and the last item has an index of 5. By the way, if I didn't mention this before, it's a good idea to name Lists using the plural form of a noun—that enables programmers reading your code to immediately recognize that the variable is referring to a List."

I paused before continuing.

"As was the case in Practice7_1," I said, "we then sum the values of all six grade List items and assign the result to the *accumulator* variable. Instead of summing six variables, however, this time we sum the individual items of the *grades* List using their index."

```
accumulator=grades[0]+grades[1]+grades[2]+grades[3]+grades[4]+grades[5]
```

"...and with this line of code we calculate the overall class average."

```
average = accumulator/len(grades)
```

"What happened to the *counter* variable that we had in Practice7_1?" Rhonda asked.

"We don't need it," I said, "The **len()** function eliminates the need for a counter variable. The len() function that we learned about a short time ago can be used with a List object as well as a String. When used with a List object, it returns a value equal to the number of items in the *grades* List, which is the number we divide the value of the *accumulator* variable by in order to calculate the average. It's 6, the same as the counter variable value in Practice7_1."

"I like that," Ward said. "That makes our program very flexible."

"Yes it does Ward," I said. "One less thing we need to worry about if the number of items in the *grades* List changes. This next section of code is similar to that from Practice7_1—it displays the values of the individual grades in the Python Console, referring to the individual items in the *grades* List to do so. In Practice7_3, this will be much more streamlined."

```
print(grades[0])
print(grades[1])
print(grades[2])
print(grades[3])
print(grades[4])
print(grades[5])
```

"Finally," I said, "this line of code displays the calculated class average in the Python Console."

```
print("\nThe class average is " + str(average))
```

The Wonders of List Processing

"I can see," Ward said, "that List processing reduces the number of variables we need to create in our program. However, to display the items of the *grades* List in the Python Console, there is still quite a bit of tedious typing required to refer to the individual items of the List. My programmer friends at work love working with Python Lists. Am I missing something? Is there a better way to do this?"

"I'm glad you asked that, Ward," I said. "We'll see in the next exercise that there is an easier way to 'iterate' through the items in a List, making displaying them in the Python Console much easier. With a List, we can use Loop processing to quickly access each item in the List, and that can be a big timesaver. This next exercise will illustrate why the programmers at your work place love Lists so much."

I then distributed this exercise for the class to complete.

Practice 7-3 The Wonders of List processing

In this exercise, you'll modify the code from Practice 7-2, using a Python For Loop to quickly and easily access the items of a List.
1. Using Notepad (or Notepad++), enter the following code.

```
#Practice7_3.py
grades = [82,90,64,80,95,75]
accumulator = 0.0

for grade in grades:
  print(grade)
  accumulator += grade

average = accumulator/len(grades)

print("\nThe class average is " + str(average))
```

2. Save your source file as <u>Practice7_3.py</u> in the \PythonFiles\Practice folder (select File | Save As from Notepad's menu bar). Be sure to save your source file with the filename extension py.

3. Execute the program. The program will then display each of the six grades, plus the calculated overall class average, which is **81.0**

```
C:\Windows\system32\cmd.exe

C:\PythonFiles\Practice>Practice7_3
82
90
64
80
95
75

The class average is 81.0

C:\PythonFiles\Practice>
```

Discussion

Only one or two students had difficulty with this exercise---either slight typos or that familiar issue of indentation. After a few minutes, they had successfully completed the exercise as well.

"Okay, I'm beginning to see the light," Ward said. "This version of the program is certainly a lot more streamlined than the other code, and I'm happy to see we never directly referred to an individual item of the List."

"That's right Ward," I said, "we saved ourselves a few lines of code with this version of the program. The more items we have in our *grades* List, the more lines of code we'll save versus the other version. In fact, no matter how many items are in our *grades* List, the code to display them and calculate the overall average will remain the same."

"Wow, that's amazing," Rhonda said. "Can you go over the code with us?"

"I'd be glad to, Rhonda," I said. "In the next version of this program, we'll allow the user to add items to the grades list, but for now, once again we declare a six item List called *grades*..."

```
grades = [82,90,64,80,95,75]
```

"We also need to create a variable called *accumulator*," I said. "As we'll see shortly, we're going to use the Augmented Addition Operator to add to the *accumulator* variable within our For Loop. Because of that, Python expects that the *accumulator* variable has already been created. If we don't create it here, Python will complain that we are trying to refer to a variable that doesn't exist and display a **NameError** Exception message when we try to execute the program---something some of you have seen a few times in this class already."

```
accumulator = 0.0
```

"At this point in our program," I continued, "the *grades* List now contains six items, with values assigned to each item. In the previous version of this program, we used six individual executions of the **print()** function to display the values for each item of the List. The problem with that version of the program—and it's one that bothered Ward quite a bit—is that if the number of students in the class changes (either increases or decreases,) we'll have to modify the code for the correct number of grades, either by adding or deleting lines of code. That's why this next section of code is so powerful: It uses a Python For Loop to access every *grade* item in the *grades* List, displaying its value in the Python Console and adding its value to the *accumulator* variable."

```
for grade in grades:
    print(grade)
    accumulator += grade
```

"Finally, this section of code calculates the average, and displays that average in the Python Console as well. As we did in Practice7_2, the *average* variable is equal to the value of the *accumulator* variable, divided by the number of items in the *grades* List, which is determined using the **len()** function."

```
average = accumulator/len(grades)
print("\nThe class average is " + str(average))
```

"The beauty of this code," I said, "is that hat it works regardless of the number of items in our grades List. It doesn't need to be modified."

"Are you saying," Linda asked, "that if we changed the *grades* List to have 250 student grades, this code wouldn't need to be changed?"

"That's exactly right, Linda," I said.

"I'm a little confused," Rhonda said. "What's happening with this For Loop?"

"This is very similar to the code we used earlier in Example7_9 and Example7_10," I said, "where we used the For Loop to iterate through the individual items in a List. In those examples, we iterated through the While Loop, and accessed and printed each individual item in the Python Console. We do that here within the body of the For Loop..."

```
print(grade)
```

"After we have displayed the value of the *grade* item in the Python Console," I said, "we then add it to the current value of *accumulator*, using the Augmented Addition Operator. In this way, the *accumulator* variable maintains a running total of the value of the List items we have displayed in the Python Console."

```
accumulator += grade
```

"We could also have written this line of code this way.," I said.

```
accumulator = accumulator + grade
```

"I'm having trouble understanding how this *accumulator* variable works," Chuck said.

"To make things easier to understand," I said, "visualize that the first time the body of the For Loop is executed, the value of the Index for the first *grade* item is 0. That would look like this to Python..."

```
accumulator = accumulator + grades[0]
```

"This would then be interpreted by Python like this..."

```
accumulator = 0 + 82
```

"The second time through the While Loop," I continued, "Python is now working on the second item in the List, whose Index value is 1, and the statement is then interpreted by Python like this."

```
accumulator = accumulator + grades[1]
```

"Or like this:"

```
accumulator = 82 + 90
```

I explained that this process is repeated until the For Loop terminates and all the items of the *grades* List have been processed.

I took a look around the classroom, and surprisingly, it appeared that everyone was OK with what we had done. There were no obvious signs of distress.

"I would love to see Lists used with the code we wrote in Practice7_1," Mary said. "Is it possible to use Lists even when the user is being prompted for grades to calculate?"

"Yes, it is possible," I said. I then distributed this exercise for the class to complete.

Practice 7-4 Using Lists with Interactive Processing

In this exercise, you'll modify the program you wrote in Practice 7-1, using Lists to make the process of calculating the average of six grades input by the user much easier.
1. Using Notepad (or Notepad++), enter the following code.

```
#Practice7_4.py

grades = []
accumulator = 0.0

loop_response = input("\nDo you want to calculate a grade? ")
```

```
while loop_response.upper() == "YES":
  grades.append(input("Enter a grade "))
  loop_response = input("\nDo you have another grade to enter? ")

print ("\nThe entered grades are \n")

for grade in grades:
  print(grade)
  accumulator += float(grade)

average = accumulator/len(grades)
print("\nThe class average is " + str(average))
```

2. Save your source file as <u>Practice7_4.py</u> in the \PythonFiles\Practice folder (select File | Save As from Notepad's menu bar). Be sure to save your source file with the filename extension py.

3. Execute your program. The program will ask if you if you have grades to enter. Enter **Yes**.

4. The program will then prompt you for a grade. Enter **82**.

5. The program will then ask if you have more grades to enter. Enter **Yes**.

6. The program will then prompt you for a grade. Enter **90**, and continue entering grades in this manner (**64** for the third grade, **80** for the fourth, **95** for the fifth, and **75** for the sixth).

7. After entering the sixth grade, the program will ask if you have more grades to enter. Enter **No**. The program will then display the entered grades, and the calculated overall average, which is **81**.0

Discussion

There were no major problems completing the exercise, although a few students initially coded their braces as parentheses.

"As you can see," I said, "the changes between this version of the program and the one from the first exercise are pretty dramatic. Using Lists to prompt for and process a series of grades like this is a great deal easier than using multiple variables to store the grades."

"I see that," Steve said, "We married the methodologies from the first three exercise to write a program that allows the user to load values directly into the items of the *grades* List themselves."

"That's right, Steve," I said. "The main difference between this version of <u>Practice7_1</u> is that the user's input of a quiz grade is assigned to an item of a List instead of to a dedicated variable declared within the program. This allows the program to dynamically deal with a variable number of grades."

I paused before continuing.

"Let's take a look at the code now," I said. "As we did in <u>Practice7_3</u>, the first thing we did was create an empty List called *grades.* We also created a variable called *accumulator.*"

```
grades = []
accumulator = 0.0
```

"Why an empty List?" Rhonda asked.

"Because all of the items in the *grades* List will be entered by the user," I said, "the *grades* List has to be initially be created as an empty List.. It contains no items."

"I remember," Steve said, "you created empty Lists earlier in the class when you showed us the **insert()** and **append()** methods."

"That's right Steve," I said, "In Example7_11, we created an empty List, and used the **append()** method to add items to it. That's similar to what we're doing here. This time we're allowing the user to enter a grade via the **input()** function, then adding that value as a new item to the *grades* List via the **append()** method of the List Object."

I paused before continuing to make sure I hadn't lost anyone.

"This looks more complicated than it really is because this takes place within a While Loop," I said. "Prior to executing the While Loop, we ask the user if he or she has a grade to enter"

```
loop_response = input("\nDo you want to calculate a grade? ")
```

"If the user answers 'yes', or any of the 8 variants of 'yes'," I said, "the While Loop processes, and the two lines of code within the body of the While Loop are executed. The first line within the body of the While Loop is the prompt for the grade, which once entered is appended as an item the *grades* List. The second line is a prompt to ask the user if he or she has another grade to enter..."

```
while loop_response.upper() == "YES":
  grades.append(input("Enter a grade "))
  loop_response = input("\nDo you have another grade to enter? ")
```

"If the answer is 'yes', or any of the 8 variants of 'yes'," I said, "the While Loop processes, and the body of the While Loop is executed once more, with the user being prompted for a second grade. The second grade (if there is one) is added as an item to the *grades* List. This process continues until the user answers something other than 'yes'. At that point, the line of code following the last line in the body of the While Loop (the indented code-) is executed. This displays the message The entered grades are' in the Python Console, followed by a blank line..."

```
print ("\nThe entered grades are \n")
```

"Next," I said, "we execute a For Loop to iterate through the items of the *grades* List, display the value of each item in the Python Console, and add its value to the *accumulator* variable. This code is identical to that found in Practice7_3."

```
for grade in grades:
  print(grade)
  accumulator += float(grade)
```

"Finally, this section of code calculates the overall class average, and displays that average in the Python Console. This also is identical to the code found in Practice7_3 in which the *average* variable is equal to the value of the *accumulator* variable, divided by the number of items in the *grades* List, which is determined using the **len()** function."

```
average = accumulator/len(grades)
print("\nThe class average is " + str(average))
```

"That is neat," Blaine said. "I'm beginning to like Lists more and more—too bad we can't include one in the Grades Calculation Program."

Adding List Processing to the Grades Calculation Program

"I don't see why we can't," I said. "Although Frank Olley never requested it, I don't think he would mind if we calculated an overall class average for the student's grade entered into the program. And I think a List would be a perfect way to do that."

I then distributed this exercise for the class to complete.

Don't Forget: If typing these long examples and exercises isn't something you want to do, feel free to follow this link to find and download the completed solutions for all of the examples and exercises in the book. Just click on the Python book, then follow the link entitled exercises ☺

http://www.johnsmiley.com/main/books.htm

Practice 7-5 Modify the Grades functions in Util.py for List processing

In this exercise, you'll take the first step in allowing the Grades program to calculate an overall class average. The first step is to modify Util.py. The modifications are minimal.---a total of 3 lines of code. You'll be adding a return statement at the end of each of the three functions in Util.py. I'm providing you the entirety of the code here, but it will be much easier if you simply add the return statement to the end of each of the three functions.

1. Using Notepad (or Notepad++) (if you are using Windows) locate and open the Util.py source file you created last week. (It should be in the \PythonFiles\Grades folder)
2. Modify each of the three functions with a return statement at the end of each definition. When you have finished util.py, your source file should look like this.

```
# util.py

def calculate_english_grade():
  ENGLISH_MIDTERM_PERCENTAGE = .25
  ENGLISH_FINAL_EXAM_PERCENTAGE = .25
```

```python
  ENGLISH_RESEARCH_PERCENTAGE = .30
  ENGLISH_PRESENTATION_PERCENTAGE = .20

  midterm=int(input("\nEnter the Midterm Grade: "))
  final_exam_grade =  int(input("Enter the Final Examination Grade: "))
  research = int(input("Enter the Research Grade: "))
  presentation = int(input("Enter the Presentation Grade: "))
  final_numeric_grade = \
   (midterm * ENGLISH_MIDTERM_PERCENTAGE) + \
   (final_exam_grade * ENGLISH_FINAL_EXAM_PERCENTAGE) + \
   (research * ENGLISH_RESEARCH_PERCENTAGE) + \
   (presentation * ENGLISH_PRESENTATION_PERCENTAGE)
  if final_numeric_grade >= 93 :
    final_letter_grade = "A"
  elif final_numeric_grade >= 85 and final_numeric_grade < 93 :
    final_letter_grade = "B"
  elif final_numeric_grade >= 78 and final_numeric_grade < 85 :
    final_letter_grade = "C"
  elif final_numeric_grade >= 70 and final_numeric_grade < 78 :
    final_letter_grade = "D"
  elif final_numeric_grade < 70 :
    final_letter_grade = "F"
  print ("\n*** ENGLISH STUDENT ***\n")
  print("Midterm grade is : ",midterm)
  print("Final Exam grade is : ",final_exam_grade)
  print("Research grade is : ",research)
  print("Presentation grade is: ",presentation)
  print("\nFinal Numeric Grade is: ",final_numeric_grade)
  print("Final Letter Grade is: ",final_letter_grade)
  return final_numeric_grade                          #New line for List processing

def calculate_math_grade():
  MATH_MIDTERM_PERCENTAGE = .50
  MATH_FINAL_EXAM_PERCENTAGE = .50

  midterm=int(input("\nEnter the Midterm Grade: "))
  final_exam_grade =  int(input("Enter the Final Examination Grade: "))
  final_numeric_grade = \
   (midterm * MATH_MIDTERM_PERCENTAGE) + \
   (final_exam_grade * MATH_FINAL_EXAM_PERCENTAGE)
  if final_numeric_grade >= 90 :
    final_letter_grade = "A"
  elif final_numeric_grade >= 83 and final_numeric_grade < 90 :
    final_letter_grade = "B"
  elif final_numeric_grade >= 76 and final_numeric_grade < 83 :
    final_letter_grade = "C"
  elif final_numeric_grade >= 65 and final_numeric_grade < 76 :
    final_letter_grade = "D"
  elif final_numeric_grade < 65 :
    final_letter_grade = "F"
  print ("\n*** MATH STUDENT ***\n")
  print("Midterm grade is : ",midterm)
  print("Final Exam grade is : ",final_exam_grade)
  print("\nFinal Numeric Grade is: ",final_numeric_grade)
  print("Final Letter Grade is: ",final_letter_grade)
  return final_numeric_grade                          #New line for List processing

def calculate_science_grade():
  SCIENCE_MIDTERM_PERCENTAGE = .40
```

```
SCIENCE_FINAL_EXAM_PERCENTAGE = .40
SCIENCE_RESEARCH_PERCENTAGE = .20


midterm=int(input("\nEnter the Midterm Grade: "))
final_exam_grade =  int(input("Enter the Final Examination Grade: "))
research = int(input("Enter the Research Grade: "))
final_numeric_grade = \
 (midterm * SCIENCE_MIDTERM_PERCENTAGE) + \
 (final_exam_grade * SCIENCE_FINAL_EXAM_PERCENTAGE) + \
 (research * SCIENCE_RESEARCH_PERCENTAGE)
if final_numeric_grade >= 90 :
  final_letter_grade = "A"
elif final_numeric_grade >= 80 and final_numeric_grade < 90 :
  final_letter_grade = "B"
elif final_numeric_grade >= 70 and final_numeric_grade < 80 :
  final_letter_grade = "C"
elif final_numeric_grade >= 60 and final_numeric_grade < 70 :
  final_letter_grade = "D"
elif final_numeric_grade < 60 :
  final_letter_grade = "F"
print ("\n*** SCIENCE STUDENT ***\n")
print("Midterm grade is : ",midterm)
print("Final Exam grade is : ",final_exam_grade)
print("Research grade is : ",research)
print("\nFinal Numeric Grade is: ",final_numeric_grade)
print("Final Letter Grade is: ",final_letter_grade)
return final_numeric_grade                    #New line for List processing
```

3. Save your file as util.py in the \PythonFiles\Grades folder (select File-Save As from Notepad's Menu Bar). Be sure to save your source file with the file name extension 'py'.

Discussion

With just three lines of code to add to util.py, this exercise didn't pose much of a challenge to the class. As my students did, you also need to be careful that the return statements you added are properly indented to match the code above them.

"Don't we need to modify the Grades.py program for List processing also?" Rhonda asked.

"You're right Rhonda," I said, "and we'll be doing that shortly. First we needed to modify each of our three functions to return the calculated *final_numeric_grade* back to the calling Grades.py program. That's what this line of code does..."

```
return final_numeric_grade                    #New line for List processing
```

"This line of code," I said, "will make more sense to you when you see how we handle the return value in the Grades.py program we're about to modify."

I then distributed the final exercise of the day for the class to complete.

Don't Forget: If typing these long examples and exercises isn't something you want to do, feel free to follow this link to find and download the completed solutions for all of the examples and exercises in the book. Just click on the Python book, then follow the link entitled exercises ☺

http://www.johnsmiley.com/main/books.htm

Practice 7-6 Modify the Grades Calculation Program to use a List

In this exercise, you'll take the second step in providing for List processing in the Grades Calculation Program by modifying the Grades.py Source Files.

1. Using Notepad (or Notepad++), locate and open the Grades.py source file you worked on last week. (It should be in the \PythonFiles\Grades folder)

2. Modify your code so that it looks like this

```
# Grades.py
# After Chapter 7

from util import calculate_english_grade,calculate_math_grade,calculate_science_grade

grades = []
accumulator = 0

print("WELCOME TO THE GRADES CALCULATION PROGRAM")

loop_response = "YES"

while loop_response.upper() == "YES":
  # What type of student are we calculating?
  response = input("\nEnter student type (1=English, 2=Math, 3=Science): ")

  if response == "":
    print("You must select a Student Type")
    continue

  if int(response) <1 or int(response) > 3 :
    print(response, "is not a valid Student Type")
    continue

  #Student type is valid, now let's calculate the grade

  #1 is an English Student
  if response =="1":
    grades.append(calculate_english_grade())

  # 2 is a Math Student
  if response == "2":
    grades.append(calculate_math_grade())

  # 3 is a Science Student
  if response == "3":
    grades.append(calculate_science_grade())

  loop_response = input("\nDo you have another grade to calculate? ")

print("\nThe calculated final grades are: \n")

for grade in grades:
  print(grade)
  accumulator += float(grade)

average = accumulator/len(grades)

print("\nThe class average is " + str(average))
print("\nTHANKS FOR USING THE GRADES CALCULATION PROGRAM!")
```

3. Save your source file as <u>Grades.py</u> in the \PythonFiles\Grades folder (select File | Save As from Notepad's menu bar). Be sure to save your source file with the filename extension py.

4. Execute your program and test it thoroughly. We need to verify that the looping behavior of the program is working correctly.

5. Indicate that you wish to calculate the grade for an **English** student. Enter **70** for the midterm grade, **80** for the final examination grade, **90** for the research grade, and **100** for the presentation. A final numeric grade of **84.5** should be displayed with a letter grade of **C**.

6. After the grade is displayed, the program should ask you if you have more grades to calculate.

7. Answer **Yes** and calculate the grade for a Math student. Enter **70** for the midterm and **80** for the final examination. A final numeric grade of **75** should be displayed with a letter grade of **D**.

8. After the grade is displayed, the program should ask you if you have more grades to calculate.

9. Answer **Yes** and calculate the grade for a Science student. Enter **70** for the midterm, **80** for the final examination, and **90** for the research grade. A final numeric grade of **78** should be displayed with a letter grade of **C**. After the grade is displayed, the program should ask you if you have more grades to calculate.

10. Answer **No**. All three final numeric grades will be displayed in the Python Console, along with an overall class average of **79.1667**. You should be thanked for using the program, and the program should end.

Discussion

There were some significant changes required to the Grades Calculation program in this exercise, and there were more than a few mistakes made in coding it. However, none of my students asked for help. I was very proud of their ability to look at any syntax errors the Python Interpreter was making, and make the changes necessary to make the program run successfully. After about 30 minutes, everyone had completed the exercise.

"I'm not sure that the changes we've just made to the Grades Calculation Program are something Frank Olley requires," I said, "but I know they will add greatly to your learning experience. Having modified the functions in util.py to return the calculated *final_numeric_grade* for the student's grades entered, we now need to use that grade to calculate an overall class average. Let's take a look at the code in Grades.py now. Not much has changed. I'll highlight the changes as we get to them. As we did in the previous version of the Grades.py program, the first thing we did was to tell Python where to find the functions we would be using in our program. We did that using the 'from util import' statement..."

```
from util import calculate_english_grade,calculate_math_grade,calculate_science_grade
```

"Next," I said, "we see two new lines of code that are required to calculate an overall class average for the student grades entered by the user. These are identical to the two lines of code we entered in Practice7_4.py. We create an empty List called *grades*, and then we create a variable called *accumulator* to which we assign the Floating point value of 0.0."

```
grades = []
accumulator = 0
```

"This code is not new," I said. "We display the 'Welcome' banner, followed by the initialization of the *loop_response* variable to 'YES'."

```
print("WELCOME TO THE GRADES CALCULATION PROGRAM")
loop_response = "YES"
```

"We then set up our While Loop and its test expression," I said. "Because we initialized the *loop_response* variable to 'YES', the test expression evaluates to True the first time we execute it, ensuring that our loop executes at least once."

```
while loop_response.upper() == "YES":
    # What type of student are we calculating?
    response = input("\nEnter student type (1=English, 2=Math, 3=Science) : ")
```

"If the user's response is invalid," I said, "we display a warning message and then execute the continue statement to start the While Loop from the beginning. Once again, this code hasn't changed from the previous version of Grades.py."

```
if response == "":
    print("You must select a Student Type")
    continue

if int(response) <1 or int(response) > 3 :
    print(response, "is not a valid Student Type")
    continue
```

"Provided the user's response is 1, 2 or 3, " I said, "we call one of the three User-defined functions we wrote to calculate the student's grade. Here, you'll notice a slight change from the previous version. In addition to calling the appropriate function, because the function is now returning a value, we assign that value to an item in the *grades* List. To do that, we use the **append()** method of the List object. This code is very similar to what we did in Practice7_4, except that this time, instead of using the return value of the **input()** function to populate the *grades* List, we're using the return value of one of our three User-defined functions."

```
#Student type is valid, now let's calculate the grade

#1 is an English Student
if response =="1":
    grades.append(calculate_english_grade())
```

```
# 2 is a Math Student
if response == "2":
  grades.append(calculate_math_grade())
```

```
# 3 is a Science Student
if response == "3":
  grades.append(calculate_science_grade())
```

"Here's the last line of code in our loop that asks the user if he or she has another grade to calculate," I said.

```
loop_response = input("\nDo you have another grade to calculate? ")
```

"If the answer is 'YES' (or one of its 8 variants), the While Loop is repeated and the process starts all over again. If the answer is not 'YES' (or one of its 8 variants), the lines of code that follow the body of the While Loop are executed. In the previous version of the Grades program, we immediately thanked the user for using the Grades Calculation program, and ended the program. In this version, however, we calculate an overall class average."

I paused before continuing.

"We first display are message," I said, "then use the same For Loop technique we used in Practice7_4 to display each of the items in the *grades* List (the individual grades), add their value to the *accumulator* variable, and then calculate and display the overall class average in the Python Console. Notice the use of the len() function to calculate a value for the *average* variable."

```
print("\nThe calculated final grades are: \n")
```

```
for grade in grades:
  print(grade)
  accumulator += float(grade)
```

```
average = accumulator/len(grades)
print("\nThe class average is " + str(average))
```

"Finally," I said, "this last line of code thanks the user for using the Grades Calculation Program…"

```
print("\nTHANKS FOR USING THE GRADES CALCULATION PROGRAM!")
```

I scanned the classroom to make sure I hadn't lost anyone. My students seemed pretty excited over what they had just done."

"Seeing the List used in the Grades Calculation Program really helped me," Rhonda said.

I waited to see if there were any questions, but there were none. I then dismissed class for the day.

Summary

In this chapter, we learned about the basics of List processing. We also learned about String processing.

- List are made up of one or more items

- String are made up of one or more characters

- Lists are useful in making your code easier to write and use

- Lists can reduce the amount of hard-coding you write in your projects

- A String is a series of characters.

- There are a number of List methods that you can perform on a List

- There are a series of String methods that you can perform on a String

Chapter 8---Errors and Exception Handling

In this chapter, you'll follow my University class as we learn how to avoid some of the common mistakes that beginner Python programmers make. You'll also learn how to detect and handle errors that slip through your fingers. Finally, we'll wrap up the course by delivering and installing the Grades Calculation program in the English department.

Errors and Exception Handling

I began the final class of my Introduction to Python course by saying that in our final meeting together, we would examine common errors that beginner Python programmers make, as we as cover the topic of Exception Handling. Finally, we'll deliver and install our Grades Calculation program on a Computer in the English department.

"Do you mean to say that we'll be delivering the Grades Calculation program today?" Ward asked.

"That's right, Ward," I said. "Frank Olley called me earlier in the week to find out if we were on target to complete the project today, and when I told him we were, he asked if it would be possible to deliver and install the program as part of today's class. I told him that would be fine with me, and he was elated. He's arranged to have two work study students come in today to get acquainted with the program. This might mean that today's class goes a little bit longer than usual. I do hope you can all hang in there and help me deliver and install our program in the English Department."

"I wouldn't miss it for anything," Linda said.

"Me either," Steve said. "I think it will be exciting to see how the work study students like the program."

From the looks on the faces of the rest of my students, I had a distinct feeling they all felt the same way and would be paying a visit to the English Department as well.

"It's a shame," Mary said suddenly, "but it doesn't look like Rose and Jack will make it back in time for our final class. Has anyone heard from them? Are they still in Liverpool?"

"I've heard from both of them," I said. "In fact, I spoke with both of them on Thursday night, and at the time, they were aboard their ship somewhere in the North Atlantic headed back to New York. They said the weather was unusually frigid for April, and when I asked them whether they would make it back on time for today's class, they told me they had spoken to the ship's captain, who assured them that at the ship's top speed of 30 knots, they'd be arriving in New York harbor early this morning—a few hours ahead of schedule. I expect both of them to be here before the end of class."

I intentionally withheld one additional piece of news concerning Rose and Jack---you'll find out shortly.

> **NOTE: For those of you who may have forgotten, Rose and Jack are Civil Engineers and were called away suddenly after Week 2 of our class to participate in sea trials for a new cruise ship they had designed.**

"That's great news," Rhonda said. "It will be good to see the two of them again."

"I suppose our delivery and installation of the Grades Calculation program on a PC in the English department will wrap up the SDLC?" Valerie asked.

"Just about," I replied. "Phase 5 of the SDLC, which is the Implementation Phase, will begin today with the delivery and installation of the Grades Calculation program, and it will conclude over the course of the next week or so as I and hopefully some student volunteers orient and train Work Study students in the English, Math, and Science departments in the use of our program. Phase 6 of the SDLC, which is the Audit and Maintenance phase, will begin today as well, as we observe and study how well the program functions under live use."

"I had totally forgotten all about the SDLC," Blaine said, "I've been having too much fun coding the last few weeks. However, I do see the need for the process. It provided us with a great design, that we've been able to easily follow."

"Besides delivering the program to Frank Olley," Ward said, "what's on the agenda today?"

"Exception Handling," I answered. "Exceptions are generated by Python when it detects an error at run time. These errors can sometimes be gracefully handled within the program, which is where the term Exception Handling comes into play."

"Are Errors and Exceptions the same thing?" Kate asked.

"Practically speaking they are," I said, "and you will frequently hear the terms Errors and Exceptions used interchangeably. Strictly speaking, when a run time error occurs Python generates an Exception."

"So a program won't necessarily bomb and stop running when an Exception is generated by Python?" Ward asked.

"That's right, Ward," I said. "Exception Handling involves writing code to handle errors that can creep into our programs, even after we do our best to ensure that they are free of errors. Good Exception Handling can anticipate the types of run time errors that might occur in a program, and write code to gracefully handle these errors and allow the program to continue running."

I then went on to explain that as a teacher of Computer Programming, it's very tempting to show my students examples of bad code early on in a class in an effort to show them what 'not' to do. However, after many years of teaching, I have learned that there's a huge danger in illustrating bad code or code that contains errors too early in the class. I had done it once or twice in this class, but it's something I try to avoid.

"For that reason," I said, "I try to wait until we've established a strong foundation in good coding techniques before discussing the types of errors you are likely to make, errors which can cause your program to bomb and quickly ruin your programming reputation. In today's class, we'll examine the types of common Python errors that beginners make. In some cases, we'll learn how to avoid them. In other cases, we'll learn how to implement Exception Handling techniques to detect and handle the errors that may occur anyway, even in the best of programs."

Common Beginner Errors

"What kinds of errors are you talking about detecting?" Dave asked. "I assume you mean Runtime Errors? You're not talking about Python Interpreter errors where something is simply misspelled. Exception Handling won't help there will it?"

"That's a good point, Dave," I said. "There are three kinds of errors that we'll be discussing today. The first kind are Python Interpreter errors that are, as you point out, usually misspellings of one kind or other. We've already seen (and made) a number of these during the class. Interpreter errors (also called Parser Errors) prevent us from ever getting to the point where we can run our program. The second kind are Logic errors, and are the most dangerous. Logic errors are not detected by the Interpreter, nor will they, for the most part, cause your program to 'bomb' or abnormally terminate at runtime. Logic errors are programming mistakes that can cause horrific results. Logic errors need to be uncovered before a program is in production, ideally during the Design Phase of the SDLC. Unfortunately, Logic errors can be very difficult to detect—some programs have run for years with subtle Logic errors that went unnoticed."

"You said there's a third kind of error" Kate asked?

"The third kind of errors," I said, "are Runtime Errors. These are errors that the Python Interpreter can't detect, and which occur (unfortunately) when we (or our users) run the program. When Python encounters a Runtime Error, it displays an Exception message that can startle and confuse the user of our program, and as a result, can hurt our programming reputation. Runtime Errors are the kinds of errors that we should be able to anticipate, and write Exception Handling code to deal with so that the user never sees an Exception message. We'll see how to do that a little later on in today's class."

Python Interpreter Errors

"Let's start by examining the most common types of Interpreter errors that beginners are likely to make," I said. "Remember, Interpreter errors are those errors which are detected by the Python Interpreter and which prevent your program from running at all."

NOTE: You will sometime see Interpreter Errors referred to as Parser Errors

Indentation Following a colon

"I thought I would start out by revisiting the issue of indentation." I said. "Indentation in Python can really confuse beginners. As some of you know, in other languages such as Java, C++, or C#, indentation is never required, but it can be used to make your program more readable. In Python, however, there are times when indentation is required. Using it at any other time (such as to make your program more readable) is a mistake. Let's take a look at this code where we have written 3 lines of code to display messages in the Python Console. The second line of code is 'accidentally' indented by one space. This single space will be enough to cause the Python Interpreter to complain and display an Error message. By the way, do you see that we have indented the second comment line. Because it's a comment, the Python Interpreter won't mind."

I then displayed this code on the classroom projector.

```
# Example8_1.py
 # 2nd comment line indented---no problem because it's a comment!

print("Line Number 1")
 print("Line Number 2")
print("Line Number 3")
```

I saved the program as Example8_1.py, and ran it for the class. The following screenshot was displayed on the classroom projector.

```
C:\Windows\system32\cmd.exe

C:\PythonFiles\Examples>Example8_1
  File "C:\PythonFiles\Examples\Example8_1.py", line 5
    print("Line Number 2")
        ^
IndentationError: unexpected indent

C:\PythonFiles\Examples>
```

"This kind of error is pretty easy to make by accident," I said. "Just a stray space which causes Python to believe that we are indenting the line of code. As you can see, the Python Interpreter displays an **IndentationError: unexpected indent error**, and displays the line of code and the line number that it has flagged as being incorrect. Because this is a Python Interpreter error, the program never has a chance to run."

I paused a moment before continuing.

"What we've seen is an example of an IndentationError where indentation is used where it shouldn't be," I said. "Let's review the six cases where indentation is required. Essentially whenever we see a colon in a Python program, the next line or lines of code need to be indented. Other than those cases, avoid indentation."

- Following an **if** statement (see Example3_29)

- Following an **else** Clause (see Example 4_2)

- Following an **elif** Clause (see Practice4_5)

- Following a **for** statement (see Example5_1)

- Following a **while** statement (see Example5_4)

- Following a **def** statement (see Example 6_2)

"Failure to indent where indentation is required," I said, "will also cause an IndentationError error. Here's an example where the line of codes following an If statement are not indented. This code is the incorrect version of Example3_29 from back in Week 3 of our class."

I then displayed this code on the classroom projector.

```
# Example8_2.py
# Incorrect version of Example3_29.py
# The line following the if statement is not properly indented---this will generate an error!

number1 = 22

if number1 == 22 :
print("number1 is equal to 22")
```

I saved the program as Example8_2.py, and ran it for the class. The following screenshot was displayed on the classroom projector.

"Once again," I said, "this is the kind of error that is pretty easy to make by accident. As was the case with the previous example, the Interpreter displays an IndentationError, but this time, the text is **IndentationError: expected an indented block**, and displays the line and line number that it has flagged as being incorrect. Because this is an Interpreter error, the program never has a chance to run."

I paused before continuing.

"Failure to indent following an Else Clause, an Elif Clause, a For statement, a While statement, or a Def statement defining a function will produce the same IndentatonError," I said. "You can test it out for yourself by modifying the Examples I cited earlier."

Python built-in Python function and method names are spelled in ALL lower case

"Here's another one," I said, "Built in Python functions and methods are <u>always</u>, without exception, spelled in lower case letters. Spelling them any other way in your program will generate a Python Interpreter error. I can't tell you how many times beginners spell built-in function names (or method names) with an initial capital letter."

"Does that apply to custom user-written functions as well" Chuck asked.

"Great question Chuck," I said. "I'm talking about built-in Python functions and methods. It's possible that one of your coworkers, disregarding Python recommendations, will create User-defined functions (or custom methods) that are not spelled in all lower case letters. In that case, you would need to call them exactly the way they are defined by the programmer. However built-in Python functions and methods are always spelled in all lower case letters. Let's see what kind of error we'll receive if we misspell a function name. Let's modify the first program we wrote together back in week 2 of our class. Notice that I have spelled the function name **print()** with a capital P."

I then displayed this code on the classroom projector.

```
# Example8_3.py
# print() is spelled with a capital letter. All built-in Python functions are spelled in lower case

Print("I love Python!")
```

I saved the program as <u>Example8_3.py</u>, and ran it for the class. The following screenshot was displayed on the classroom projector.

"As you can see," I said, "The Python Interpreter displays a **NameError: name 'Print' is not defined** error, and displays the line of code and the line number that it has flagged as being incorrect. The Interpreter is confused because it knows that Print is not the name of a function, and the Interpreter also knows that Print is not the name of a variable defined in the program. The error isn't as explicit as the others we've seen today, but it should point you in the right direction."

"Is there a list of Python functions available anywhere?" Mary asked.

"Yes there is Mary," I replied, "you can access a list of all the built in Python functions via the Internet. Just follow this link..."

https://docs.python.org/3/library/functions.html

"This is very useful," Mary said, "what about a list of Python methods?"

"Finding a list of Python methods is a little more difficult," I said, "You first need to locate the Python object whose method you wish to learn more about, then access a list of its available methods. To do that, start with the official Python documentation here, then look up the appropriate Python object."

https://docs.python.org/3/

Defining a variable with the name of a Python function disables the function

"Another thing I've seen beginners do," I said, "is to define variables with the same name as a Python built-in function. You might think that Python would stop you from doing this (as some other programming languages do,) but Python let's you create the variable. However, once you create the variable, you then disable the built-in function for the duration of your program. It's as if the function doesn't exist. Here's an example of an error that I see beginners make all of the time. For some reason, beginners love to define a variable called *input* in their program, then attempt to use the Python **input()** function later on. Once you create a variable called *input* in your program, you can't execute the **input()** function."

I then displayed this code on the classroom projector.

```
# Example8_4.py
# Oops, we've defined input as variable and then tried to use the input() function

input = 0

response = input("How old are you?")
```

I saved the program as Example8_4.py, and ran it for the class. The following screenshot was displayed on the classroom projector.

```
C:\PythonFiles\Examples>Example8_4
Traceback (most recent call last):
  File "C:\PythonFiles\Examples\Example8_4.py", line 6, in <module>
    input = input("How old are you?")
TypeError: 'int' object is not callable

C:\PythonFiles\Examples>
```

"The Python Interpreter," I said, "displays a **TypeError: 'int' object is not callable** error, and displays the line of code and the line number that it has flagged as being incorrect."

"That's a bit of an obscure message," Kate said.

"I agree Kate," I said. "This can be a very tricky error to correct, especially for beginners. The Python Interpreter is confused because as far as it is concerned, *input* is no longer a built-in function, it's an Integer variable that you defined earlier in the program. However, the parentheses are telling the Python Interpreter to treat the variable as a function. In general, if you see an error message that an object is not callable, look to see if the name is spelled correctly, and if it is, check to see if you haven't created a variable with the name of a built-in function or method."

"Wow," Rhonda said smiling, "I don't think I ever would be able to solve this one. But I can almost guarantee you it's a mistake I might make in the future."

Just about all Python statements are spelled in all lower case

"In keeping with the lower case theme," I said, "all of the major Python statements (keywords) that we've covered in the course are spelled in lower case."

"Such as?" Blaine asked.

"if, else, elif, for, while, range, to name a few," I replied. "The only keywords that aren't spelled in all lowercase are True, False and None."

"Is there a list of Python statements and how they are spelled?" Ward asked.

"There are two online references to Python Statements," I said, "This one is for simple statements..."

https://docs.python.org/3/reference/simple_stmts.html

"... and this one for what Python calls complex statements..."

https://docs.python.org/3/reference/compound_stmts.html

"Spelling Python statements (keywords) in any other manner than the correct spelling," I said, "will generate a Python Interpreter error. Something I see quite often is beginners spelling the word 'if' with a leading capital letter. Look at this code which you may recognize as similar to the code in Example3_29.py. Notice that the word 'if' has been spelled as 'If' beginning with the capital letter I."

I displayed this code on the classroom projector.

```
# Example8_5.py

number1 = 22

If number1 == 22 :
    print("number1 is equal to 22")
```

I then saved the program as Example8_5.py, and ran it for the class. The following screenshot was displayed on the classroom projector.

"The Python Interpreter," I said, "displays an unusually vague **SyntaxError: invalid syntax** error, and displays the line of code and the line number that it has flagged as being incorrect. Notice that the Interpreter has placed a circumflex, or carat (^) underneath the *number1.*"

"That error message isn't telling us very much, is it? Barbara said.

"No it isn't Barbara," I agreed. "This is about as confused as you will see the Python Interpreter get. The Interpreter believes the problem is with the variable *number1.* In reality, the problem is that it has no idea what the statement as a whole is doing, since as far as the Interpreter is concerned, 'If' is not a Python statement."

"Wow," said Rhonda, " I guess I didn't realize we could confuse the Python Interpreter. I thought it could figure out anything. This is another kind of error that I would be pulling my hair out trying to solve."

"Just remember," I said, "just about everything in Python is going to be spelled in all lower case letters, with the exception of variables, functions and objects (such as Lists) that you create on your own. And in that case, you may have noticed that every variable, function and List that we created in this class has also been named in all lower case letters (in accordance with the recommendations of the Python community.) Doing this makes things easier. The only exception to that rule was the way we named Constants in all Capital Letters (this is also in accordance with the recommendations of the Python community.) Even though Python doesn't have true constants the way other languages do, if we create a variable whose value is not intended to change, it should be named in all Upper Case letters."

True and False (and None) are spelled with an initial Capital letter

"Having just told you that just about everything in Python is spelled in all lower case letters," I said, "let me now remind you of an exception to that rule. The Boolean values True and False (and the special value None) are spelled with an initial Capital letter. Spelling 'True' as 'true' will confuse Python, as will spelling 'False' as 'false.' and 'None' as 'none'. Here's a variation of Example3._10.py that we wrote back in Week #3, this time with the Boolean values True and False intentionally spelled incorrectly...."

> NOTE: Other programming languages, such as Java and C++ spell True and False in all lower case letters, but Python wants True spelled with a capital T and False spelled with a capital F, otherwise you will get this error message."

I displayed this code on the classroom projector.

```
# Example8_6.py
# Working with Boolean Variables
# True and False intentionally spelled wrong

married = true    # Intentionally spelled wrong
retired = false   # Intentionally spelled wrong

print("The value of married is",  married)
print("The value of retired is ",  retired)
```

I then saved the program as Example8_6.py, and ran it for the class. The following screenshot was displayed on the classroom projector.

```
C:\Windows\system32\cmd.exe

C:\PythonFiles\Examples>Example8_6
Traceback (most recent call last):
  File "C:\PythonFiles\Examples\Example8_6.py", line 5, in <module>
    married = true        # Intentionally spelled wrong
NameError: name 'true' is not defined

C:\PythonFiles\Examples>
```

"As you can see," I said, "The Python Interpreter displays a **NameError: name 'true' is not defined** error, and displays the line of code and the line number that it has flagged as being incorrect. This error message should point you in the right direction."

"I notice that the Python Interpreter didn't complain the line of code with the word False spelled in all lower case letters," Barbara said.

"That's right Barbara," I said, "the Python Interpreter flags only the first error it finds. As a result, if we correct the spelling of the word 'true' to 'True', and run the program again, the Python Interpreter will then flag the line of code where 'false' is spelled incorrectly. The Python Interpreter will never display more than one error at a time. If you have a program that has several errors, you're going to need to identify and correct them, one line of code at a time."

Python is Case Sensitive

"As we've just seen," I said, "Python is case sensitive. Python statements are almost always spelled in lower case, and True, False and None begin with a capital letter. This case sensitivity impacts everything we do in Python, particularly when we start creating names of our own---variables, functions, Lists (and Classes when we learn about them in our upcoming course on Classes and Objects.) If you follow the guidelines I previously provided for naming in Python, you should be fine. Let's continue to review some common errors I've seen beginners make."

Referring to a variable that doesn't exist will generate an Interpreter Error

"One common problem beginners make," I said, "is to define a variable in all lower case letters (as I've suggested) but then later refer to it spelled in some other way. Let's illustrate this by declaring a variable called *number1*, assigning it a value, then try to display its value using the **print()** function. The only problem—we are trying to display the value of a variable called *Number1* (with a Capital N), not *number1*."

I then displayed this code on the classroom projector.

```
# Example8_7.py

number1 = 22

print("The value of number1 is",  Number1)
```

I saved the program as Example8_7.py, and ran it for the class. The following screenshot was displayed on the classroom projector.

```
C:\Windows\system32\cmd.exe

C:\PythonFiles\Examples>Example8_7
Traceback (most recent call last):
  File "C:\PythonFiles\Examples\Example8_7.py", line 5, in <module>
    print("The value of number1 is",  Number1)
NameError: name 'Number1' is not defined

C:\PythonFiles\Examples>_
```

"The Python Interpreter," I said, displays a **NameError: name 'Number1' is not defined** error, and displays the line of code and the line number that it has flagged as being incorrect. This error is displayed because we are trying to display the value of a variable called *Number1*, but we never created a variable with that name, we created a variable called *number1*. Whenever you see the Python Interpreter display a **NameError** message, immediately check the spelling and case sensitivity of the line in question."

"It would be great," Kate suggested, "if Python made the suggestion that perhaps we meant *number1* when we typed *Number1*," Kate suggested.

"That would be a great feature," I said. "Perhaps in the next major release of the Python language. Of course, if you follow the Python naming guidelines and name your variables, functions and objects in lowercase letters, most of these kinds of errors won't occur."

Referring to a function that doesn't exist will generate an Interpreter Error

"Referring to a function name that doesn't exist will generate the same type of NameError Exception," I said. "Here's some code that incorrectly tries to execute the **print()** function spelled with a capital letter P..."

I then displayed this code on the classroom projector.

```
# Example8_8.py

number1 = 22

Print("The value of number1 is",  number1)
```

I saved the program as Example8_8.py, and ran it for the class. The following screenshot was displayed on the classroom projector.

"The Python Interpreter," I said, displays a **NameError: name 'Print' is not defined** error, and displays the line of code and the line number that it has flagged as being incorrect. This is the same error we saw with the undefined variable name. As far as the Python Interpreter is concerned, it doesn't know if Print is an undefined variable or an undefined function---it just knows it doesn't exist either in its list of built in functions, or defined anywhere within our program. As was the case with the Example8_7.py, whenever you see the Python Interpreter display a **NameError** message, immediately check the spelling and case sensitivity of the line that it flags as being in error."

Referring to a method that doesn't exist will generate an Interpreter Error

"Interestingly," I said, "if we attempt to execute a method of a Python object that isn't spelled correctly we get an entirely different error displayed. Methods are different from Python functions in that they 'belong' to a particular Python class or object. A good example would be the List Object, which has an **append()** method that we used last week to add an item to the end of a List. Let's see what happens if we spell the method name **append()** incorrectly."

I then displayed this code on the classroom projector.

Example8_9.py

list1 = [1,2,3]

list1.apend(4)

print (list1)

I saved the program as Example8_9.py, and ran it for the class. The following screenshot was displayed on the classroom projector.

"As I told you," I said, "the Python Interpreter displays a different error for a misspelled method name than it does for a misspelled function or variable name. The reason for that is that it knows we are working with a List object, and figures that what follows the period is out attempt to specify either a method name of the List object or a property of the List object (more on that in the Classes and Objects course.) When we spell the name of an Object method incorrectly, the Python Interpreter displays an **AttributeError: 'list' object has no attribute 'append'** error, and displays the line of code and the line number that it has flagged as being incorrect. This message provides us with two important pieces of information to help us determine what the problem is--the name of the object, in this case the Python List object, and the name of the misspelled method (what the Interpreter calls an attribute.) Provided you aren't working in the middle of the night on your program, and your eyes can see clearly, you should see that the method name 'append' is spelled incorrectly as 'apend'."

"Speaking of eyes," Dave said, "Might I suggest obtaining a second set of eyes when you receive errors like this?" "I've spent hours looking over errors in code I've written like this, only to ask a coworker to look at it who then immediately finds the problem."

"That's a great tip Dave," I said. "I've also found that a good night's sleep can help with a troublesome error."

Using an Augmented Assignment operator on a variable that does not exist

"I know I mentioned this very early in the class," I said, "and some of you may have discovered this the hard way, but using an Augmented Assignment Operator on a variable that has not first been created will produce an error. It's an extremely easy error to make, particularly since Python doesn't require you to formally declare variables before assigning a value to them. However, that's a problem if you use an Augmented Assignment Operator on a variable that hasn't first been created. Here's some code we wrote in Example3_24.py in Week 3 of our class. It takes the value of the variable *number1*, and using the Augmented Addition Operator (+=) adds 24 to it..."

I then displayed this code on the classroom projector.

```
# Example3_24.py

number1 = 10
number1 += 22

print("The value of number1 is now", number1)
```

I ran the program for the class and the following screen shot was displayed on the classroom projector.

"As expected," I said, "after the Augmented Addition Operation, the value of *number1* is now 32. Now look what happens if we forget to first create *number1* before using the Augmented Addition Operator on it..."

I then displayed this code on the classroom projector.

```
# Example8_10.py

number1 += 22

print("The value of number1 is now", number1)
```

I saved the program as Example8_10.py, and ran it for the class. The following screenshot was displayed on the classroom projector.

"The Python Interpreter," I said, "displays a **NameError: name 'number1' is not defined** error, and displays the line of code and the line number that it has flagged as being incorrect. Although Python is clear that the problem is with number1, this can be a very frustrating error for a beginner to find because the line of code that is highlighted appears to be defining the variable *number1*, but it isn't. The Augmented Addition Operation we see here is the equivalent of this line of code..."

```
number1 = number1 + 24
```

"The right side operation," I said, "**number1 + 24** is the culprit here. Since the variable *number1* does not exist, you can't add 24 to it, and the Python Interpreter halts the execution of the program with this error."

"I agree," Rhonda said, "this would be a frustrating error for me to correct. I'm glad you presented it formally to us here."

Confusing the sorted() function with the sort() method

"A potential problem we saw last week" I said, "is confusing the **sorted()** function with the **sort()** method of the List object. If they both worked the same way, it wouldn't be a problem, but they don't, and if you confuse the two, you'll receive a Python Interpreter error. To review, here's the code we wrote last week in Example7_30.py in which we used the **sorted()** function to sort a List called *names* and *numbers*..."

```
# Example7_30.py
# Using the sorted() function to display a List sorted alphabetically or numerically

names = ["John","Linda","Tom","Kevin","Rita","Gil","Melissa"]
print(sorted(names))
print(names)

numbers = [11,26,3,12,8,18]
print(sorted(numbers))
print(numbers)
```

"...and the **sort()** method in Example7_31.py, to sort the same two Lists..."

```
# Example7_31.py
# Use the sort() method to sort the original List

names = ["John","Linda","Tom","Kevin","Rita","Gil","Melissa"]
print(names)
names.sort()
print(names)

numbers = [11,26,3,12,8,18]
print(numbers)
numbers.sort()
print(numbers)
```

"Executing the **sorted()** function requires that we pass, as an argument, the name of the List. Executing the **sort()** method is performed by naming the List, followed by a period, then specifying the method name. Let's take the first example, Example7_30.py, and modify it by exchanging the function name **sorted()** for the method name **sort()** and see what happens. For brevity, we'll work just with the names List..."

I displayed this code on the classroom projector.

```
# Example8_11.py

names = ["John","Linda","Tom","Kevin","Rita","Gil","Melissa"]
print(sort(names))                    # Oops, should be the sorted() function
print(names)
```

I then saved the program as Example8_11.py, and ran it for the class. The following screenshot was displayed on the classroom projector.

```
■ C:\Windows\system32\cmd.exe                              ─ □ X

C:\PythonFiles\Examples>Example8_11
Traceback (most recent call last):
  File "C:\PythonFiles\Examples\Example8_11.py", line 4, in <module>
    print(sort(names))              # Oops, should be sort()
NameError: name 'sort' is not defined

C:\PythonFiles\Examples>
```

"The Python Interpreter," I said, displays a **NameError: name 'sort' is not defined** error, and displays the line of code and the line number that it has flagged as being incorrect. Python knows that **sort()** is not a function name, but unfortunately, the Interpreter doesn't realize that we intended to execute the **sorted()** function. As Kate suggested earlier, it would be great if Python asked us if we meant to use the **sorted()** function, but unfortunately it doesn't."

I paused before continuing.

"Let's take Example7_31.py," I said, "and modify it by mistaking the function name **sorted()** for the **sort()** method of the List object. Once again, for brevity, we'll work only with the *names* List. I'm predicting a slightly different error message."

I displayed this code on the classroom projector.

```
# Example8_12.py

names = ["John","Linda","Tom","Kevin","Rita","Gil","Melissa"]
print(names)
names.sorted()          # Oops, should be the sort() method
print(names)
```

I then saved the program as Example8_12.py, and ran it for the class. The following screenshot was displayed on the classroom projector.

```
■ C:\Windows\system32\cmd.exe                              ─ □ X

C:\PythonFiles\Examples>Example8_12
['John', 'Linda', 'Tom', 'Kevin', 'Rita', 'Gil', 'Melissa']
Traceback (most recent call last):
  File "C:\PythonFiles\Examples\Example8_12.py", line 5, in <module>
    names.sorted()              # Oops, should be the sort() method
AttributeError: 'list' object has no attribute 'sorted'

C:\PythonFiles\Examples>
```

"As predicted," I said, "the Python Interpreter displays a different error when we confuse the method name sort() with the function name **sort()**. It displays an **AttributeError: 'list' object has no attribute 'sorted'** error, and displays the line of code and the line number that it has flagged as being incorrect. Because the Python Interpreter believes we are trying to execute a non-existent method of an object, it provides us with two important pieces of information to help us--the name of the object, in this case the Python List object, and the name of the misspelled method (what the Interpreter calls an attribute.)"

Brackets (and Parentheses) Must Occur in Matching Pairs

"Here's an error that not only happens to beginners," I said, "it can happen to an experienced Python programmer as well. Parentheses and brackets must always occur in matching pairs."

"Matching pairs?" Rhonda asked.

"That's right Rhonda," I said, "Matching pairs means that in a Python statement, you must have the same number of left parentheses as right parentheses. If the statement contains brackets---for instance, if you are working with Lists---you must have the same number of left brackets as you have right brackets. Also, though we haven't discussed them in this class, Tuples and Dictionaries are created using curly braces, and they must appear in matching pairs as well in a Python statement."

> NOTE: We haven't discussed them in this class, but Tuples and Dictionaries are created using curly braces {}, and they must appear in matching pairs in a Python statement."

"That doesn't seem to be that difficult a rule to follow," Blaine said. "If you have two left parenthesis, you must have two right parenthesis."

"Blaine, in a simple Python statement," I said, "I would agree with you. How can you possibly lose track of the number of left and right parenthesis? But experienced Python programmers have been known to create some very complex (and long) Python statements, sometimes containing large numbers of nested parentheses."

"Nested parentheses?" Rhonda asked. "What is a nested parentheses?"

"Nested parentheses," I said, "occur when a statement is contained within a pair of parentheses which may themselves be contained within another pair of parentheses, which may also be contained within another pair of parentheses. One easy example of nested parentheses I mentioned earlier in the class is the way in which you can specify the order in which you want your Python operations executed by enclosing the Operation within parentheses. This is called the Order of Operations. The statement or operation within the innermost pair of parentheses is performed first. Let's look at a simple example that we wrote back in Week 3 of our class, Example3_28.py."

I displayed this code on the classroom projector.

```
# Example3_28.py
print((3 + 6 + 9) / 3)
```

"Nothing fancy here," I said, "just a line of code to display the sum of 3+6+9 divided by 3. Can you see that the statement..."

```
(3 + 6 + 9) / 3
```

"...is nested within parentheses as an argument to the **print()** function?"

"I see that," Rhonda said. "This nesting business can get pretty complicated."

"Exactly Rhonda," I said. "The statement needs to have the same number of left and right parentheses. In this case, we have two of each which is perfect."

I then executed Example3_28.py, and ran it for the class. The following screenshot was displayed on the classroom projector.

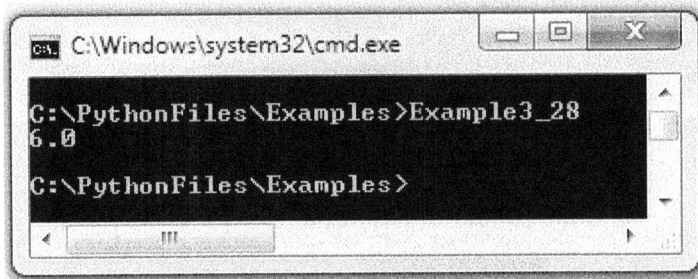

"This code runs without problems," I said, "and displays a result of **6.0**. Let's see what happens if we forget one of the left parentheses, giving us unequal numbers of left and right parentheses in the statement."

I then displayed this code (containing 1 left parenthesis and 2 right parenthesis) on the classroom projector.

```
# Example8_13.py
print(3 + 6 + 9) / 3)          #Oops, unequal numbers of left and right parenthesis
```

I saved the program as Example8_13.py, and ran it for the class. The following screenshot was displayed on the classroom projector.

"As you can see," I said, "the Python Interpreter displays a **SyntaxError: invalid syntax** error, and displays the line of code and the line number that it has flagged as being incorrect. It also places a circumflex or carat(^) underneath the right most parenthesis. The Interpreter in this case does a pretty good job of telling us that there is one more right parentheses than there is a left parenthesis. This should be enough to give you a clue that the number of left and right parenthesis are not matching. By the way, whenever you see a SyntaxError message, the Interpreter is giving you its best guess as to what is wrong with the statement. That means you'll still need to do a little detective work of your own to figure out what is wrong with your code."

I paused before continuing.

"Let's see what happens if we forget the **right most** parenthesis," I said. "We'll still receive a SyntaxError but the Interpreter's guess as to what is the problem is will be much different..."

I then displayed this code (containing 2 left parenthesis and 1 right parenthesis) on the classroom projector.

Example8_14.py

print((3 + 6 + 9) / 3   #Oops, one less right parenthesis than left

I saved the program as Example8_14.py, and ran it for the class. The following screenshot was displayed on the classroom projector.

"As you can see," I said, "the Python Interpreter once again displays a SyntaxError, but this time the message says **SyntaxError: unexpected EOF while parsing**, and displays a line number (but not an actual line of code) that it has flagged as being incorrect. In this case, the Interpreter has totally missed the mark. There is no line number 4 in our program--we only have three lines of code, which explains the 'unexpected EOF' part of the error message. EOF stands for End of File and the Interpreter is saying that it was expecting more on the previous line of code (perhaps a right parenthesis) and that it came to an end of our program before it could make any sense of it."

"In other words," Rhonda said, "we have totally confused the Interpreter."

"I couldn't have said it better myself Rhonda," I said. "When you receive this sort of SyntaxError, check for unequal numbers of parentheses or brackets or braces---but it can just as well be another error entirely. At that point, all you can do is examine your code as carefully as possible looking for possible errors. And remember to take Dave's advice---another set of eyes examining your code may come in handy here."

I paused before continuing.

"The same rule about matching pairs of parentheses," I said, "also applies for brackets when we are working with Lists and List elements. Here's some code we wrote last week in Example7_9.py in which we created a List called *baseball_greats* that has four left brackets and four right brackets."

I then displayed this code on the classroom projector.

```
# Example7_9.py
```

```
baseball_greats = [["Hank Aaron",755], ["Babe Ruth",714],["Willie Mays",660]]

for player in baseball_greats:
  print(*player)
```

I then executed Example7_9.py, and ran it for the class. The following screenshot was displayed on the classroom projector.

"As you can see," I said, "this program runs with no problem. Now let's see what happens if we forget the left bracket in front of Babe Ruth. "

I then displayed this code (with a missing bracket in front of Babe Ruth) on the classroom projector.

```
# Example8_15.py
```

```
baseball_greats = [["Hank Aaron",755], "Babe Ruth",714],["Willie Mays",660]]

for player in baseball_greats:
  print(*player)
```

I saved the program as Example8_15.py, and ran it for the class. The following screenshot was displayed on the classroom projector.

"That's similar to the error we received with a missing left parenthesis, isn't it?" Kate said.

"That's right Kate," I said. "As was the case with the missing left parenthesis in Example8_13.py, here the Python Interpreter displays a **SyntaxError: invalid syntax** error, and displays the line of code and the line number that it has flagged as being incorrect. It also places a circumflex or carat(^) underneath the right most bracket. The Interpreter is telling us that there is one more right bracket than there is a left bracket. This should be enough to give you a clue that the number of left and right brackets are not matching. Let's see what happens if forget the **right most** bracket..."

I then displayed this code (with a missing right most bracket) on the classroom projector.

```
# Example8_16.py
```

```
baseball_greats = [["Hank Aaron",755], ["Babe Ruth",714],["Willie Mays",660]

for player in baseball_greats:
  print(*player)
```

I saved the program as Example8_16.py, and ran it for the class. The following screenshot was displayed on the classroom projector.

```
C:\Windows\system32\cmd.exe

C:\PythonFiles\Examples>Example8_16
  File "C:\PythonFiles\Examples\Example8_16.py", line 5
    for player in baseball_greats:
      ^
SyntaxError: invalid syntax

C:\PythonFiles\Examples>
```

"Once again," I said, "the Python Interpreter displays a **<u>SyntaxError: invalid syntax</u>** error, and displays the line of code and the line number that it has flagged as being incorrect. It also places a circumflex or carat(^) underneath the word for in the For Loop."

"Wow, the Python Interpreter really got confused on this one," Bob said, "There's nothing wrong with that line of code. The error is on the previous line of code."

"That's right Linda," I said, "the Interpreter is saying that the Syntax Error is on the line following the one with the missing right parenthesis. As I mentioned earlier, whenever you see a <u>SyntaxError</u> message, the Interpreter is giving you its best guess as to what is wrong with the statement. That means you'll still need to do a little detective work of your own to figure out what is wrong with your code. As I've learned in my many years of programming: When in doubt about an error, check the line of code above the one that the Python Interpreter flags as being in error. That may be where the actual error is."

> NOTE: When in doubt about an error, check the line of code above the one that the Python Interpreter flags as being in error. That may be where the actual error is.

Confusing the Equality Operator (==) with the Assignment Operator (=)

"This next error is one I see all the time from beginners," I said, "and occurs when a programmer confuses the equality operator (==) with the assignment operator (=). Remember, the single equal to sign (=) is an Assignment Operator, used to assign a value to a variable. The double equal to sign (==) is the Equality Operator, generally used in a test expression to check is two operands are equal. Here's Example3_29.py from Week 3 where we first worked with the Equality Operator."

I then displayed this code on the classroom projector.

```
# Example3_29.py

number1 = 22

if number1 == 22 :
    print("number1 is equal to 22")
```

"Notice that the value 22 is assigned to the variable number1," I said, "and then the value of the variable number1 is tested, via the Equality Operator, to determine if it's equal to 22. Beginners frequently confuse the two Operators, particularly if they've programmed in other Programming languages where the Equality and Assignment Operators are the same. Look at this code in which I incorrectly use the Assignment Operator to test for equality."

I then displayed this code on the classroom projector.

```
# Example8_17.py

number1 = 22

if number1 = 22 :
    print("number1 is equal to 22")
```

I saved the program as <u>Example8_17.py</u>, and ran it for the class. The following screenshot was displayed on the classroom projector.

"Once again," I said, "the Python Interpreter displays a **SyntaxError: invalid syntax** error, and displays the line of code and the line number that it has flagged as being incorrect. It also places a circumflex or carat(^) underneath the equal to sign in the If statement. In this case, the Python Interpreter has correctly identified the issue---it's just a matter of recognizing it if you see it."

String Literals must be enclosed within quotation mark

"Continuing along with our discussion of Syntax Errors," I said, "here's another one that is pretty common for beginners to make. String Literals must be enclosed within quotation marks---either single quotes, double quotes, or triple quotes. Here's the very first program we wrote back in Week 2. Notice how the String Literal 'I love Python!' is enclosed within quotation marks."

I displayed this code on the classroom projector.

```
# This program displays "I love Python!"
print("I love Python!")
```

"Let's see what happens," I said, "if we fail to enclose the String within quotation marks."

I then displayed this code on the classroom projector.

```
# Example8_18.py
print(I love Python!)
```

I saved the program as Example8_18.py, and ran it for the class. The following screenshot was displayed on the classroom projector.

"As you can see," I said, "the Python Interpreter displays a **SyntaxError: invalid syntax** error, and displays the line of code and the line number that it has flagged as being incorrect. Interestingly, it also places a circumflex or carat(^) underneath the letter 'e' in the word 'love' in the String 'I love Python!'. It's not a perfect diagnosis of the error, but it does point you to the line of code in error."

"I would have thought the Interpreter would identify the letter 'I' as the beginning of the String as the problem," Valerie said. "Or even that the String needs to be enclosed within quotation marks, but I guess we should be grateful for what it gives us."

"That would be great if it did that Valerie," I said, "but as I said earlier, the Interpreter is giving us its best guess as to the problem. At least the Python Interpreter has correctly identified the line of code with the problem. Remember, whenever you see an error flagged by the Python Interpreter, the actual error may be something else on the line it has flagged, or even a line or two above it."

I paused before continuing.

"Similarly," I said, "Strings assigned to variables must also be enclosed within single quotes, double quotes or triple quotes as we saw in Week 3 with Example3_12.py..."

I displayed this code on the classroom projector.

```
# Example3_12.py
# A String variable

string1 = "John Smiley"
print("The value of string1 is",  string1)
```

"Let's see what happens," I said, "if we try to assign a String to a variable without the enclosing quotation marks."

I then displayed this code on the classroom projector.

```
# Example8_19.py

string1 = John Smiley
print("The value of string1 is",  string1)
```

I saved the program as Example8_19.py, and ran it for the class. The following screenshot was displayed on the classroom projector.

```
C:\Windows\system32\cmd.exe

C:\PythonFiles\Examples>Example8_19
  File "C:\PythonFiles\Examples\Example8_19.py", line 3
    string1 = John Smiley

SyntaxError: invalid syntax

C:\PythonFiles\Examples>
```

"Once again," I said, "the Python Interpreter displays a **SyntaxError: invalid syntax** error, and displays the line of code and the line number that it has flagged as being incorrect. Here, it has placed a circumflex or carat (^) underneath the last letter in the String 'John Smiley'. Again, it's not a perfect diagnosis of the error, but it does point you to the line of code in error."

Trying to concatenate a non-String value to a String value

"Since we're discussing Strings," I said, "let's take a quick look at String Concatenation and a very common error that can trip you up. We know that when we concatenate, we join one String to another using the Plus (+) Operator. We've been concatenating Strings since week 4 when we wrote this line of code..."

```
print("You have great taste. " + response + " is a great language.")
```

"In that example," I said, "we concatenated a String variable onto a String Literal, and then concatenated a String Literal onto that combination. With String Concatenation, the possibilities are endless---but the important thing to remember is that you can only concatenate two Strings."

"What do you mean?" Rhonda asked.

"I mean that you cannot concatenate a String and a number," I said. "Or a String and any other kind of Data Type. For instance, two weeks ago, in Example6_7.py, we saw that if we want to concatenate a number to a String, we must first convert the number to a String using the **str()** function..."

I displayed this code on the classroom projector.

```
# Example6_7.py
```

```
def lets_multiply(x,y):              #Function Definition
  return x*y                          #Return the result of the multiplication

retval = lets_multiply(3,5)          #Call of User-defined function
print("The result of 3 multiplied by 5 is " + str(retval))
```

> NOTE: Converting a number to a String or one Data Type to another is also known as 'casting'

"Here's another example," I said, "where we create a variable called *age*, assign it my age, and then use String Concatenation to display my name and age in a neatly formatted sentence."

I displayed this code on the classroom projector.

```
# Example8_20.py

age = 29

print("John Smiley is "  + str(age) + " years old")
```

I then saved the program as Example8_20.py, and ran it for the class. The following screenshot was displayed on the classroom projector.

"As you can see," I said, "the programs runs fine. There is no problem with this concatenation since we used the **str()** function to convert the Integer value to a String prior to concatenation it. Let's see what happens if we forget to do the conversion..."

I then displayed this code on the classroom projector.

```
# Example8_21.py

age = 29

print("John Smiley is " + age + " years old")
```

I saved the program as Example8_21.py, and ran it for the class. The following screenshot was displayed on the classroom projector.

"A different story this time," I said. "The Python Interpreter displays a **TypeError: Can't convert 'int' object to str implicitly** error, and displays the line of code and the line number that it has flagged as being incorrect. The Concatenation has failed."

"Wow," Rhonda said, "this is probably the most confusing error we've seen today. What's this about an object?"

"This error can seem pretty confusing at first," I said, "but fortunately, it's straightforward.. As soon as you see the word 'convert' in the error message, you should be thinking about Concatenation. The Python Interpreter is saying that it can't execute the int to str conversion implicitly---in other words, automatically. We have to do it ourselves using the **str()** function."

> NOTE: Some programming languages would perform the conversion automatically for us. Python does not.

Calling a Function before you define it

"I'd like to turn our attention now to Functions," I said, "and the common errors we can make when working with User-defined functions (functions that we create ourselves.) Some of these errors you may recognize from the class we had two weeks ago in Week 6. At that time, I promised that we would cover them again. It never hurts to review them again."

I paused before continuing.

"One of the most common errors I see," I said, "is that beginners sometimes forget that they must define a function in their code **before** they execute code to call the function. This might seem obvious to us, but some other programming languages permit the Function Definition to appear at the bottom of the code file. Python does not. For that reason, I recommend defining all of your functions at the 'top' of your code file. If you have placed your functions in an external file, be sure the import statement to include those functions is at the top of your code before any other code is executed. The Python Interpreter reads through your code in a linear fashion. It needs to see the Function Definition before it can execute the code to call it. Here's some code we wrote in Week 6 in Example6_2.py that uses a User-defined function to display 'I love Python!' in the Python Console. Notice how the Function Definition appears at the top of the code before the function is called."

I displayed this code on the classroom projector.

```
# Example6_2.py

def display_message():          #Function Definition
    print("I love Python!")

display_message()               #Call of User-defined function
```

I then executed Example6_2.py, and ran it for the class. The following screenshot was displayed on the classroom projector

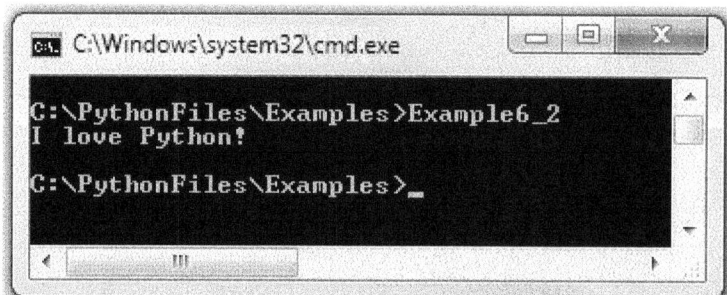

```
C:\Windows\system32\cmd.exe

C:\PythonFiles\Examples>Example6_2
I love Python!

C:\PythonFiles\Examples>_
```

"This code executes with no problem," I said. "Now let's see what happens if we try to call the function before we define it. Notice how the definition for the function appears after the line of code to call the function."

I displayed this code on the classroom projector.

```
# Example8_22.py

display_message()               #Call of User-defined function before the definition

def display_message():          #Function Definition
    print("I love Python!")
```

I then saved the program as Example8_22.py, and ran it for the class. The following screen shot was displayed on the classroom projector:

```
C:\Windows\system32\cmd.exe

C:\PythonFiles\Examples>Example8_22
Traceback (most recent call last):
  File "C:\PythonFiles\Examples\Example8_22.py", line 3, in <module>
    display_message()                          #Call of Custom Function
NameError: name 'display_message' is not defined

C:\PythonFiles\Examples>
```

"The Python Interpreter," I said, "displays a **<u>NameError: name 'display_message' is not defined</u>** error, and displays the line of code and the line number that it has flagged as being incorrect. As far as error messages go, this is fairly illustrative, although at first you might think, wait a minute, I have defined the function **display_message()** in my code. A perfect error message would say that **display_message()** is called before it's defined, but I think Python gives you enough to work with here."

"Why does the Interpreter say name, not function?" Barbara asked.

"To the Python Interpreter," I replied, "just about everything it sees in your program is a Name--the name of a built in function, the name of a class or object, the name of a variable, the name of an intrinsic operation. When it sees something it doesn't recognize, 9 times out of 10 it will display a NameError message."

> NOTE: I discussed the concept of names in Python in Chapter 3 when we had a brief discussion of the Python Namespace.

When you define a function with no arguments, it's very easy to forget the ()

"So many beginners," I said, "forget the empty pair of parentheses when they call a function that requires no arguments. Let's take another look at <u>Example6_2.py</u>. Notice how the **display_message()** function requires no arguments, and that we call it using the name of the function, followed by an empty pair of parentheses."

I displayed this code on the classroom projector.

```
# Example6_2.py

def display_message():        #Function Definition
  print("I love Python!")

display_message()             #Call of User-defined function
```

"We've already seen that this code executes fine," I said, "Now let's see what happens if we forget the empty pair of parentheses after the function name when we try to call it. Trust me, it's very easy to forget them. Take a look at what happens."

I then displayed this code on the classroom projector.

```
# Example8_23.py

def display_message():        #Function Definition
  print("I love Python!")

display_message               #Call of User-defined function
```

I saved the program as <u>Example8_23.py</u>, and ran it for the class. The following screenshot was displayed on the classroom projector.

```
C:\Windows\system32\cmd.exe

C:\PythonFiles\Examples>Example8_23

C:\PythonFiles\Examples>_
```

"Nothing was displayed in the Python Console," I said. "That's because the **display_message()** function never executed. When a function is called without parentheses, as we did here, it doesn't execute. Instead, a reference to the function is returned to the program that calls it."

> **NOTE: If you call a function requiring one or more arguments without the parentheses (and the arguments) Python will return a reference to the function. Doing this intentionally is beyond the scope of this class**

"Reference?" Rhonda asked.

"A reference," I said, "is just the memory address of a defined function in our program's memory. This address can be returned to a program, and can be used by advanced Python programmers to do some very interesting things. Things that are well beyond the scope of this class. We may touch upon them in the University's Advanced Python course next year."

"Can we see what a memory address looks like?" Kate asked.

"Let's do that Kate," I said. "In this program, since we weren't expecting a return value from the incorrect function call, we lost the reference. Let's modify Example8_23.py to store the returned reference it in variable called *address*. Once stored, we can then display the value of the variable *address* in the Python Console."

I displayed this code on the classroom projector.

```
# Example8_24.py

def display_message():            #Function Definition
    print("I love Python!")

address = display_message         #Call of User-defined function
print(address)
```

I then saved the modified program as Example8_24.py, and executed it <u>four</u> times for the class. The following screenshot was displayed on the classroom projector.

```
C:\Windows\system32\cmd.exe

C:\PythonFiles\Examples>Example8_24
<function display_message at 0x007825D0>

C:\PythonFiles\Examples>Example8_24
<function display_message at 0x003625D0>

C:\PythonFiles\Examples>Example8_24
<function display_message at 0x005025D0>

C:\PythonFiles\Examples>Example8_24
<function display_message at 0x022125D0>

C:\PythonFiles\Examples>
```

> **NOTE: If you are following along at home, the address you see displayed in the Python Console may be different from the one displayed here.**

"What's going on?" Rhonda asked. "What are those numbers displayed each time you ran the program? Are those the values for the variable address?"

"That's right Rhonda," I said. "Each time I ran the program, because we called the **display_message()** function without a pair of parentheses, the Python Interpreter found the definition for the function stored in the computer's memory allocated for our program. The memory address of the **display_message()** function was then returned to our program, stored in the variable *address*, and then displayed in the Python Console."

"Why were the results <u>different</u> each time we ran the program?" Ward asked. "Was the function stored in a different memory location each time?"

"That's exactly what happened Ward," I said. "In addition to running our program, the computer is performing other work in the background, constantly shuffling programs in and out of memory. It's very likely that the memory location allocated to our program will change each time we run the program---although there might be times when it is identical, and the result will be the same."

I saw some confused looks in the classroom.

"I can't imagine doing anything with a memory address," Rhonda said. "I'm hopeful by the time I take the Advanced Python programming class, this will all make sense to me."

"I'm sure you'll be ready for the Advanced Python Programming class Rhonda," I answered. "The important lesson here is: in Python, in order to call a function, be sure to include the parentheses, even if the function requires no arguments."

Failing to pass the correct number of arguments to a function

"Back in Week 6," I said, "we wrote a variation of the **display_message()** function that required 2 arguments. Here is Example6_4.py."

I displayed this code on the classroom projector.

```
# Example6_4.py

def display_message(language,how_much):          #Function Definition
  print("I love " + language + " " + how_much)

display_message("Java","a lot!")                 #Call of User-defined function
display_message("C++", "a little bit.")          #Call of User-defined function
display_message("Python", "more than any other!") #Call of Custom Function
```

I then executed Example6_4.py, and ran it for the class. The following screenshot was displayed on the classroom projector

```
C:\Windows\system32\cmd.exe

C:\PythonFiles\Examples>Example6_4
I love Java a lot!
I love C++ a little bit.
I love Python more than any other!

C:\PythonFiles\Examples>
```

"This code executes fine," I said, "**display_message()** expects two arguments, and that's exactly what we provided. Now watch what happens if we forget to include one of the arguments when we call the function."

I then displayed this code on the classroom projector.

```
# Example8_25.py
# Function requires 2 arguments, we pass only 1
# This code will not execute!!!

def display_message(language,how_much):          #Function Definition
  print("I love " + language + " " + how_much)

display_message("Java")                          #Call of User-defined function
display_message("C++", "a little bit.")          #Call of User-defined function
display_message("Python", "more than any other!") #Call of Custom Function
```

I saved the program as Example8_25.py, and ran it for the class. The following screenshot was displayed on the classroom projector.

"The Python Interpreter," I said, "displays a **TypeError: name 'display_message' missing 1 required position argument: 'how_much'** error, and displays the line of code and the line number that it has flagged as being incorrect. This is probably the most straightforward error message we've seen so far today. It tells us exactly what is wrong with our code, and even tells us the name of the argument that is missing."

"I'll agree with that," Bob said, "there should be no doubt as to what's wrong with our program if we receive this error message. I wish they were all like this."

So too, I suspect, did the rest of my class.

Forgetting to return a value from a User-defined function

"Back in Week 6," I continued, "we also learned how to pass a value from our function back to the calling program via a return statement. Here's Example6_8.py that accepts two numbers as arguments, multiplies them and returns the result back to the calling program, which then displays the result in the Python Console."

I then displayed this code on the classroom projector.

```
# Example6_8.py
# Call function and use the return value directly in the print() function

def lets_multiply(x,y):                    #Function Definition
    return x*y

print(lets_multiply(3,5))                  #Call of User-defined function
```

I then executed Example6_8.py, and ran it for the class. The following screenshot was displayed on the classroom projector

"This code executes fine," I said, "our program expects **lets_multiply()** to return a value and that's exactly what it does. We then use display it in the Python Console. Now let's see what happens if we forget to code the return statement in the Function Definition"

I then displayed this code in the classroom projector.

```
# Example8_26.py
# Oops---we forgot the return statement in the function
# A function without a return statement returns the None Object

def lets_multiply(x,y):                    #Function Definition
    x*y                                    #Perform the multiplication but forget to return the result
print(lets_multiply(3,5))                  #Call of User-defined function.
```

"Does everyone see," I said, "that we performed the multiplication in the **lets_multiply()** Function Definition but neglected to return the calculated result as a return value. This would be OK if our calling function wasn't expecting that return value and using it as an argument to the **print()** function. Let's see what happens when I execute this program."

I saved the program as Example8_26.py, and ran it for the class. The following screenshot was displayed on the classroom projector:

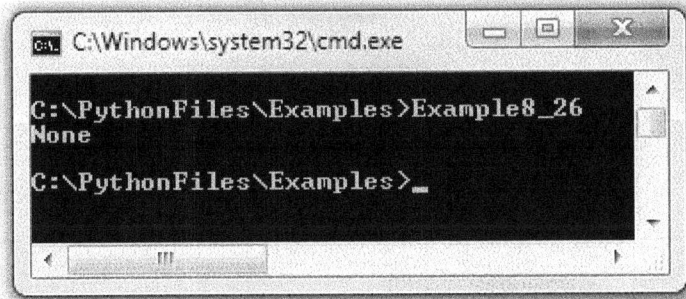

"What happened?" Ward asked. "I didn't expect the program to execute, but it did."

"That's right Ward," I said, "In Python, failing to include a return statement in a Function Definition when you intend to do so is an example of a Logic Error, not a Syntax Error. Other languages such as Java and C++ protect against this by having you explicitly define, in the Function Header, whether the function returns a value and if so, its Data Type. Python doesn't do that. As a result, the Python Interpreter has no way of knowing that you intended your function to return a value, but simply forgot to code the return statement."

"I think we looked at the None Object in Chapter 6, didn't we?" Mary said.

"That's right Mary," I said. "We learned then that every Python Function that is defined without a return statement actually returns the None Object. For that reason, when we used the return value of **lets_multiply()** as an argument to the **print()** function, because no return value was explicitly coded, the word None was displayed in the Python Console."

"You told us Python was very Object-Oriented," Ward said. "To return an object called None is very thorough on the part of its designers."

Referencing an Index value that doesn't exist

"Let's turn our attention," I said, "to some errors that can occur when we work with Lists. We've seen these before, but again, it never hurts to review them. Lists can be tricky to work with, particularly because their Index value begins with 0. We can update existing List items using their indices in combination with an assignment statement. Any attempt to reference a List item that doesn't exist will result in an error. I see this sometimes with beginners who attempt to use an assignment statement to add an item to a List. List items can be added to a List through the **append()**, **insert()** or **extend()** methods of the List object, or through List Concatenation. Items cannot be added via an assignment statement referencing an Index value that does not yet exist. Likewise, items are deleted from a List through the **remove()** method of the List object or the generic Delete (del) Statement. Referencing a List item that doesn't exist will also result in an error in these cases as well. Here's a program we wrote in Week 7, Example7_4.py, in which we created a List with 3 items, then updated the value of the third item using an assignment with its Index value of 2…"

I displayed this code on the classroom projector.

```
# Example7_4.py

grades = [82,90,66]          #Create a List with 3 items

print (grades[0])
print (grades[1])
print (grades[2])

grades[2] = 64               #Assign the value 64 to the element whose Index is 2 and value is now 66

print()
print (grades[0])
```

```
print (grades[1])
print (grades[2])
```

I then executed Example7_4.py, and ran it for the class. The following screenshot was displayed on the classroom projector.

"This code executes fine," I said, "Using an assignment statement, we were able to update the value of the third item in the *grades* list from 66 to 64. Now let's see what happens if we try to add a fourth grades to the grades() list by referencing an Index value of 3."

I then displayed this code in the classroom projector.

```
# Example8_27.py

grades = [82,90,66]              #Create a List with 3 items

print (grades[0])
print (grades[1])
print (grades[2])

grades[3] = 64                   #Oops. Attempt to add a new item to the List. This item doesn't exist

print()
print (grades[0])
print (grades[1])
print (grades[2])
```

I saved the program as Example8_27.py, and ran it for the class. The following screenshot was displayed on the classroom projector:

"It looks like the program started to execute," Ward said, "before the Python Interpreter discovered a problem."

"That's right Ward," I said, "I'm not sure if we've had an example like that today. You're right. The program started to run, and some lines of code were successfully executed---the display of the numbers 82,90 and 62---before the Python Interpreter detected that something was wrong. At that point, the Interpreter displayed an **IndexError: list assignment index out of range** error, and displayed the line of code and the line number that it believed had a problem. In this case, the Python Interpreter is right on the mark. It knows the problem is with this line of code…"

```
grades[3] = 64          #Oops. Attempt to add a new item to the List. This item doesn't exist
```

"The code looks fine," I said, "but an assignment statement like this can only be used to update an existing item with an Index value of 3. Right now the *grades* List has items with Index values of 0, 1 and 2, so this line results in a message that the assignment index is out of range. Whenever you see an error like this, right away you should suspect that something is wrong with the code that is referencing a List."

> NOTE: Not only Assignment Operations, but any statement or method that references an Index value that does not exist will result in the same index out of range error.

List Object is not callable

"Here's an error that is easy to make," I said, "not only with the List object, but any time you attempt to execute the method of any Python object (including Objects you will create on your own in our Classes and Objects course.) It's very easy to reference the Object name, but forget the period and the method name that need to follow. Doing so will produce a pretty obscure error message. Take a look at Example7_15.py from Week 7 where we used the **insert()** method of the List object to insert a new item---Tuesday--between two existing items in the *days_of_the_week* List..."

I displayed this code on the classroom projector.

```
# Example7_15.py

days_of_the_week = ["Monday","Wednesday","Thursday","Friday","Saturday","Sunday"]
print(days_of_the_week)

days_of_the_week.insert(1,"Tuesday")
print(days_of_the_week)
```

I then executed Example7_12.py, and ran it for the class. The following screenshot was displayed on the classroom projector.

"This code executes fine," I said. "As you can see, Tuesday has been properly inserted in the *days_of_the_week* List between Monday and Wednesday. Now, suppose, in your excitement to insert an item in the *days_of_the_week* List, you totally forget to code the insert method of the List object. In other words, this line of code…

```
days_of_the_week.insert(1,"Tuesday")
```

"…will look like this…"

```
days_of_the_week(1,"Tuesday")
```

"Wow," Rhonda said, "that's a subtle difference. I can see myself doing something like that."

I then displayed this code on the classroom projector.

```
# Example8_28.py

days_of_the_week = ["Monday","Wednesday","Thursday","Friday","Saturday","Sunday"]
print(days_of_the_week)

days_of_the_week(1,"Tuesday")
print(days_of_the_week)
```

I saved the program as Example8_28.py, and ran it for the class. The following screenshot was displayed on the classroom projector:

```
C:\Windows\system32\cmd.exe

C:\PythonFiles\Examples>Example8_28
['Monday', 'Wednesday', 'Thursday', 'Friday', 'Saturday', 'Sunday']
Traceback (most recent call last):
  File "C:\PythonFiles\Examples\Example8_28.py", line 6, in <module>
    days_of_the_week(1,"Tuesday")
TypeError: 'list' object is not callable

C:\PythonFiles\Examples>
```

"The Python Interpreter," I said, "displays a **TypeError: 'list' object is not callable** error, and displays the line of code and the line number that it has flagged as being incorrect. The Interpreter has identified the correct line of code, but the message is poor."

"You're right," Lou said. "that is a pretty obscure message. There's nothing in there about a missing method."

"Exactly Lou," I said. "I've seen beginners, and also some experienced programmers, receive this error and stare at their code for hours trying to figure it out. By telling us that a List object is not callable, Python is trying to tell us that we are using our List object as if it were a function. Better to say we're missing a method. If you see this error with the List object (or any other Python object,) you should immediately look for a missing method name following the name of the object."

Logic Errors

"The types of errors that we've examined so far this morning," I said, "have been exclusively Python Interpreter errors that either immediately generated an error that prevented our program from running or, as was the case in Example8_27.py, stopped the program from running sometime after it began to run. In both cases, the Python Interpreter discovered something wrong with our code, stopped the program from running, displayed an error message, and did its best to display the line of code that it believed to be in error."

> NOTE: You can argue that Example8_27.py was an example of a Runtime Error since the program actually did 'something' prior to stopping. However, because it contained a not so obvious syntax error, I prefer to categorize it as a Python Interpreter error.

"I think you mentioned earlier there are also Logic Error and Runtime Errors?" Mary asked.

"That's right Mary," I said. "Let's examine Logic Errors next. Unlike Syntax errors, Logic errors are not discoverable by the Python Interpreter, and therefore the program is not terminated. As a result, programs with Logic Errors run normally, appearing to work just fine, when in reality they're producing incorrect results."

"So that's the hallmark of a Logic Error," Ward said. "Incorrect results?"

"That's' right Ward," I said. "If you are lucky, you'll detect the Logic Error yourself while you are developing the program. It may be a so-called 'Eureka' moment in which you say to yourself 'how could I ever have written my code like that?'. It may be that the user of the program detects your Logic Error, hopefully during the Testing phase of your program. It might be that the user discovers your Logic Error shortly after the program is implemented, thereby minimizing its damage. Worse yet, it may be that the Logic Error isn't discovered for a long period of time, potentially causing much more damage."

"Can you give us some examples of Logic Errors?" Rhonda asked.

"I can think of a few examples," I said. "Generating a paycheck for an employee for one million dollars instead of one thousand dollars. Causing a robot to dispense a dosage of medicine for a patient that is potentially fatal. Opening a valve on the engine of a space craft prematurely. Granted, these are extreme cases, but I think you see the point. What causes Logic Errors? Many times, incorrect specifications from a user during the Design Phase, but also sometimes erroneous assumptions on the part of a programmer. For instance, I've seen code written that assumed there are 365 days in a year (not quite true.) Code written that assumes there are exactly 24 hours in a day (not true.) Code written that assumes there are 3 yards in a meter (not true.) I've seen code that runs fine every day of the year, but fails to run on February 29th, which occurs every 4 years (with some exceptions.)"

"Will you be showing us any of those errors today?" Joe asked.

"Those errors are very application specific," I said, "I won't be showing you any of those types of errors, but we will review some very basic Logic Errors that many beginners to Python make---some of which we've already seen. With the exception of one of them, the examples will run without error and will appear to work fine. That's the most dangerous type of error we can have."

Failing to include two expressions in an or statement

"We've already seen a number of Logic errors during the class," I said. "although I'm not sure I formally termed them that. Back in Week 3, for example, we wrote code in Example3_36.py in which we failed to include two expressions in an Or statement. Mistakes like this one are the types of errors that an over-confident beginner Python programmer might make and, without realizing it, produce erroneous results."

I displayed this code on the classroom projector.

```
# Example3_36.py

number1 = 99

if number1 == 22 or 88:
  print("One or both sides of the OR expression are True")
```

"Let's modify the program slightly," I said. "so that we can more obviously see the Logic Error."

I then displayed this code on the classroom projector

```
# Example8_29.py

number1 = 99

if number1 == 22 or 88:
  print("number1 is equal to the number 22 or the number 88")
else:
  print("number1 is NOT equal to the number 22 or the number 88")
```

I saved the program as Example8_29.py, and ran it for the class. The following screen shot was displayed on the classroom projector:

Something was wrong.

"That answer is definitely not correct," Rhonda said. "the value of the variable *number1* is equal to 99. It definitely isn't equal to either 22 or 88. What did we do wrong?"

"We confused Python," I said. "Although our code is very English-like, we failed to adhere to the requirements for a Python Or expression. We don't have two valid expressions on either side of the Or operator. Our left-hand test expression is 'number1 == 22', which can evaluate to True or False., depending upon the value of the variable *number1.* However, the right-hand test expression is only the number 88."

```
if number1 == 22 or 88:
```

"In Python's eyes," I continued, "the right-hand test expression is asking, is 88 equal to 88? The answer, of course, is yes! 88 is equal to 88. The right-hand test expression will always evaluate to True. Because of that, the entire Or expression also always evaluates to True. I know it's difficult not to fall into this trap of writing Python code the way we speak. Unfortunately, here you can't code the way we speak to a friend. This is an error I've seen many, many times."

"And this is most definitely a Logic error," Ward said, "since the program produced incorrect results, yet wasn't flagged as being in error or bomb at runtime."

"Exactly Ward," I said.

"So how do we fix it?" Rhonda asked.

"By supplying," I answered, "a valid expression that can evaluate to True or False on both sides of the Or Operator. Like this..."

I then displayed this code on the classroom projector.

```
# Example8_30.py

number1 = 99

if number1 == 22 or number1 == 88:
  print("number1 is equal to the number 22 or the number 88")
else:
  print("number1 is NOT equal to the number 22 or the number 88")
```

"Do you see the difference between this?" I asked.

```
if number1 == 22 or 88:
```

"…and this?"

```
if number1 == 22 or number1 == 88:
```

"Yes," Rhonda said, "you repeated the variable name *number1*."

I saved the modified program as Example8_30.py, and ran it for the class. The following screen shot was displayed on the classroom projector:

```
C:\Windows\system32\cmd.exe

C:\PythonFiles\Examples>Example8_30
number1 is NOT equal to the number 22 or the number 88

C:\PythonFiles\Examples>_
```

"That's better," I heard Ward say. "*number1* is not equal either to the number 22 or the number 88."

"And I just changed the program so that number1 was equal to 22 and received a message saying exactly that," Rhonda said. "I guess that's good testing at work!"

"Yes, it is Rhonda," I said, "the program is now behaving as it should. Good testing will prove that."

Not Providing a Way for a While Loop to End/Forgetting to Increment a Counter Variable

"Another type of Logic Error that is common for beginners to make," I said, "is to code a While Loop and forget to provide a way for the While Loop to end. Sometimes this is caused by forgetting to increment a counter variable."

"Counter variable?" Steve asked.

I continued by explaining that many of the programs we had written during the class depended, to some degree, on creating, incrementing, and examining a counter variable somewhere within a program. Most often, but not always, the counter variable was named *counter*.

"Counter variables," I explained, "are variables that you create to do exactly that—count something. For example, three weeks ago in Example5_4.py, we used a counter variable appropriately named *counter* to assist us in displaying the numbers 1 through 10 in the Python Console. We incremented the *counter* variable, and used it in a test expression so that our Loop would eventually stop running..."

I displayed this code on the classroom projector.

```
# Example5_4

counter = 1
```

```
while counter < 11:
  print (counter)
  counter += 1
print("\nAll Done!")
```

I then executed Example5_4.py, and ran it for the class. The following screenshot was displayed on the classroom projector.

"This code executes fine," I said. "As you can see, the numbers 1 through 10 have been displayed in the Python Console. Also, the message 'All done!' has been displayed indicating that the While Loop terminated normally. Crucial to this program running correctly, is incrementing the value of the *counter* variable, within the body of the While Loop, each time the While Loop executes."

```
counter +=1
```

"Beginner Python programmers," I said, "when they make an error with the While Loop, tend to do one of two things. They either forget to increment the value of the *counter* variable entirely, or they increment the value of the *counter* variable <u>outside</u> the body of the While Loop. Either one of these mistakes will result in an Endless Loop, something we saw back in Week 5. Let's modify Example5_4.py so that we 'accidentally' increment the value of the *counter* variable outside of the body of the While Loop. Because the body of the While Loop needs to be indented, this is an easy thing to do. All we need to do is fail to indent that line of code properly..."

I then displayed this code on the classroom projector.

```
# Example8_31

counter = 1

while counter < 11:
  print (counter)
counter += 1
print("\nAll Done!")
```

I saved the program as Example8_31.py and ran it for the class. The following screen shot was displayed on the classroom projector---a series of scrolling 1's.

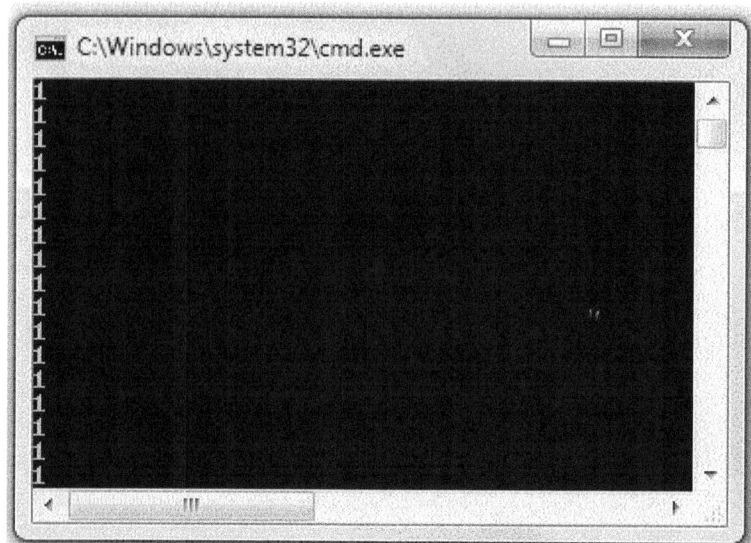

"The Python Console is displaying the number 1 continuously," Rhonda said.

"That's right Rhonda," I said. "That's because the incrementation of the *counter* variable was accidentally placed outside of the body of the While Loop. Because of that, the test expression will always evaluate to True--- *counter* will always be less than 11. This results in an Endless Loop, and as we can see, Python will continue to display the number 1 in the Python Console. In fact, if we left the program running at the end of today's class, it would still be scrolling when we arrived in the Computer Lab next week for the start of our Classes and Objects course."

"According to my notes from Week 5," Linda said, "pressing the Control and the letter C together will end the program, is that correct?"

"That's perfect, Linda" I said, "Let's do that now."

I pressed Control+C simultaneously. The following screenshot was displayed on the classroom projector.

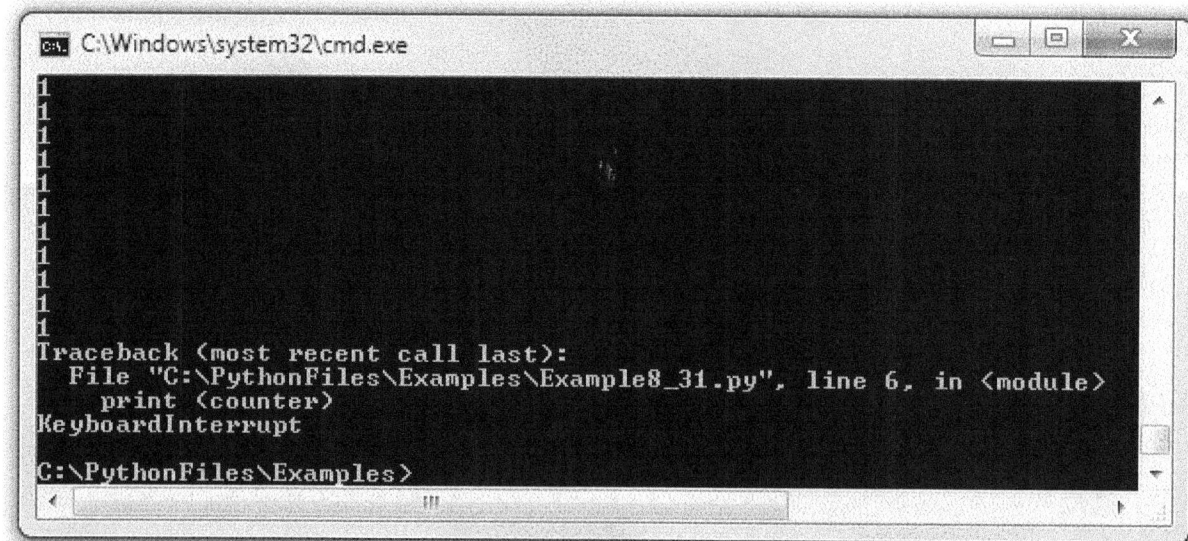

"Didn't you say that Logic Errors don't generate explicit error messages?" Rhonda asked.

"That's right Rhonda," I said, "but this message isn't an error message. It's the message we received when we interrupted the program. As far as Python is concerned, an Endless Loop isn't an error---although I think we would certainly disagree. Furthermore, this message doesn't point us in the direction of an Endless Loop or a problem with the *counter* variable not being incremented. The Python Interpreter merely displays the line of code that was executing when we interrupted it, which is the line of code to display the current value of the *counter* variable in the Python Console. Hopefully a continuous scrolling of the same value in the Python Console will alert you to a potential Endless Loop condition. But there will also be cases where the program you write doesn't display anything, but just runs and runs continuously. If you know that the program should end processing after a few minutes, and it's hours later, hit the Control+C combination and start looking for an Endless Loop in your program."

I waited to see if anyone had any questions before continuing.

"Forgetting to increment the *counter* variable doesn't always result in an Endless Loop," I said, "sometimes it just results in incorrect output. Remember this program, <u>Practice5_8.py</u>, from Week 5, where we counted numbers until the user told us to stop?"

I displayed this code on the classroom projector.

```
# Practice5_8.py

counter = 1

loop_response = input("Should I start counting? ")

while loop_response.upper() == "YES":
  print (counter)
  counter += 1
  loop_response = input("Should I continue? ")
print("\nThanks for counting with me!")
```

"What would happen," I said, "if we forget to increment the value of the *counter* variable in this program, like this..."

I then displayed this code on the classroom projector.

```
# Example8_32.py

counter = 1

loop_response = input("Should I start counting? ")

while loop_response.upper() == "YES":
  print (counter)
  loop_response = input("Should I continue? ")
print("\nThanks for counting with me!")
```

I saved the program as <u>Example8_32.py</u> and ran it for the class. I answered 'Yes' to the prompt 'Should I start counting? '. The number 1 was displayed. I then answered 'Yes' to the prompt 'Should I continue? Again, the number 1 was displayed. Again I answered 'Yes' to the prompt 'Should I continue?". Again the number 1 was displayed. Something was obviously wrong. My students saw the following screen shot displayed on the classroom projector.

"Something's wrong," Barbara said. "The number 1 continues to be displayed in the Python Console. The program is no longer counting forward."

"That's right Barbara," I said. "This is because we forgot to increment the value of the *counter* variable. As a result, the value of the *counter* variable displayed in the Python Console is always the same---the number 1. You might argue that the problem this time is not as severe as an Endless Loop, but the results are still incorrect. And again, there no error message generated by the Interpreter error. The program seems to run fine, but the results are erroneous---the worst kind of error possible in programming."

Again, I waited to see if anyone had any questions before continuing.

Forgetting to Add to an Accumulator Variable

"Forgetting to add values to an accumulator variable," I said, "is similar to forgetting to increment a *counter* variable. An *accumulator* variable is used to hold a running total of something, such as the total scores of all the quiz grades taken or the total value of all employee salaries in a company. Last week, we wrote a program that calculated the overall average of grades entered by the user. In order to properly calculate an overall average, we needed to add the value of each entered grade to an *accumulator* variable. If we had forgotten to do that we would have displayed an incorrect average in the Python Console—most likely zero."

"And there goes our reputation!" Rhonda said.

"That's right, Rhonda" I agreed. "It only takes a few mistakes to tarnish it. Here's the code from Practice7_4.py that we wrote last week."

I displayed the code from Practice7_4.py on the classroom projector...

```
#Practice7_4.py

grades = []
accumulator = 0.0

loop_response = input("\nDo you want to calculate a grade? ")

while loop_response.upper() == "YES":
  grades.append(input("Enter a grade "))
  loop_response = input("\nDo you have another grade to enter? ")

print ("\nThe entered grades are \n")

for grade in grades:
  print(grade)
  accumulator += float(grade)

average = accumulator/len(grades)
print("\nThe class average is " + str(average))
```

"This code will work fine," I said, and to prove it I executed Practice7_4.py and entered 3 grades, before telling the program I was finished.

"As promised," I said, "this program works fine. The key to this program working correctly is adding the entered grade to the *accumulator* variable. We do that by iterating through each *grade* in the *grades* List via a For Loop and use the Augmented Addition Operator to add its value to the *accumulator* variable..."

```
accumulator += float(grades)
```

"Forgetting to add to the *accumulator* variable is a very common type of Logic Error," I explained. "Let's see what happens if we delete the line of code within the For Loop that does that."

I then deleted the line of code in the For Loop where we add the value of the *grade* item in the *grades* List to the *accumulator* variable, and displayed the code on the classroom projector.

```python
# Example8_33.py

grades = []
accumulator = 0.0

loop_response = input("\nDo you want to calculate a grade? ")

while loop_response.upper() == "YES":
  grades.append(input("Enter a grade "))
  loop_response = input("\nDo you have another grade to enter? ")

print ("\nThe entered grades are \n")

for grade in grades:
  print(grade)

average = accumulator/len(grades)
print("\nThe class average is " + str(average))
```

I then saved the program as Example8_33.py and ran it for the class, entering the same 3 grades I did when I executed Practice7_4. The following screen shot was displayed

```
C:\Windows\system32\cmd.exe                        _  □  X

C:\PythonFiles\Examples>Example8_33

Do you want to calculate a grade? Yes
Enter a grade 70

Do you have another grade to enter? Yes
Enter a grade 80

Do you have another grade to enter? Yes
Enter a grade 90

Do you have another grade to enter? No

The entered grades are

70
80
90

The class average is 0.0

C:\PythonFiles\Examples>
```

"Exactly as you predicted," Steve said. "An erroneous class average of 0.0."

"For a moment there," Rhonda said, "I thought the program worked fine--but now I can see that the class average is displayed as 0.0. That's wrong."

"That's right," I said. "Because we forgot to increment the value of the *accumulator* variable, its value remained at its initial value of zero. Because of that, when we divided the *accumulator* variable by the number of grades in the *grades* List—in this case 3—our result was zero. The program didn't bomb, but it did result in an incorrect answer, which as I've been preaching to you for several minutes, is the worst kind of error you can make."

A problem with the Or Operator

"The last Logic Error I have to discuss this morning," I said, "is one we saw back in Week 3, when I showed you a potential problem with the Or Operator. Specifically, when the expressions on both sides of the Or Operator use the not equal to (!=) sign. This is a very common Logic Error. Unfortunately, it's almost the most difficult one to explain and understand. Here's the code from Example3_39.py that illustrates the problem."

I displayed this code on the classroom projector.

```
# Example3_39.py

x = int(input("Enter a number from 1 to 100: "))

if x != 22 or x != 44:
  print("Your number is not equal to 22 or 44. It is",x)
else:
  print("Your number is equal to 22 or 44. It is",x)
```

I gave my students a chance to study the code.

"I vaguely remember this problem," Barbara said, "but I'm not totally sure I understood the issue then."

"Let's run the program. That should help illustrate the Logic Error," I said, "We'll ask the user to enter a number from 1 to 100, and we want the program to determine if the number is not equal to 22 or not equal to 44. If it isn't, we'll display a message to that effect, otherwise we'll display a message that the number is equal to 22 or is equal to 44."

I could see some puzzled looks on the faces of my students.

"I admit that this is an awkward expression," I said, "but this is such a common error for beginners to make, I need to illustrate it for you."

> **NOTE:** Sharp students will undoubtedly realize that we could have written this code using the equality operator (==) and totally avoided the problem we're about to see.

"Are we agreed," I continued, "that if we run the program and enter the number 99, we would expect a message to be displayed that the entered number is <u>not equal to</u> 22 or 44?"

"Yes, that's what I would expect," Ward said.

I ran the program for the class, and entered the number 99. The following screen shot was displayed on the classroom projector:

```
C:\Windows\system32\cmd.exe

C:\PythonFiles\Examples>Example3_39
Enter a number from 1 to 100: 99
Your number is not equal to 22 or 44. It is 99

C:\PythonFiles\Examples>_
```

"No problem here," I said, "99 is <u>neither</u> 22 nor 44, and we display a message saying exactly that. The program seems to be running perfectly. Now let's run the program again, this time entering the number 22. Are we agreed that if we enter the number 22, the program should display a message that the entered number is either 22 or 44?"

"That's right," Rhonda said. "The program's If statement is checking if the entered number is <u>not equal to</u> 22 or <u>not equal to</u> 44. If it's <u>not equal to</u> one of those two numbers that means it must be <u>equal to</u> 22 or 44."

"My head is starting to spin," Mary said.

I ran the program for the class again, this time entering the number 22. The following screen shot was displayed on the classroom projector:

```
C:\Windows\system32\cmd.exe

C:\PythonFiles\Examples>Example3_39
Enter a number from 1 to 100: 22
Your number is not equal to 22 or 44. It is 22

C:\PythonFiles\Examples>
```

"Uh oh," Blaine said. "We have a problem. The program is telling us that the number 22 is not equal to 22 or 44. However, it is equal to one of them."

"That's a Logic Error if ever I saw one," Rhonda said.

"That's right Rhonda," I said. "Furthermore, if we run the program again and enter the number 44, the same problem will occur. The program will tell us that 44 is not equal to 22 or equal to 44---but of course it is equal to one of them."

I ran the program for the class again, this time entering the number 44. The following screen shot was displayed on the classroom projector:

```
C:\Windows\system32\cmd.exe                          ─  □   X

C:\PythonFiles\Examples>Example3_39
Enter a number from 1 to 100: 44
Your number is not equal to 22 or 44. It is 44

C:\PythonFiles\Examples>_
```

'Wow, we have a real problem on our hands with this code," Barbara said. "Except for the first case, when we entered 99, it's produced <u>erroneous</u> results."

"In fact, Barbara" I said, "if we were to run the program and enter every number from 1 to 100, every number will result in the same message being displayed---that the entered number is <u>not equal to</u> 22 or 44---including the two numbers that are, 22 and 44!"

"As I recall when we discussed this error in Week 3," Dave said, "you gave us a very simple rule of them. When we have 'not equal to' expressions on both sides of an Or Operator, change the Or operator to an And operator and the code should behave correctly."

"That's right Dave," I said. "That's exactly what we did back in Week 3, when we modified the code in <u>Example 3_39.py</u> to look like this..."

I displayed this code on the classroom projector.

```
# Example3_40.py

x = int(input("Enter a number from 1 to 100: "))

if x != 22 and x != 44:
  print("Your number is not equal to 22 or 44. It is",x)
else:
  print("Your number is equal to 22 or 44. It is",x)
```

I ran <u>Example3_40</u> for the class, and entered the number 99. The following screen shot was displayed on the classroom projector:

```
C:\Windows\system32\cmd.exe                          ─  □   X

C:\PythonFiles\Examples>Example3_40
Enter a number from 1 to 100: 99
Your number is not equal to 22 or 44. It is 99

C:\PythonFiles\Examples>
```

"This is correct," I said, "Since 99 is neither 22 nor 44, we display a message saying exactly that. Now let's run the program again, this time entering the number 22. We should receive a different message this time."

I ran the program for the class again, this time entering the number **22**. The following screen shot was displayed on the classroom projector:

"That's better," Ward said. "The program is correct this time. 22 is most definitely 22 or 44."

I ran the program for the class again, this time entering the number **44**. The following screen shot was displayed on the classroom projector:

"Again," I said, "the program is correct. 44 is most definitely 22 or 44. You'll see, if we run through all of the numbers between 1 and 100 that the program is running perfectly. Changing the Or Operator to an And Operator made all the difference."

> NOTE: When you have not equal to expressions on both sides of an Or statement, change the Or to an And---you'll be fine. For a fuller explanation of the problem (including our good friend the Truth Table), refer back to Chapter 3

"I mentioned earlier that the construction of the If statement was awkward," I said. "As we saw back in Week 3, alternatively, we could have written the code in Example3_39.py to look like this, which we did in Example3_41.py."

I displayed this code on the classroom projector.

```
# Example3_41.py

x = int(input("Enter a number from 1 to 100: "))

if x == 22 or x == 44:
  print("Your number is equal to 22 or 44. It is",x)
else:
  print("Your number is not equal to 22 or 44. It is",x)
```

"Changing the construction of the If statement," I said, "by first checking for the 2 numbers we are looking for, and allowing the else clause to handle all the other possibilities allows us to avoid the troublesome not equal to (!=) Operator. As you've heard me say more than once, there are many ways to paint a picture, and in programming, there is usually more than one way to solve the same problem. Example 3_40 and Example3_41 both work correctly. Which one you prefer is up to you."

Runtime Errors

"The final type of error I want to discuss today," I said "is the Runtime Error. So far today, we've discussed Syntax errors, which are obvious coding mistakes by a programmer. Logic Errors are subtle mistakes made by a programmer. Runtime Errors, on the other hand, are generally not the fault of the programmer. Having said that, however, experienced programmers should anticipate potential Runtime Errors and deal with them using a technique called Exception Handling."

"Can you give us an example of a Runtime Error?" Barbara asked.

"Runtime Errors," I said, "can occur when our program is interacting with a user. For example, the user may enter their name when the program asks for their birth date. This can cause the program to abnormally terminate (in programming jargon 'bomb') if the program then uses that entry to calculate how old the user is."

"Wow, who would have thought the user would do such a thing?' Rhonda asked.

"Experienced Python programmers, and of course, those who took this computer class," I said smiling.

I paused before continuing.

"When we write programs," I continued, "we should do our best to test the program for all possible scenarios, but sometimes the programmer is too 'close' to the situation.. As Rhonda said, after writing code to accept the user's name and age, most programmers wouldn't test the program by entering an age when a name is asked for, and their name when the age is requested. As a result, the programmer believes the program is fool proof, when in actuality, it's just a step away from producing a Runtime Error. For this reason, it is often best to let another programmer test your program. Some companies employ dedicated software testers for exactly this reason.

"Can you give us any other Runtime Error examples?" Joe asked.

"Here are a few Joe," I said. "A program that interacts with external files or databases is the kind of code that can trigger Runtime Errors. For instance, you may write code that anticipates finding and opening a file or database that exists somewhere on a computer network. If the file or database is not there---through not fault of your program--- your program will bomb with a Runtime Error. Because modern Python programs are so powerful and flexible, in the future you may write programs that interact with all kinds of different hardware (i.e. phones, thermostats, watches, satellite, lights, Artificial Intelligence Devices, etc.). These too are also susceptible to triggering Runtime Errors."

"You mentioned that we can 'handle' Runtime Errors through Exception Handling?" Kathy asked. "Are you going to show us how to do that?"

Runtime Error Illustrated---Division by Zero

"We'll get to that shortly," I said. "Before we do that, I'd like to show you an example of a Python Runtime Error. It's a very common one, Division by Zero, and because it's so easy to trigger ourselves, it's a great way to learn about Exception Handling."

"Division by Zero?" Steve asked. "Is that a problem."

"Yes it is Steve," I said. "In Python, like most programming languages, Division by Zero will generate a Runtime Error."

I continued by stating that in the computer world, Division by Zero is a big no-no.

"What's 12 divided by 1?" I asked.

"12," Mary replied.

"Now what about 12 divided by 1/2?" I continued.

After a moment's hesitation, Dave answered, "24."

"Correct," I said. There were some puzzled faces.

"I know I've caught those of you with math phobia on that one," I said. "A number, divided by a number *smaller* than 1 always results in an answer *larger* than the original number."

"In Mathematics terms," Ward said, "I believe you mean to say that when we divide a number (called the <u>dividend</u>) by another number (called the <u>divisor</u>) that's smaller than 1, we take the *reciprocal* of that number and multiply by it. In other words, 12 divided by 1/2 becomes 12 multiplied by 2, whose result is 24."

"Well said, Ward," I replied smiling. "You must have been a Math major in College."

I then displayed the following chart on the board:

Number 1 (Dividend)	Number 2 (Divisor)	Answer
12	1	12
12	1/2	24
12	1/3	36

12	1/4	48
12	1/10	120
12	1/100	1200
12	1/1000	12000

I continued by telling my students that as the divisor approaches zero, the answer becomes larger and larger. In fact, when the <u>divisor</u> is zero, the answer becomes an infinite number, which is impossible to represent in a computer.

"For that reason," I continued, "dividing a number by 0 in your computer program causes programs in most programming languages to bomb, and Python is no exception. Let's take a look at this code."

I displayed this code on the classroom projector.

```
# Example8_34.py

x = 4
y = 0

z = x/y

print ("The value of z is ", z)
```

"As you can see," I said, "this code will divide the value of the variable x, which is 4, by the value of the variable y, which is 0."

I then saved the program as <u>Example8_34.py</u> and ran it for the class. The following screen shot was displayed

```
C:\PythonFiles\Examples>Example8_34
Traceback (most recent call last):
  File "C:\PythonFiles\Examples\Example8_34.py", line 6, in <module>
    z = x/y
ZeroDivisionError: division by zero

C:\PythonFiles\Examples>
```

"As you can see," I said, "the Python Interpreter displays a **<u>ZeroDivisionError: division by zero</u>** error, and displays the line of code and the line number that it has flagged as being incorrect. Unlike some of the other error messages we've seen today, this error message is very explicit. This Runtime Error is almost always the fault of the programmer for not anticipating the possibility of division by zero."

I went on to explain that most beginner programmers aren't aware of the problems with Division by Zero and that their immediate response would most likely be that they aren't dividing by zero anywhere within their program."

"That's what I was going to say," Dave said. "However, I can imagine that this kind of error can occur in many different ways—for instance, input from a user via the Python **input()** function."

"That's excellent, Dave," I said. "That's exactly one way it could happen. The user might enter zero at runtime in answer to a prompt. If the program then divides by that value, we have a Division by Zero error. As a rule of thumb, whenever division is occurring anywhere within your program, it's a good idea to write Exception Handling Code to deal with the Division by Zero error."

"Isn't that something we could prevent with an If statement?" Barbara suggested.

"That's another way to handle it Barbara," I said, "and we'll be discussing that shortly when we return from our 15-minute break."

Dealing With Errors/Exceptions in Your Program

Fifteen minutes later I was about to begin discussing Exception Handling in a Python program when I noticed two people approach the classroom door. It was Rose and Jack, back from their long journey!

"Rose and Jack," I said, "welcome back. It's great to see you! I was getting a little worried that you might not make it back in time for our final class."

"Professor Smiley has been keeping us apprised of the development of the Grades Calculation Program," Rose explained to the class. "And of course, we took our laptops along with us so we could work along the rest of the class. We're right on pace—well, just about on pace—to complete the course, and the project, with all of you. I don't think we've missed a beat."

"I'm glad that you're both able to be with us today," I said. "We've missed you. Your attendance will help put a nice close to the project we all started together eight weeks ago."

Back to Exception Handling, I reminded my students that during the first part of our class, as a learning experience, we had intentionally created errors to cause our programs to bomb. During the last half of the class, we would be examining ways of gracefully handling those errors in such a way that our programs don't come to a grinding halt.

"As I've mentioned several times today," I said, "nothing can ruin your reputation faster than having one of your customers proclaim that they love your programs but that they 'bomb' once in a while. As you can imagine, this can be very bad for business! Exception Handling can prevent that."

"I'm still not sure I understand the concept of Exception Handling," Rhonda said. "Are you saying that the program won't stop running? That the user won't see an error? Or that the user will see a custom error?"

"Rhonda," I said, "let me give you a real world example of Exception Handling in a program you probably use all of the time---a Word Processing program. Suppose you start up your favorite Word Processor, and tell it you wish to open a file on Drive E---your DVD drive, but you forget to insert the DVD into the DVD Drive. Does your Word Processor simply bomb and stop working?"

"No I don't think so," Rhonda answered. "I would think that it would display a message telling me that there's no DVD in the DVD drive, and that I should insert one."

"That's exactly right Ronda," I replied. "Much like the examples I cited earlier about missing files or databases, the programmers who wrote your Word Processor anticipated that the user might want to open a file that it couldn't find. In this case a DVD not being inserted into a DVD drive. To handle this, the programmers implemented Exception Handling in their program, substituting a user-friendly message in place of a system-generated Runtime Error that would cause the program to stop running. Those are the important components of good Exception Handling: A user friendly message, and a program that continues running instead of coming to a grinding halt. This is our goal for the Python programs we write."

"So we can intercept those nasty Runtime Error messages we saw earlier today," Barbara said, "and replace them with user-friendly messages of our own?"

"Yes we can Barbara," I said. "We can anticipate Runtime Errors, check for them and handle them if they occur. For instance, in the case of the Division By Zero error we saw just before out break, we can test whether the user has supplied our program with a denominator of zero—and if they have, we can then display a warning message. If we write a program that prompts the user for a file to open, we can first check for the existence of the file prior to trying to open it. This is very basic Exception Handling. As you'll see, we can also use Python Try...Except Blocks to handle Runtime Errors that may occur. Which technique you choose (and it's possible to use both) will be up to you."

I paused before continuing.

"Let's begin our look at Python Exception Handling," I said, "by completing an exercise in which we write a program that allows the user to cause a Division By Zero Runtime Error. When we test the program, we'll intentionally generate that error."

I then distributed this exercise to the class.

Practice 8-1 Intentionally Generate an Error

In this exercise, you'll write a program that prompts the user for two numbers, then divides the first number by the second number. After verifying the result of one calculation, you will then run the program again, intentionally generating a Division By Zero error. But don't worry---in the next exercise, you'll implement Basic Exception Handling to gracefully deal with the error.

1. Using Notepad (or Notepad++), enter the following code.

```
#Practice8_1.py
```

```
number1 = int(input("Enter number 1: "))
number2 = int(input("Enter number 2: "))

answer = number1/number2

print("The answer is", answer)
```

2. Save your source file as <u>Practice8_1.py</u> in the \PythonFiles\Practice folder (select File | Save As from Notepad's menu bar). Be sure to save your source file with the filename extension py

3. Execute your program. When prompted, enter 9 for the first number and 4 for the second. The program will display a result of **2.25** in the Python Console.

4. Now run the program again. When prompted, enter **9** for the first number and **0** for the second. The program will terminate with a <u>ZeroDivisionError: division by zero</u> error, as shown here:

Discussion

This may have been the simplest exercise my students had completed in the course---no one had any issues coding it.

"As you can see," I said, "the Python Interpreter displays a **ZeroDivisionError: division by zero** error, and displays the line of code and the line number that it has flagged as being incorrect. This error message is identical to the error we received when we executed <u>Example8_34</u>. The difference here is that the error was generated by user input, unlike <u>Example8_34</u> where the division by zero was hard coded into the program. Again, this error message is very explicit. However, it's an error that the user of the program should never see, since it's totally avoidable. A Python programmer, knowing that division is occurring anywhere within his or her program, should always implement Exception Handling in the program: Basic Exception Handling, as I'm about to show you in the next practice Exercise or Exception Handling using Try...Except blocks that I will show you after that."

"So will we be able to prevent this type of problem?" Kate asked.

"We can't prevent the user from entering zero for the second number Kate," I said, "but we can detect if they've done so and prevent the program from bombing."

"Is a Python Exception the same thing as a Python error?" Steve asked. "I think you've used both terms in the last few minutes."

"In Python," I said, "when a Runtime Error occurs the way it did here, an Exception Object is created that contains information about the error, such as the name of the error and the line of code where the error occurred. It is this information from the Exception Object that is displayed by the Python Interpreter."

"So an error occurs, and an Exception Object is created," Rose said. "I can see how the terms Error and Exception are almost interchangeable."

"You're right Rose," I said, "and you will also probably see and hear the terms Error Handling and Exception Handling used interchangeably as well. In this case, I'll defer to the official Python Reference Guide that calls a Runtime Error an Exception, and refers to the process of handling these Runtime Errors as Exception Handling."

"Regardless of what we call it," Jack said, "Using Exception Handling, what can we do when a Python Runtime Error or exception occurs?"

Strategies for dealing with Exceptions

"There are several strategies for dealing with possible Exceptions," I said.

I then quickly displayed this chart on the classroom projector.

- Ignore the possible Runtime Error

- Basic Exception Handling

- Exception Handling using Try...Except Blocks

"What's that?" Mary asked, "Ignore a possible Runtime Error?"

"That's right, Mary" I said, "Some programmers, when they write their programs, provide for no error or Exception Handling of any kind. Either they believe that their programs will not suffer from a Runtime Error or they simply don't care. Of course, some programmers are writing programs for home or personal use and don't see the need for Exception Handling in these programs."

"Even for home use," Ward said, "I think that is a little foolish on their part."

"Right or wrong," I said, "we can choose to ignore potential Runtime Errors, and simply let the program bomb. As Ward said, it's foolish to ignore a Runtime Error that you suspect may occur, and you should do your best to anticipate the error and react to it."

"How will we know what they are?" Rhonda asked.

"As you gain experience in Python programming," I said, "you'll learn that most of the code you write won't result in Runtime Errors. You'll also learn the kind of code that is likely to trigger a runtime Error, and the types of errors likely to be triggered. Not every line of code you write needs to be written to handle Exceptions. In fact, most don't."

"So what should we do when we realize that the code we've written **might** result in a Runtime Error?" Ward asked.

"Implement either basic Exception Handling," I said, "or Exception Handling using Try...Except blocks."

I paused before continuing.

"Python allows us to sandwich error prone code within a Try...Except block," I said. "When a Runtime Error occurs, the code in the Except block is then executed. It's not terribly complicated, but before we learn that technique, there's a simpler approach which is to write code that detects the error condition before the Runtime Error is generated. I call that Basic Exception Handling."

Basic Exception Handling

"Let's implement Basic Exception Handling in Practice8_1," I said. "As we discovered when we executed Practice8_1 a few minutes ago, there's a very real possibility of a Runtime Error if the user enters a value of zero for the second number. We'll modify the program by determining if the user has entered a value of zero for the second number, and if so, we'll notify the user of the problem with division by zero. Finally, we need to decide what the program should do next."

I then distributed this exercise for the class to complete.

Practice 8-2 Basic Exception Handling

In this exercise, you'll implement Basic Exception Handling by modifying the program from Practice 8-1 to use a simple If statement to deal with the possible Division by Zero error.
1. Using Notepad (or Notepad++), enter the following code.

```
#Practice8_2.py

number1 = int(input("Enter number 1: "))
number2 = int(input("Enter number 2: "))

if number2 == 0:
  print("Sorry, you may not divide by zero")
else:
  answer = number1/number2
  print("The answer is", answer)
```

2. Save your source file as Practice8_2.py in the \PythonFiles\Practice folder (select File | Save As from Notepad's menu bar). Be sure to save your source file with the filename extension py.
3. Execute your program. When prompted, enter **9** for the first number and **4** for the second. The program will

display a result of **2.25** in the Python Console.

4. Now run the program again. When prompted, enter **9** for the first number and **0** for the second. This time, instead of terminating with a Runtime Error, the program will display a warning message to the user indicating that Division by Zero is not permitted and then gracefully end.

Discussion

Again, no one had any problems completing this exercise.

After they were finished the exercise, I ran the program myself, entering 9 for the first number and 0 for the second. The following screenshot was displayed on the classroom projector:

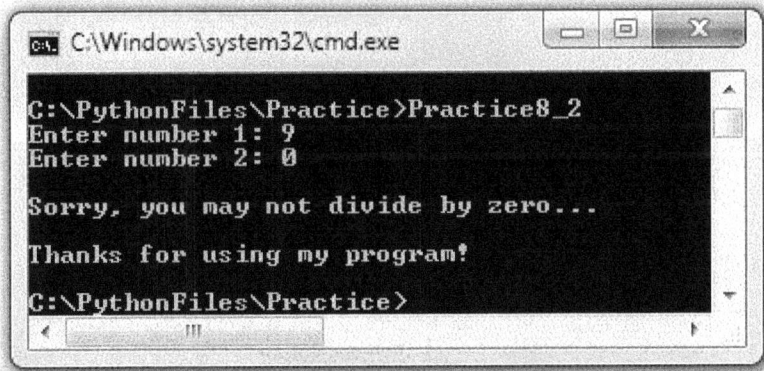

"As you can see," I said, "the additional code we wrote detected the impending Division by Zero error and avoided the Runtime <u>ZeroDivisionError: division by zero</u> Exception. To do that, all we needed to do was code a simple If statement to determine if the user had entered a zero for the second number..."

```python
if number2 == 0:
```

"If so," I continued, "then we display a warning message to the user telling them that Division by Zero is not permitted."

```python
print("Sorry, you may not divide by zero")
```

"Otherwise," I said, "we perform the division and display the result in the Python Console."

```python
else:
    answer = number1/number2
    print("The answer is", answer)
```

"By the way," I said, "If we had written the program to perform more than one calculation through a Loop structure, we could have placed a continue statement after the warning message to the user which would have allowed the user to have another chance at entering two numbers into the program."

"That seemed to work fine," Rhonda said. "Is that all there is to Basic Exception Handling?"

"You can frequently implement Basic Exception Handling through the use of an If statement," I said, "but sometimes writing multiple If statements can get pretty cumbersome. In that case, coding the Python Try...Except block may be a better option. We'll be looking at the Try...Except Block next. After that, we'll look at the Try...Except...Finally Blocks."

Try...Except Block

"The idea behind a Try...Except block," I said "is that we tell Python to 'try' the indented code within the Try block. This tells Python that the code may potentially cause a Runtime Error to occur, and if it does, to execute the code in the Except block that follows it instead of displaying the Exception message that we normally see when an Exception is raised."

"So no error message will be displayed?" Barbara asked.

"That's right Barbara," I said, "no Exception message will be displayed, provided we have coded an Except block to handle the specific Exception that Python raised. We can code an Except block for a specific Runtime Error, or as you'll learn later, any Runtime Error that may occur with a generic Except block."

"Can we have more than one Try block?" Dave asked.

"You can have as many Try blocks as you want," I said. "Programmers typically have more than one in their program, placing potentially troublesome code with the Try block. Here's the format for the Try block. Notice that the word Try is spelled in lower case letters, and it ends with a colon. The line of code or code to execute is then indented on the following lines."

```
try:
  indented code to try
  more indented code to try
```

"The format for the <u>Except Block</u> follows the end of the <u>Try block</u>," I said. "Here's the format for an Except Block to handle the Division by Zero Exception. Notice the word except is in all lower case letters, followed by the Exception we are handing, followed by a colon. As is the case with all Python blocks (the If statement, the For and While Loops), the code within the block is indented."

```
except ZeroDivisionError:
  print("\nSorry, you may not divide by zero")
```

"Let me see if I understand," Mary said. "The code within the Try block is code that we would ordinarily execute---such as a Division Operation---and the code in the following Except Block is the code to execute if an Exception does occur."

"That's perfect, Mary," I replied. "Usually we code the Except block for the exact Runtime Error we are anticipating. We do that using the name of the Runtime Error that we wish to handle. For example, if we are anticipating a Division by Zero error, we would code an Except block specifically for the <u>ZeroDivisionError</u> Exception."

"How do we know the name of the Exception to code in the Except Block?" Joe asked.

"As you gain experience," I said, "you'll know in advance what Runtime Errors may occur in your program and code your Except Block accordingly. You'll develop a list of common Exceptions as your learn more and more. If it's something that you haven't seen before, you can make a note of it when you discover it in testing."

"I'm going to need to see this in action," Rhonda said. "I think this is all pretty confusing."

"Let's take the code in <u>Practice8_2</u>," I said, "and modify it to include a Try...Except block. I think that will clear things up greatly for you."

I then distributed this exercise for the class to complete.

Practice 8-3 Try...Except Block

In this exercise, you'll modify the program from <u>Practice 8-2</u> to use Try...Except blocks to deal with the Division by Zero Runtime Error. Be very careful of your indentation!
1. Using Notepad (or Notepad++), enter the following code.

```
#Practice8_3.py

number1 = int(input("Enter number 1: "))
number2 = int(input("Enter number 2: "))

try:
  answer = number1/number2
  print("The answer is", answer)

except ZeroDivisionError:
  print("\nSorry, you may not divide by zero")
```

2. Save your source file as <u>Practice8_3.py</u> in the \PythonFiles\Practice folder (select File | Save As from Notepad's menu bar). Be sure to save your source file with the filename extension py.
3. Execute your program. When prompted, enter **9** for the first number and **4** for the second. The program will display a result of **2.25** in the Python Console.
4. Now run the program again. When prompted, enter **9** for the first number and **0** for the second. This time, instead of terminating, the program will display a warning message indicating that division by zero is not permitted and gracefully end.

Discussion

There were just a few problems completing the exercise. Several students spelled 'try' with an initial Capital letter 'T'. Try and Except are both spelled in all lowercase letters. One student placed a colon after the word 'except' in the

Except Block, and one student entirely forgot to indent both the <u>try</u> and the <u>Except Blocks</u>. One other student accidentally inserted the code to calculate the value of the *answer* variable between the end of the Try block and the beginning of the Except Block. This generated a Syntax Error.

"The Python Interpreter," I said, "wants the Except Block to immediately follow the Try block. Inserting just a single line of code in between the two of them will confuse the Interpreter."

> **NOTE: Python will look for at least one Except Block immediately following a Try block. If it doesn't see one, the Python Interpreter will halt with a Syntax Error.**

These were minor issues, easily fixable, and after a few minutes, we were ready to discuss the program.

I then ran the program myself, entering 9 for the first number and 0 for the second. The following screenshot was displayed on the classroom projector:

"The output is the same as that from <u>Practice8_2</u>," I said, "but this time, the user friendly error message displayed comes from the code in the Except block, not an If statement. Most importantly, the Exception message that Python would normally display isn't displayed to the user."

I paused before continuing.

"Let's take a look at the code now," I said. "We took the code that could potentially lead to a Division by Zero error, the Division Operation, and placed it within a Try block. As you can see, the Try block starts with the word try (in lowercase letters) followed by a colon. The actual code in the Try block is then indented on the following lines."

```
try:
 answer = number1/number2
 print("The answer is", answer)
```

"The Try block contains only the code that might cause an error," I continued. "Some programmers might have included the code containing the input() function within the Try block also. There's certainly no harm in it."

"Yes, I noticed that," Ward said. "I was wondering why you didn't include the code to prompt the user for the 2 numbers in the Try block."

"Since the troublesome code is the Division Operation," I said, "I included only that code in the Try block. Most Python programmers include only the code that may generate a Runtime Error in the Try block."

"I see we discarded the If statement to determine if the value of *number2* is equal to 0?" Ward said.

"That's right Ward," I said, "It's no longer needed. We're now allowing the Division by Zero error to occur, and when it does, the Exception will be 'raised' by Python and we will react to that Exception with the code in the Except Block."

> **NOTE: When a Runtime Error occurs, Python 'raises' an Exception. You may also hear the term 'trigger' but raise is the proper term**

"When an error occurs in the code within a Try block," I said, "Python will look to see if there is an Except Block following the Try block that matches the Exception that has been raised. If there is, Python will execute the indented code within the Except Block. That was the case here when the **ZeroDivisionError** Exception was raised. Notice the format of the Except Block. It begins with the word except (in lowercase letters), followed by the specific Exception we are handling, followed by a colon. The code to be executed if the Exception is raised appears in the indented line or lines of code that follow."

```
except ZeroDivisionError:
 print("\nSorry, you may not divide by zero")
```

"Can you have more than one Except Block?" Peter asked, "to handle more than one Exception."

"That's an excellent question, Peter," I said, "and the answer is yes. Your program can contain multiple Except Blocks, each one designed to handle a specific raised Exception from the preceding <u>Try block</u>. For instance, in Practice 8-3.py, we could have coded these two Except Blocks, one to handle the **ZeroDivisionError** Exception and another one to handle an **IndexError** Exception. The second Except block follows the first."

```
try:
 answer = number1/number2
 print("The answer is", answer)
except ZeroDivisionError:
 print("\nSorry, you may not divide by zero")
except IndexError:
 print("\nOops, something has gone wrong. Contact John Smiley")
```

"Notice the Exception Handling code for the **IndexError** Exception," I said. "This is an example of an Except Block that does nothing more than soothe the nerves of the user, exiting the program gracefully, and perhaps suggesting that the user call Tech support. More complex Except Blocks may try to recover from the raised Exception, but as you might imagine, it takes a great deal of experience to know exactly what to do in those cases."

Generic Except Block

"You mentioned a Generic Except Block earlier," Barbara said.

"Thanks for reminding me Barbara," I said, "Generic Except Blocks are executed if an Exception is raised out of a Try block, and there is no specific Except Block coded to handle it. For instance, in Practice 8-3.py, we could have coded these two Except Blocks, one to handle the **ZeroDivisionError** Exception, and the Generic Except Block to handle every other Exception that might be raised out of the Try block. Notice the format of the Generic Except Block. It's the word except (in lower case) followed by the word Exception, followed by a colon. There is no specific Exception listed..."

```
try:
 answer = number1/number2
 print("The answer is", answer)
except ZeroDivisionError:
 print("\nSorry, you may not divide by zero")
except Exception:
 print("\nAn unanticipated error has occurred. Contact John Smiley")
```

"If the **ZeroDivisionError** Exception occurs," I said, "that specific Except Block will handle the Exception. If any other Exception occurs, the generic Except Block will handle the Exception, and my preference is to display a message stating that an unanticipated error has occurred, and to contact Tech Support."

I paused before continuing.

"There's a second variation of the Generic Except Block," I said. "written this way. It's the word except (in lower case) followed immediately by a colon. This variation of the Generic Except Block can handle even more than the first variation."

```
except:
 print("\nAn unanticipated error has occurred. Contact John Smiley")
```

"What do you mean handle more? Barbara asked.

"It's a subtle difference," I said, "but this format tells Python to handle not only Exceptions that are raised from within code in the Try Block but Python warnings as well."

"Warning?" Ward pondered.

"That's right Ward," I said. "Do you remember when we coded the Endless Loop a few weeks ago. We stopped the program by pressing the Control+C combination. When we did, Python displayed a message that a

KeyboardInterrupt had occurred. Technically, this isn't an Exception but a warning---although it did cause the program to come to an abrupt halt."

I quickly ran Example5_5 for the class, which was the program with the Endless Loop. I hit the Control+C combination to stop the program, and display the Python warning.

"So you're saying," Dave said, "that we could handle this warning message using the first Generic Except Block but that the second form of the Generic Except Block wouldn't handle it?"

"That's right Dave," I said. "This format would handle the KeyboardInterrupt warning…"

```
except:
  print("\nAn unanticipated error has occurred. Contact John Smiley")
```

"…but this one wouldn't and the program would simply stop with the Python warning message…"

```
Except Exception:
  print("\nAn unanticipated error has occurred. Contact John Smiley")
```

"Of course," Dave said, "we can always write a specific Except block for the KeyboardInterrupt warning."

"Right again Dave," I said. "That would be a good idea if you have any reason to believe that the user would press the Control+C combination, and you wanted to gracefully handle it. It might look something like this."

```
Except KeyboardInterrupt:
  print("\nYou pressed Control+C and I'm not sure why…")
```

> **NOTE:** This is the most exhaustive coverage of the two Generic Except blocks in print that I've seen, and I've done a great deal of research. If the topic is boring to you, I include it here for the reader or two who might find it interesting. When in doubt, write explicit Except Blocks.

"I guess if a programmer wanted to," Blaine said, "he or she could choose to code just a single Generic Except Block to handle every possible Exception in their program."

"That's true Blaine," I said. "Some programmers prefer to code just a single Generic Except Block following the Try Block. In our case, that would mean that every Exception raised would result in a message being displayed to 'Contact John Smiley'."

"That seems like a lazy way to program," Steve said.

"I agree with you Steve," I said, "although it's better than no Exception Handling at all. Ideally, you should code specific Except Blocks for Exceptions that you anticipate will occur. Hold off coding the Generic Except Block (which must come last) for truly unanticipated Exceptions."

"Is the order in which the Except Blocks appear significant?" Dave asked.

"If you have a generic Except Block," I said, "it needs to be placed after all of the other specific Except Blocks are coded."

Try...Except...Finally Block

"I think you made a reference earlier to a Finally Block earlier, didn't you?" Barbara asked.

"Once again Barbara," I said, "thanks for reminding me. The Finally Block is optional, and if coded, it follows the last Except Block. The Finally Block specifies code that is to be executed whether an Exception occurs or doesn't occur with the code within the Try Block. The code in the Finally block is always executed."

"Do you recommend coding a Finally Block?" Linda asked.

"Since the Finally Block is optional," I said, "some programmers code it and others do not. Code within the Finally block typically performs some kind of housekeeping such as closing files, or thanking the user for using the program. For that reason, I tend to use a Finally Block with a Try Block that contains an Except Block for an exception that the program can't recover from, and in which resources (such as files, network connections, etc) need to be closed."

"Suppose we have more than one Try Block coded in our program?" Joe asked. "Does that mean we can have multiple Finally Blocks?"

"That's right Joe," I said. "Each Finally Block will execute after its corresponding Try and Except Blocks execute."

> **NOTE: The concept of a Finally Block can be confusing since to many beginners it sounds like it's code that is executed when your program ends, but that's not the case. The Finally Block contains code that executes when its corresponding Try...Except Blocks are complete. And remember, the code in the Finally Block executes whether the code within the Try Block triggers an Exception or not.**

"Let me make sure I understand the order of what's happening here," Joe said. "We have the Try Block, followed by one or more Except Blocks, optionally followed by a single Finally Block. And there can be multiple sequences of Try...Except...Finally Blocks in our program?"

"That's perfect Joe," I said.

"I think you said this earlier," Jack said, "but just to emphasize. Not every part of our program needs to be contained within a Try Block?"

"That's correct Jack," I said. "I've seen some beginners 'sandwich' their entire program within a huge Try Block, but advanced programmers create Try Blocks only for the code they know from experience may raise Runtime Exceptions. Experience is the best teacher. As you (or your users) encounter Runtime Errors in your programs (hopefully during the testing phase,) you'll place that troublesome code within a Try Block and code specific Except Blocks to handle it. The next time you write a similar program, almost without thinking about it, you'll place that code within a Try Block."

"I think it's about time we saw an example of the Finally Block in action, don't you think?" Rhonda asked.

"That's a great idea Rhonda," I said, "Here's an exercise that gives you a chance to code both a Generic Except Block and a Finally Block."

I then distributed this exercise for the class to complete.

Practice 8-4 Try...Except...Finally With a Generic Except Block

In this exercise, you'll modify the program from Practice 8-3 to include a Generic Except Block and also a Finally Block.

1. Using Notepad (or Notepad++), enter the following code.

#Practice8_4.py

```
number1 = int(input("Enter number 1: "))
number2 = int(input("Enter number 2: "))

try:
  answer = number1/number2
  print("The answer is", answer)

except ZeroDivisionError:
  print("\nSorry, you may not divide by zero")

except:
  print("\nAn unanticipated error has occurred. Contact John Smiley")

finally:
  print("\nThanks for using my program!")
```

2. Save your source file as <u>Practice8_4.py</u> in the \PythonFiles\Practice folder (select File | Save As from Notepad's menu bar). Be sure to save your source file with the filename extension py.

3. Execute your program. When prompted, enter **9** for the first number and **4** for the second. The program will display a result of **2.25** in the Python Console. Because of the Finally Block, the program will display a message thanking the user for using it.

4. Now run the program again. When prompted, enter **9** for the first number and **0** for the second. The program will display a warning message indicating that division by zero is not permitted and gracefully end. Because of the Finally Block, the program will also display a message thanking the user for using it.

Discussion

Adding a Generic Except Block and a Finally block didn't pose much of a problem for my students. A few minutes later, everyone in the class had completed the exercise.

I then ran the program myself, entering 9 for the first number and 4 for the second. The following screenshot was displayed on the classroom projector:

"As you can see," I said, "the program has properly calculated the result of 9 divided by 4 and displayed it in the Python Console. In addition, because of the Finally Block, our program has also displayed the message 'Thanks for using my program!' As you can see, the code in the Except Block was bypassed, but the code in the Finally Block was executed, even when there was no Exception triggered."

```
finally:
  print("\nThanks for using my program!")
```

"That's right," Rhonda said, "The code to display the thank you message is now in the Finally Block. I didn't realize that when I was completing the exercise."

I ran the program myself again, this time entering 9 for the first number and 0 for the second. The following screenshot was displayed on the classroom projector:

"This time," I said, "Division by Zero results in an Exception being triggered, and the code in the Except Block for the **ZeroDivisionError** Exception is executed. Also, because of the Finally Block, our program also displays the message 'Thanks for using my program!' As you can see by the order of the messages in the Python Console, the code in the Finally Block was executed **after** the code in the Except Block was executed."

"Uh Oh," I heard Rhonda say. "I accidentally typed a letter instead of a number for the first number---and the program bombed with a **ValueError** Exception Why didn't the Generic Except Block handle that?"

"I think I know why," Dave said. "The input of the two numbers isn't within the Try Block. The **ValueError** Exception was raised outside of the Try Block,"

"Excellent Dave," I said. "See what I mean by experience being the best teacher? Executing the **input()** function doesn't seem like a very error prone activity, but in reality it is."

"How can we fix this?" Rhonda asked.

"To begin with," I said. "include the **input()** functions within the Try Block. Then write an Except Block to handle the Exception."

"Should we code a specific Except Block for the **ValueError** Exception?" Valerie asked. "Or just let the Generic Except Block handle it?"

"My preference," I said, "is to always write specific Except Blocks for the Runtime Error I'm anticipating. Since we know it's a possibility that the **ValueError** Exception will be raised---Rhonda just proved it---a custom message telling the user that he or she must enter a number would be best. Allow the Generic Except Block to handle errors we don't anticipate. Write specific Except Blocks for those errors you do anticipate. Here's what the modified code would look like..."

```
# Example8_35.py

try:
    number1 = int(input("Enter number 1: "))
    number2 = int(input("Enter number 2: "))

    answer = number1/number2
    print("The answer is", answer)
except ZeroDivisionError:
    print("\nSorry, you may not divide by zero")
except ValueError:
    print("\nSorry, your input value must be a number")
except:
    print("\nAn unanticipated error has occurred. Contact John Smiley")
finally:
    print("\nThanks for using my program!")
```

I then saved the program as Example8_35.py.

"Let's run the program now and type the letter x for the value of number 1 and see what happens," I said.

I did exactly that, and the following screen shot was displayed on the classroom projector:

"Entering the letter x instead of a number," I said, "in the previous version of the program would have produced an unhandled **ValueError** Exception. Because we included the **input()** functions within a Try Block and wrote a custom Except Block for the **ValueError** Exception, we were able to graciously handle the Exception."

"I wish there was a way for the program to continue running instead of stopping after the display of the custom error message," Rose said.

"We can do that pretty easily," I said, "by placing all of this code within a While Loop, and executing the continue statement from within the Except block."

"And you're saying we can place code after the Finally Block?" Linda asked.

"Absolutely Linda," I said, "we can have code following the Finally Block. And if we don't have a Finally Block, we can have code following the last Except Block. Let's modify Example8_35 to display a statement in the Python Console, and the code to do that will be after the Finally Block..."

I then displayed this code on the classroom projector.

```
# Example8_36.py

try:
  number1 = int(input("Enter number 1: "))
  number2 = int(input("Enter number 2: "))

  answer = number1/number2
  print("The answer is", answer)

except ZeroDivisionError:
  print("\nSorry, you may not divide by zero")

except ValueError:
  print("\nSorry, your input value must be a number")

except:
  print("\nAn unanticipated error has occurred. Contact John Smiley")

finally:
  print("\nThanks for using my program!")

print("To prove that code will execute after the Finally Block.")
```

I saved it as Example8_36.py and executed it, entering 9 for the first number and 4 for the second number. The following screen shot was displayed on the classroom projector.

```
C:\Windows\system32\cmd.exe

C:\PythonFiles\Examples>Example8_36
Enter number 1: 9
Enter number 2: 2

The answer is 4.5

Thanks for using my program!

To prove that code will execute after the finally clause.

C:\PythonFiles\Examples>
```

"Notice," I said, "that the answer was displayed, followed by the thank you message contained in the Finally Block, followed by the display message that is the last line of code in the program. There's no doubt here that we can write code that follows the Finally block."

I executed the program again, this time entering the letter x for the value of the first number---this is what Rhonda had done accidentally a few minutes ago. The following screen shot was displayed on the classroom projector:

```
C:\Windows\system32\cmd.exe

C:\PythonFiles\Examples>Example8_36
Enter number 1: x

Sorry, your input value must be a number

Thanks for using my program!

To prove that code will execute after the finally clause.

C:\PythonFiles\Examples>
```

"This time," I said, "the code in the ValueError Except block was executed, followed by the code in the Finally Block, followed by the last line of code in the program. Once again, we've proven that any code following the Finally Block will most definitely execute."

I waited for questions but there were none.

"That ends our discussion of Error and Exception Handling," I said. "I think in the future, as you work on projects of your own, you may want to consult the notes from today's class. At least I hope you do."

Adding Exception Handling to the Grades Calculation Program

"Are we going to modify the Grades Calculation Program to provide for Exception Handling?" Kate asked.

"I think that's a great idea Kate," I said. "We've already implemented some very Basic Exception Handling in the Grades Calculation Program, by checking for valid keyboard entries made by the user. However, as we've discovered in the last few minutes, that may not be enough."

I then distributed this final exercise of the day (and the course) for the class to complete.

Don't Forget: If typing these long examples and exercises isn't something you want to do, feel free to follow this link to find and download the completed solutions for all of the examples and exercises in the book. Just click on the Python book, then follow the link entitled exercises ☺

http://www.johnsmiley.com/main/books.htm

Practice 8-5 Modify the Grades Calculation Program to use a Try...Except...Finally Block

In this exercise, you'll modify the Grades.py Source Files to use a Try...Except Finally Block. Prior to modifying the program, you'll first execute it and see that there's a hidden bug in the program!

1. Locate the Grades.py source file you worked on last week. (It should be in the \PythonFiles\Grades folder.)
2. Execute the program. It should ask you if you have a grade to calculate.
3. Instead of entering the number 1, 2 or 3 to calculate the grade for an English, Math or Science student, enter the letter 'd' and watch the program 'bomb' with a **ValueError Exception**.

```
C:\Windows\system32\cmd.exe

C:\PythonFiles\Grades>Grades
WELCOME TO THE GRADES CALCULATION PROGRAM

Enter student type (1=English, 2=Math, 3=Science): d
Traceback (most recent call last):
  File "C:\PythonFiles\Grades\Grades.py", line 21, in <module>
    if int(response) <1 or int(response) > 3 :
ValueError: invalid literal for int() with base 10: 'd'

C:\PythonFiles\Grades>
```

4. Execute the program again.
5. Specify that you wish to calculate the grade for an English student by entering the number 1.
6. You will be prompted for the midterm grade. Instead of entering a number, enter the letter 'd' for the midterm grade and watch the program 'bomb' with a **ValueError Exception**.

```
C:\Windows\system32\cmd.exe

C:\PythonFiles\Grades>Grades
WELCOME TO THE GRADES CALCULATION PROGRAM

Enter student type (1=English, 2=Math, 3=Science): 1

Enter the Midterm Grade: d
Traceback (most recent call last):
  File "C:\PythonFiles\Grades\Grades.py", line 29, in <module>
    grades.append(calculate_english_grade())
  File "C:\PythonFiles\Grades\util.py", line 9, in calculate_english_grade
    midterm=int(input("\nEnter the Midterm Grade: "))
ValueError: invalid literal for int() with base 10: 'd'

C:\PythonFiles\Grades>
```

7. Now let's modify the Grades program to handle these errors. Using Notepad (or Notepad++), locate and open the Grades.py source file you worked on last week. (It should be in the \PythonFiles\Grades folder)
8. Modify your code so that it looks like this. You will be sandwiching much of your existing code (that pertaining to user input) within a Try Block, so you will need to be very careful with your indentation! If you are using Notepad++, it has a nice feature that allows you to select one or more lines of code, and then select Edit-Indent to indent the selected lines of code. You will also be adding two Except Blocks.

```
# Grades.py
# After Chapter 8

from util import calculate_english_grade,calculate_math_grade,calculate_science_grade

grades = []
accumulator = 0.0
```

```
print("WELCOME TO THE GRADES CALCULATION PROGRAM")

loop_response = "YES"

while loop_response.upper() == "YES":
  # What type of student are we calculating?
  try:
    response=input("\nEnter student type (1=English, 2=Math, 3=Science): ")

    if response == "":
      print("You must select a Student Type")
      continue

    if int(response) <1 or int(response) > 3 :
      print(response, "is not a valid Student Type")
      continue

    #Student type is valid, now let's calculate the grade
    #1 is an English Student
    if response =="1":
      grades.append(calculate_english_grade())

    # 2 is a Math Student
    if response == "2":
      grades.append(calculate_math_grade())

    # 3 is a Science Student
    if response == "3":
      grades.append(calculate_science_grade())

  except ValueError:
    print("\nI was expecting a number and you entered a letter. Please try again.")

  except:
    print("\nAn unanticipated error has occurred---call John Smiley")

  loop_response=input("\nDo you have another grade to calculate? ")

if len(grades) == 0:
  print("\nTHANKS FOR USING THE GRADES CALCULATION PROGRAM!")
  exit()

print("\nThe calculated final grades are: \n")

for grade in grades:
  print(grade)
  accumulator += float(grade)

average = accumulator/len(grades)

print("\nThe class average is " + str(average))
print("\nTHANKS FOR USING THE GRADES CALCULATION PROGRAM!")
```

9. Save your source file as <u>Grades.py</u> in the \PythonFiles\Grades folder (select File | Save As from Notepad's menu bar). Be sure to save your source file with the filename extension py.

10. Execute your program.

11. When the program asks you to enter 1, 2 or 3 to calculate the grade for an English, Math or Science student, instead enter the letter 'd'. The program will display a message that it was expecting a number, tell you to try again, and ask you if there any more grades to enter. . The program has gracefully recovered from an Exception.

12. Answer **Yes**. You will be prompted for the student type. This time, specify that you wish to calculate the grade for an English student. Enter the letter 'd' for the midterm grade. The program will display a message that it was expecting a number, tell you to try again, and ask you if there any more grades to enter. . The program has gracefully recovered from an Exception.

13. Answer **Yes**. To prove that the program can handle unanticipated errors, Press Control+C at the student prompt and see what happens. You should receive a message that an unanticipated error has occurred, to call John Smiley, and once again be asked if there are any more grades to enter. The program has gracefully recovered from an Exception.

```
C:\Windows\system32\cmd.exe - Grades

C:\PythonFiles\Grades>Grades
WELCOME TO THE GRADES CALCULATION PROGRAM

Enter student type (1=English, 2=Math, 3=Science): d

I was expecting a number and you entered a letter. Please try again.

Do you have another grade to calculate? Yes

Enter student type (1=English, 2=Math, 3=Science): 1

Enter the Midterm Grade: d

I was expecting a number and you entered a letter. Please try again.

Do you have another grade to calculate? Yes

Enter student type (1=English, 2=Math, 3=Science):
An unanticipated error has occurred---call John Smiley

Do you have another grade to calculate?
```

14. The program continues to run. We need to verify that the program still works as it should, even with the Exception Handling code that we've added.

15. Answer **Yes**, then indicate that you wish to calculate the grade for an English student. Enter **70** for the midterm, **80** for the final examination, **90** for the research grade, and **100** for the presentation. A final numeric grade of **84.5** should be displayed with a letter grade of **C**.

16. After the grade is displayed, the program should ask you if you have more grades to calculate.

17. Answer **Yes** and calculate the grade for a Math student. Enter **70** for the midterm and **80** for the final examination. A final numeric grade of **75** should be displayed with a letter grade of **D**.

18. After the grade is displayed, the program should ask you if you have more grades to calculate.

19. Answer **Yes** and calculate the grade for a Science student. Enter **70** for the midterm, **80** for the final examination, and **90** for the research grade. A final numeric grade of **78** should be displayed with a letter grade of **C**. After the grade is displayed, the program should ask you if you have more grades to calculate.

20. Answer **No**. All three final numeric grades will be displayed in the Python Console, along with an overall class average of **79.1666**. You should be thanked for using the program, and the program should then end.

Discussion

Placing existing code within a Try Block was not quite as easy as it seemed. Indentation, of course, is always an issue in Python. After about 30 minutes, and a few problems, my students had completed the final exercise of the class.

"As I indicated before we started the exercise," I said, "Grades.py already had some basic Error Handling in it. For instance, we already check to ensure that a number between 1 and 3 is entered for a student type. If it's not, we prompt the user to try again and allow them to start over by using the Continue statement. The problem that still existed with our code comes when the user enters something other than a number when a number is what is required. As we saw in Step 5 of the exercise, the program will bomb with a **ValueError** Exception. Likewise, if the user enters something other than a number for one of the component grade pieces, the program will also bomb with a **ValueError** Exception, as we saw in Step 9. That's what the changes we made to Grades.py are meant to deal with. To more gracefully handle the ValueError exception, we placed everything within the While Loop within a Try Block. Here's just a portion of the code in the Try Block..."

```
while loop_response.upper() == "YES":
  # What type of student are we calculating?
  try:
    response=input("\nEnter student type (1=English, 2=Math, 3=Science): ")
```

"Knowing that there's a possibility the user will generate a **ValueError** Exception if he or she enters anything other than a number for the Student type or the component grade pieces, we have coded an Except Block for that specific Exception..."

```
except ValueError:
  print("\nI was expecting a number and you entered a letter. Please try again.")
```

"It's great that the program simply didn't end here," Ward said. "After displaying the error message, the program begins again with the first line of code within the body of the While Loop."

"That is a nice feature Ward," I said. "That's because the Try...Except Blocks are coded within the While Loop. If an Except Block is executed, it's the last lines of code within the body of the While Loop, and so the While Loop executes once more, until its test expression is no longer true."

I gave my students a chance to think about that.

"Here's our generic Except Block," I said, "It's our intention to use the Generic Except Block to handle any unanticipated Exception that is generated during the running of the Grades program. Of course, we tested it in Step #13 of the exercise by pressing the Control+C combination, which we know generated a **KeyboardInterrupt** Exception. We could have written a specific Except Block for that Exception, but using the Generic Except block here instead gave us a chance to test it..."

```
except:
  print("\nAn unexpected error occurred. Please contact John Smiley.")
```

"There's no Finally Block in the program," Ward said.

"There's no need for it here Ward," I said, "Because our Exception Handling is contained within the While Loop, there's nothing that a Finally Block could accomplish here. We're not opening files, databases, or network connections. Those are the typical uses for a Finally Block."

"What happens if an error occurs in one of the functions in our external module?" Rose asked.

"Actually, Rose," I said, "that's exactly what happened. When we entered an invalid midterm grade for an English student, the Exception was raised in the **EnglishStudent()** function. Python will look within the function for an Exception Handler, and if there's none there, will look for an Exception Handler in the main portion of our program to handle it."

"I think it handled it quite nicely," Rhonda said, with quite a bit of pride.

"I have to agree Rhonda," I said, "While testing our program, it encountered a few errors, responded to them, and still permitted the user to continue working with it. That's a sign of a good Exception Handler."

Testing the Program

"Does that mean we're done?" Ward asked..

"Yes it does Ward," I said. "The Grades Calculation Program is finished, and so is the class!"

"I'm a little sad to think about that," Linda said. "It's been a fun class."

"Register for our next class," I said, "Python GUI Programming and Python Classes and Objects. I guarantee you even more fun in those classes. We may even work on a new version of the Grades Calculation Program in there."

"When do we deliver the program?" Mary asked.

"And what version do we deliver?" Linda asked. "Will you be installing your version of the project?"

"When I spoke to Frank Olley earlier in the week," I said, "I explained to him that, excluding my version of the program, we had 18 different versions of the program—and that because this was a student project, I'd would prefer that he use one of yours, not mine."

I could see some excitement building among the students in the class.

"I invited Frank to visit us today to select the 'winning' project," I said, "but in Frank's mind, you're all winners—and I have to agree. It's going to be hard to select one project over another to install in the English department."

"So what are we going to do?" Ward asked.

"Frank had a good suggestion," I said, "He suggested that prior to traveling over to the English department at the end of today's class, we all select one project as 'the' one to install in the English department. So here's what I'm going to ask you to do. I would like everyone to take a few moments to test their own version of the program to verify that it's working properly, then walk up to the front of the classroom and pick up a voting ballot that I've prepared. Take the ballot, walk around the classroom and observe everyone's project, and then anonymously record your vote for what you consider to be the best project you see. The project that receives the most votes will be the one that we install in the English department. By the way, I'm removing my version of the project from consideration—so please don't vote for mine! This is your project and one of you deserves to have the place of honor in Frank Olley's English department."

"Can you give us some guidelines on testing our programs?" Linda asked, after a moment or two.

"That's a good question," I said. "Obviously, at a minimum, the program must work—that is, it needs to properly calculate the grade for each one of the three types of students. You should also make sure that the Python Console interface, as far as possible, is attractive and easy to use. And Exception Handling, of course, is a big plus."

"I would think that most of the bugs have been discovered by now," Valerie commented.

"I'm not sure we can say that with 100-percent certainty," I said. "There's always the possibility that something has slipped through our fingers. But I would say that I'm fairly confident our programs are bug free. Obviously, the more complicated the programs you write, the less certain you can feel, and the more thorough your testing needs to be."

"Is it possible to test each and every combination of grades and student types?" Rhonda asked.

"You're right, Rhonda," I said. "There are quite a few possible combinations of different student types and grades, and testing every one of them would be next to impossible. We've been testing our programs all along with a scenario for each type of student—and we should take this testing one step further. For instance, you should test scenarios where each component grade is zero, where one or more component grades, but not all, are zero, where all component grades are 100 percent, and where only some are 100 percent. Above all, make sure you calculate the grades manually first so that you know what the correct answer should be."

"In other words," Dave said, "test the extreme limits of each component."

"That's right, Dave," I said. "We saw today how the introduction of a zero into a program can produce errors. Try to 'break' your program now, before you give it to one of the work study students in the English Department to work with."

"I've been testing my project all along using a similar methodology," Chuck said, "except that I used Microsoft Excel to develop a worksheet of possible scenarios, along with the correct answers, and then ran my program to test as many of these scenarios as I could, verifying each correct answer."

"That's a great idea, Chuck," I said.

I then gave the class 30 minutes to test their projects one last time and then asked them to review and evaluate their fellow students' projects and anonymously vote for the project they thought was "best." As I collected their ballots and tallied the results, I asked my students to provide me a copy of their project on a USB Stick as well.

"Class is officially dismissed for today," I said. "I hope to see you all in the English Department in a few minutes!"

I called Dave aside.

Dave had volunteered to coordinate the installation of Python on a PC in the English department, along with the installation of the 'winning' program's Python Source code. I handed Dave a USB Stick containing the project that had received the most votes.

"Would you mind installing Python and the winning Project on the English Department PC?" I asked him. "I have a few things to wrap up here."

"Not at all," Dave said, as he glanced at the student's name on the USB Stick and smiled. "That project was excellent. I guess it pays to ask a lot of questions! I'll take care of this."

Delivering and Implementing the Grades Calculation Program

No sooner had I packed up my things and was preparing to make my way out the door of the classroom than a former student of mine approached me with a problem. Half an hour later, I finally arrived in the English Department.

As I entered, I could hear a great deal of excited talk and conversation. I could see an incredible amount of activity taking place. The area was packed with students—my eighteen students, plus two students whom I recognized as work study students—plus Frank Olley, David Burton, and Robin Aronstam were there."

Frank Olley caught sight of me.

"John, this program is absolutely great," Frank said excitedly. "I can't believe what an excellent job your students did with this. I, David, and Robin really love it—plus the two people who really count, the work study students who will be using it."

Amid all the hullabaloo, I glanced toward the middle of the open space in the English department and noticed a small table with a computer sitting on it. Seated at the table were the two work study students, and there was Rhonda, standing in front of the computer, training the Work Study students who would be using her version of the program to calculate grades for the English, Math, and Science departments!

"Rhonda's been proudly demonstrating her program to our work study students for the last 15 minutes," Frank explained. "She's obviously very proud of it, and they love it also—they haven't gotten up from their chairs yet. Rhonda did a great job with it."

I wandered over to them and caught Rhonda's eye.

"I'm flabbergasted that the class voted for my version of the project," Rhonda said. "To say that this has made my week in an understatement—more like my year! I'm just so honored that someone like me, with absolutely no programming background, could write a program like this. I felt like I asked so many stupid questions during the course."

"You know what I always say Rhonda," I interrupted, "the only stupid question is the question you don't ask. Your questions were always good ones, plus I know they were questions that some of the other students in the class were dying to ask. By the way, when I put this Python course together, I had someone just like you in mind—an inquisitive person, anxious to learn, but with no programming background. You did a great job."

"Really?" Rhonda said. "You know I enjoyed the course very much. You should consider taking those notes of yours and writing an Introductory Python book."

"Maybe I'll do that someday," I told her.

I spent the next few minutes observing the two work study students—Rita and Gil—experiment with the program. They had no problem whatsoever with it. Rhonda's Python Console interface was neat, easy to read, and easy to use—both of them obviously seemed to be enjoying working with it.

"Believe me," Rita said, "this is a lot better than the method we were using before."

"You can say that again," Gil said, "calculating these grades using a calculator was a real pain in the neck."

"From what I can see," I told the assembled class as they gathered around us, "the system works as designed. The ultimate users of the project—Rita and Gil—have been using the program for the last few minutes to calculate grades, and as you've all probably seen, they're extremely pleased with it. I want to thank Dave for installing Python and Rhonda's version of the project on this PC. By installing the software, we have begun phase 5 of the SDLC, the Implementation phase. Installation, fine-tuning, and training are all part of this phase."

Frank Olley came over and stood next to me, obviously pleased at the time savings and accuracy the program would achieve. I turned to him and told him that this phase of the SDLC would last for at least the next week.

"Pairs of students have volunteered to be 'on site' during the week to make observations and assist with any problems that might come up," I explained.

"It's comforting to know they'll be here," Frank said. "What are those notes I've seen you taking?"

"I'm making notes about Phase 6 of the SDLC," I said. "Even though we're now in Phase 5 of the SDLC, we can proceed concurrently with Phase 6, which is the Feedback and Maintenance phase—and observation is an important part of the Feedback and Maintenance phase."

"Feedback and Maintenance?" Frank asked.

"We want to make sure the program is behaving according to the Requirements Statement you and I agreed upon before the class began," I explained. "A big part of this phase is observing the system to see how it's being used."

"And how it's being admired," Frank Olley added.

"Positive feedback is a wonderful thing," I said, smiling.

"What about program maintenance?" Frank asked.

"The Maintenance phase handles any changes to the program that are necessitated by governmental regulations, changes in business rules, or changes that you decide you want to make to the program," I replied.

"After seeing the great work you've done on the project," Frank said, "I'm sure I'll have more work for your class."

"Sadly though," I said, "this is the end of our Introductory Python course. But many, if not all of these students, will be signed up for my Python Classes and Objects course starting next Semester. Maybe we can work on any enhancements you have then. And then in the following Python GUI class, perhaps we'll produce a version with a graphical user interface like Windows."

Frank Olley seemed happy with that idea and left to chat with the two work study students. Linda, meanwhile, stopped by to see me and asked to see the notes I had taken.

"Interesting observations," Linda said. "I can see we still have some work to do."

I approached Frank Olley, Rhonda and the two Work Study students.

"Frank," I said, "on behalf of the class, I want to thank you for a wonderful learning experience. I'm sure we'll be in touch."

I shouted across the room to the rest of my students, "I've got to take off now. Everyone please be mindful of your coverage schedules, and if you have any problems at all, you know where to find me—remember, my e-mail address is johnsmiley@johnsmiley.com. I hope to see you all in a few weeks."

One Final Word

Congratulations! You've finished the Introductory Python class and completed and implemented the Grades Calculation Program. I hope you felt the excitement of completing, delivering, and installing the Grades Calculation program as much as the students in my class did, because you were a big part of it.

What's next? At this point, you should feel confident enough to tackle a variety of Python programs.

I hope that by following my Introductory Computer Programming class, you've seen how real-world applications are developed. The step-by-step methodology that we followed to complete the program should be one that you follow in your own programming work.

That's not to say that all projects go as smoothly as this one did. You can expect your share of mistakes, misinterpretations, and misunderstandings along the way. Nonetheless, developing a computer program is always exciting, and if you love it as I do, it's always fun.

Everyone makes mistakes when they start programming. Never let this discourage you. When you first learn something new, it's a strange and awkward experience as you become familiar with it. But it's also an exciting time. Never let the frustrations of learning something new thwart that excitement. As time goes by, experience ill help you make fewer mistakes.

As I close, I just want to give you a few words of advice.

First, remember that in programming there's rarely a single 'correct' solution. Ultimately, if your program achieves the desires of the person who needs to use it, you've developed the 'correct' solution. In the beginning of your programming experience, don't waste your time trying to achieve the best solution. Move on to other projects to broaden your experience.

Second, always be your own best friend. Inevitably, while trying to work through a solution, there will be frustrating moments. Never doubt yourself, and never get "down" on yourself.

Finally, remember that there is always more to learn. The world of programming is an endless series of free learning seminars. All you need to do is open up a manual, read a Help file, surf the Internet, or pick up a copy of a good book (like this one,) and you are well on your way.

Few people know it all, fewer still master it all. But always move in that direction. Good luck, and I hope to see you in another Python class some day!

Summary

This chapter was designed to show you the various types of errors that all programmers---especially beginners---can make in their programs. We've covered three different types of errors here: Interpreter errors, Runtime Errors, and Logic Errors.

Interpreter errors are errors which the Python Interpreter catches before permitting our program to execute. All that's required on our part is to figure out what's wrong and to correct them, then re-run the program.

Runtime Errors occur when our program is executing, and a condition occurs that causes the program to fail (such as an input from the user.) Runtime Errors are the types of errors that can and should be dealt with gracefully through the use of Python Exception Handling.

The third type of error we dealt with was a Logic error, which unfortunately, is the most difficult type of error to detect and can be the most dangerous, since it rarely causes our program to 'bomb'. Logic errors can exist for years in programs without ever being detected.

We learned that Python Exception Handling can be used to deal with Runtime Errors through the use of Try...Except...Finally Blocks. You can't code for every eventuality, but you should code for the ones that you anticipate. We learned that you should definitely code an Exception handler when you're working with user input.

Index

F

R

S

T

U

V

W

Z